PROBLEMS IN
THE ORIGINS AND DEVELOPMENT
OF THE ENGLISH LANGUAGE

Second Edition

PROBLEMS IN THE ORIGINS AND DEVELOPMENT OF THE ENGLISH LANGUAGE

SECOND EDITION

John Algeo
UNIVERSITY OF GEORGIA

HARCOURT BRACE JOVANOVICH, INC.
New York   Chicago   San Francisco   Atlanta

COVER: From British Museum Manuscript Cotton Julius E vii, folio 59,
which is reproduced in its entirety on page 68 of this book.

© 1966, 1972 by Harcourt Brace Jovanovich, Inc.

ISBN: 0-15-567604-0
Library of Congress Catalog Card Number: 78-182336

Printed in the United States of America

Preface

This manual is intended as a supplement for courses in the development of the English language. Though it has been specifically designed to accompany Thomas Pyles's *The Origins and Development of the English Language*, Second Edition (Harcourt Brace Jovanovich, 1971), it can also be used with other textbooks to illustrate how English has evolved from its prehistoric beginnings. The second edition, like the first, assumes that a good knowledge of any language in its historical development can best be gained by working with samples of the language in its various historical stages. Exercises have been revised, and new material, such as that on phonological features, has been added. The treatment, however, remains basically conservative. Students are introduced to the history of English without being asked to master at the same time a new view of grammar. The instructor is consequently free to reinterpret the data in whatever theoretical framework he likes.

The problems included are of various types. Some ask the student to demonstrate knowledge of specific facts to be derived from the textbook or a similar source. Others provide supplementary data for the student to analyze and draw conclusions from. Still others are open-ended problems, notably the illustrative passages at the end of several chapters, which can be used in a variety of ways to demonstrate the structure of English at various periods in its history. Some of the exercises are intended for class discussion; others are designed to be worked out independently, with the answers to be written in a form that permits easy checking.

The manual contains a wealth of material, and selectivity in its use may well be a necessity. Some of the problems, such as 1.17, on the history and plan of the *OED*, might be assigned to individual students for oral reports. Others, such as 1.20, on the process of dictionary-making, can be the basis for an extensive research assignment. Still other exercises, such as 1.19, on using the *OED*, are large enough for the questions to be divided among the students in a class so that no undue strain need be placed on limited library facilities.

Experience suggests that the chapters can profitably be taken up in more than one order. The most obvious order, that of passing from first to last, can be varied by following the three introductory chapters with chapters 10, 11, and 12 on the lexicon, and then returning to the central chapters 4 through 9; the advantage of this arrangement is that drill on the sounds of modern English can be continued during the study of the lexicon to lay a firmer basis for the consideration of historical sound changes that begins with chapter 4.

The materials presented here have been derived from many sources. Specific acknowledgments have been made wherever possible, and reference is provided to the fuller original treatments. Historical studies such as those by Jespersen, the Wrights, Abbott, Campbell, Mossé, Prokosch, Wyld, Dobson, and Visser have been cheerfully pillaged for examples, but no list of authors could encompass the debts that are owed. Special acknowledgment is due the workbook by H. A. Gleason, Jr., which provided the first model for this book, and that by Winfred P. Lehmann, which showed how historical material could be handled. I am also indebted to Virginia G. McDavid, who gave suggestions for the plan of the first edition; to I. Willis Russell, for his many helpful suggestions, which I have incorporated in the second edition; to various users of the book, especially my own students, who have made comments from which the second edition has benefited; to Nina Gunzenhauser, for invaluable editorial help with the first edition; and to Cecilia Gardner and Anthony Kurland for their work on the second edition.

Thomas Pyles, whose name should rightfully appear on the title page, has helped with every chapter and saved me from many an error. Whatever is good in this manual derives from his text or his teaching; only its failings are my contribution. Adele S. Algeo assisted in every stage of the book's preparation; indeed her continual aid and encouragement made possible its completion.

JOHN ALGEO

Contents

PROBLEMS IN
THE ORIGINS AND DEVELOPMENT
OF THE ENGLISH LANGUAGE

Second Edition

Facts, Assumptions, and Misconceptions About Language

1.1 QUESTIONS FOR REVIEW AND DISCUSSION

1. Below are some terms relating to the study of language. Most of them are used in Chapter I of Thomas Pyles's *Origins and Development of the English Language*, 2nd ed., where they are defined either explicitly or by the context in which they occur. You should be familiar with all of them. Consult a recent dictionary for any whose meaning is not clear to you.

Language Variation
language
dialect
idiolect
universals of language
particulars of language
language-acquisition
  device
competence
performance
paralanguage
kinesis
secondary response
  (metalanguage)
tertiary response
usage
prescriptivism
colloquial(ism)

Speech and Writing
translation
transliteration
intonation
stress
transition (juncture)
homonym
homograph
homophone

Levels of Language
phonology
morphology
syntax
surface (grammatical)
  structure
deep (conceptual)
  structure
semology

Grammatical Categories
phoneme
morpheme
tagmeme
immediate constituent
phrase-structure rules
transform(ation)
well-formed sentence
inflection
word order
function word
case
tense
mood
gender

Approaches to Language Study
mentalistic linguistics
mechanistic (behaviorist)
  linguistics
generative linguistics
taxonomic linguistics
synchronic linguistics
diachronic linguistics
external linguistic history
internal linguistic history
sociolinguistics
psycholinguistics

Schools of Linguistics
comparative-historical
  grammar
descriptive-structural
  grammar
transformational-
  generative grammar
tagmemic grammar
systemic grammar
stratificational grammar

2. How old is language? What evidence can be advanced to suggest an answer to this question?

3. What theories have been suggested to explain how language first began? What are the weaknesses of these theories?

4. What are the characteristics of human language that distinguish it from animal communication?

5. What are the major differences between speech and writing as expressions of language?

6. What means other than speech or writing do human beings use in communicating with one another?

7. What is meant by the statement that language is *systematized*? What levels or varieties of system does language have?

8. What devices does language use to indicate grammatical relationships?

9. The distinguished philologist Otto Jespersen invented an artificial language called Novial. Of Jesperson's project, G. B. Shaw said, "Everybody can learn Novial, there is very little grammar in it; but one must be English to understand how one can get along splendidly without grammar." What did Shaw probably mean by the word *grammar*?

10. Which of the following provide the best characterization of "good English": *pure, correct, aesthetic, commonly used, prestigious, literary, appropriate*?

11. What is the function of a dictionary?

12. What effect does the arbitrary and conventional nature of language have on its historical development?

13. Make a summary list of misconceptions and popular errors about language.

14. During the past hundred years what have been the chief movements in the scholarly study of language, and how do they differ from one another?

15. The history of the English language is customarily divided into three periods: Old English, Middle English, and Modern English. Look up those terms in several dictionaries to find the dates assigned to the periods. Can you suggest an explanation for the discrepancies which you are likely to find?

1.2 *HUMAN LANGUAGE AND ANIMAL COMMUNICATION*

In each of the pairs below, one statement is typical of human language while the other is more characteristic of animal communication. Mark them HL and AC respectively.

1. _____ The system produces an unlimited number of novel utterances.
_____ There is a closed repertory of distinctive utterances.

2. _____ The topic of communication is present in the immediate environment of the utterance.
_____ The utterance may be displaced in time or space from the events with which it deals.

3. _____ Meanings are represented by combinations of sounds which are individually meaningless.
_____ Each meaning is represented by an individual sound in a one-to-one relation.

4. _____ The system is acquired by learning.
_____ The system is transmitted through genetic inheritance.

5. _____ The connection between the signal and its meaning is usually arbitrary and conventional.
_____ The connection between the signal and its meaning is often iconic and natural.

6. _____ The signals of the communication vary continuously and analogically represent continuous meanings, like the length of a bar on a bar graph or the loudness of a cry.

_____ The signals of the communication are discrete and represent discrete, clearly separate meanings, like the difference between the numbers 1, 2, 3 . . . .

7. _____ The response to an utterance may be to the way the utterance was expressed rather than to what was said (secondary response).

_____ The response is usually to what the utterance was about rather than to its form (primary response).

1.3 WRITING AND SPEECH

1. Speech has certain resources for conveying meaning that writing can represent imperfectly at best. Say this sentence aloud in a way that will convey each of the meanings indicated below: *He's a very enthusiastic person.*

I am simply giving you the fact.
I like him; his enthusiasm is to his credit.
I dislike him; enthusiasm is depressing.
I am hesitant or reluctant to describe him.
I mean him, not her.
I am asking you, not telling you.
Is that what you said? I can hardly believe it.
The degree of his enthusiasm is quite remarkable.
Enthusiasm is the only good thing about him, and it isn't much; I could say more, but I won't.

Describe as precisely as you can how the various meanings are signaled. Can any of these meanings be shown in writing by punctuation or typographical devices?

2. Can these pairs be distinguished in speech? If so, how?

blue blood (aristocrat)   blue blood (cyanotic condition)
red eye (cheap whiskey)   red eye (bloodshot eye)
hot line (direct telephone line to Moscow)   hot line (heated cord)
New Year (January 1)   new year (fresh year)
long shot (a kind of bet)   long shot (shot-putting at a far distance)
short order (quickly cooked food)   short order (brief command)
big head (conceit)   big head (large skull)
a man's store (store selling men's clothing)   a man's store (store owned by a man)
a fishing pole (rod for fishing)   a fishing Pole (Polish fisherman)
a bull's-eye (center of a target)   a bull's eye (eye of a bull)

3. Can these pairs be distinguished in speech? If so, how does the distinction differ from that of the pairs in the preceding list?

New Jersey (the state)   new jersey (blouse purchased recently)
old maid (spinster)   old maid (serving-woman of advanced years)
little woman (wife)   little woman (small female)
Long Island (the place)   long island (any elongated island)
good and hot (very hot)   good and hot (hot and good)

4. Each of these sentences is ambiguous in writing. Say each sentence in two different ways to make the potential meanings clear. Describe the means you use to make the spoken sentences unambiguous.

Old men and women should be the first to abandon ship.

The doorman asked her quietly to telephone the police.

She gave him an order to leave.

They went by the old highway.

He painted the picture in the hall.

5. Are these sentences usually distinguished in speech? Can they be distinguished?

He came to.

He came too.

He found a pear.

He found a pair.

The straight way is best.

The strait way is best.

The mathematics department is teaching plane geometry.

The mathematics department is teaching plain geometry.

The directions read, "Leave address with Miss Jones."

The directions read, "Leave a dress with Miss Jones."

1.4 *WRITING IS NOT LANGUAGE*

All four of the following passages, as well as this paragraph, are representations of the same language, although they may look somewhat dissimilar. They are merely alternate ways of recording English which are useful for different purposes. You should be able to read them in spite of the unfamiliar symbols and combinations.

ꞇhis iꞩ printeḑ in an augmenteḑ rœman alfabet, ꞇhe purpoꞩ ov whiꞔ iꞩ not, aꞩ miet bєє suppœꞩḑ, tꙍ reform our spelliꞃ, but tꙍ imprꙍv ꞇhe lerniꞃ ov rєєḑiꞃ. it iꞩ intendeḑ ꞇhat when ꞇhe beginner haꞩ aꞔєєvḑ ꞇhe iniꞩhal suksess ov flꙍꙍensy in ꞇhis speꞩhally єєꞩy form, hiꞩ fuetuer progress ꞩhꙍḑ bєє konfiend tꙍ rєєḑiꞃ in ꞇhe preꞩent alfabets anḑ spelliꞃꞩ ov ꞇhem œnly.[1]

ðis iz printəd in ə fənetik ælfəbet, ðə pərpəs əv wič iz nat, æz mayt biy səpowzd, tə rəform awr speliŋ ər tuw impruwv ðə lərniŋ əv riydiŋ, bət tə rikord ðə prənənsiyeyšən əv ingliš æz ækyərətliy æz pasəbəl. ðis ælfəbet iz yuwzd bay meniy liŋgwists in ðə yuwnaytəd steyts fər raytiŋ ðə sawndz əv madərn ingliš.

~~this~~ iz printəd in ə fənetik alfəbet, ~~the~~ pûrpəs əv wich iz not, az mīt bē səpōzd, tə rəfôrm our speling ôr tōō imprōōv ~~the~~ lûrning əv rēding, bət tə rikôrd ~~the~~ prənunsēāshən əv wûrdz in dikshənârēz. ~~this~~ alfəbet, yōōzd in ~~the~~ standərd kolij dikshənârē, iz tipikəl əv such sistəmz.

This is printed in a reformd speling kauld Angglik, the purpos of which is to maek the orthografi of our langgwij moer regueler and eezier to lurn, and dhus to impruuv the lieklihood that Ingglish mae be adopted as an internashonl augzilyeri langgwij. This alfabet, aultho wiedli noetist at wun tiem, is not much uezd nou.

[1] I. J. Pitman, "Intermedia," *The Linguistic Reporter* (Supplement Number 3), 3.

1. Which of the four writing systems looks most like the conventional spelling of English, and which least? _____

2. What special difficulties are presented by each system? _____
_____
_____
_____
_____

3. In 1961, when the Augmented Roman Alphabet was first noticed by the American press, *Time* magazine said of it, "If successful, it may revolutionize English." What misconception is implicit in that statement? _____
_____
_____

4. Another writing system for English is the Shaw Alphabet, chosen as the best design for a totally new alphabet in a contest established by G. B. Shaw's will. With the aid of the reading key below, transcribe the following sentence into normal orthography:

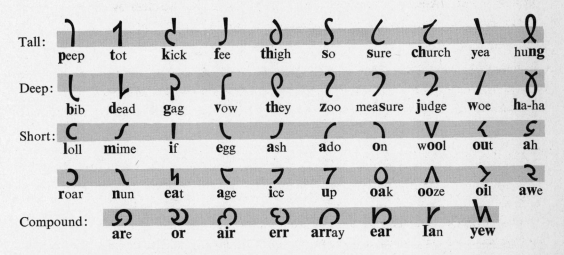

THE SHAW ALPHABET READING KEY
The letters are classified as Tall, Deep, Short, and Compound.
Beneath each letter is its full name: its *sound* is shown in **bold** type.

Tall:	**p**ee**p**	**t**o**t**	**k**i**ck**	**f**ee	**th**igh	**s**o	**s**ure	**ch**ur**ch**	**y**ea	hu**ng**
Deep:	**b**i**b**	**d**ea**d**	**g**a**g**	**v**ow	**th**ey	**z**oo	mea**s**ure	**j**ud**g**e	**w**oe	**h**a-**h**a
Short:	**l**o**ll**	**m**i**m**e	**i**f	**e**gg	**a**sh	**a**do	**o**n	w**oo**l	**ou**t	**ah**
	roar	**n**u**n**	**ea**t	**a**ge	**i**ce	**u**p	**oa**k	**oo**ze	**oi**l	**awe**
Compound:	**are**	**or**	**air**	**err**	**array**	**ear**	**Ian**	**yew**		

The four most frequent words are represented by single letters: **the** ϱ, **of** ſ, **and** ι, **to** 1.
Proper names may be distinguished by a preceding 'Namer' dot: e.g. ꞏꞇoſ, Rome.
Punctuation and numerals are unchanged.

5. English can be represented by many other writing systems, some of them—such as Gregg shorthand—very different in appearance from our conventional orthography. What other such systems can you mention? Do any of them stand for normal spelling rather than for language directly? _____

_____

_____

_____

1.5 THE SOUND-SYSTEM: CONSONANT SEQUENCES

The sound-system of Modern English permits certain combinations of sounds and precludes others. Here is a list of the regular sequences of consonants that can begin a word. The sequences are given both in their most common spelling and in phonetic symbols within square brackets. The phonetic symbols will be explained in Chapter 2; they are given here so that you may refer to them later. For each sequence, write a word that begins with that combination of sounds. If you have difficulty thinking of a word, use a dictionary.

pr-	[pr]	_pray_		cl-	[kl]	_clamor_
tr-	[tr]	_trust_		bl-	[bl]	_blue_
cr-	[kr]	_crash_		gl-	[gl]	_glow_
br-	[br]	_brouse_		fl-	[fl]	_flower_
dr-	[dr]	_dredge_		sl-	[sl]	_slit_
gr-	[gr]	_grow_		sp-	[sp]	_spill_
fr-	[fr]	_free_		st-	[st]	_stop_
thr-	[θr]	_throughly_		sk-	[sk]	_skill_
shr-	[šr] or [sr]	_shred_		sph-	[sf]	_sphinx_
tw-	[tw]	_tweed_		sm-	[sm]	_smile_
qu-	[kw]	_queen_		sn-	[sn]	_snail_
dw-	[dw]	_dwell_		spr-	[spr]	_spray_
gw- or gu-	[gw]	_Gwendolyn_		spl-	[spl]	_splash_
thw-	[θw]	_thwart_		str-	[str]	_straw_
sw-	[sw]	_swim_		scr-	[skr]	_scramble_
wh-	[hw] or [w]	_which_		squ-	[skw]	_squash_
pl-	[pl]	_plastic_		scl-	[skl]	_sclera_

The foregoing list of initial consonant sequences could have been extended with other combinations:

1. The initial sounds of words like *pew, cue, bugle, gules, few, view, mew, hew, spume, skew, smew,* and for some speakers *tune, dew, new, student, thew, suit, zeugma, lewd,* include a consonant or consonant-like sound that is not recorded in the spelling. What is this sound?
   _y_

2. Some combinations are rare or recent in English, such as the [pw] sound used in some pronunciations of *puissant* or the [bw] sound of *bwana.* Four quite recent consonant sequences begin with the initial sound of *ship.* Can you supply words to illustrate them?

   schl- [šl] _Schlitz_   schm- [šm] _schmaltz_
   schw- [šw] _schwa_   schn- [šn] _____

3. Dictionaries often record sequences that are seldom heard because they violate the system of English. What dictionary pronunciations do you find for the initial consonants of *phthisis, svelte,* and *tmesis?* _____

_____

4. There are a number of foreign names like *Mrumlinski, Pforzheim,* and *Pskov* that English speakers sometimes make an effort to pronounce "properly." Can you think of any other foreign words or names that contain initial consonant sequences not permitted by the habits of English? _____

_____

The consonant sequences that begin English words are not merely a random selection of sounds combined in any order. They follow a precise system which we will not detail but which you should be able to describe after you have studied Chapter 2.

A quite different and more complex system obtains among the consonant sequences that end English words. In final position, English permits such combinations as [mpst] as in *glimpsed,* [mpts] as in *exempts,* [lkts] as in *mulcts,* and even [mpfst] as in the admittedly contrived "Methinks thou *humphst* too much." Good descriptions of the permitted sound sequences of English can be found in Bloomfield's *Language* and in Malone's "The Phonemes of Current English," which are cited on page 42 of Pyles's *Origins and Development.*

1.6 *THE GRAMMATICAL SYSTEM: PLURAL SUFFIXES*

The common plural ending of nouns, written -*s* or -*es,* is pronounced in three ways. Thus *duck* adds an *s*-sound; *dog,* a *z*-sound; and *horse,* a vowel plus the *z*-sound. This kind of systematic variation in the pronunciation of a meaningful form is called morphophonemic alternation.

Write each of these nouns in the appropriate column, according to the *pronunciation* of its plural ending: ace, almanac, bag, book, burlesque, church, cough, cup, dish, dress, fall, graph, hat, house, hunch, judge, lad, lash, lathe, maze, moor, myth, oaf, pillow, room, tax, thing, train, wisp.

s-SOUND	*z*-SOUND	VOWEL + *z*-SOUND
almanac	bag	ace
book	fall	church
burlesque	lad	dish
cough	lathe	dress
cup	moor	house
graph	pillow	hunch
hat	room	judge
myth	thing	lash
oaf	train	maze
wisp		tax

1.7 THE GRAMMATICAL SYSTEM: TWO CLASSES OF NOUNS

There are various patterns in which nouns can be used, some of which are illustrated by these frame-sentences:

A. He likes _____.
B. The _____ is good.
C. He wants a(n) _____.
D. _____(e)s are good.

Consider these words:

ambition	chicken	fun	light
amiss	courage	home	loathe
ask	cup	house	news
bank	desk	illumine	noise
cash	dessert	lamp	seldom

1. Which of the words will fit into none of the patterns and thus are not nouns?
    amiss, ask, illumine, loathe, seldom

2. Which of the words will fit into patterns A and B, but not into C and D?
    cash, courage, fun, news
    Such words are called *uncountable nouns* or *mass-nouns*.

3. Which of the words will fit into patterns B, C, and D, but not into A? *bank, cup,*
    Such words are called *countable nouns* or *unit-nouns*. *desk, house, lamp*

4. Which of the words will fit into all four of the patterns? *ambition, home*

    Such words function as both mass- and unit-nouns. You may be able to detect some change of meaning in these nouns between their use in pattern A and their use in pattern C.

List five different examples for each of the three noun subclasses:

MASS-NOUNS	UNIT-NOUNS	MASS- AND UNIT-NOUNS
cash	bank	ambition
courage	cup	chicken
fun	desk	dessert
news	house	home
	lamp	light
		noise

1.8 THE GRAMMATICAL SYSTEM: TWO FUNCTION WORDS

Although native speakers of a language manage its complex system with ease, they often have difficulty describing the system which they habitually and unconsciously use. Function words, described on page 15 of Pyles's *Origins and Development*, are especially complex in their use. For example, what is the difference in use between the function words *some* and *any*?

1. Observe the use of unstressed *some* and *any* in the sentences below. The starred sentences are ungrammatical as long as *some* and *any* are pronounced without stress.

    I know some examples.   *I know any examples.
    The class needs some liveliness.   *The class needs any liveliness.

*I don't know some examples. I don't know any examples.
*The class doesn't need some liveliness. The class doesn't need any liveliness.

Do you know some examples? Do you know any examples?
Does the class need some liveliness? Does the class need any liveliness?

Don't you know some examples? Don't you know any examples?
Doesn't the class need some liveliness? Doesn't the class need any liveliness?

Describe the systematic difference you observe in the use of *some* and *any*.

_____

_____

2. The use of *some* and *any* is more complex than the sentences above would suggest. Consider these sentences:

The book has some exámples.
The book has sóme examples.   The book doesn't have sóme examples.

What is the difference in use and meaning between unstressed and stressed *some*? Which *some*, stressed or unstressed, can be omitted without changing the meaning of the sentence?

_____

_____

3. Now consider these sentences, in which a relative clause follows the noun:

The book has some examples you want. _____C_____
The book doesn't have some examples you want. _____D_____
The book has any examples you want. _____A_____
The book doesn't have any examples you want. _____B_____

In the blank after each sentence, indicate the appropriate meaning:

A. 'all examples'   C. 'some but probably not all examples'
B. 'no examples'   D. 'not all but probably some examples'

1.9   THE GRAMMATICAL SYSTEM: DEVICES TO INDICATE RELATIONSHIP

The following constructions, which are written in bad newspaper-headline style, are ambiguous. Rephrase each headline in at least two different ways to make the potential meanings clear. You may need to change the word order, change words, add function words, or alter the inflections.

Heavyweight Fights Tonight _Heavyweights Fight Tonight_

Bank Rates High _High Bank Rates_

Presidents Elect to Appear _President Elect Appears_

Closed Truck Stops _Truck Stops Closed_

Whiskey Still Illegal _Illegal Whiskey Still_

State Wins over Opponent *Wins over State Opponent*

New Student Assembly Held *Held New Student Assembly*

Army Cashiers Failure

1.10 *THE GRAMMATICAL SYSTEM: RELATED SENTENCES*

1. The matrix below contains sentences that are generally similar in meaning though quite different in syntax:

	ACTIVE		PASSIVE	
	Affirmative	*Negative*	*Affirmative*	*Negative*
Statement	Adam has seen Eve.	Adam hasn't seen Eve.	Eve has been seen by Adam.	Eve hasn't been seen by Adam.
Yes/No question	Has Adam seen Eve?	Hasn't Adam seen Eve?	Has Eve been seen by Adam?	Hasn't Eve been seen by Adam?
Wh- questions	Who has seen Eve?	Who hasn't seen Eve?	Who has Eve been seen by?	Who hasn't Eve been seen by?
	Who has Adam seen?	Who hasn't Adam seen?	Who has been seen by Adam?	Who hasn't been seen by Adam?

Complete the following similar matrix:

	ACTIVE		PASSIVE	
	Affirmative	*Negative*	*Affirmative*	*Negative*
Statement	Socrates is drinking hemlock.	*Socrates isn't drinking hemlock.*	*Hem. has been drunk by Soc.*	*Hem. hasn't been drunk by Soc.*
Yes/No question	*Is Soc. drink. hem.?*	Isn't Socrates drinking hemlock?	*Has hem. been drunk by Soc.*	*Hasn't hem. been drunk by Soc.?*
Wh- questions	*Who has drunk hem?*	*Who hasn't drunk hem?*	Who is hemlock being drunk by?	*Who is hem. not being drunk by?*
	What has Soc. drunk?	*What hasn't Soc. drunk?*	*What is being drunk by Soc?*	What isn't being drunk by Socrates?

10

2. There are yet other transformations a sentence can undergo. Supply the appropriate form of *Socrates is drinking hemlock* to match the sentences on the left.

Adam has seen Eve.　　　　　　　　Socrates is drinking hemlock.
It is Adam who has seen Eve.　　　It is Soc. who has drunk hem.
It is Eve that Adam has seen.　　　It is hem. that Soc. has Dr.
Adam is the one who has seen Eve.　Soc. is the one who has Dr. hem.
Eve is who Adam has seen.　　　　Hem. is what Soc has Dr.
Seen Eve is what Adam has done.　 Dr. Hem. is what Soc. has Done.

3. Write the appropriate negative for each affirmative sentence on the left.

He can play the *Minute Waltz*.　　He can't play the *Minute Waltz*.
The rain will stop.　　　　　　　Th. r. won't st.
He is growing a beard.　　　　　　He isn't gr. a be:
The movie has started.　　　　　　The movie hasn't st.
That movie has an X rating.　　　　That mo. doesn't have an X ra.
The sun came up this morning.　　　Th. su. didn't come up th. mo.

4. Write the appropriate passive for each active sentence on the left. If there is no correct passive write "none."

Eve ate the apple.　　　　　　　　The apple was eaten by Eve.
Xanthippe was emptying the pot.　　Th. po. was emptied by Xa.
The fat lady weighs 580 pounds.　　NONE
Mr. Holmes will look after the problem.　Th. pr. was looked af. by Mr. Ho.
Dr. Watson will look before Mr. Holmes.　NONE
The hijacker made the pilot fly to Havana.　Th. pl. was made to fly to Ha.

5. Make a question out of each sentence on the left by using the appropriate question word for the italicized items and making any neccessary changes in wording and order.

Ishmael was the sole survivor.　　Who was the sole survivor?
Ishmael was his name.　　　　　　What wa. hi. na.?
Captain Ahab was looking for *a white whale*.　What was Ca. Ah. lo. for?
He nailed a gold coin *to the mast*.　Where did he na. a go. co.?
The crew want to *return to port*.　What does th. cr. wa.?
The voyage will be done *very* soon.　When will the voy. be done?

1.11　*MORPHEMES*

Divide the following words into morphemes by writing them with slashes at the morpheme boundaries. For example: hat/s, pre/view, power/house.

boomerangs boomer/angs　likelihood like/li/hood　somersaulted somer/sault/ed
deforest de/forest　　　normal norl mal　　　songwriter song/write/er
freedom free/dom　　　pineapple pine/apple　sovereignty sovereign/ty
growth gro/wth　　　　playwright play/wright　spelunking spelunk/ing
indoors in/doors　　　 reflexive reflex/ive　　unthankfully un/thank/ful/ly

11

Language systems differ from one another in many ways. Here are four sets of equivalent expressions from different languages. The second column is Melanesian Pidgin, spoken in New Guinea,[2] the third is Latin, and the fourth is Esperanto, an artificial language invented in the nineteenth century.

ENGLISH	PIDGIN	LATIN	ESPERANTO
a good man	gudfela man	vir bonus	bona viro
a good woman	gudfela meri	femina bona	bona virino
a big house	bigfela haus	casa magna	granda domo
a little book	smolfela buk	liber parvus	malgranda libro
a man's wife	meri bilong man	virī uxor	edzino de viro
a woman's house	haus bilong meri	feminae casa	domo de virino
a wall of a house	wol bilong haus	casae paries	muro de domo
I look.	Mi luk.	Videō.	Mi rigardas.
He looks.	Em i-luk.	Videt.	Li rigardas.
She looks.	Em i-luk.	Videt.	Ŝi rigardas.
I see a man.	Mi lukim man.	Virum videō.	Mi rigardas viron.
He sees a woman.	Em i-lukim meri.	Feminam videt.	Li rigardas virinon.
She reads a book.	Em i-ridim buk.	Librum legit.	Ŝi legas libron.
I see him.	Mi lukim.	Eum videō.	Mi rigardas lin.
He sees her.	Em i-lukim.	Eam videt.	Li rigardas ŝin.
She reads it.	Em i-ridim.	Eum legit.	Ŝi legas ĝin.
You look.	Yu luk.	Vidēs.	Vi rigardas.
You looked.	Yu luk.	Vīdistī.	Vi rigardis.
They (are) read(ing) a book.	Em i-ridim buk.	Librum legunt.	Ili legas libron.
They (have) read a book.	Em i-ridim buk.	Librum lēgērunt.	Ili legis libron.
This man is big.	Disfela man i-bigfela.	Magnus hīc vir.	Tiu-ĉi viro estas granda.
This woman is good.	Disfela meri i-gudfela.	Bona haec femina.	Tiu-ĉi virino estas bona.
He is a man.	Em i-man.	Vir est.	Li estas viro.
It is a book.	Em i-buk.	Liber est.	Ĝi estas libro.
It rains.	I-ren.	Pluit.	Pluvas.

Each of the following statements describes the grammatical system of one or more of the four languages. If we were considering a larger body of material, some of the statements would need qualification, but for this exercise you should suppose that the expressions given above represent the complete corpus of each language. Circle the names of the languages to which each statement applies.

1. Nouns must be modified by an article, a pronoun, or a possessive noun.   Eng. Pid. Lat. Esp.

---

[2] The Pidgin material has been adapted from Robert A. Hall, Jr., *Hands Off Pidgin English!* (Sydney, Australia, 1955), *Melanesian Pidgin English* (Baltimore, 1943), and *Melanesian Pidgin Phrase Book and Vocabulary* (Baltimore, 1943).

2. Nouns, as a part of speech, can always be identified by their endings. Eng. (Pid.) (Lat.) (Esp.)

3. Adjectives, as a part of speech, can always be identified by their endings. Eng. (Pid.) (Lat.) (Esp.)

4. Adjectives have endings that change according to the nouns they modify. (Eng.) Pid. Lat. Esp.

5. Adjectives usually follow the nouns they modify. (Eng.) Pid. Lat. Esp.

6. "Possession" is sometimes shown by a function word. Eng. Pid. Lat. Esp.

7. "Possession" is sometimes shown by inflection. Eng. Pid. Lat. Esp.

8. The pronoun of the third person has different forms for different genders. Eng. Pid. Lat. Esp.

9. Nouns change their form when they are the object of a verb. Eng. Pid. Lat. Esp.

10. Pronouns change their form when they are the object of a verb. Eng. Pid. Lat. Esp.

11. Verbs have an ending that signals that the action is directed toward some goal. Eng. Pid. Lat. Esp.

12. Verbs change their form to agree with certain subjects. Eng. Pid. Lat. Esp.

13. Verbs change their form to show the time of the action. Eng. Pid. Lat. Esp.

14. Grammatical meaning is shown by changes of vowel pronunciation within a word as well as by endings. Eng. Pid. Lat. Esp.

15. A linking verb is required in all sentences of the type "X is Y." Eng. Pid. Lat. Esp.

16. Verb inflections can be added to nouns and adjectives. Eng. Pid. Lat. Esp.

17. Every sentence must have a subject. Eng. Pid. Lat. Esp.

18. The usual word order of sentences is subject–verb–object. Eng. Pid. Lat. Esp.

Translate these expressions into each of the other three languages:

ENGLISH	PIDGIN	LATIN	ESPERANTO
a big man	bigfela man	magnus vir	granda viro
a little woman	smolfela meri	parvus bona	malgranda virin
a big wall	bigfela wol	paries magnus	granda muro
a man of the good book	_____	_____	bona libro de viro
She is a woman.	_____	_____	_____
_____	Disfela haus i-smolfela.	_____	_____
_____	_____	Eum legunt.	_____
_____	_____	_____	Vi rigardis libron.

13

1.13 LANGUAGE SYSTEMS ARE CONVENTIONS

Even echoic words are conventional. On the left are a number of words designating various noises and on the right are the sources of those noises. Match the two columns. The correct answers are printed below, but try your ear before you look at the key.

_____ guau	1. a Spanish dog	
_____ glouglou	2. an Irish dog	
_____ kuckeliku	3. a Serbo-Croatian dog	
_____ plof	4. a Hebrew cat	
_____ bim-bam	5. an Italian sheep	
_____ amh-amh	6. a Swedish horse	
_____ bats	7. a Hungarian pig	
_____ gakgak	8. a French turkey	
_____ tsiltsul	9. a Swedish cock	
_____ bè	10. a Turkish duck	
_____ yimyum	11. an English nightingale	
_____ av-av	12. a Dutch door slamming	
_____ gnägg	13. a Russian door slamming	
_____ jug jug tereu	14. a German bell ringing	
_____ röff-röff	15. a Hebrew bell ringing	

KEY: 1, 8, 9, 12, 14, 2, 13, 10, 15, 5, 4, 3, 6, 11, 7.

1.14 LANGUAGE CHANGE AND LINGUISTIC CORRUPTION

Here are three translations of the paternoster corresponding to the three major periods in the history of our language: Old English (or Anglo-Saxon), Middle English, and early Modern English. The first was made about the year 1000, the second is from the Wyclif Bible of 1380, and the third is from the King James Bible of 1611.

OLD ENGLISH: Fæder ūre, þū þe eart on heofonum, sī þīn nama gehālgod. Tōbecume þīn

[handwritten: Father our thou that art in heaven be thy name hallowed come ~~thy kingdom~~]

rīce. Gewurðe þīn willa on eorðan swā swā on heofonum. Ūrne gedæghwāmlican hlāf syle ūs tō

[handwritten: thy ~~kingdom~~ Be done thy will on earth so as in heaven Our substance and office loaf]

dæg. And forgyf ūs ūre gyltas, swā swā wē forgyfað ūrum gyltendum. And ne gelǣd þū ūs on

[handwritten: ~~treats~~ give to us today And forgive us our debts so as we forgive our debtors]

costnunge, ac ālȳs ūs of yfele. Sōðlice.

[handwritten: And no lead thous us in temptaction but deliver us from Evil. Amen.]

MIDDLE ENGLISH: Oure fadir that art in heuenes halowid be thi name, thi kyngdom come to, be thi wille don in erthe as in heuene, yeue to us this day oure breed ouir other substaunce, & foryeue to us oure dettis, as we foryeuen to oure dettouris, & lede us not in to temptacion: but delyuer us from yuel, amen.

EARLY MODERN ENGLISH: Our father which art in heauen, hallowed be thy Name. Thy kingdome come. Thy will be done, in earth, as it is in heauen. Giue vs this day our dayly bread. And forgiue vs our debts, as we forgiue our debters. And leade vs not into temptation, but deliuer vs from euill: For thine is the kingdome, and the power, and the glory, for euer, Amen.

1. Try to make a word-for-word translation of the Old English by comparing it with the later versions. Write your translation in the blank spaces under the Old English words.

2. Some Old English words that may look completely unfamiliar have survived in Modern English in fixed expressions or with changed meanings. Finding the answers to these questions in a dictionary may help you to translate the Old English paternoster:
What is a 'bishop*ric*'? (cf. *rīce*) office of a bishop
What is the meaning of *worth* in 'woe *worth* the day'? (cf. *gewurðe*) _____
What are the Old English words from which came Modern English *so* and *as*? (cf. *swā swā*)
_____
What is the Old English source-word for Modern English *loaf*? hlāf
What is the meaning of *sooth* in *soothsayer* or *forsooth*? (cf. *sōðlice*) _____

3. What three letters of the Old English writing system have been lost from our alphabet?
þ ð æ

4. At first sight, the letters *v* and *u* seem to be used haphazardly in the King James translation, but there is a system in their use. Which is used at the beginning of a word? v Which is used medially? u

5. What different forms does Old English have for the word *our*? ūre ūrne
Can you suggest why Old English has more than one form for this word?
_____
_____

6. List three phrases from the Wyclif translation in which the use of prepositions differs from that in the King James version. kingdom come to

7. List three phrases from the Wyclif translation in which the word order differs from that in the Old English version. Our father hallowed be thy name, and lead us not

8. In general, does the Middle English version appear to be more similar to the Old English translation or to the King James translation? Give several reasons to support your answer.
_____
_____
_____

9. The King James version of the paternoster may be familiar, but in many ways its language is archaic. Rewrite the prayer in normal, contemporary English. Notice the kinds of change you must make to avoid an ecclesiastical flavor.

10. What reasons might an Elizabethan have for thinking the language of your version to be "corrupt"? What reasons might an Englishman of the year 1000 have for thinking the language of the King James version "corrupt"? Why would they both be wrong?
_____
_____

1.15 *THE QUESTION OF USAGE*

Which of the following expressions are considered good usage today? Which would you yourself say differently?

_____ 1. "These kind of knaves, I know." (Shakespeare, *King Lear*)

_____ 2. "I want to take this opportunity of thanking you on behalf of the Duchess of Windsor and I." (Edward, Duke of Windsor, in a radio speech, January 1965)

_____ 3. "and this she did . . . with a certain melancholy, as if life were all over for her and she was only shouting a few last messages to the fading shore." (J. B. Priestley, *The Good Companions*)

_____ 4. "I shall return." (General Douglas MacArthur on leaving Corregidor, March 1942)

_____ 5. "I only asked the question from habit." (B. Jowett, *The Dialogues of Plato*)

_____ 6. "The great point of honor on these occasions was for each man to strictly limit himself to half a pint of liquor." (Thomas Hardy, *The Mayor of Casterbridge*)

_____ 7. "No data is as yet available on how far this increase continues." (New York *Times*, August 10, 1958)

_____ 8. "Those assemblies were not wise like the English parliament was." (J. C. Morison, *Macaulay*)

_____ 9. "Here there does seem to be, if not certainties, at least a few probabilities." (H. G. Wells, *Mankind in the Making*)

_____ 10. "Whom do men say that I the Son of man am?" (Matthew 10:13)

1.16 USAGE AND THE DICTIONARY

1. Below are a number of usage labels employed in some dictionaries. Which of them appear in the entries of the desk dictionary you use, and what does your dictionary say in its prefatory material about the meaning of those terms?

archaic	dialect	incorrect	localism	poetic	slang
argot	formal	informal	nonstandard	rare	standard
British	humorous	jargon	obsolescent	regional	substandard
colloquial	illiterate	literary	obsolete	shop talk	vulgar

_____

_____

_____

_____

_____

2. The following expressions evoke varying reactions among English speakers. First decide whether you regard each as acceptable or not; then look up each in three or four dictionaries and note the usage labels or comments that are given for it.

ain't (as in "ain't I") _____

anxious (in the sense 'eager') _____

but what ("no doubt but what . . .") _____

contact (as a verb, as in "I will contact you.") _____

disinterested (in the sense 'not interested') _____
_____

finalize _____
irregardless _____
nauseous (in the sense 'nauseated') _____
_____

thusly _____
type (without *of*, as in "a new type car") _____
_____

1.17 *THE* OXFORD ENGLISH DICTIONARY: *HISTORY AND PLAN*

One of the most useful tools for studying the history of the English language is the *Oxford English Dictionary* (*OED*), originally named *A New English Dictionary on Historical Principles* (*NED*). It is the best dictionary of its kind for any language in the world. Abridged versions of this work have been made, but the student of English should make himself familiar with the thirteen volumes of the complete *OED*. Examine the dictionary and read the prefatory material, noting especially these points:

1. The *OED* is based on a large collection of quotations. How were the quotations gathered and by whom?

2. From what kind of material and from what historical periods were the quotations taken?

3. How many quotations were gathered as the basis for the *OED*, and how many quotations actually appear as illustrative citations in the dictionary?

4. What "new principles in lexicography" were followed by the editors of the *OED*?

5. Who was responsible for the initial preparation of the dictionary materials, and in what year was the work begun?

6. Who were the chief editors of the *OED*?

7. What difficulties did the editors encounter as they prepared the material for publication?

8. In what year was the first part of the dictionary published, and in what year was the publication completed?

Write a short report on the *OED*, considering the questions above and explaining why the *OED* is uniquely valuable among dictionaries. For what purposes is it most useful? What limitations does it have? That is, for what kind of information or for what uses might you prefer another dictionary?

1.18 *THE* OXFORD ENGLISH DICTIONARY: *THE TREATMENT OF ENTRIES*

As an example of the kind of information you will find in the *OED*, examine the sample entry that follows on page 18.

There are four parts to the treatment of each entry:

I. The **identification** begins with the *main form* in boldface type. It is the usual or typical spelling under which the rest of the information for the word is entered. Next follows the *pronunciation*, within parentheses; the symbols used in writing the sound of the word are explained

Enthusiasm (enþiū·zi¡æ̆z'm). Also 7 enthusiasme, (entousiasm, 8 enthysiasm). [ad. late L. *enthūsiasm-us*, Gr. ἐνθουσιασμός, f. ἐνθουσιά-ζειν, f. ἐνθουσία (Zonaras *Lex.*) the fact of being ἔνθεος possessed by a god. Cf. Fr. *enthousiasme*.

The word ἐνθουσία has been explained by Leo Meyer as for *ἐνθεουσία, abstr. sb. f. ἐνθεοῦντ- stem of pr. pple. of *ἐνθεεῖν to be ἔνθεος.]

†1. Possession by a god, supernatural inspiration, prophetic or poetic frenzy; an occasion or manifestation of these. *Obs.*

[**1579** E. K. *Gloss. Spenser's Sheph. Cal.* Oct. *Argt.*, A certaine ἐνθουσιασμός and celestiall inspiration. **1608** SYLVESTER *Du Bartas* 210, I feel the vertue of my spirit decayed, The Enthousiasmos of my Muse allaid.] **1603** HOLLAND *Plutarch's Mor.* 1342 The Dæmons use to make their prophets and prophetesses to be ravished with an Enthusiasme or divine fury. **1620** J. PYPER tr. *Hist. Astrea* I. v. 146 The Bacchanals runne thorow the streets raging and storming, full of the Enthusiasme of their god. **1651** BAXTER *Inf. Bapt.* 87 Doth he think they knew it by Enthusiasm or Revelation from Heaven? **1674** HICKMAN *Hist. Quinquart.* (ed. 2) 8 Nothing made the Anabaptists so infamous as their pretended enthusiasms or revelations. **1693** URQUHART *Rabelais* III. Prol., It is my sole Entousiasm. **1807** ROBINSON *Archæol. Græca* III. xii. 253 The second sort of θεομάντεις..were such as pretended to enthusiasm.

† b. (cf. 3.) Poetical fervour, impassioned mood or tone. *Obs.*

1693 DRYDEN *Juvenal* Pref. (J.), Poetry, by a kind of enthusiasm, or extraordinary emotion of soul, makes it seem to us that we behold, etc. **1779-81** JOHNSON *L. P., Cowley* Wks. II. 70 He [Cowley] was the first who imparted to English numbers the enthusiasm of the greater ode, and the gaiety of the less.

2. Fancied inspiration; 'a vain confidence of divine favour or communication' (J.). In 18th c. often in vaguer sense: Ill-regulated or misdirected religious emotion, extravagance of religious speculation. *arch.*

1660 H. MORE *Myst. Godl.* To Rdr., If ever Christianity be exterminated, it will be by Enthusiasme. **1711** SHAFTESB. *Charac.* § 7 (1737) I. 53 Inspiration is a real feeling of the Divine Presence, and Enthusiasm a false one. **1747** DODD-RIDGE *Life Col. Gardiner* § 137. 163 There is really such a Thing as Enthusiasm, against which it becomes the true Friends of the Revelation to be diligently on their Guard. **1766** WALPOLE *Let.* 10 Oct., Towards the end he [Wesley] exalted his voice and acted very ugly enthusiasm. **1772** PRIESTLEY *Inst. Relig.* (1782) I. 121 Enthusiasm [makes us] imagine that we are the peculiar favorites of the divine being. **1829** I. TAYLOR *Enthus.* ii. (1867) 20 The most formal and lifeless devotions..are mere enthusiasm unless, etc. **1841-4** EMERSON *Ess. Over-Soul* Wks. (Bohn) I. 118 Everywhere the history of religion betrays a tendency to enthusiasm.

3. The current sense: Rapturous intensity of feeling in favour of a person, principle, cause, etc.; passionate eagerness in any pursuit, proceeding from an intense conviction of the worthiness of the object.

1716 KENNETT in Ellis *Orig. Lett.* II. 429 IV. 306 The King of Sweden..must have much more enthusiasm in him to put it in execution. **1766-7** MRS. S. PENNINGTON *Lett.* III. 167 Different religions have introduced prejudices, Enthusiasms, and Scepticisms. **1792** *Anecd. W. Pitt* I. xviii. 282 A passion for glory which was nothing short of enthusiasm. **1808** SIR JOHN MOORE in Jas. Moore *Camp. Spain* 76 The armies you see are also without enthusiasm, or even common obstinacy. **1817** MISS MITFORD in L'Estrange *Life* II. i. 11 Enthusiasm is very catching, especially when it is very eloquent. **1863** MARY HOWITT tr. *F. Bremer's Greece* I. ii. 56 Enthusiasm for the ideals of his country and of humanity.

From the *Oxford English Dictionary*. Reprinted by permission of the Clarendon Press, Oxford.

in the front of each volume of the dictionary. The pronunciation will often be followed by an abbreviation designating the part of speech, for example, *a* for adjective or *v* for verb; these abbreviations are also explained in the front of each volume. If no part of speech is designated for a word, as in the case of "Enthusiasm," the word is a substantive or noun. If the word is a technical term restricted to one field of knowledge, the restriction will be indicated next by an abbreviated *specification of use*, such as Mus. (music) or Bot. (botany). Or if the word is otherwise limited in its use because it is obsolete, archaic, colloquial, dialectal, and so forth, its *status* will be indicated by an appropriate abbreviation. Neither of these restrictions applies to "Enthusiasm." Next follows a list of *earlier forms* or spellings. For "Enthusiasm," three such earlier spellings are given: the spelling "enthusiasme" was used in the seventeenth century (hence the 7 preceding the form), and less commonly the spellings "entousiasm" and "enthysiasm" were used in the seventeenth and eighteenth centuries respectively. The identification ends with a list of *inflections* if they are in any way irregular. Since "Enthusiasm" has only the regular noun plural in -*s*, no inflections are listed for it.

II. Next the **form history** of the word is given within square brackets. The *etymology* or origin of the word is traced as far back as the editors were able to track it. "Enthusiasm" is an adaptation (ad.), that is, a scholarly borrowing, from the late Latin *enthūsiasmus* or from the Greek *enthousiasmos*, which was formed from (f.) the verb *enthousiazein*, in turn formed from the noun *enthousia*, which means "the fact of being *entheos*, possessed by a god." With the English word, we might compare the French *enthousiasme*, which has a similar etymology. The "Cf." indicates that although the English and French words have a similar origin, they are not directly connected with each other. The remainder of the etymology in small type traces the earlier history of the Greek word *enthousia*. We need not be concerned with it except to point out that the asterisk which occurs before several of the words has a special significance; it means that the word it precedes is not actually preserved in written records but is a reconstructed form. The asterisk says, in effect, "The word *entheousia* does not occur in the Greek writings that have come down to us, but in discussing the history of the word it is useful to postulate the existence of some such form." We will have occasion to use the asterisk in this way in Chapter 4 (see Pyles, p. 90, n. 21).

III. The third part of the treatment is the **signification** or meaning of the word. "Enthusiasm" has had three different meanings in English, so all three of these meanings are listed and numbered in roughly chronological order. The dagger before the first definition, as well as the abbreviation *Obs.* after it, indicates that this sense is obsolete; the word is no longer used with this meaning. The earliest English meaning of the word, "possession by a god," gave rise to a subsidiary meaning, "poetical fervour," which is sublettered **b** and also marked obsolete. The comment "cf. 3" in parentheses refers the reader to the third sense of the word and implies some connection between the two senses. It is likely that the current meaning of the word developed out of sense 1b. For the second major sense of the word, "fancied inspiration," the editors of the *OED* have quoted a definition from Samuel Johnson's dictionary (J.): "a vain confidence of divine favour or communication." They have also added some information about the use of the word in the eighteenth century. The abbreviation *arch.* stands for *archaic*, which indicates that this meaning of the word survives in current English only in highly specialized use, in this case chiefly in discussions of eighteenth-century religious practices. The third meaning is the "current sense," that is, the sense current at the time the *OED* was compiled.

IV. The last part of the treatment is the **illustrative quotations** which follow each meaning and show the word being used in that sense. Thus the first quotation under the first meaning of "Enthusiasm" is from Spenser's *Shepheardes Calender*, the October Eclogue. More precisely, the quotation is from the Argument to that eclogue, which is part of the Gloss written by the otherwise anonymous E. K. The work was published in 1579. In Volume XIII of the *OED* there is a bibliography of the works from which the quotations were most often taken. It is usually possible to find there the full title of a source abbreviated in the quotations. Occasionally, however, the reader must simply use his own ingenuity.

The first quotation given for every meaning is the earliest use in that sense which the editors of the *OED* were able to find. It would, of course, be unwarranted to assume that the word had not been used earlier, but it is likely in most cases that the earliest date given is close to the initial appearance of the word in English. The quotations for each meaning are given in roughly chronological order. For practical purposes, we can use the quotations given in the *OED* as reliable indications of the appearance, frequency, and desuetude of the word. Further, the quotations supply more information about the history of the word than might be apparent from a casual glance. Some of this information will be pointed out in the questions below.

After you have examined the entry for "Enthusiasm" and have made yourself familiar with the treatment accorded the word, answer these questions:

1. Why might you be cautious about using the pronunciation given for *enthusiasm*? (Consult the preface of the *OED* to find when the dictionary was compiled and where.)

   _____

2. In the form history, *enthusiasm* is said to have been adapted (ad.) as a scholarly loan-word. Other words, such as *entice*, are said to have been adopted (a.) as popular loan-words. What evidence do the quotations supply that *enthusiasm* in fact entered English as a scholarly word rather than as a common word used freely by the people?_____

   _____

   _____

3. The quotation from 1608 is out of chronological order. Why are it and the quotation from 1579 put in square brackets? (Notice the form of the word in these two quotations.)

_____

4. Several recent dictionaries trace the etymology of *enthusiasm* directly to the Greek *enthousiasmos* without mentioning the Latin *enthūsiasmus* at all. Judging from the quotations, which of the two possible etymologies would you think more likely to be correct?

_____

5. How do the quotations from 1579, 1603, 1651, 1674, and 1693 (Dryden) especially help to define the word? _____

_____

6. Do those five quotations suggest that the word would have been a familiar or unfamiliar one to readers in the late sixteenth and the seventeenth centuries? Why?_____

_____

_____

7. The last quotation for the meaning "possession by a god" is from 1807. What indication is there that this meaning may in fact have been archaic by the early nineteenth century?

_____

_____

8. The meaning "poetical fervour" has been included as a subdivision of the earliest sense of the word. How do the quotations from 1579 and 1608 justify its inclusion there?

_____

_____

9. Why did the editors of the *OED* quote Johnson's definition as part of the second meaning of the word?_____

_____

_____

10. The second definition is "fancied inspiration," but inspiration can be poetical, political, religious, scholarly, and so forth. What kind of inspiration is meant by *enthusiasm* in the quotations for the second definition?_____

_____

11. Which quotations from the sense "possession by a god" most clearly foreshadow the typical eighteenth-century meaning "fancied inspiration"?_____

_____

12. Which quotation from the third or current sense suggests most clearly how that sense developed out of the second meaning? _____

13. Does the contemporary use of *enthusiasm* differ in any respect from the definition given by the *OED* for the "current sense" of the word? If so, how? In answering this question, decide which of these two phrases seems more natural:

    an enthusiasm which was nothing short of passion
    a passion which was nothing short of enthusiasm

and compare it with the quotation from 1792. _____

_____

_____

14. Quite apart from its denotation or literal meaning, a word may change its connotation or emotional value. Of the twenty-three quotations cited to illustrate the denotations of

enthusiasm, some use the word with an unfavorable connotation, some with a favorable connotation, and some with a neutral or indeterminate connotation. Which connotation has predominated during the entire history of the word in English? _____
Of what subject matter has *enthusiasm* been used most often with an unfavorable connotation? _____
With a favorable connotation? _____
What connotation does the word most often have in current use? _____
_____

15. When you consult the *OED* for the history of a word, in what part of the treatment will you find the most information? _____
_____

1.19   *USING THE* OXFORD ENGLISH DICTIONARY

The questions about each of these words can be answered from the information in the *Oxford English Dictionary*.

1. **algebra**   From what language is this word ultimately derived? _____
   What nonmathematical meaning has the word had? _____
   According to Burton in his *Anatomy of Melancholy*, who invented algebra?
   _____
   Was he right? _____

2. **anatomy**   What was the earliest spelling of this word in English? _____
   What misunderstanding created the word *atomy*? _____
   _____
   In what century did the word come into common use, as opposed to the century of first occurrence? _____

3. **anesthetic**   Under what "main form" is this word entered in the *OED*? _____
   In what century was the word first used? _____
   Who is credited with proposing the term? _____

4. **ask** *v.*   In what centuries was the spelling *axe* used? _____
   From what dialect did the spelling *ask* enter Standard English? _____
   What prepositions other than *of* have been used in the expression "ask (something) *of* a person"? _____

5. **belfry**   In what century did the *l* first appear in the spelling of *belfry*? _____
   In what century did the word acquire the meaning "bell-tower"? _____
   Name another word in which an *r* has been replaced by an *l*. _____

6. **cheap**   The adjective *cheap* results from the shortening of what phrase? _____
   _____
   What was the meaning of *cheap* in that phrase? _____
   Are cognates (related forms) of this word common in other Germanic languages?
   _____

7. **child** *sb.*   Are cognates (related forms) of this word common in other Germanic languages?
   _____
   The word has had five varieties of plural. Identify them by citing one spelling for each.
   _____
   What does the word mean in Byron's poem *Childe Harold*? _____

8. **collate**   What other English verb is derived from the same Latin source as *collate*?

_____

What is the oldest English meaning of this word?_____

What technical meaning does the word have in bookbinding? _____

9. **crocodile**   What is the oldest spelling of this word in English?_____

In what century was the modern spelling introduced, and what was the motive for its introduction? _____

Who was the first English author to refer to a crocodile's weeping?_____

10. **dip**   Are *dip* and *deep* cognate (historically related) forms?_____

Was *dip* first a noun or a verb?_____

What does the noun mean in thieves' slang? _____

11. **diploma**   What two plural forms has the word had in English? _____

What is the literal sense of the Greek word from which *diploma* ultimately derives?

_____

What meaning of *diploma* connects it with *diplomat*? _____

12. **error**   In what century was the spelling *errour* generally replaced by the current form?

What sense does the word have in Tennyson's "The damsel's headlong error thro' the wood"? _____

How did the word acquire that sense?_____

13. **ether**   What was the earliest sense of this word in English? _____

When was the word first used to name the anesthetic substance? _____

Which English spelling is earlier: *aether* or *ether*? _____

14. **father**   In what century did the spelling with *th* become common? _____

What medial consonant did the word have in earlier times? _____

In what other words has a similar change taken place? _____

15. **fiber**   What is the main entry form of this word in the *OED*? _____

What is the earliest English meaning of the word? _____

How do the quotations of 1598 and 1601 suggest that the earliest meaning is modeled on Latin usage? _____

16. **glamour**   *Glamour* is an altered form of what common English word?_____

What is the oldest sense of *glamour*? _____

Who is responsible for popularizing the word in standard literary English?

_____

17. **gossip**   This word was originally a compound of what two words?_____

What was the earliest meaning of the word? _____

In what century was the word first used in the meaning "idle talk"?_____

18. **humour** *sb.*   Which pronunciation is older: the one with or the one without the *h*-sound?

_____

What did Shakespeare mean by the word in this phrase from *Julius Caesar*: "the humours / Of the danke Morning"? _____
In what century did the meaning "amusement, jocularity" become common?

_____

19. **inn** *sb.* Is the word related to the modern preposition-adverb *in*? _____
James Howell wrote, "Queen Mary gave this House to Nicholas Heth, Archbishop of York, and his successors for ever, to be their Inne." Are we to suppose that the archbishop ran a public house? If not, what? _____
What are the Inns of Court? _____

20. **jail** *sb.* Briefly explain why this word has two spellings in contemporary use.

_____
Give the date of a quotation which suggests that the word formerly had two pronunciations. _____
Examine the quotations cited for the first definition. Which spelling is more common in official records? _____

21. **knave** *sb.* With what contemporary German word is *knave* cognate? _____
What is the earliest recorded meaning of *knave*? _____
As a name for a playing-card, which word is older, *knave* or *jack*? _____

22. **leech** *sb.*[1] What semantic connection is there between this word and the homophonous *leech, sb.*[2]? _____
Can you offer any explanation for the lack of figurative uses of the word after the sixteenth century? _____

_____
Why was the *leech-finger* so called? _____

23. **legend** What is the etymological sense of the word, that is, the meaning it had in the language from which it is ultimately derived? _____
What is its earliest recorded meaning in English? _____
In what century does the sense "unauthentic or non-historical story" appear?

_____

24. **Mrs.** What is the origin of the title? _____
In what century did the abbreviation become common? _____
Mrs. Bracegirdle was a popular actress on the Restoration stage. Why would it be wrong to assume that a Mr. Bracegirdle was her husband? _____

_____

25. **nostril** This word was originally a compound of what two words? _____

_____
In what century was the *r* first metathesized (reversed in order) with the vowel?

_____
Judging from all the quotations, which spelling has been more usual: that with *th* (þ) or that with *t*? _____

26. **off** What is the origin of this word? _____
In what century did *off* become the only standard spelling of the word? _____

_____
Explain how *off* has come to function sometimes as a verb. _____

_____

27. **pandemonium**   What is the earliest meaning of the word?_____

    Who coined the word?_____

    In what year is the sense "uproar," as opposed to "place of uproar," first recorded?

    _____

28. **plow**   What is the main entry form of this word in the *OED*?_____

    What is the difference between the two spellings in current English use?_____

    _____

    What is the earliest recorded meaning of the word in English?_____

29. **prestige**   What is the earliest meaning of the word in English?_____

    Although there are quotations from 1870 and 1881 illustrating the word in its earliest meaning, how do they suggest that the meaning was already obsolete?_____

    _____

    What evidence is there in the quotations that the meaning "influence or reputation" was derived from French?_____

    _____

30. **protocol**   What is the etymological sense of *protocol* (its meaning in the ultimate source-language from which the word is derived)?_____

    What is the earliest sense of the word in English?_____

    If the editors of the *OED* were rewriting the fifth definition today, what changes might they make? Specifically, which two qualifications might they omit?_____

    _____

31. **quiz**   In what century did the word first appear in English?_____

    What was its earliest meaning?_____

    When and where did the meaning "short test" develop?_____

    _____

32. **rooster**   What is the source of the word?_____

    How is its use limited geographically?_____

    In what century was it first used?_____

33. **salmagundi**   From what language was the word derived?_____

    Which two occasional spellings of the word show the influence of folk etymology (see Pyles, pp. 302–05)?_____

    Cite a quotation which clearly shows the connotations of the word when it is used figuratively._____

    _____

34. **shift** *sb.*   What is the origin of the noun?_____

    How did the word acquire the meaning "garment"?_____

    _____

    What meanings not listed in the *OED* has the word acquired in contemporary English?

    _____

35. **snob**   What is known about the origin of the word?_____

    _____

    What was its earliest meaning?_____

    Who do the quotations suggest popularized the word in its current sense?

    _____

36. **sphinx**   What plurals does the word have?_____

    In what century was the spelling *spynx* used?_____

Was the English word first applied to the Greek or the Egyptian creature?

37. **story** *sb.*² What is the apparent origin of this word?_____

According to the *OED*, what distinction is usually made in England between the first story and the first floor?_____

Which meaning of *story* is reflected in *clerestory*? _____

38. **swing** *v.*¹ Which past tense form is older: I *swung* or I *swang*?_____
During what centuries was the past participle *swinged* used?_____
A fifteenth-century recipe says, "Recipe [take] brede gratyd, & eggis; & swyng tham togydere." What is the cook supposed to do? _____

39. **thimble** Describe the origin of this word. _____

Name another word which has developed an excrescent *b*. _____
Give the earliest quotation you can find that implies that thimbles were made of metal.

40. **tomato** What is the oldest English form of the word? _____
How is the spelling *tomato* explained?_____
What earlier English name did the tomato have? _____

41. **uncouth** What is the earliest English sense of the word?_____
In what century is the modern sense "uncomely, awkward" first recorded?

Explain the meaning and origin of *unco* in Burns's poem "Address to the Unco Guid."_____

42. **victual** *sb.* In what century does the *c* first appear in Standard English, as contrasted with Scottish, spellings of the word?_____
What is the origin of the *c*?_____
Examine all the quotations dated after 1800. Describe any change you detect in the use of the word during the nineteenth century. _____

43. **wretch** *sb.* What is the meaning of the Modern German cognate of this word?

What is the earliest meaning of the word in English?_____
Judging from the spellings of this word, by what century had final *a* sounds changed in pronunciation?_____

44. **Yankee** What origin of this word do the editors of the *OED* think most plausible?

Why do they prefer it to the other possibilities they list?_____

The word apparently originated as a derisive term. How early does it seem to have acquired a neutral connotation in some uses? _____

45. **zest** If a recipe calls for a teaspoon of grated zest, what ought the cook to use?

Does the seventeenth-century quotation suggest that the word was in common English use at that time? Explain your answer. _____

_____

How early was the word used metaphorically? _____

1.20 THE PROCESS OF DICTIONARY-MAKING, OR EVERY MAN HIS OWN LEXICOGRAPHER

Because the publication of the *Oxford English Dictionary* extended over some forty-five years and even the supplement was completed a generation ago, this greatest of all dictionaries is less than satisfactory as a record of present-day English. For the historical study of our language, the *OED* is unsurpassed, but for contemporary usage, it is inadequate.

Take any one of the following words, or some similar term that has come into use since the publication of the *OED*, and investigate its meaning by using a technique similar to that of the *OED*.

1. Consult books and magazines or newspaper stories dealing with the subject area of the word to find examples of its use. The library catalog, the *Readers' Guide to Periodical Literature*, the *New York Times Index*, or similar indexes will help you locate relevant material. Look especially for quotations in which the context helps to define the word or in which there is an indication that the word has recently come into use in English.

2. For each use of the word that you find, prepare an index card giving the information described in the "Historical Introduction" to the *OED*.

3. When you have collected enough useful quotations, frame a definition for the word and illustrate it with the quotations. Your definition should be based on all the quotations that you have collected. If the quotations justify it, you may need to recognize more than one sense for the word. List the "main form" of the word and write the definition and quotations in the style of the *OED* (you need not write further identification or form history).

SOME RECENT ENGLISH WORDS

acid rock	cop-out	mini (skirt)	shtick
bag 'specialty'	crash pad	mod	skylounge
bikeway	extravehicular	pantihose	space walk
camp(y)	flares 'trousers'	psychedelic	telelecture
clout 'influence'	hang-up	pulsar	think tank
computerize	kitsch	put-on	uptight
condominium 'apartment'	(Chemical) Mace	roll bar	Yippies

1.21 RECENT SCHOLARLY STUDY OF LANGUAGE

In each of the pairs below, one characteristic is more typical of descriptive-structural grammar and the other of transformational-generative grammar. Mark each characteristic DS or TG.

1. _____ Emphasizes a nonmentalistic or mechanistic view of human behavior.
   _____ Emphasizes that language behavior is primarily mental and creative in nature.

2. _____ Emphasizes the methods of analyzing the signaling devices in language.

_____ Emphasizes a system of rules that relate meaning to sound.

3. _____ Moves from the study of deep or conceptual structure to surface structure to phonological representation.

_____ Moves from the study of phonology to morphology to syntax.

4. _____ Conceives of a grammatical description as the result of segmenting and classifying the elements of a sentence.

_____ Conceives of a grammar as a device that defines and characterizes all the grammatical sentences of a language and none of the ungrammatical ones.

5. _____ Believes that the proper study of linguistics is competence—what a person knows, although nondiscursively, about his language—rather than actual performance.

_____ Believes that what people actually say is the primary object of linguistic study.

6. _____ Stresses universals—the ways in which all languages are alike.

_____ Stresses particulars—the ways in which each language uniquely differs from all others.

2

The Sounds and Spelling of
Current English

2.1 *QUESTIONS FOR REVIEW AND DISCUSSION*

1. Define the following terms:

phonetic transcription—	velar	off-glide
broad or narrow	glottal	diphthong
distinctive sounds	manner of articulation	schwa
contrastive pair	stop (plosive, explosive)	front vowel
phoneme	fricative (spirant)	back vowel
allophone	affricate	central vowel
aspiration (aspirate)	liquid	high vowel
complementary distribution	lateral	low vowel
place of articulation	retroflex	mid vowel
labial	nasal	rounded vowel
bilabial	voice (vibrancy)	tense vowel
labiodental	linking [r]	lax vowel
dental	intrusive [r]	vowel quantity (length)
interdental	intrusion (svarabhakti,	stress
alveolar	epenthesis, anaptyxis)	virgules
alveolopalatal	consonant	macron
palatovelar	vowel	
palatal	semivowel	

2. The discussion of the phoneme in Pyles's *Origins and Development* includes seven characteristics which might be summarized as in the following list. Look up the word *phoneme* in
several recent dictionaries. How many of these characteristics are included in the dictionary
definitions?
   (1) A phoneme is a group, class, or set of sounds used in speech.
   (2) The sounds of which a phoneme consists are phonetically similar to one another.
   (3) The sounds of which a phoneme consists alternate with one another in different phonetic
   environments (that is, they occur in complementary distribution).
   (4) The difference between two phonemes is contrastive (that is, phonemes serve to distinguish utterances from one another).
   (5) The difference between two sounds belonging to the same phoneme is not contrastive
   (that is, allophones do not serve to distinguish utterances).
   (6) The speakers of a language commonly regard the sounds that make up a single phoneme
   as the "same sound."

(7) Two sounds that belong to the same phoneme in one language may belong to different phonemes in another language.

3. The difference between vowels in the English words *sit* and *seat* is not phonemic in Spanish. On the other hand, the difference between [t] sounds in English *tone* and *stone* is phonemic in Chinese, Classical Greek, and Sanskrit.

If you are sufficiently familiar with some foreign tongue, cite some similar variations between the phonemic systems of that language and of English.

4. Describe the place and manner of articulation of the English consonants.

5. Describe the articulatory positions of the English vowels.

6. What are the most regular spellings for each of the phonemes of English?

7. A Korean general who wanted Westerners to pronounce his name not [pæk] but rather [pɑk] changed its Romanized spelling from *Pak* to *Park*. What dialect of English had he probably learned? How would most Americans pronounce the new spelling? For most Americans what spelling would most adequately represent the pronunciation General Park wanted?

8. What is the meaning of each of these symbols as used in transcribing sounds?

$$[\ ] \qquad / \ / \qquad \bar{\ } \qquad ´ \qquad ` \qquad ^$$

2.2 WRITING PHONETIC SYMBOLS

Phonetic symbols should always be in printed, never in cursive, form. Do not try to join them together like the letters of the longhand alphabet. Write [bo t], not [*bot*].

Phonetic notation does not use upper case and lower case letters like those of our conventional spelling. All phonetic symbols are lower case. *Jones* is transcribed phonetically as [jonz].

Always enclose phonetic symbols within square brackets. The brackets indicate that the symbol stands for a sound. When you refer to a symbol as a written letter of the alphabet or as part of a normal spelling, it should be underlined or italicized. Thus, *boat* represents a spelling; [bot] represents a pronunciation. Use one opening bracket ([) at the beginning of a phonetic transcription and one closing bracket (]) at the end; do not set off each word or each symbol with a separate set of brackets.

Notice the wedge over [š ž č ǰ]. Always write it as part of these symbols. Distinguish it from the circumflex mark which may be used over vowels, as in *rôle*.

Distinguish clearly between these pairs of letters:

[n] and [ŋ]   [d] and [ð]   [i] and [ɪ]   [u] and [ʊ]   [e] and [ɛ]

Write [æ] with one continuous stroke of the pen:

Write [ə] with the loop at the bottom:

Here is a list of most of the phonetic symbols you will have occasion to use. Each symbol is given in both printed and handwritten form. Practice writing the symbols distinctly and legibly.

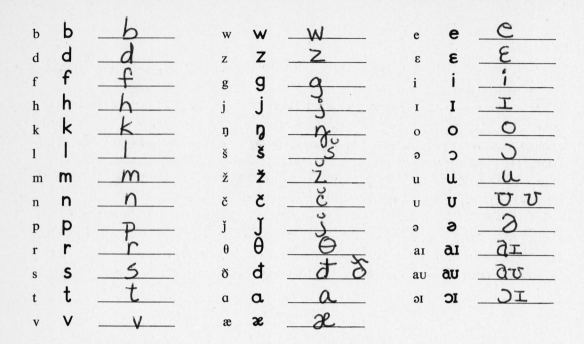

2.3 TRANSCRIPTION FOR READING PRACTICE

Since English varies somewhat from one dialect to another, no transcription can represent the speech of all readers. The pronunciation indicated by this transcription may differ from yours in various ways.

Read the words aloud. Write each word in conventional spelling. Some of the pronunciations correspond to more than one spelling.

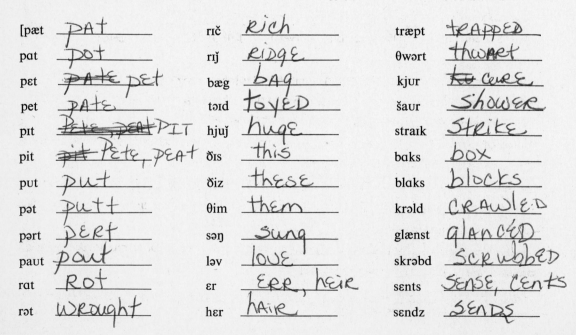

rot	_WROTE_	ɪr	_EAR_	šərts	_shirts_
rut	_ROOT_	wər	_WERE_	čərč	_church_
raɪt	_WRITE_	wɛr	_WEAR_	jəŋk]	_junk_

2.4 MORE READING PRACTICE

Here are some sentences in phonetic notation. To assist you, the punctuation and word division of conventional writing have been used. In a strictly phonetic transcription, they would be replaced by symbols for pitches and junctures, which would more accurately indicate what is said. (The use of punctuation marks in a phonetic transcription, though rare in American books, has the practical advantage of helping interpretation and is common in the journal of the International Phonetics Association.) Stress has not been indicated.

Read these sentences aloud using the pronunciation represented by the symbols. Notice any instances in which your own pronunciation differs from the one transcribed here. Unstressed vowels may very likely differ. Also notice that the pronunciation a word has in isolation may change considerably when the word is spoken normally in a sentence.

[æfərɪzəmz

frəm eč ɛl meŋkən[1]

wɛn ə mæn læfs æt ɪz trəbəlz, hi luzəz ə gʊd mɛni frɛnz. ðe nɛvər fərgɪv ðe ləs əv ðɛr prərəgətɪv.

frɛnšɪp ɪz ə kamən bəlif ɪn ðə sem fæləsiz, maʊntəbæŋks æn habgablənz.

kančənts ɪz ði ɪnər vɔɪs wič wornz əs ðæt səmwən me bi lʊkɪŋ.

ivəl ɪz ðæt wič wən bəlivz əv əðərz. its ə sɪn tə bəliv ivəl əv əðərz, bət its sɛldəm ə məstek.

æn aɪdiələst ɪz wən hu, ɑn notəsɪŋ ðæt ə roz smɛlz bɛtər ðæn ə kæbɪǰ, kəŋkludz ðæt it wɪl olso mek bɛtər sup.

suəsaɪd ɪz ə bəletəd ækwiɛsənts ɪn ði əpɪnjən əv wənz waɪfs rɛlətɪvz.

tɛmptešən ɪz ən ɪrəzɪstəbəl fors æt wərk ɑn ə muvəbəl badi.

bəfor ə mæn spiks, its olwiz sef tu əsum ðæt hiz ə ful. æftər i spiks, its sɛldəm nɛsəseri tu əsum it.

wɛn wɪmɪn kɪs, it olwiz rəmaɪnz wən əv praɪzfaɪtərz šekɪŋ hænz.

if wɪmɪn bəlivd ɪn ðɛr həzbənz, ðe wʊd bi ə gʊd dil hæpiər. æn olso ə gʊd dil mor fulɪš.

ə bæčlər ɪz wən hu wɑnts ə waɪf, bət ɪz glæd i hæzənt gat ər.

dəmakrəsi ɪz ðə θɪri ðæt ðə kamən pipəl no wət ðe wɑnt, æn dəzərv tə gɛt it gʊd ən hard.

pjurətənɪzəm ɪz ðə həntɪŋ fɪr ðæt səmwən, səmwɛr, me bi hæpi.

ə pæstər ɪz wən implɔɪd baɪ ðə wɪkəd tə pruv tə ðɛm baɪ hɪz ɪgzæmpəl ðæt vərču dəzənt pe.

ə kætəkɪzəm. kwɛščən—if ju faɪn so məč ðæt ɪz ənwərði əv rɛvrənts ɪn ðə junaɪtəd stets, ðɛn waɪ du ju lɪv hɪr? ænsər—waɪ du mɛn go tə zuz?

ɛpətæf. if, æftər aɪ dəpart ðɪs vel, ju ɛvər rəmɛmbər mi æn hæv θot tə pliz maɪ gost, fərgɪv səm sɪnər æn wɪŋk jər aɪ æt səm homli gərl.]

[1] From H. L. Mencken, *A Mencken Chrestomathy* (New York, 1953), pp. 616–27 *passim*. Reprinted by permission of the publisher, Alfred A. Knopf, Inc.

2.5 CONTRASTIVE SETS

A contrastive set is a group of words which differ from one another by a single sound. Thus *hat–bat–rat* are a contrastive set which differ only in their initial consonants; *hat–had–ham* are another set which differ in their final consonants; and *hat–hot–hit* are a set which differ in their vowels. A contrastive set like *causing–caulking–coughing–calling* differ only in their medial consonants. Notice that it is a difference in sound, not in spelling, that we are concerned with. Furthermore, notice that *shawl–tall* are a contrastive pair because they differ only in their initial sounds, [š]–[t], but that *shawl–stall* are not a contrastive pair because they have more than a minimum difference, [š]–[st].

On this and the next pages are a number of contrastive sets which show variation in (1) the vowel, (2) the initial consonant, and (3) the final consonant. Make each set as complete as you can by adding words which show a minimum contrast in sound. For example, on the page devoted to initial consonants, the next word in the third column might be *dough* or *doe*.

VOWELS

[i]	leak	feel	lead	~~toose~~	___	beat	peel	meat	keyed	bead
[ɪ]	lick	fill	lid	miss	kit	bit	pill	mitt	kid	bid
[e]	lake	fail	laid	mace	___	bait	pail	mate	___	bade
[ɛ]	___	fell	led	mess	___	bet	___	met	___	bed
[æ]	lack	___	lad	mass	cat	bat	pal	mat	cad	bad
[u]	Luke	fool	lewd	moose	___	boot	pool	___	cooed	booed
[ʊ]	look	full	___	___	___	___	pull	___	could	___
[o]	___	foal	load	___	coat	boat	pole	moat	code	___
[ɔ]	___	fall	lawd	moss	caught	bought	pall	mall	cawed	___
[ɑ]	lock	___	___	___	cot	___	___	___	cod	___
[ə]	luck	___	___	muss	cut	but	___	mutt	cud	bud
[ər]	lurk	furl	___	___	cuet	___	pearl	___	curd	bird
[aɪ]	like	file	lied	mice	kite	bite	pile	might	___	bide
[aʊ]	___	foul	loud	mouse	___	bout	___	___	cowed	bowed
[ɔɪ]	___	foil	___	___	___	___	___	___	___	___

	pie	pooh	Poe	pay	peas	pore	pain	pill	pail	peer	pair
[p]	pie	pooh	Poe	pay	peas	pore	pain	pill	pail	peer	pair
[b]	by	boo	beau	bay	bees	bore	___	bill	bail	beer	bare
[t]	tie	two	toe	___	tease	tore	___	till	tail	tier	tear
[d]	die	do	doe	day	___	door	___	dill	dale	deer	dare
[k]	Chi	coo	___	___	keys	core	___	kill	kale	___	care
[g]	guy	goo	go	gay	___	gore	gain	gill	gale	___	___
[č]	___	chew	___	___	cheese	chore	chain	chill	___	cheer	chair
[j]	___	Jew	___	jay	___	___	___	___	jail	jeer	___
[f]	fie	___	foe	___	fees	fore	fain	fill	fail	fear	fair
[v]	vie	___	___	___	___	___	vain	___	veil	veer	___
[θ]	thigh	___	___	___	___	___	___	___	___	___	___
[ð]	thy	___	though so	they	these	___	___	___	___	___	there
[s]	sigh	sue	sew	say	seas	sore	___	sill	sail	seer	___
[z]	Xi	zoo	___	___	___	___	___	___	___	___	___
[š]	shy	shoe	___	___	___	___	___	___	shale	sheer	share
[m]	my	moo	___	may	___	more	main	mill	mail	___	mayor
[n]	nigh	new	no	nay	knees	nor	___	nill	nail	near	___
[l]	lie	lieu	low	lay	leas	lore	lain	___	___	leer	lair
[r]	rye	rue	row	ray	___	roar	rain	___	rail	reer	rare
[w]	wye	woo	woe	way	___	wore	___	will	wail	___	wear
[j]	___	you	___	yea	___	yore	___	___	___	year	___
[h]	high	who	hoe	hay	___	whore	___	hill	hail	hear	hair

33

[p]	reap	lip	ape	ripe	cap	roup	sip	——	rap	——	lope
[b]	——	lib	Abe	——	cab	rube	——	babe	——	Bab	lobe
[t]	——	lit	Ate	write	CAT	Root / ROUTE	Sit	bait	RAT	bAt	——
[d]	read	lid	Aid	Ride	CAD	RUDE	Sid	bade	——	bAD	lODE / bAD
[k]	reek	lick	Ache	——	——	——	Sick	bAke	RACK	bACk	——
[g]	——	——	——	——	——	——	~~bag~~	——	RAg	bAg	——
[č]	reach	——	——	——	CAtch	——	——	——	——	batch	loAch
[j]	——	——	Age	——	——	Rouge	——	beige	——	badge	——
[f]	reef	——	——	——	——	Rufe	——	——	——	——	loAf
[v]	reeve	live	——	——	CAlve	——	——	——	——	——	——
[θ]	wreath	——	——	——	——	Ruth	——	——	wrAth	bAth	loAthe
[ð]	wreathe	——	——	writhe	——	——	——	bathe	——	——	loAthe
[s]	Rhys	——	ACE	RICE	——	——	——	bass / bAse	——	bAss	——
[z]	——	Liz	——	RISE	——	RUES	——	bays	——	——	lows
[š]	——	——	——	——	CASH	——	——	——	RAsh	bAsh	——
[ž]	——	——	——	——	——	Rouge	——	——	——	——	——
[m]	ream	limb	Aim / ~~tame~~	Rhyme	——	Room	——	——	RAM	bAM / ~~bam~~	loAM
[n]	——	Lynn	——	Rine	CAn	——	Sin	~~bane~~	RAn	bAn	loan
[ŋ]	Ring	——	——	——	——	——	~~sit~~	——	RAng	bang	——
[l]	reel	——	Ail / Ale	Rile	——	Rule	bail / bale	——	——	——	——
[r]	REAR	——	AIR	——	CARE	——	——	——	RARE	bear / bare	lore

34

This diagram, a conventionalized cross section of the head, identifies some of the important organs used in producing speech.

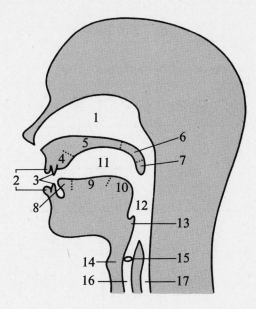

Identify each of the following organs by its number from the diagram above.

_____ alveolar ridge	_____ nasal cavity	_____ dorsum or back of tongue
_____ epiglottis	_____ oral cavity	_____ trachea
_____ esophagus	_____ pharynx	_____ uvula
_____ hard palate	_____ teeth	_____ velum (soft palate)
_____ larynx	_____ apex or tip of tongue	_____ vocal cords
_____ lips	_____ blade or front of tongue	

2.7 *A CLASSIFICATION OF ENGLISH CONSONANTS*

Complete the following chart by writing the phonetic symbols in the appropriate boxes so as to show the place and manner of articulation for each sound. For simplicity's sake, the stops and affricates are combined in this chart although because the latter are part stop, part fricative they are often treated separately. A dash in a box means that no English consonant phoneme has that place and manner of articulation. Such sounds, however, do occur in other languages (for example, the Spanish voiced bilabial fricative in *haber*) and even in English, as allophonic variants (for example, the common labiodental nasal in *emphatic*). You need not be concerned with such seemingly exotic sounds for a description of English phonemes, but you should be aware that they exist.

Consonants [b, d, f, h, k, l, m, n, p, r, s, t, v, w, z, g, j, ŋ, š, ž, č, ǰ, θ, ð]

			PLACE OF ARTICULATION						
			labial		*dental*			*palatovelar*		*glottal*
			bilabial	labio-dental	inter-dental	alveolar	alveolo-palatal	palatal	velar	
MANNER OF ARTICULATION	*stops and affricates*	voiced	b	—	—	d	ǰ		g	—
		voiceless	p	—	—	t	č		k	—
	fricatives	voiced	—	v	ð	z	ž	—	—	—
		voiceless	—	f	θ	s	š	—	—	h
	nasals		m	—	—	n	—	ŋ		
	liquids	lateral	—	—	—	l	—			
		retroflex	—	—	—	R				
	semivowels		w	—	—	—	—	j (ɥ)	w	—

2.8 THE ARTICULATORY DESCRIPTION OF CONSONANTS

Write the phonetic symbol for the sound that is described:

voiceless bilabial stop _p_

voiced labiodental fricative _f_

voiced velar stop _g_

★ voiceless affricate _≠ č_

voiced interdental fricative _ð_

glottal fricative _h_

voiced alveolar fricative _z_

alveolar nasal _n_

lateral _l_

(bilabial) velar semivowel _w_

voiceless alveolopalatal fricative _š_

bilabial nasal _m_

Give a phonetic description, like those above, for each of these sounds:

[t] voiceless alveolar ~~affricate~~ stop

[s] " " fricative

[ŋ] velar nasal

[ǰ] voiced alveolopalatal affricate

[θ] voiceless interdental fricative

[g] voiced velar stop

[b] voiced bilabial stop

[ž] " alveolopalatal fricative

[j] palatal semivowel

[f] voiceless labio-dental fricative

[k] " velar stop

[r] ~~alveolar~~ retroflex

36

Write the phonetic symbol for the *initial* consonant sound.

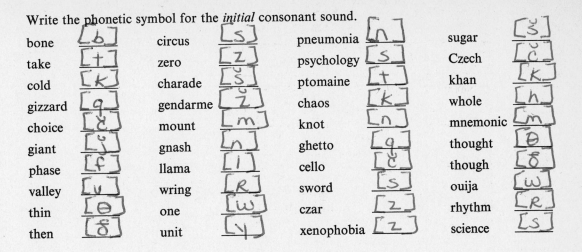

bone [b]	circus [s]	pneumonia [n]	sugar [š]
take [t]	zero [z]	psychology [s]	Czech [č]
cold [k]	charade [š]	ptomaine [t]	khan [k]
gizzard [g]	gendarme [ž]	chaos [k]	whole [h]
choice [č]	mount [m]	knot [n]	mnemonic [m]
giant [ǰ]	gnash [n]	ghetto [g]	thought [θ]
phase [f]	llama [l]	cello [č]	though [ð]
valley [v]	wring [R]	sword [s]	ouija [w]
thin [θ]	one [w]	czar [z]	rhythm [R]
then [ð]	unit [y]	xenophobia [z]	science [s]

Write the phonetic symbol for the *final* consonant sound.

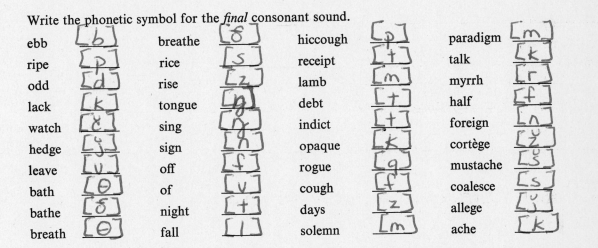

ebb [b]	breathe [ð]	hiccough [p]	paradigm [m]
ripe [p]	rice [s]	receipt [t]	talk [k]
odd [d]	rise [z]	lamb [m]	myrrh [r]
lack [k]	tongue [ŋ]	debt [t]	half [f]
watch [č]	sing [ŋ]	indict [t]	foreign [n]
hedge [ǰ]	sign [n]	opaque [k]	cortège [ž]
leave [v]	off [f]	rogue [g]	mustache [š]
bath [θ]	of [v]	cough [f]	coalesce [s]
bathe [ð]	night [t]	days [z]	allege [ǰ]
breath [θ]	fall [l]	solemn [m]	ache [k]

Write the phonetic symbol for the *medial* consonant sound or cluster.

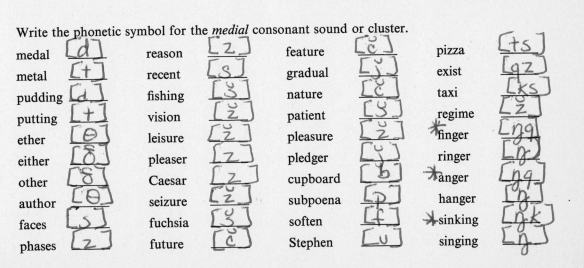

medal [d]	reason [z]	feature [č]	pizza [ts]
metal [t]	recent [s]	gradual [ǰ]	exist [gz]
pudding [d]	fishing [š]	nature [č]	taxi [ks]
putting [t]	vision [ž]	patient [š]	regime [ž]
ether [θ]	leisure [ž]	pleasure [ž]	*finger [ŋg]
either [ð]	pleaser [z]	pledger [ǰ]	ringer [ŋ]
other [ð]	Caesar [z]	cupboard [b]	*anger [ŋg]
author [θ]	seizure [ž]	subpoena [p]	hanger [ŋ]
faces [s]	fuchsia [š]	soften [f]	*sinking [ŋk]
phases [z]	future [č]	Stephen [v]	singing [ŋ]

2.12 A CLASSIFICATION OF ENGLISH VOWELS

Complete the following charts by writing the phonetic symbols in the appropriate boxes to show the place of articulation for each vowel. For the distinction between tense and lax and between rounded and spread vowels, see exercise 2.26.

Vowels [ɑ, æ, e, ɛ, i, ɪ, o, ɔ, u, ʊ, ə]

			FRONTNESS OF TONGUE		
			front	*central*	*back*
HEIGHT OF TONGUE	*high*	tense	i	—	u
		lax	ɪ	—	ʊ
	mid	tense	e	—	o
		lax	ɛ	ə	—
	low	rounded	—	—	ɔ
		spread	æ	—	ɑ

Diphthongs [aɪ, aʊ, ɔɪ]

A diphthong is a combination of two vowels pronounced in a single syllable. The tongue moves from the position for the first vowel to that for the second vowel. The arrows in this diagram indicate the direction of movement. Write the phonetic symbol for each diphthong at the beginning of the appropriate arrow. The vowel [a] is low central.

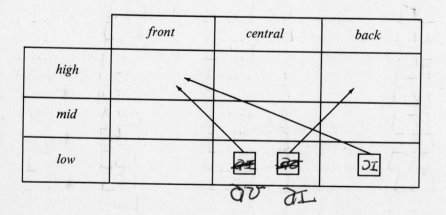

	front	*central*	*back*
high			
mid			
low		aɪ aʊ	ɔɪ

aʊ   aɪ

Write the phonetic symbol for the sound that is described:

high front tense vowel [i]　　　　　　　high back lax vowel [ʊ]
mid back tense vowel [o]　　　　　　　mid central lax vowel [ə]
low back rounded vowel [ɔ]　　　　　　low central to high back diphthong [aɪ]
mid front lax vowel [ɛ]　　　　　　　low back to high front diphthong [ɔɪ]

Give a phonetic description, like those above, for each of these sounds:

[u] high back tense vowel　　　　　　[ɑ] low back spread vowel
[ɪ] high front lax vowel　　　　　　　[æ] low front spread vowel
[e] mid front tense vowel　　　　　　[aɪ] low central to high back
　　　　　　　　　　　　　　　　　　　　diphthong

2.14 *TRANSCRIPTION: VOWELS AND CONSONANTS*

Transcribe the following words in their entirety, thus: *hat* [hæt].

dip	[dɪp]	hug	[hǝg]	thing	[θɪŋ]
deep	[dip]	curt	[kɔrt]	glows	[gloz]
shell	[šɛl]	wife	[waɪf]	verse	[vɛrs]
shake	[šek]	slouch	[slɔč]	sedge	[sɛǰ]
fool	[ful]	moist	[mɔɪst]	cow	[kǝ]
wool	[wʊl]	hue	[hju]	soy	[sɔɪ]
soap	[sop]	teach	[tič]	tall	[tɔl]
saw	[sɔ]	path	[pæθ]	chuck	[čǝk]
job	[jɑb]	youth	[juθ]	prize	[praɪz]
pad	[pæd]	pull	[pʊl]	they	[ðe]

2.15 *TRANSCRIPTION: HOMOGRAPHIC SPELLINGS*

Transcribe the following words.

lose	[luz]	plaid	[plæd]	blade	[bled]
loose	[lʊs]	laid	[led]	bade	[bæd]
plough	[plɔ]	said	[sɛd]	façade	[fɑsɑd]
though	[ðo]	done	[dǝn]	sweat	[swɛt]
move	[muv]	tone	[ton]	treat	[trit]
wove	[wov]	touch	[tɔč]	great	[gret]
dove	[dǝv]	couch	[kaʊč]	gaunt	[gɔnt]
tomb	[tum]	blood	[blǝd]	kraut	[krɔt]
comb	[kom]	good	[gʊd]	thyme	[taɪm]
bomb	[bam]	mood	[mud]	theme	[θim]

2.16 TRANSCRIPTION: SILENT LETTERS

Transcribe the following words.

through	[θru]	hour	[aʊr]	indict	[ɪndaɪt]
wrong	[rɔŋ]	lamb	[læm]	answer	[ænsər]
psalm	[salm]	gnaw	[nɔw]	solder	[soldər]
hymn	[hɪm]	folk	[folk]	plumber	[pləmər]
build	[bɪld]	phlegm	[flɛgəm]	rhythm	[rɪðəm]
calf	[kæf]	reign	[ren]	renege	[rənɛž]
two	[tu]	corps	[kor]	salmon	[sæmən]
who	[hu]	queue	[kju]	subpoena	[səpinə]
sigh	[saɪ]	kiln	[kɪln]	cologne	[kəlon]
know	[no]	gauge	[gej]	croquet	[kroke]

2.17 TRANSCRIPTION: SUFFIXES

Transcribe the following words.

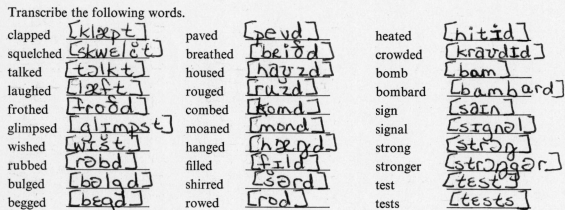

clapped	[klæpt]	paved	[pevd]	heated	[hitɪd]
squelched	[skwɛlčt]	breathed	[breɪðd]	crowded	[kraʊdɪd]
talked	[tɔlkt]	housed	[haʊzd]	bomb	[bam]
laughed	[læft]	rouged	[ruzd]	bombard	[bambard]
frothed	[froθd]	combed	[komd]	sign	[saɪn]
glimpsed	[glɪmpst]	moaned	[mond]	signal	[sɪgnəl]
wished	[wɪšt]	hanged	[hæŋd]	strong	[strɔŋ]
rubbed	[rəbd]	filled	[fɪld]	stronger	[strɔŋgər]
bulged	[bəlǰd]	shirred	[sərd]	test	[tɛst]
begged	[bɛgd]	rowed	[rod]	tests	[tɛsts]

2.18 TRANSCRIPTION: VOWELS BEFORE [r]

Transcribe the following words.

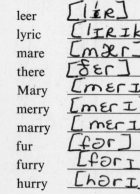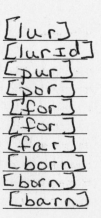

leer	[lɪr]	lure	[lur]	story	[storɪ]
lyric	[lɪrɪk]	lurid	[lurɪd]	sorry	[sorɪ]
mare	[mær]	poor	[pur]	starry	[storɪ]
there	[ðɛr]	pore	[por]	hire	[haɪr]
Mary	[mɛrɪ]	four	[for]	higher	[haɪər]
merry	[mɛrɪ]	for	[for]	flour	[flaʊər]
marry	[mɛrɪ]	far	[far]	flower	[flaʊər]
fur	[fər]	borne	[born]	pure	[pjur]
furry	[fərɪ]	born	[born]	fewer	[fjər]
hurry	[hərɪ]	barn	[barn]	fury	[fjurɪ]

Transcribe the following words.

suite _____	shred _____	luxury _____
greasy _____	schnitzel _____	tournament _____
syrup _____	wash _____	thither _____
bouquet _____	roof _____	chicanery _____
brooch _____	orange _____	garage _____
dais _____	hog _____	homage _____
creek _____	egg _____	vehicle _____
catch _____	aunt _____	spinach _____
with _____	million _____	junta _____
onion _____	height _____	strength _____

2.20 *TRANSCRIPTION: HOMOPHONES AND NEAR HOMOPHONES*

Transcribe the following words.

candid _____	maw _____	shut _____
candied _____	ma _____	shirt _____
taut _____	can 'able' _____	do _____
tot _____	can (n.) _____	due _____
yon _____	have _____	hole _____
yawn _____	halve _____	whole _____
bomb _____	tarred _____	ladder _____
balm _____	tired _____	latter _____
witch _____	wife's _____	click _____
which _____	wives _____	clique _____

2.21 *PRIMARY STRESS*

Indicate the primary stress in each of these words by writing an accent mark over the vowel symbol (or over the first symbol of a digraph) thus: *sófa*, *abóut*.

abyss	ketchup	gluttonous	consecutively
almond	massage	heresy	debauchery
basket	message	improvement	executive
beguile	abolish	industry	fashionable
decent	accredit	platinum	immediate
descent	collector	successor	nominative
engaged	detective	alternative	obtainable
figure	division	annually	parenthesis
harangue	element	caressingly	sensuousness
impose	fallacious	circumference	servility

2.22 PRIMARY AND SECONDARY STRESS

Indicate the primary and secondary stresses with accent marks: ´ for primary, ` for secondary. Write the marks over the vowel symbol of the stressed syllable.

backlash	almighty	adversary	assimilation
cartoon	attitude	aftereffect	attitudinize
concourse	incorrect	confidential	depository
foresee	iota	halfheartedly	philosophical
good-by	panhandle	necessitate	expeditionary

2.23 TRANSCRIPTION WITH PRIMARY STRESS

Transcribe these words phonetically and indicate primary stress on the transcription; for example, [əbáut].

seldom	_____	visit	_____	except	_____
image	_____	command	_____	produce (v.)	_____
adjust	_____	comic	_____	above	_____
oppose	_____	stomach	_____	pleasure	_____
martyr	_____	accept	_____	genial	_____

2.24 TRANSCRIPTION WITH PRIMARY AND SECONDARY STRESS

Transcribe these words phonetically; mark both primary and secondary stress.

local	_____	oblige	_____	analog	_____
locate	_____	obligate	_____	analogical	_____
location	_____	obligation	_____	consolidate	_____
locative	_____	obligatory	_____	consolidation	_____
absolve	_____	apply	_____	migrate	_____
absolution	_____	application	_____	migration	_____
propose	_____	applicable	_____	migratory	_____
proposition	_____	applicability	_____	intellect	_____
actual	_____	operating	_____	intellectual	_____
actuality	_____	operation	_____	intelligent	_____

2.25 THE PRODUCTION OF SPEECH SOUNDS

The diagrams in this exercise represent in conventionalized form the positions of the speech organs for certain English sounds. Notice the position of the velum, the lips, the tongue, and the vocal cords (a straight line indicates voicelessness, a jagged line indicates vibration and voice). For vowels, a grid has been added to help in estimating the tongue's position; for diphthongs, the tongue's final position is indicated by a dotted line.

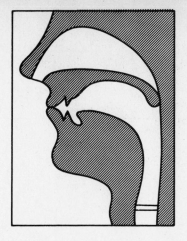

[p]

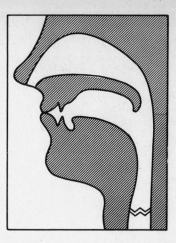

[b]

[m]

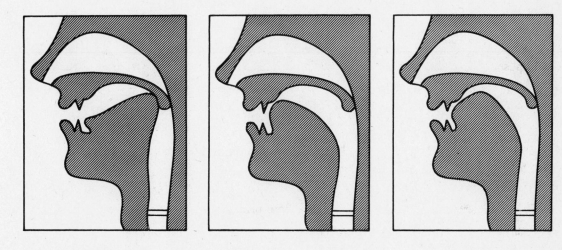

[k]

[s]

[š]

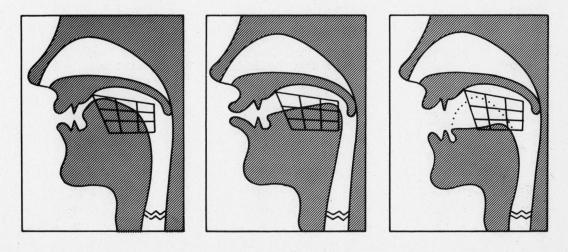

[i] or [ɪ]

[u] or [ʊ]

[aɪ]

What sound is indicated by each of these diagrams?

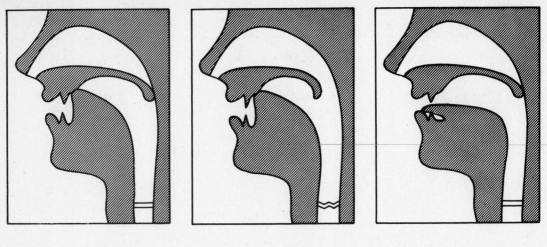

[   ]   [   ]   [   ]

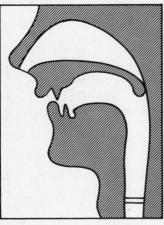 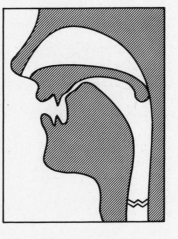 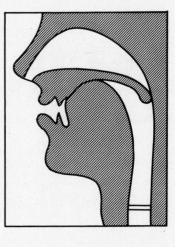

[   ]   [   ]   [   ]

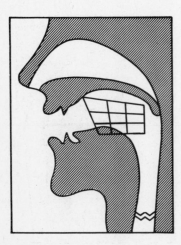 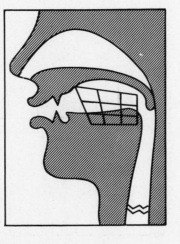

[   ]   [   ]   [   ]

Complete these diagrams by adding the velum, lips, tongue, and vocal cords to indicate the sounds called for.

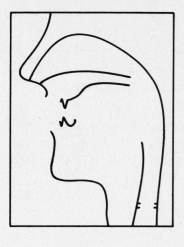

[g]

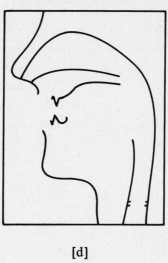

[d]

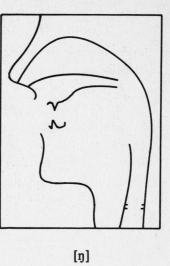

[ŋ]

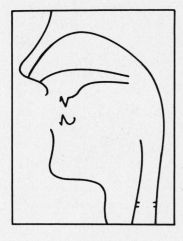

[z]

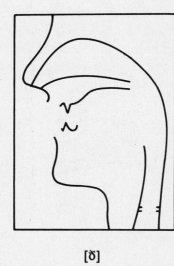

[ð]

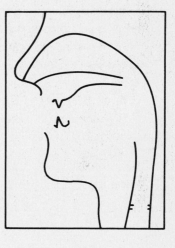

[v]

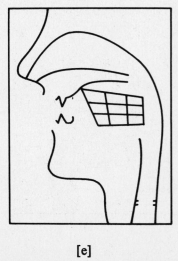

[e]

[ɑ]

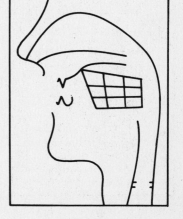

[aʊ]

Sounds can be looked at in different ways. On the one hand, we can think of them as individual segments that follow one another in the chain of speech like beads on a string; this is the view implied by normal phonetic transcription, which is the most useful way of recording sounds for practical purposes. On the other hand, we can think of each sound, not as an indivisible unit, but rather as a bundle of "features." Each feature is the consequence of an articulatory movement of the speech organs, has characteristic acoustical properties that can be recorded by instruments designed for the purpose, and produces its own special effect on the ear of a listener.[2] All the world's languages draw from the relatively small number of these phonetic features to create the many diverse phonological systems of human speech. The features are the real elements of phonology—the atomic building blocks from which a sound system is constructed.

Below are listed the features that are of importance for English; there are other features that are not used by English speakers but are relevant to other languages.[3] Each feature listed here has a binary value—that is, it is either present (indicated by a plus mark: +) or absent (indicated by a minus mark: −); none can occur in part or by degrees.

1. **Sonorant** sounds are produced in such a way that spontaneous vibration of the vocal cords is possible; they are, consequently, normally voiced and only exceptionally voiceless. Nonsonorants, also called obstruents, are produced with the air passage so constricted that voicing requires a special effort; they typically occur both with and without voice.

    + sonorant: vowels, semivowels, nasals, liquids
    − sonorant (obstruent): stops, affricates, fricatives

2. **Consonantal** sounds are produced with a radical obstruction along the midline of the vocal tract.

    + consonantal: stops, affricates, fricatives except [h], nasals, liquids
    − consonantal: vowels, semivowels, [h]

3. **Syllabic** sounds occur at the peak of a syllable, with just as many syllabics as there are syllables in each word uttered. Nonsyllabics cluster around syllabics on the margins of syllables. Nasals and liquids can be either syllabics or nonsyllabics, depending on their use in an utterance (see Pyles's *Origins and Development*, p. 35).

    + syllabic: vowels, syllabic nasals, syllabic liquids
    − syllabic: stops, affricates, fricatives, semivowels, nonsyllabic nasals,
      nonsyllabic liquids

[2] The articulatory, acoustic, and auditory correlates of a somewhat older set of features than that used here are described in Roman Jakobson, C. Gunnar M. Fant, and Morris Halle, *Preliminaries to Speech Analysis: The Distinctive Features and Their Correlates* (Cambridge, Mass., 1951); a useful survey of the theory can be found in Robert T. Harm, *Introduction to Phonological Theory* (Englewood Cliffs, N.J., 1968).

[3] The features listed here, with the exception of number 9, are taken from Noam Chomsky and Morris Halle, *The Sound Pattern of English* (New York, 1968), pp. 298–329.

4. **Continuant** sounds are produced by an air flow that is not completely interrupted at any time during the production of the sound. Noncontinuants, also called stops, completely block the air flow at some point in their articulation.

> \+ continuant: fricatives, nasals, liquids, semivowels, vowels
> − continuant (stop): stops, affricates

5. **Nasal** sounds are produced with the velum lowered, so that air escapes through the nose.

> \+ nasal: nasals
> − nasal: stops, affricates, fricatives, liquids, semivowels, vowels

6. **Lateral** sounds are produced by directing the air flow out of the mouth through a side channel, normally around one or both sides of the tongue.

> \+ lateral: [l]
> − lateral: all other sounds

7. **Anterior** sounds are those made with an obstruction in the front part of the mouth, from the alveolar ridge forward, and with no obstruction from the palatal region back.

> \+ anterior: labials, interdentals, alveolars
> − anterior: alveolopalatals, retroflexes, palatovelars, semivowels, vowels

8. **Coronal** sounds are those made with the blade or front of the tongue raised from a neutral position.

> \+ coronal: interdentals, alveolars, alveolopalatals
> − coronal: labials, palatovelars, semivowels, vowels

9. **Sibilant** sounds are produced by forcing the air through a narrow opening produced by a groove in the midline of the tongue; they have a characteristic "hissing" effect.[4]

> \+ sibilant: [s, z, š, ž, č, ǰ]
> − sibilant: all other sounds

10. **Voiced** sounds are produced with vibration of the vocal cords.

> \+ voiced: [b, d, ǰ, g, v, ð, z, ž], nasals, liquids, semivowels, vowels
> − voiced (voiceless): [p, t, č, k, f, θ, s, š, h]

---

[4] The sibilant feature has been chosen here instead of the more widely used "strident" feature because the sibilants form a grammatically relevant class in English (for determining the pronunciation of the noun plural, genitive, and verbal -s ending) whereas the stridents do not. Moreover, the sibilants are, on purely phonetic grounds, a better defined set than the stridents.

11. **Back** sounds are produced with the body of the tongue retracted from a neutral position. In English this feature applies only to vowels and semivowels.

    + back: [u, ʊ, o, ɔ, ɑ, ə, w]
    − back (front): [i, ɪ, e, ɛ, æ, j]

12. **Rounded** sounds are produced with the lip opening narrowed by "rounding" the lips, that is, by protruding the lips and pressing their side edges together. In English the feature is characteristic mainly of vowels and semivowels.

    + rounded: [u, ʊ, o, ɔ, w] and the Old English vowel [y]
    − rounded (spread): [i, ɪ, e, ɛ, æ, ə, ɑ, j]

13. **High** sounds are made with the body of the tongue raised above a neutral position. In English this feature applies only to vowels.

    + high: [i, ɪ, u, ʊ]
    − high: [e, ɛ, æ, o, ɔ, ɑ, ə]

14. **Low** sounds are made with the body of the tongue lowered below a neutral position. In English this feature applies only to vowels. The mid vowels are nonhigh and nonlow.

    + low: [æ, ɔ, ɑ]
    − low: [i, ɪ, e, ɛ, u, ʊ, o, ə]

15. **Tense** sounds are produced with tense muscles of the tongue and with relatively more effort; they are held longer and give an effect of greater forcefulness. The feature is relevant mainly to vowels, although in the most common forms of American English it does not apply to the low vowels.

    + tense: [i, e, u, o]
    − tense (lax): [ɪ, ɛ, ʊ, ə]

These fifteen features will account for most of the contrasts one might wish to make among English sounds, although there are still others available if they are needed. For example, sounds can be distinguished as + abrupt versus − abrupt (delayed) in their release, depending on whether or not a closure in the vocal tract is released quickly and cleanly. Stops are + abrupt, and affricates are − abrupt. Such distinctions, however, need not be made unless they are useful for some purpose.

Complete the chart on the next page by writing a plus or minus, as appropriate, in each box. The "plus over minus" entered in five boxes indicates that the syllabic feature can be either present or absent for those sounds. The completed chart will show the value of each feature for every phonemic segment of English.

THE PHONETIC FEATURES OF ENGLISH

	p	b	t	d	k	g	č	ǰ	f	v	θ	ð	s	z	š	ž	h	m	n	ŋ	l	r	w	j	æ	a	i	i	e	ɛ	ʌ	u	o	ə
sonorant																																		
consonantal																																		
syllabic																		±	±	±	±	±												
continuant																																		
nasal																																		
lateral																																		
anterior																																		
coronal																																		
sibilant																																		
voiced																																		
back																	*not applicable*																	
rounded																																		
high																																		
low																																		
tense																																		

DISCARD

Identify the phonetic feature, plus or minus, that defines each of the following sets:

1. [l] _____
2. [m, n, ŋ] _____
3. [θ, ð, t, d, s, z, n, l, r, č, ǰ, š, ž] _____
4. [p, t, č, k, f, θ, s, š, h] _____
5. [u, ʊ, o, ɔ, w] _____
6. [e, ɛ, æ, o, ɔ, ɑ, ə] _____
7. [i, e, u, o] _____
8. [p, t, č, k, b, d, ǰ, g, f, v, θ, ð, s, z, š, ž, h] _____
9. [i, ɪ, e, ɛ, æ, u, ʊ, o, ɔ, ɑ, ə, j, w, h] _____
10. [p, t, č, k, b, d, ǰ, g] _____
11. [p, b, m, f, v, θ, ð, t, d, s, z, n, l] _____
12. [s, z, š, ž, č, ǰ] _____
13. [i, ɪ, e, ɛ, æ, j] _____
14. [æ, ɔ, ɑ] _____
15. [i, ɪ, e, ɛ, æ, u, ʊ, o, ɔ, ɑ, ə, m̩, n̩, ŋ̩, l̩, r̩] _____

Each of the following sets can be uniquely defined by specifying two features. What are they?

16. [f, v, θ, ð, s, z, š, ž, h] _____ and _____
17. [h] _____ and _____
18. [i, ɪ, e, ɛ, æ, u, ʊ, o, ɔ, ɑ, ə] _____ and _____
19. [i, ɪ] _____ and _____
20. [p, b, f, v, m] _____ and _____

2.27 *SYSTEMATIC PHONEMES*

In addition to the kind of phoneme we have been dealing with, which is a class of phonetic events, there is another, called the systematic phoneme, which accounts for phonetically diverse sounds in related words. For example, in *mean/meant, clean/cleanlier, please/pleasure, repeat/repetitive, weal/wealth,* and *seam/sempstress,* the first word in each pair has the stressed vowel [i], whereas the second has [ɛ]. The alternation of [i] in a root with [ɛ] when certain suffixes are added is too widespread and too regular to be fortuitous. One way to account for it is to say that there is an underlying vowel, a systematic phoneme, that we might symbolize as [ē] although it is more accurately described as a cluster of features like those in the preceding exercise. Under certain circumstances that can be stated by general rules this systematic phoneme is realized as [i], and under other circumstances as [ɛ].[5] One of the interesting aspects of this way of accounting for the alternation of sounds in present-day English is that it mirrors, at least approximately, the historical changes English sounds have gone through. Not only is our present sound system the result of past changes, but it still carries within it the evidence of its history.

In each of the following groups of words, the italicized spellings stand for phonetic segments that correspond to one systematic phoneme. Write the phonetic symbols for those segments. In later chapters we will investigate the historical changes that produced the vowel alternations illustrated by the first five groups. The last four groups show consonant alternations that English inherited from Romance languages.

---

[5] That is, the systematic phoneme is a vowel with the features [− back, − low, − high, + tense]. The rules make it [+ high] in *mean, please,* and so on, and [− tense] in *meant, pleasure,* and so on.

1. vi*ce*/vi*ci*ous, div*i*ne/div*i*nity, der*i*ve/der*i*vative, l*i*ne/l*i*near _____

2. obsc*e*ne/obsc*e*nity, app*ea*l/app*e*lative, supr*e*me/supr*e*macy, m*e*ter/m*e*tric _____

3. gymn*a*sium/gymn*a*stic, prof*a*ne/prof*a*nity, gr*a*teful/gr*a*titude, expl*ai*n/expl*a*natory _____

4. teleph*o*ne/teleph*o*nic, cons*o*le/cons*o*latory, epis*o*de/epis*o*dic, verb*o*se/verb*o*sity _____

5. prof*ou*nd/prof*u*ndity, pron*ou*nce/pron*u*nciation, ab*ou*nd/ab*u*ndant, ann*ou*nce/ann*u*nciate

   _____

6. corro*d*e/corro*s*ive/corro*s*ion, divi*d*e/divi*s*ive/divi*s*ion/indivi*d*ual _____

7. democra*t*/democra*c*y, par*t*/par*t*ial, habi*t*/habi*t*ual, ac*t*/ac*t*ion/ac*t*ual _____

8. logi*c*/logi*c*ize/logi*c*ian, impli*c*ate/impli*c*it, musi*c*/musi*c*ian _____

9. analo*g*/analo*g*ize, pedago*g*/pedago*g*y, theolo*g*/theolo*g*ical _____

2.28   *OTHER METHODS OF TRANSCRIBING ENGLISH VOWELS*

Phonemes, whether they are the traditional kind or the "systematic" kind mentioned in the preceding exercise, are abstractions from actual speech. Because it is possible to abstract in more than one way, there can be different systems for transcribing the sounds of any language. For example, the vowels of *laid* and *led* are both mid-front (that is, [− high, − low, − back]), but they differ from each other phonetically in several ways:

1. Position: the vowel of *led* is somewhat lower and less front than that of *laid*. If we use the same basic symbol [e] for both vowels, we could show this difference by writing the vowel of *led* as [e[∨][>]] with the arrows showing the direction in which the tongue is shifted.

2. Length: the vowel of *laid* is somewhat longer than that of *led*. Using a colon to indicate phonetic length, we could show this difference as [e:] for *laid* versus [e] for *led*.

3. Diphthongization: *laid* has a vowel that is diphthongized with a glide toward the high-front region: [eɪ] (or [ej] or [ey]), whereas *led* has either no diphthongization or a glide to the mid-central region: [eə].

4. Tenseness: the vowel of *laid* is pronounced with the tongue muscles relatively tense and *led* with the muscles lax. This difference can be indicated by a macron for the tense vowel: [ē] versus [e]. (The macron is also, and more commonly, used to mean length, but can be pressed into service here as a signal of tenseness.)

If we were to indicate all these phonetic distinctions, the vowel of *led* might be written [e[∨][>]ə] and the vowel of *laid* [ēɪ:]. Such a relatively narrow phonetic transcription, although accurate as a description of the actual sounds, is wasteful because it records the difference between the two vowels in four different ways. Most styles of transcription show only one or two of the differences explicitly, leaving the others to be inferred. When the vowels are written with different symbols ([e] for *laid* and [ɛ] for *led*), the distinction in symbols can be taken as standing for any (or, indeed, all) of the phonetic differences.

The Trager-Smith phonemic transcription of English is mentioned on page 42 of Pyles's *Origins and Development* along with certain British systems of phonetic transcription, of which Daniel Jones's is best known. Moreover, dictionaries generally use their own systems, which vary greatly from those just mentioned. Because several styles of transcription are widely used for current English, you are likely to encounter them in your reading. The following table will show how the Jones and the Trager-Smith analyses of English vowels correlate with the analysis used in Pyles's text and this workbook. (In several cases, the Jones transcription reflects a difference in pronunciation between British and American speech.) In the fourth column of the following list write the symbol found in the dictionary you use; and in the blank following the example, transcribe the key word according to the dictionary's system. Indicate which dictionary you use: _____

PYLES	JONES	T-S	DICTIONARY	EXAMPLES
[ɪ]	[i]	/i/	_____	*it:* [ɪt], [it], /it/, _____
[ɛ]	[ɛ]	/e/	_____	*elf:* [ɛlf], [ɛlf], /elf/, _____
[æ]	[a]	/æ/	_____	*at:* [æt], [at], /æt/, _____
[ʊ]	[u]	/u/	_____	*bull:* [bʊl], [bul], /bul/, _____
[ɑ]	[ɔ]	/a/	_____	*stop:* [stɑp], [stɔp], /stap/, _____
[ə]	[ʌ]	/ə/	_____	*sun:* [sən], [sʌn], /sən/, _____
[ə]	[ə]	[ə]	_____	*attack:* [ətǽk], [əˈtæk], /ətǽk/, _____
[ə]	[ə]	[h]	_____	as a replacement of final and preconsonantal [r] in the stressed syllables of *r*-less speech: *tour:* [tʊə], [tuə], /tuh/, _____
[i]	[i:]	/iy/	_____	*eat:* [it], [i:t], /iyt/, _____
[e]	[ei]	/ey/	_____	*ape:* [ep], [eip], /eyp/, _____
[aɪ]	[ai]	/ay/	_____	*buy:* [baɪ], [bai], /bay/, _____
[ɔɪ]	[ɔi]	/ɔy/	_____	*boy:* [bɔɪ], [bɔi], /bɔy/, _____
[u]	[u:]	/uw/	_____	*ooze:* [uz], [u:z], /uwz/, _____
[o]	[ou]	/ow/	_____	*oats:* [ots], [outs], /owts/, _____
[aʊ]	[au]	/aw/	_____	*how:* [haʊ], [hau], /haw/, _____
[ɔ]	[ɔ:]	/ɔh/	_____	*law:* [lɔ], [lɔ:], /lɔh/, _____
[ər]	[ər]	/ər/	_____	as in *r*-ish *urn:* [ərn], [ərn], /ərn/, _____
[ə̄]	[ə:]	/əh/	_____	as in *r*-less *urn:* [ə̄n], [ə:n], /əhn/, _____
[a]	[a:]	/æh/	_____	as in eastern New England *ask:* [ask], [a:sk], /æhsk/, _____
[ɑ̄]	[ɑ:]	/ah/	_____	as in *r*-less *art:* [ɑ̄t], [ɑ:t], /aht/, _____
[æ]	[ɛ:]	/eh/	_____	as in New York City *halve:* [hǽv], [hɛ:v], /hehv/, _____

Transcribe each of the following words twice, first according to Pyles's phonetic notation and then according to one of the other systems (indicate which).

	PYLES	OTHER		PYLES	OTHER
big	_____	_____	tie	_____	_____
beep	_____	_____	toy	_____	_____
less	_____	_____	vow	_____	_____
lace	_____	_____	fume	_____	_____
look	_____	_____	calf	_____	_____
loop	_____	_____	about	_____	_____
dud	_____	_____	gallon	_____	_____
burr	_____	_____	fear	_____	_____
mote	_____	_____	lure	_____	_____
raw	_____	_____	more	_____	_____
pop	_____	_____	harm	_____	_____
cap	_____	_____	bear	_____	_____

Letters and Sounds:
A Brief History of Writing

3.1 QUESTIONS FOR REVIEW AND DISCUSSION

1. Define the following terms:

ideographic writing	dieresis	futhorc
phonogram	acute accent mark	Insular hand
rebus	grave accent mark	thorn
syllabary (syllabic writing)	circumflex accent mark	eth
alphabetic writing	wedge (*haček*)	wynn
boustrophedon	tilde	æsc ('ash')
majuscule	cedilla	yogh
minuscule	digraph	orthoëpy
Cyrillic alphabet	ligature	etymological respelling
diacritical markings	runes (runic alphabet)	spelling pronunciation

2. How do the drawings of preliterate societies, such as those of the cave men or of the American Indians, differ from true writing?

3. In modern times, stylized drawings are still used for some purposes, for example on road signs. Cite some specific examples.

4. Arabic numerals and symbols like & or % are basically ideograms. Can you cite other examples of ideograms in current use?

5. What evidence is there that the Greeks acquired their writing system from the Semites?

6. In the Semitic script there was no way of writing vowel sounds. Explain the origins of the Greek vowel letters.

7. What accounts for the difference between the angular (Γ, Δ, Σ) and the rounded (C, D, S) forms of what are historically the same letters?

8. What letters and ligatures, formerly used in the English writing system, have passed out of common use?

9. Chaucer's Wife of Bath used to berate her husbands by asking such questions as "What rowne ye with oure mayde?" and in *The Winter's Tale* Leontes says, "They're here with me already, whispering, rounding, 'Sicilia is a so-forth.'" What is the etymological connection between the obsolete verb *rown* or *round* and *runic* writing?

10. In what ways has the Roman alphabet been adapted for writing the un-Latin sounds of such a language as Polish, German, or English?

11. What is the origin of the dot over the letter *i*?

12. Why do the vowel letters in Modern English spelling represent sounds that differ greatly from the sounds represented by the same letters in other languages?

13. Old English spelling was a reasonably good representation of the sounds of the language. Modern English spelling is notoriously bad in this respect. What causes for the widened gap between English sound and spelling can you suggest?

14. Describe the logical development, which is not necessarily the actual historical development, of writing systems. Use an outline like the following one to classify the kinds of writing systems.

> Pictures (American Indian)
> Ideographs (Egyptian ideographs, Sumerian ideographs)
> Phonograms
>> Rebuses
>> Syllabaries
>>> Full syllabaries (Cherokee, Japanese)
>>> Consonantal syllabaries (Egyptian phonograms, Semitic)
>> Alphabets (Greek, Roman, Cyrillic, runic)

15. What is the relationship between writing and speech as expressions of language? In what ways is writing secondary? Does writing ever influence speech?

3.2 *A PICTOGRAPH*

The Indian "letter" mentioned by Pyles on page 50 of *Origins and Development* is adapted here from Henry R. Schoolcraft, *Information Respecting the History, Condition, and Prospects of the Indian Tribes of the United States.*[1] An interpretation of the pictograph is also given. Compare the interpretation with the drawing to discover the conventions the "writer" used. How is each of the following concepts expressed in the pictograph?

an agreement of opinion _____

an offering of friendship_____

the rank of chief (vs. mere warrior) _____

the rank of a more important chief _____

a settled or civilized way of life _____

the location of the writer's home _____

the totem-group to which the Indians belong _____

_____

INTERPRETATION: A chief of the eagle totem, four of his warrior-kinsmen, a fifth warrior (of the catfish totem), and another chief, who is more powerful than the first leader, are all

[1] (Philadelphia, 1853), Vol. I, pp. 418–19.

54

agreed in their views. They extend friendship to the president of the United States in the White House. The eagle chief intends to settle at a location on a river, and his kinsmen will occupy houses, thus adopting the white man's culture. It is hoped the president will understand the offer of friendship and return it.

3.3 *ANOTHER PICTOGRAPH*

The following "letter" was sent by an Ojibwa girl to a young man, inviting him to her lodge. The lover is given directions for finding his way and other information appropriate to such an invitation. Only the R.S.V.P. is lacking. (The letters have been added to the original for purposes of identification.)

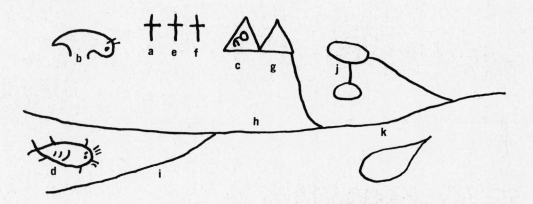

INTERPRETATION: The writer of the letter is a girl of the bear totem (   ). She and two companions, all three of whom are Christians (   ) (   ) (   ), live in two lodges (   ) (   ) near some lakes (   ). A trail leads from the lodges to a main road (   ), which runs near another lake (   ) not far from the lodges. The letter is being sent to a man of the mud puppy totem (   ), who is reminded of a trail (   ) which leads from his lodge to the main road. A hand extending through the door of one of the dwellings (   ) both invites the young man (the purpose of the letter) and tells him which lodge he should visit.[2]

1. Complete the interpretation by writing within the parentheses the letters from the drawing.

2. Although the drawing represents various objects important to the message, the import of the letter is not explicitly stated. Nothing in the drawing actually says, "Come up and see me sometime." That message must be inferred because picture writing has no way of being so specific. In what other ways does pictography differ from genuine writing? For example, would two persons be likely to "read" the message in exactly the same way? Is there any one correct order for interpreting the parts of the message? Does the message tell anything about the pronunciation, word order, or inflections of the Ojibwa language?

_____
_____
_____
_____
_____

[2] Adapted from Garrick Mallery, *Picture Writing of the American Indians* (Tenth Annual Report of the Bureau of Ethnology, 1888–89 [Washington, D.C., 1893]), pp. 362–63.

3.4 IDEOGRAPHS: SUMERIAN CUNEIFORM

The Sumerians, who lived in southern Mesopotamia, were enthusiastic bookkeepers. The phrases in this exercise are adapted from a collection of records, invoices, and receipts which were written between 2400 and 2300 B.C.[3] Although the cuneiform style was also used for phonograms, the Sumerian in this sample is written in ideographs.

two bulls

five pastured cows

_____

two lambs

seventeen pastured bulls

_____

four sheep

twenty suckling bull calves

_____

one suckling lamb

(an) offering (for the) king

_____

ten fattened bulls

offerings (for the) goddess Nina

_____

1. Translate the last five phrases in the blanks above.

2. Consult a dictionary for the literal meaning of the word *cuneiform.*_____

3. How did the writing materials that were used for cuneiform influence the shape of the symbols? _____

4. Cuneiform symbols were originally pictures of the objects they represent. Find at least one that still has some pictorial value. Suggestion: Rotate the page 90 degrees clockwise.

5. The symbol for "offering" is a combination of which two other symbols?

6. How is the plural of nouns indicated when there is no accompanying numeral?

7. How is the plural of nouns indicated after a numeral?_____

8. What is the position of modifiers with relation to the noun they modify? Is there more than one kind of modifier? _____

[3] William M. Nesbit, *Sumerian Records from Drehem,* "Columbia University Oriental Series," Vol. VIII (New York, 1914).

9. List two or three ways in which these ideographs differ from the pictograph of the preceding exercise. _____

_____

_____

_____

10. How might "ten fattened bulls" be expressed in a pictograph? _____

_____

3.5 *EGYPTIAN HIEROGLYPHICS*

Egyptian writing is a mixture of phonograms, which represent sounds, and ideographs, which represent ideas or general concepts. The phonograms stand for consonants only; vowels were not represented in Egyptian writing. Consequently the exact pronunciation of Egyptian is unknown. Here are some typical hieroglyphs:

PHONOGRAMS AND TRANSLITERATION			IDEOGRAPHS AND MEANING	
⟨y glyph⟩	y	⟨m glyph⟩ m	⟨sun glyph⟩	sun
⟨glottal glyph⟩	' (a glottal sound)	⟨n glyph⟩ n	⟨light glyph⟩	light, shine
⟨w glyph⟩	w	⟨r glyph⟩ r	⟨heaven glyph⟩	heaven
⟨b glyph⟩	b	⟨h glyph⟩ h	⟨moon glyph⟩	moon
⟨p glyph⟩	p	⟨t glyph⟩ t		

From these hieroglyphs, the following sentences can be made:[4]

HIEROGLYPHS	TRANSLITERATION	TRANSLATION
⟨glyphs⟩	wbn r' m pt	The sun rises in the sky.
⟨glyphs⟩	yw r' m pt	The sun is in the sky.
⟨glyphs⟩	wbn y'ḥ	The moon rises.
⟨glyphs⟩	_____	_____
⟨glyphs⟩	_____	_____

1. Transliterate and translate the last two sentences in the blanks above.

2. What is the Egyptian word order for subject, verb, and adverbial phrase? _____

_____

[4] Adapted from Sir Alan Henderson Gardiner, *Egyptian Grammar* (London, 1950).

3. The hieroglyphs above are written from left to right, but other orders of writing are possible. For example: ⊙ ⌒ 𓆓 𓃭 𓆑

   What is the translation of this sentence? _____

4. How can you tell from looking at hieroglyphic writing whether it is to be read from right to left or from left to right? _____

5. The ideographs used in these sentences are called determinatives. What useful functions do they serve? _____
   _____

6. In what way are these hieroglyphs a more adequate representation of language than the cuneiforms of the preceding exercise? _____
   _____

3.6 HEBREW WRITING

1. The Semitic writing systems are in many ways like Egyptian phonograms, which were, indeed, probably the model for the first Semitic writing. Hebrew script, one variety of Semitic, is written from right to left. At its simplest it is like Egyptian phonograms in making no provision whatever for representing the vowels; however, since Hebrew is still a spoken language, the vowels can be supplied in a transcription.

אבא	'abbā'	papa	חדש	chădăsh	new
בת	bath	daughter	ילד	yeled	child
בית	bayith	house	כל	kol	all
בקר	bōqer	morning	נער	na'ar	boy
גז	gēz	mowing	פסח	pesach	Passover
הר	har	hill	עט	'ēt	pen
וו	wāw	hook	צמח	tsemach	plant
חדש	chodesh	month	שמש	shemesh	sun

Here are the twenty-two letters of the Hebrew script. Supply a transliteration for each.[5]

א ____   ו ____   כ ____   ס ____   ק ____

ב ____   ז ____   ל ____   ע ____   ר ____

ג ____   ח ____   מ ____   פ ____   שׁ ____

ד ____   ט ____   נ ____   צ ____   ת ____

ה ____   י ____

[5] Some of the letters represent two pronunciations: (1) a stop before a vowel or when doubled, in which case the letter has a dot (called *dagesh*) written inside it, and (2) a fricative after a vowel. The letter transliterated *sh* also represents two pronunciations, distinguished by the position of the dot over it. For simplicity's sake, only one variety of each letter is shown here.

2. Sometimes letters which normally stand for consonants are used to represent vowels. When so used, they are called *matres lectionis*, 'mothers of reading.'

מִי	mī	who		סוס	sūs	horse
אִישׁ	'īsh	man		כוס	kōs	goblet
מיתר	mēthār	string		אור	'ōr	light
בית	bēth	the house of		מה	mā	what
סִפּוּר	sippūr	story		בחורה	bachūrā	girl

These three Hebrew letters are used as *matres lectionis;* what vowels can each represent?

י _____   ו _____   ה _____

3. In the sixth century A.D., a group of scholars called the Massoretes, from *massōrā* 'tradition,' invented a system of diacritics for a more precise writing of the Hebrew vowels. These scholars were motivated by a desire to preserve the exact pronunciation of the Scriptures and were probably influenced by the alphabetic system which the Greeks had developed much earlier. The diacritic marks they invented are called massoretic points.

DIACRITICS ADDED TO SIMPLE SPELLINGS			DIACRITICS ADDED TO *matres lectionis*		
בַּת	bath	daughter	מָה	mā	what
וָו	wāw	hook	בֵּית	bēth	the house of
שֶׁמֶשׁ	shemesh	sun	מִי	mī	who
גֵּז	gēz	mowing	אוֹר	'ōr	light
בַּיִת	bayith	house	סוּס	sūs	horse
כָּל	kol	all			
בֹּקֶר	bōqer	morning			
נֻפַּח	nuppach	blown up			

The points, except for those that represent long *o* and *u*, are written beneath the consonant that they follow. Notice that the same diacritic is used for long *a* and short *o*; in some dialects of Hebrew these two sounds are pronounced alike. Even when distinct from long *a*, short *o* is relatively rare.

Transliterate these Hebrew words:

חִידָה _____ riddle   עֵז _____ she-goat

שֹׁמֵר _____ watchman   נוּס _____ flee

שַׁחַר _____ dawn   חַיִל _____ power

קוֹל _____ voice   אֶחָד _____ one

4. The Hebrew writing system is sometimes referred to as an alphabet, but has also been called a syllabary. How does it represent a transitional stage between syllabaries and alphabets?_____

_____

_____

3.7 *THE CHEROKEE SYLLABARY*

In 1821 Sequoya, who has been called the Cherokee Cadmus, invented a script for writing his native language. Sequoya's invention made Cherokee the only Indian tongue to have an indigenous, fully developed writing system. Although he seems to have known no English, many of Sequoya's symbols are clearly derived from the Latin alphabet. The Cherokee writing system is, however, not an alphabet, but a syllabary, as the chart on the next page makes clear.[6]

Transliterate the following Cherokee words by consulting the chart.

CHEROKEE	TRANSLITERATION	TRANSLATION
ᏣᏔᎩ	_____	Cherokee
ᏍᏋᏬ	_____	Sequoya
ᏍᎭᏃᏊ	_____	October, harvest month
ᎣᏋᏇᎴᏣ	_____	instantly
ᎠᎳᏇ	_____	war club

[6] Grant Foreman, *Sequoyah* (Norman, Okla., 1959); and John K. White, "On the Revival of Printing in the Cherokee Language," *Current Anthropology*, III (1962), 511–14. Cherokee syllabary type courtesy of the Carnegie Corporation Cross-Cultural Education Project of the University of Chicago, Tahlequah, Oklahoma.

a	e	i	o	u	^
Ꭰ	Ꭱ	Ꭲ	Ꭳ	Ꭴ	Ꭵ
ka Ꭷ · ga Ꭶ	ge Ꭸ	gi Ꭹ	go Ꭺ	gu Ꭻ	g^ Ꭼ
ha Ꭽ	he Ꭾ	hi Ꭿ	ho Ꮀ	hu Ꮁ	h^ Ꮂ
la Ꮃ	le Ꮄ	li Ꮅ	lo Ꮆ	lu Ꮇ	l^ Ꮈ
ma Ꮉ	me Ꮊ	mi Ꮋ	mo Ꮌ	mu Ꮍ	
hna Ꮏ · nah Ꮐ · na Ꮎ	ne Ꮑ	ni Ꮒ	no Ꮓ	nu Ꮔ	n^ Ꮕ
kwa Ꮖ	kwe Ꮗ	kwi Ꮘ	kwo Ꮙ	kwu Ꮚ	kw^ Ꮛ
s Ꮝ · sa Ꮜ	se Ꮞ	si Ꮟ	so Ꮠ	su Ꮡ	s^ Ꮢ
da Ꮣ	de Ꮥ	di Ꮧ	do Ꮩ	du Ꮪ	d^ Ꮫ
ta Ꮤ	te Ꮦ	ti Ꮨ			
dla Ꮬ · tla Ꮭ	tle Ꮮ	tli Ꮯ	tlo Ꮰ	tlu Ꮱ	tl^ Ꮲ
tsa Ꮳ	tse Ꮴ	tsi Ꮵ	tso Ꮶ	tsu Ꮷ	ts^ Ꮸ
wa Ꮹ	we Ꮺ	wi Ꮻ	wo Ꮼ	wu Ꮽ	w^ Ꮾ
ya Ꮿ	ye Ᏸ	yi Ᏹ	yo Ᏺ	yu Ᏻ	y^ Ᏼ

3.8 *JAPANESE KATAKANA*

Japanese is normally written with a combination of ideographic signs borrowed from Chinese and phonographic characters called *kana*. There are two varieties of *kana*: the *hiragana*, used for most ordinary purposes, and the *katakana*, used for transcribing foreign words and for formal, official writing. The latter system is illustrated here.

KATAKANA	TRANSLITERATION	TRANSLATION
ワタシ	watashi	I
アナタ	anata	you
イチ	ichi	one
ヨル	yoru	night
ハイ	hai	yes
シロ	shiro	white
カモク	kamoku	thing
ヨイ	_____	good
ハナ	_____	flower
シカル	_____	blame

1. Transliterate the last three words in the blanks above.

2. What kind of writing system is the katakana? _____

3. How does the katakana differ from the Semitic writing system? _____

_____

_____

_____

4. Languages differ from one another not only in the sounds they use, but also in the order in which their sounds may be arranged. The possible arrangements of sounds (technically, *phonotactics*) have some bearing on the kind of writing system most appropriate for a language. In Japanese each syllable tends to be composed of a single consonant (C) followed by a single vowel (V). Thus we can describe the canonical, or regular, form of the Japanese syllable as CV. The words *yo-ru* and *wa-ta-shi* are made entirely of syllables of this sort. Notice that the spellings *sh* and *ch* in the transliterations stand for single consonants each. There are, of course, other possibilities; for example, any of the five vowels of Japanese may form a syllable by itself with no preceding consonant. The word *i-chi* begins with such a syllable, and the word *ha-i* ends in one. Moreover, certain consonants, such as the *n*-sound, can form a syllable without a vowel. The Japanese word *hon* 'book' consists of two syllables: *ho-n*. Unlike English, Japanese has no syllables of the form VC or CVC and no syllables beginning with consonant combinations like *st*, *tr*, *sw*, or *spl*. Consequently, when the Japanese language borrows words from a language like English, it must adapt the arrangement of sounds to its own patterns. Thus *beer* appears in Japanese as *bīru*, and *butter* as *bata*. Such loan-words have become so common that a large portion of Don C.

Bailey's *Glossary of Japanese Neologisms* (Tucson: University of Arizona Press, 1962) is devoted to recording them. According to Mr. Bailey, Western culture has introduced Japanese politicians to the *firibasutā* 'filibuster,' businessmen to the *wōru-sutorīto-jānaru* '*Wall Street Journal*,' and suburbanites to the lawn *supurinkurā* 'sprinkler' and the *disukaunto-hausu* 'discount house.' My fair Japanese lady has the benefit of *kosuchūmu-jueru* 'costume jewelry,' the *negurije* 'negligee,' or a *fēsu-rifuto* 'face lift.' The *jitabagu* 'jitterbug' has been replaced by *puroguresshibu-jazu* 'progressive jazz' as the *kūru* 'cool' form of music preferred by those who put a *sutereo-rekōdo* 'stereo record' on the *rekōdo-pureyā* 'record player' and adjust the *tsuītā* 'tweeter' and the *ūfā* 'woofer.' Others merely watch the *terebi* 'TV,' swallow a *torankiraizā* 'tranquilizer,' and shout *Yankī-go-hōmu!*

Explain why the phonotactics of Japanese makes the katakana an appropriate kind of writing system for the language. _____

_____

_____

5. Compare the phonotactics of Japanese with that of Cherokee. Are they generally similar or dissimilar? _____

How appropriate is Sequoya's writing system for Cherokee? _____

_____

6. Compare the phonotactics of Japanese with that of Hebrew. What are the canonical forms (consonant and vowel patterns) for Hebrew words of one syllable? _____

How does Hebrew differ most noticeably from Japanese in its phonotactic patterns?

_____

Which language probably has the larger number of different syllables—Hebrew or Japanese?

_____

7. Compare the phonotactics of Japanese with that of English. What are the C and V forms for the following monosyllabic English words?

a _____   at _____   pant _____   spit _____   prompts _____
no _____   pan _____   pants _____   split _____   splints _____

Would a syllabary be an appropriate writing system for English? Explain your answer.

_____

_____

_____

3.9 *THE DEVELOPMENT OF THE ALPHABET*

The invention of the alphabet is one of those rare events in human history that seem to have occurred only once. Some apparently independent alphabets, like that used for Korean, probably evolved under the influence of the Roman script as it was disseminated by missionaries. The first and archetypal alphabet came into existence when the Greeks adapted the Semitic syllabary to their own language, using some of the extra consonant letters to write vowels. All subsequent alphabets spring from this bit of Greek cleverness. The chart on the next page traces, in greatly simplified fashion, the development of the alphabet from Semitic to Greek to Latin to English. By referring to pages 51–55 of Pyles's *Origins and Development* and to the table that can be found under the entry *alphabet* in most desk dictionaries, you can complete the chart.

SEMITIC			GREEK		ROMAN	
Hebrew letters	*Hebrew letter names*	*Phoenician letters*	*letters*	*letter names*	*Classic Latin letters*	*Modern English letters*
א	aleph		A	alpha	A	A
ב						
ג						
ד						
ה						
ו				F	digamma		
ז						
ח						
ט						
י						
כ						
ל						
מ						
נ						
ס						
ע						
פ			Q	koppa		
צ						
ק						
ר						
ש						
ת						

The Cyrillic alphabet, used in Russian and some other Slavic languages, is a development of the Greek alphabet. A comparison of the Cyrillic letter-shapes with those of Greek will reveal many similarities. The alphabet given here is the form of Cyrillic used in writing Russian; there are slight differences for other languages.

LETTER	TRANSLITERATION	LETTER	TRANSLITERATION	LETTER	TRANSLITERATION
А а	a	Л л	l	Ц ц	ts
Б б	b	М м	m	Ч ч	ch
В в	v	Н н	n	Ш ш	sh
Г г	g	О о	o	Щ щ	shch
Д д	d	П п	p	Ъ ъ	none
Е е	e	Р р	r	Ы ы	y
Ж ж	zh	С с	s	Ь ь	' (palatalization)
З з	z	Т т	t	Э э	e
И и	i	У у	u	Ю ю	yu
Й й	i (in diphthongs)	Ф ф	f	Я я	ya
К к	k	Х х	kh		

Transliterate these Russian words:

Чехов	_____	Пушкин	_____
Хрущев	_____	самовар	_____
Толстой	_____	спутник	_____
дрожки	_____	рубль	_____
степь	_____	бабушка	_____
интеллигенция	_____	тройка	_____

3.11 *THE RUNIC INSCRIPTION OF THE RUTHWELL CROSS*

The Ruthwell Cross is a Scottish stone monument that has engraved upon it part of an Old English poem, "The Dream of the Rood." The inscription, which is in runic symbols, has been badly damaged by the ravages of the weather and of the Scottish Covenanters, who objected to "idolatrous monuments." In the 1640's the cross was broken into pieces and cast into the churchyard; consequently the inscription is now fragmentary. Most of what survives is reproduced here, with some of the missing letters supplied; the text has also been divided into words, although in the original the runes follow one another without spaces. The speaker in the poem is the True Cross, which relates the events of the Crucifixion as the Old English poet conceived them. The poem dates from the early eighth century and is in the Northumbrian dialect.[7]

[7] Bruce Dickins and Alan S. C. Ross, *The Dream of the Rood* (London, 1954); and Ralph W. V. Elliott, *Runes* (New York, 1959).

NE FRAGMENT

ᚠᚪᚷᛖᚱᛗᛇᚠ ᚻᛁᚾᚪ ᚷᚪᛇ ᚠᛚᚪᛖᛋᛏᛏᛁᚷ ᚦᚪ
ᚻᛖ ᚹᚪᛚᚻᛖ ᚪᚾ ᚷᚪᛚᚷᚢ ᚷᛁᛋᛏᛁᚷᚪ ᛗᚪᚻᛁᚷ

TRANSLITERATION AND GLOSS

ongeredæ hinæ ḡod almeȝttig þa he walde on ḡalḡu gistiḡa modig
Unclothed himself god almighty. For he would onto the cross ascend courageous.

SE FRAGMENT

ᚠᚪᚻᚠ ᛁᚻ ᚱᛁᛁᚻᚾᚪ ᚸᛏᛁᚻᛉᚻ ᚻᛇᚠᚢᚾᚪᛋ
ᚻᛚᚪᚠᚪᚱᚻ ᚻᚪᛚᚻᚪ ᛁᚻ ᚾᛁ ᚻᚪᚱᛋᛏᚪ
ᛒᛁᛋᛗᚪᚱᚪᚻᚢ ᚢᛉᚸᛖᛏ ᛗᛖᚾ ᛒᚪ ᚠᛏᚷᚪᚻᚱᚪ
ᛁᚻ ᚹᚪᛋ ᛗᛁᚦ ᛒᛚᚪᚻᚪ ᛒᛁᛋᛏᛖᛗᛁᚻ

TRANSLITERATION AND GLOSS

ahof   ic riicnæ k̄yniŋc héâfunæs hlafard hælda ic ni   dorstæ bismærædu uŋ̄ket men
Lifted up I   a great king,   heaven's Lord.   Bow   I   did not dare.   Mocked   us two men

ba   ætḡadræ ic wæs miþ blodæ bistemid
both together.[8] I was with blood bedewed.

SW FRAGMENT

ᛏᚱᛁᛋᛏ ᚹᚪᛋ ᚪᚾ ᚱᚪᚻᛁ ᚻᚹᛖᚦᚱᚪ ᚦᛖᚱ
ᚠᚢᛋᚪ ᚠᛇᚱᚱᚪᚾ ᛏᚹᚪᛗᚢ ᚪᚦᚦᛁᛚᚪ ᛏᛁᛚ ᚪᚾᚢᛗ
ᛁᚻ ᚦᚪᛏ ᚪᛚ ᛒᛁᚻᛇᛚᚻ ᛋᚪᚱᚪ ᛁᚻ
ᚹᚪᛋ ᛗᛁᚦ ᛋᚪᚱᚷᚢᛗ ᚷᛁᚻᚱᛟᚠᛁᚻ

TRANSLITERATION AND GLOSS

krist wæs on rodi   hweþræ þer fusæ   féârran kwomu æþþilæ   til
Christ was on the cross. And   there hastening from afar came   noblemen[9] towards (me)

anum ic þæt al bihéâld saræ ic wæs miþ sorgum gidrœfid
alone. I that all beheld. Sorely I was with sorrows troubled.

[8] That is, "Men mocked both us two together."
[9] Joseph of Arimathea and Nicodemus.

NW FRAGMENT

ᛗᛁᚠ ᛋᛏᚱᛖᛚᚢᛗ ᚷᛁᚹᚢᚾᛞᚨᚠ   ᚠᚳᛖᚷᚨᛞᛏ
ᚻᛁᚠ ᚻᛁᚾᚠ ᛚᛁᛗᚹᛟᚱᛁᚷᛏᚠ   ᚷᛁᛋᛏᚨᛞᛞᛏ
ᚻᛁᛗ ᚠᛏ ᚻᛁᛋ ᛚᛁᚻᚨᛋ ᚻᛖᚩᚻᛞᛗ   ᛒᛁᚾᛏᚠᛞᛏ
ᚻᛁᚠ ᚦᛖᚱ ᚻᛖᚩᛖᚾᚠᛋ ᚻᚱᛗᚻᛏᛖᛞ

TRANSLITERATION AND GLOSS

___ ___ ___ ___ ___ ___ ___

(*I was*) *with*   *arrows*   *wounded.*   *Laid down*   *they*   *him*   *weary in limb.*

___ ___ ___ ___ ___ ___

They stood   *by him*   *at*   *his*   *body's*   *head.*

___ ___ ___ ___ ___

Beheld   *they*   *there*   *heaven's*   *Lord.*

1. Complete the chart below by giving the transliteration for each rune.

2. Transliterate the runic letters of the fourth fragment in the blanks provided above.

3. What does the style in which the letters are made—angular with few curves—suggest about the original material and method for writing runes?

THE FUTHORC

RUNE	TRANS.	RUNE	TRANS.	RUNE	TRANS.	RUNE	TRANS.
ᚠ	___	ᚻ	___	ᛏ	___	ᚪ	___
ᚢ	___	ᛏ	___	ᛒ	___	ᚫ	___
ᚦ	___	ᛁ	___	ᛖ	___	ᛗ	___
ᚩ	___	ᛉ	îo	ᛗ	___	ᛣ	___
ᚱ	___	ᛄ	___	ᛚ	___	ᛠ	___
ᚳ	___	ᛢ	p	ᛥ	___	ᛤ	___
ᚷ	___	ᛦ	x	ᛝ	___	ᛞ	___
ᚹ	___	ᛋ	___	ᚻ	___		

The illustration below is a page from an Old English manuscript written in the Insular hand, probably in the early eleventh century.[10]

---

[10] British Museum Manuscript Cotton Julius E vii, folio 59.

In the middle of the page, at the large capital letter, there begins a homily with the Latin title "VII ID*US* M*ARTIAS* NAT*ALE* S*ANCTORUM* QUADRAGINTA MILITUM," that is, "The Seventh Day Before the Ides of March: Feast of the Holy Forty Soldiers." (Italics or underlining can be used to indicate an expanded abbreviation.) You will find this passage transliterated and translated on pages 147–48 of Pyles's *Origins and Development*. Notice that word division does not always conform to modern practice. Notice also the letter shapes that differ significantly from modern forms, especially *g*, *r*, the three forms of *s*, the letter called *eth*, and the runes *thorn* and *wynn*. Occasionally and inconsistently the scribes used a mark like an acute accent over a vowel to show length; it can be transliterated with a macron.

At the top of the page is the end of another homily which includes the story of the virgin St. Felicula, who was a companion of St. Peter's daughter, Petronilla. Felicula had received unwanted amorous attention from an important and powerful pagan named Flaccus. The fragment of the story on this page tells how she spurned Flaccus and how he took revenge. The passage is translated and partly transliterated here; complete the transliteration.

(Ne beo)   ic næfre þin wif· forðan þe ic sylfwylles   eom criste   gehalgod·ne ic
(*Not shall be*) *I   never thine wife because   I of my own will am to Christ hallowed, nor I*

þam hæþenum godum lac   ne geoffrige·forðan þe ic on crist gelyfe · Þa hēt
to the heathen   gods sacrifice not will offer because   I in Christ believe. Then commanded

se arleasa flaccus· þa femnan gebringan   on þysterfullu*m* cwearterne · & cwæþ·
the merciless Flaccus the virgin to be brought into a dark   prison   and said

þæt man ne sceolde ænigne bigleofan hire dōn binnon seofon nihton·
that one not should any   food   her give for   seven nights.

She   dwelt   then   so   seven   nights   meatless,   and   afterwards   was

---

tortured   for   the   true   faith   and   for   her   maidhood   until   she

---

was   martyred,   and   her   ghost   fared   free   to   heaven.   Then   came

---

Nicomedis   the   foresaid   mass-priest,   and   buried   her   body   to

---

praise   of the   Almighty.   Then   seized   Flaccus   the   faithful

---

priest,   and   because   he   would not   to the   foul   gods   offer,

---

commanded   him   to be scourged   until   he   died.   He   departed   then

---

to   heaven   to   the Savior   Christ,   to whom   is   glory   and   honor

---

in   all   worlds'   worlds.[11]   *Amen.*

[11] That is, 'world without end.'

After the Norman Conquest, the Insular hand, which Englishmen had learned from Irish scribes, was replaced by a form of writing often called "Gothic." On the next page is the opening of Chaucer's *Canterbury Tales*,[12] written in this style by an unknown scribe. The first twenty-seven lines are transcribed in exercise 6.9, where the italicized letters are expansions of abbreviations indicated by lines of various sorts above the words in the manuscript. Opposite line 8, there is a marginal comment in Latin, *sol in ariete* 'sun in Aries.'

Having compared the first half of the page with its transcription, you can transcribe the bottom twenty-one lines here:

---

[12] From *The Ellesmere Chaucer Reproduced in Facsimile*, Part I (Manchester, Eng., 1911).

Whan that aprill with his shoures soote
The droghte of march hath perced to the roote
And bathed euery veyne in swich licour
Of which vertu engendred is the flour
Whan zephirus eek with his sweete breeth
Inspired hath in euery holt and heeth
The tendre croppes and the yonge sonne
Hath in the Ram his half cours yronne   *sol in ariete*
And smale foweles maken melodye
That slepen al the nyght with open eye
So priketh hem nature in hir corages
Thanne longen folk to goon on pilgrimages
And palmeres for to seken straunge strondes
To ferne halwes kowthe in sondry londes
And specially from euery shires ende
Of engelond to Caunterbury they wende
The hooly blisful martir for to seke
That hem hath holpen whan þt they were seeke

Bifil that in that seson on a day
In Southwerk at the Tabard as I lay
Redy to wenden on my pilgrymage
To Caunterbury with ful deuout corage
At nyght were come in to that hostelrye
Wel nyne and twenty in a compaignye
Of sondry folk by auenture yfalle
In felaweshipe and pilgrimes were they alle
That toward Caunterbury wolden ryde
The chambres and the stables weren wyde
And wel we weren esed atte beste
And shortly whan the sonne was to reste
So hadde I spoken with hem euerichon
That I was of hir felaweshipe anon
And made forward erly for to ryse
To take oure wey ther as I yow deuyse

But nathelees whil I haue tyme & space
Er that I ferther in this tale pace
Me thynketh it acordaunt to resoun
To telle yow al the condicioun
Of ech of hem so as it semed me
And whiche they were and of what degree
And eek in what array that they were inne
And at a knyght than wol I first bigynne   *Knyght*

A knyght ther was and that a worthy man
That fro the tyme that he first bigan
To riden out he loued chiualrie
Trouthe and honour fredom and curteisie
Ful worthy was he in his lordes werre
And therto hadde he riden no man ferre

Every sound in present-day English can be spelled in more than one way. Although some of the variation is not predictable by general rule and depends merely on what word the sound occurs in, much of it is systematic. What spelling is used for a vowel depends on such factors as (1) whether the vowel is lax [æ, ɛ, ɪ, ɑ, ɔ, ə, ʊ] or tense [e, i, o, u] or diphthongal [aɪ, aʊ, ɔɪ]; (2) whether the vowel occurs in the last syllable of a word or some other; (3) whether a tense or diphthongal vowel is followed by a consonant or not. The spelling patterns illustrated here apply to stressed vowels only; unstressed vowels must be treated in a somewhat different way.

The following list contains examples of the principal vowel spellings. In two-syllable words, the significant vowel is italicized.

bait	deuce	lye	pi	rude	soul
bay	dew	lyre	p*i*lot	rue	sow [o]
but	d*u*ty	made	proud	scene	sty
b*u*tter	Hind*u*	Mae	prow	sea	st*y*lus
coat	laud	me	p*u*llet	seat	tide
coc*oa*	law	m*e*ter	put	see	tie
c*o*ffer [ə]	let	pa [ɑ]	qua [e]	seed	toe
cog [ɔ]	l*e*tter	p*a*pa	qu*a*si [e]	shook	tone
coil	lit	pat	rot	so	too
coy	l*i*tter	p*a*tter	r*o*tten	s*o*fa	toot

1. There are two regular spelling patterns for lax vowels: (1) the VC pattern, when the vowel is in the last (or only) syllable of a word such as *sum*, and (2) the VCCV pattern, when the vowel is in other than the last syllable of a word such as *summer* and is followed by at least two consonant letters in the spelling.

   Provide examples of both spelling patterns from the above list for each of the following lax vowels:

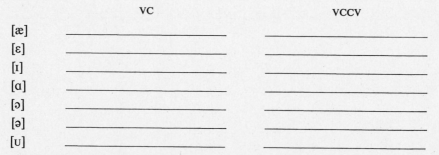

	VC	VCCV
[æ]	_____	_____
[ɛ]	_____	_____
[ɪ]	_____	_____
[ɑ]	_____	_____
[ɔ]	_____	_____
[ə]	_____	_____
[ʊ]	_____	_____

2. There are several regular spelling patterns used primarily for tense vowels and diphthongs:

   (1) The vowel may be spelled with a single letter if it is followed by a single consonant and another vowel (VCV as in *veto*) or sometimes if it is the final sound of a word (V as in *we*).

   (2) When it is followed by a word-final consonant, the vowel may be spelled by a single letter and a "silent *e*" after the consonant (VC*e* as in *pine*). If there is no following consonant, so that the vowel comes at the end of the word, the "silent *e*" may still be used (V*e* as in *pie*).

   (3) The vowel may be spelled by a digraph consisting of two vowel letters whether there is a following consonant (VVC as in *read*) or not (VV as in *tree*). The second vowel in this pattern will be *a*, *e*, or *o*.

(4) The vowel may be spelled with a digraph ending in *i* or *u* before a consonant (V*i,u*C as in *pout*) or ending in *y* or *w* otherwise (V*y,w* as in *pow*).

Provide examples from the list for each of the following vowels (the last three are lax vowels that use the tense patterns):

	VCV	V	VC*e*	V*e*	VVC	VV	V*i,u*C	V*y,w*
[e]	___	___	___				___	___
[i]	___	___	___		___			
					___	___		
[aɪ]	___	___	___					
	___	___	___	___				
[o]	___	___	___	___	___	___	___	___
[u]	___	___	___	___	___	___		
[aʊ]							___	___
[ɔɪ]							___	___
[ə]							___	___
[ɑ]	___	___						
[ʊ]					___			

3.15   *MODERN SPELLING: CONSONANTS*

1. The consonants, like the vowels, have some spellings that are unpredictable and others that fall into regular patterns. The following list illustrates the simplest spelling of each consonant: *fed, jag, kin, chip, bosh, thing, them, visual, haze, yes, rot, we.*
   Which five consonant sounds illustrated above are spelled with digraphs?

   _____

   In the above list what two phonemes does *th* stand for? _____
   s? _____
   The remaining seventeen consonants have relatively unambiguous single-letter spellings. What are the sounds? _____

   _____

2. After a lax vowel, a nonfinal single consonant sound is typically spelled with a digraph. Spell the words indicated by the following transcriptions.

   [súpər] _____ [rúdər] _____ [kómə] _____
   [sə́pər] _____ [rə́dər] _____ [kámə] _____
   [létər] _____ [táɪgər] _____ [pínəl] _____
   [lǽtər] _____ [trígər] _____ [pénənt] _____
   [pókər] _____ [réčəl] _____ [hélo] _____
   [pákət] _____ [sǽčəl] _____ [hǽlo] _____
   [fáɪbər] _____ [kójənt] _____ [sófə] _____
   [fíbər] _____ [stáji] _____ [tófi] _____

   What spellings are used instead of double letters for [k] _____, [č] _____, and [j] _____?

3. Consider the spellings for the following words:

   [stəf]   [dɪč]   [briz]
   [pæs]   [dɑǰ]   [čiz]
   [fɪz]   [gɪv]   [hɪnǰ]

[tɛl]   [lis]   [vælv]
[pæk]   [pis]   [brið]

Which consonants have special spellings used at the end of a word after a lax vowel? Give the spellings:_____

Which consonants have special spellings used at the end of a word after a tense vowel or a consonant? Give the spellings:_____

The letters *v* and *j* only very rarely occur at the end of a word. List any words you can with final *v* or *j*._____

3.16 *CHANGES IN THE ENGLISH WRITING SYSTEM*

Many influences have contributed to the shaping of Modern English orthography. The origins of our spellings are discussed on pages 58–73 of Pyles's *Origins and Development*. Summarize what is said there about the source of each of the following spellings.

w		_____
th	in *thin*	_____
y	in *Ye Olde Antique Shoppe*	_____
z	in *Kenzie*	_____
gh	in *knight*	_____
g	in *gem*	_____
j	in *judge*	_____
v	in *driven*	_____
h	in *honor*	_____
th	in *throne*	_____
th	in *author*	_____
th	in *Gotham*	_____
ph	in *philosophy*	_____
ph	in *Ralph*	_____
ch	in *child*	_____
ch	in *chorus*	_____
ch	in *schedule*	_____
gh	in *ghost*	_____
gh	in *ghoul*	_____
sh	in *shall*	_____
sc	in *scene*	_____
sc	in *scissors*	_____
wh	in *what*	_____
wh	in *whole*	_____
c	in *city*	_____
k	in *kin*	_____
que	in *critique*	_____
z	in *freeze*	_____
qu	in *queen*	_____
gu	in *guest*	_____
ee	in *feet*	_____
oo	in *rood*	_____
ai	in *raid*	_____

oa	in *road* _____
o	in *son* _____
ou	in *house* _____
ow	in *dower* _____
y	in *marry* _____
b	in *debt* _____
mp	in *comptroller* _____
l	in *fault* _____

3.17 *LEARNED AND PSEUDOLEARNED RESPELLINGS*

The spellings of some words have been changed by men with more sense of historical continuity than of contemporary reality. Thus a learned *b* was inserted in Middle English *det* to show that it is ultimately derived from Latin *debitum*. Sometimes these learned respellings, such as the *h* added to earlier *trone*, have resulted in new pronunciations. Occasionally, those who like to tinker with orthography have possessed more enthusiasm than knowledge. As a result some words have been respelled to show a wrong etymology; the pseudolearned *comptroller* for *controller* is a case in point.

1. The following Modern English words have remodeled spellings. Compare their current spellings with earlier written forms of the words, which you will find in the etymological entry of a desk dictionary or in the *Oxford English Dictionary*. In the blanks, write the *consonants* that have been added to the spellings. Be prepared to discuss whether the respelling has influenced the pronunciation of the word and whether the respelling is a learned one such as *debt* and *throne* or a pseudolearned one such as *comptroller*.

_____	adventure	_____	island	_____	schedule
_____	aisle	_____	limb 'arm or leg'	_____	schism
_____	anthem	_____	mortgage	_____	school
_____	asthma	_____	myrrh	_____	scythe
_____	bankrupt	_____	nephew	_____	soldier
_____	could	_____	palm	_____	sovereign
_____	delight	_____	perfect	_____	subtle
_____	falcon	_____	receipt	_____	vault
_____	foreign	_____	rhyme	_____	verdict
_____	indict	_____	salmon	_____	victual

2. Consult the *OED* to find the centuries in which the foregoing words were first respelled to include the new consonants. Indicate here the number of words respelled in each century:

before 1200	_____	1400–1500	_____	1700–1800	_____
1200–1300	_____	1500–1600	_____	1800–1900	_____
1300–1400	_____	1600–1700	_____	after 1900	_____

3.18 *SPELLING PRONUNCIATIONS*

1. Pyles, in *Origins and Development*, mentions, as examples of words that have acquired spelling pronunciations, *often, forehead, clapboard, grindstone,* and the proper names *Daventry, Shrewsbury, Cirencester, Magdalen(e),* and *Theobald*. Below are some additional examples. For some of these words, a spelling pronunciation is uncommon in educated speech; for

others, it is almost universal and completely respectable. By comparing your normal pronunciation of these words with their spelling and with the pronunciations listed in a dictionary, try to determine the traditional pronunciation and the spelling pronunciation.

balk	draught	holm	thither
bass 'drum'	falcon	human	thyme
blackguard	forecastle	isthmus	tortoise
boatswain	gooseberry	kiln	toward
bourbon 'whiskey'	grovel	lichen	wainscot
breeches	guerdon	lightwood	waistcoat
brooch	gunwale	oboe	Wednesday
Christmas	halfpenny	pestle	wont
coxswain	handkerchief	steelyard	worsted
dour	hiccough	sumac	yolk
Birmingham	Edinburgh	Milne	Pembroke
Concord	Greenwich	Norfolk	St. John
Cowper	Home	Norwich	Southwark

2. Suggest some additional examples of spelling pronunciation from your own experience.

_____

_____

The Backgrounds of English

4.1 QUESTIONS FOR REVIEW AND DISCUSSION

1. Define the following terms:

   analogical change (analogy)
   sound change (sound shift)
   monosyllabic language
   agglutinative language
   incorporative language
   inflective language
   typological (generic) classification
   genetic (historical) classification
   language family
   Indo-European (Proto-Indo-European)
   comparative linguistics
   inflection
   grammatical functions (for example,
      case, number, person, tense, mood,
      aspect, and so forth)
   word root
   affix (suffix, prefix, infix)
   stem
   thematic vowel
   thematic and athematic verbs

   reconstruction (reconstructed form)
   cognate (cognate words)
   sound correspondences
   loan-words
   koine
   Vulgar Latin
   Romance languages
   Germanic (Pre-Germanic)
   preterit
   dental suffix
   strong and weak verbs
   strong and weak adjectives
   stress and pitch accent
   First Sound Shift (Grimm's Law, Germanic
      Consonant Shift)
   grammatical change (Verner's Law)
   Second Sound Shift (High German
      Consonant Shift)
   rhotacism
   metathesis

2. How can similarities between languages be explained? Consider, for example, English *ma* and Chinese *ma* 'mother,' English *bong* and German *Bam* 'noise of a bell,' English *filly* and French *fille* 'girl,' English *goober* and Bantu *nguba* 'peanut,' English *brother* and Russian *brat'* 'brother.'

3. To what extent can we explain why languages change? Consider the passage of time, geographical separation, and analogy as contributing factors.

4. Some grammarians believe that, because language can be described as behavior governed by rules, most language change is rule change. That is, a speaker learns a new rule or drops an old rule or modifies it, thus altering his grammar or pronunciation. Does the idea of rule change favor the view that language change is sudden or that it is gradual?

5. What metaphors are commonly used to describe the connections that exist among languages?

6. What are some of the more important non-Indo-European language groups?

7. Summarize the contributions of Jones, Bopp, Rask, and Grimm to the comparative-historical study of Indo-European.

8. What linguistic features are shared by all Indo-European languages; that is, how are all Indo-European languages alike?

9. What is the special meaning in linguistics of an asterisk before a word?

10. What kinds of words are shared by all Indo-European languages?

11. On what kind of evidence do we base our conclusions about Indo-European culture and the original Indo-European homeland?

12. What are the main subgroups of Indo-European?

13. What is the distinction between *satem* languages and *centum* languages?

14. What linguistic features, shared by all Germanic languages, differentiate them from other branches of Indo-European?

4.2 *LANGUAGE TYPES*

The older and often imprecise classification of languages into four types (monosyllabic, agglutinative, inflective, and incorporative) has been greatly refined by modern scholars. Joseph H. Greenberg discusses the history of the four-way classification and suggests a number of indexes by which the type of a language can be determined quite precisely.[1] For a rough and ready classification, however, the four terms are still useful, although linguists no longer use them to imply an evolutionary development in language. The following examples will illustrate the four types.

1. A *monosyllabic* or *isolating* language is one in which words tend to be one syllable long and invariable in form. They take no inflections or other suffixes. The function of words in a sentence is shown primarily by word order.

    CHINESE: Ni men ti hua wo pu tu tung.

    'I do not entirely understand your language.'

    Ni　men　ti　　　　hua　　　wo　pu　tu　tung
    you / plural / possessor / language / I / not / all / understand

2. An *agglutinative* language is one in which words tend to be made up of several syllables. Typically each word has a base or stem and a number of affixes. The affixes are quite regular; they undergo very little change regardless of what base they are added to.

    TURKISH: Babam kardeşime bir mektup yazdırdı.

    'My father had my brother write a letter.'

    Baba　-m[2]　kardeş　-im[2]　-e　　　　　bir　mektup　yaz　-dır　　-dı
    father / my / brother / my / dative case / a / letter / write / cause to / past tense

3. *Inflective* languages are like agglutinative ones in that each word tends to have a number of suffixes. In an inflective language, however, the suffixes often show great irregularity in varying their shape according to the word-base to which they are added. Also, a single suffix tends to express a number of different grammatical concepts.

    LATIN: Arma virumque canō.

    'I sing about weapons and a man.'

    Arm　-a　　　　　　　　vir　-um　　　　　　　　　　-que
    weapon / neuter accusative plural / man / masculine accusative singular / and

    can　-ō

    sing / first person singular present indicative

---

[1] "A Quantitative Approach to the Morphological Typology of Language," *International Journal of American Linguistics*, XXVI (1960), 178–94.

[2] *m* is used after vowels; *im*, after consonants.

4. An *incorporative* language is one in which the verb and the subject or object of a sentence may be included in a single word. What we would think of as the main elements of a sentence are joined in one word and have no independent existence.

ESKIMO: Qasuiirsarvigssarsingitluinarnarpuq.
          'Someone did not at all find a suitable resting place.'

Qasu -iir -sar   -vig   -ssar   -si   -ngit -luinar
tired | not | causing to be | place for | suitable | find | not | completely |

-nar   -puq
someone | third person singular indicative mood[3]

To which of the four types does each of these languages seem to belong?

1. Ya dumayu, chto eto samyĭ malen'kiĭ iz vsekh gorodov Rossii.
   'I think that this is the smallest of all the cities of Russia.'

Ya duma -yu   chto eto   sam
I | think | first person singular present tense | that | this | most |

-yĭ   malen'k -iĭ   iz
masculine nominative singular | small | masculine nominative singular | out of |

vs -ekh   gorod -ov   Rossi -i
all | genitive plural | city | masculine genitive plural | Russia | feminine genitive singular

TYPE: _____

2. Lần-lần dân-chúng học làm chính-trị.
   'Little by little the masses are learning to engage in politics.'

Lần lần dân   chúng   học   làm   chính   trị
time | time | people | multitude | learn | make | government | rule

TYPE: _____

3. La maljuna viro kreskigis malgrandan pomarbaron.
   'The old man cultivated a small apple orchard.'

La mal- jun -a   vir -o   kresk -ig   -is   mal-
the | un- | young | adjective | man | noun | grow | cause to | past tense | un- |

grand -a   -n   pom -arb -ar   -o   -n
large | adjective | accusative | apple | tree | collection | noun | accusative

TYPE: _____

4. Ua mau ke[4] ea o ka 'aina i ka pono.
   'The life of the land is preserved in righteousness.'

Ua   mau   ke   ea o ka   'aina i ka   pono
perfect aspect | constant | the | life | of | the | land | in | the | goodness

TYPE: _____

5. Tis ara houtos estin, hoti kai ho anemos kai hē thalatta hypakouei autōi?
   'Who then is this, that both the wind and the sea obey him?'

Ti -s   ara   hout -os
who | masculine nominative singular | then | this | masculine nominative singular |

es -tin   hoti kai
be | third person singular present indicative | that | and |

[3] Suggestion: Read the gloss by starting at the end and working toward the beginning.
[4] *ke* occurs before words beginning with *e, a, o,* and *k; ka,* otherwise.

h	-o		anem	-os		kai

the | masculine nominative singular | wind | masculine nominative singular | and |

h	-ē		thalatt	-a

the | feminine nominative singular | sea | feminine nominative singular |

hypakou	-ei		aut	-ōi

obey | third person singular present indicative | same | masculine dative singular

TYPE: _____

6. Kahä'eisibäti.

'He fractured his skull.'

Kah	-ä'ei	-si	-bä	-ti

blow, strike | head | be in condition of | cause to | third person singular intransitive verb

TYPE: _____

7. Watu walivitaka vitabu vikubwa vyote.[5]

'The men wanted all the big books.'

Wa-	tu	wa-	li-	vi-	taka	vi-	tabu	vi-	kubwa	vy-	ote

plural | person | they | past | them | want | plural | book | plural | big | plural | all

TYPE: _____

8. Wa'shagnihwehtonie' bil.[6]

'We made a snowsnake [stick used in winter games] for Bill.'

Wa'-	shag-	ni-	hweht-	oni	-e

nonfuture definite event | I-him | dual subject | snowsnake | make | for |

_'	bil

event occuring only once | Bill

TYPE: _____

The eight languages above are Russian, Vietnamese, Esperanto, Hawaiian, Greek, Arapaho, Swahili, and Onondaga.

The four language types are, of course, merely abstractions. No real language belongs entirely to any one type. For example, the English use of monosyllables like *to, for, when, not, must, the,* and *or,* and its reliance on word order to signal grammatical meaning would seem to make it a monosyllabic language. However, the existence of paradigms like *ox, ox's, oxen, oxen's; show, shows, showing, showed, shown; good, better, best* is typical of inflective languages. Words like *activistic* which are built up by adding suffixes one by one to a stem (*act, active, activist, activistic*) are characteristic of agglutinative languages. And verb forms like *to baby-sit* or *horseback-riding* are the hallmark of an incorporative language. It is difficult to pigeonhole English, or for that matter most other languages, when we are using only four classifications. Greenberg's article, cited earlier, provides more than ten indexes that can be used in describing the type to which a language belongs. His first measurement is called the "index of synthesis," and is arrived at in this way: Take a passage written in the language you wish to type; the longer the passage, the more accurate the index will be. Count the number of words in the passage (W). Count the number of morphemes, that is, the smallest meaningful elements, in the passage (M). Divide the number of morphemes by the number of words (M/W). The result will be the index of synthesis. For example, the Chinese sentence we examined earlier has eight words; it also has eight morphemes. The index of synthesis is thus 8/8, or 1.00.

[5] Data from Henry Allan Gleason, Jr., *Workbook in Descriptive Linguistics* (New York, 1955), p. 49.

[6] Data from Wallace L. Chafe, *Meaning and the Structure of Language* (Chicago, 1970), pp. 269–86.

The Turkish sentence has five words, but ten morphemes, as we see when the sentence is broken into its smallest meaningful units. The index of synthesis is 10/5, or 2.00. The Eskimo example is a single word, but it has ten morphemes. The index of synthesis is 10/1, or 10.00.

The index of synthesis for a language tells us on the average how many morphemes are present in each word. If our results for the three languages we examined were accurate, we could say that Chinese words have on the average one morpheme each, Turkish words have an average of two morphemes each, and Eskimo words have an average of ten morphemes each. However, these samples are far too short for reliable results. For Eskimo especially our conclusion is highly suspect; we used only one word to figure the average, and an index of 10.00 is unbelievably high for any language.

A low index of synthesis, something approaching 1.00, tells us that the language is *analytic*. Monosyllabic languages are analytic. A higher index of synthesis, somewhere between 1.50 and 2.50, characterizes the language as *synthetic*. Agglutinative and inflective languages are both synthetic. A very high index of synthesis, something around 3.00 or above, identifies the language as *polysynthetic*. Incorporative languages are polysynthetic.

Now go back to the Latin sentence we used to illustrate an inflective language, and compute the index of synthesis for it.

Number of words in the sentence (W): _____

Number of morphemes in the sentence (M): _____

Number of morphemes divided by number of words (M/W) equals an index of: _____
The correct answer is 2.33 (round off the division to the second decimal place).

This single index is a very useful device for comparing languages. Below are four versions of the same Biblical passage in Latin, Old English, Middle English, and early Modern English. To assist you, the words have been divided by hyphens into their constituent morphemes. Words are separated from one another by spaces. Some words, for example *sawe* in the early Modern English passage, count as two morphemes. One morpheme is the basic meaning of the word, 'see'; the second morpheme is the meaning 'past time,' and is shown by the changed vowel sound. Such internal change is represented by the symbol ∅; ∅ should be counted as a separate morpheme. Compute the index of synthesis for each of the four passages and give your results in the space provided at the end of the exercise.

Latin[7]

Moses aut-em pasce-ba-t ov-es Jethro co-gna-t-i su-i sac-er-dot-is Madian: cum-que min-a-sse-t greg-em ad in-ter-ior-a de-sert-i, ven-i-t ad mont-em De-i Horeb. Ap-par-ui-t-que e-i Dom-in-us in flamm-a ign-is de medi-o rub-i: et vide-ba-t quod rub-us arde-re-t, et non com-bure-re-t-ur. Dix-i-t ergo Moses: Vad-a-m, et vide-b-o vis-ion-em hanc-∅ magn-am, qu-a-re-∅ non com-bura-t-ur rub-us. Cerne-n-s aut-em Dom-in-us quod per-ge-re-t ad vide-nd-um, voca-vi-t e-um de medi-o rub-i, et a-i-t: Moses, Moses. Qu-i re-spond-i-t: Ad-su-m. At ill-e: Ne ap-propi-e-s, in-qu-i-t, huc: solv-e calc-e-ament-um de ped-ibus tu-is: loc-us enim, in qu-o sta-s, terr-a sanc-t-a es-t.

Old English

Sōð-līc-e Moyses hēold-∅ hy-s mæg-es scēap-∅, þ-æs sācerd-es, on Mādian; þ-æs nam-a wæ-∅-s Iethro. And ðā hē drāf-∅ hi-s heord-e tō inn-e-weard-um þ-ām wēsten-e, hē cōm-∅ tō God-es dūn-e þe man Ōreph nemn-eþ. And Drihten hi-m æt-ēow-de on fīr-es līg-e on-midd-an ān-re brēmel-þyrn-an, and hē ge-seah-∅ þæt s-ēo ðyrn-e barn-∅ and n-æ-∅-s for-burn-an. Ðā

[7] Vowel length is not marked in this passage because it had probably ceased to be phonemic in the language of the Vulgate. See Thomas Pyles, "The Pronunciation of Latin Learned Loan Words and Foreign Words in Old English," *PMLA*, LVIII (1943), 891–910.

cwæð-∅ Moyses: Ic gā and ge-sēo þ-ā micl-an ge-sih-ð-e, hw-ī þ-ēos þyrn-e ne sȳ-∅ for-bærn-ed. Sōð-līc-e Drihten ge-seah-∅ þæt hē fēr-de tō ge-sēo-nn-e; hē clyp-ode of midd-re þ-ǣre brēmel-þyrn-an, and cwæþ-∅: Moyses! Moyses! And hē and-wyr-de, and cwæþ-∅: Hēr ic eo-m. And hē cwæþ-∅: Ne ge-nēa-lǣc-e ðū hy-der; dō þī-n ge-scȳ-∅ of ðī-n-um fōt-um: sōþ-līc-e s-ēo stōw þe ðū on stent-st y-s hāl-ig eorð-e.

Middle English

Moyses for-soþ fed-∅ þe schepe-∅ of Iethro, hi-s wyu-ys fader, þe prest of Madyan, and whenn he ha-d dreu-en þe flock to þe inn-er-mo-re part-y of desert, he comme-∅ to þe hyll of god, Oreb, and þe lord a-peer-id to hy-m in a flawme of fyre from þe mydyll of a bosche. And he seyȝ-∅ þat þe bosch wa-∅-s a-fyre, and wa-∅-s not bren-t. Þann say-d Moyses, "I schall go and see þis grete siȝ-t, why þe bosch i-s not bren-t." And þe lord by-hold-yng þat he ȝe-de to see-n, clep-ed hy-m from þe mydyll of þe bosche and sey-þ, "Moyses, Moyses," þe which answer-d, "I a-m nyȝ." And he, "Ne come þou," he sei-þ, "no ne-rre hyþer, bot louse þou þi-n scho-ing frome þi-∅ fete-∅. The place for-soþ þat þou stond-is inne i-s a hol-y londe."

Early Modern English

Nowe Moses kep-t the flocke of Iethro hi-s father in law, the Priest of Midian: and hee led-∅ the flocke to the back-side of the desert, and came-∅ to the mountaine of God, even to Horeb. And the Angel of the Lord appear-ed un-to hi-m, in a flame of fire out of the mid-st of a bush, and he look-ed, and be-hold, the bush burn-ed with fire, and the bush wa-∅-s not con-sume-d. And Moses sai-de, I will nowe turne a-side, and see this great sigh-t, why the bush i-s not burn-t. And when the Lord sawe-∅ that he turn-ed a-side to see, God call-ed un-to hi-m out of the mid-st of the bush, and sai-d, Moses, Moses. And he sai-de, Here a-m I. And he sai-d, Drawe not nigh hither: put off thy-∅ shoo-es from off thy-∅ feete-∅, for the place where-on thou stand-est, is hol-y ground.

	LATIN	OLD ENGLISH	MIDDLE ENGLISH	MODERN ENGLISH
NUMBER OF WORDS				
NUMBER OF MORPHEMES				
INDEX OF SYNTHESIS				

Is Old English closer to Latin or to Modern English in its synthetic complexity?

As measured by the synthetic complexity, did the greatest grammatical change in our language take place between Old and Middle or between Middle and Modern English?

4.3 THE WORLD'S LANGUAGES (I)

This map shows the geographical distribution of non-Indo-European language groups with relation to Indo-European in the eastern hemisphere. Language groups in the western hemisphere are both more complex and less well defined. Complete the following key by writing the numbers from the map in the appropriate blanks.

_____ Hamito-Semitic	_____ Japanese	_____ Finno-Ugric
_____ Sudanic	_____ Korean	_____ Altaic
_____ Bantu	_____ Malayo-Polynesian	_____ Indo-European
_____ Hottentot-Bushman	_____ Australian	_____ Caucasian
_____ Dravidian	_____ Papuan	
_____ Indo-Chinese	_____ Basque	

4.4 THE WORLD'S LANGUAGES (II)

Using the numbers 1 through 16 from the preceding exercise, plus 17 for American Indian languages, identify the group to which each of the following belongs. You may need to consult a dictionary.

_____ Amharic	_____ Dinka	_____ Indonesian	_____ Nahuatl
_____ Arabic	_____ Eskimo	_____ Javanese	_____ Quechua
_____ Aymara	_____ Estonian	_____ Lappish	_____ Swahili
_____ Berber	_____ Fijian	_____ Malayalam	_____ Tagalog
_____ Bushman	_____ Finnish	_____ Manchu	_____ Tamil
_____ Chinook	_____ Georgian	_____ Mandarin	_____ Tibetan
_____ Coptic	_____ Hawaiian	_____ Maori	_____ Turkish
_____ Creek	_____ Hebrew	_____ Menomini	_____ Xhosa
_____ Cushitic	_____ Hungarian	_____ Mongolian	_____ Zulu

4.5 THE LOCATION OF THE INDO-EUROPEAN LANGUAGES

The map that follows shows the main Indo-European language groups and some important non-Indo-European languages of Europe and the Near East. Complete the key by writing the numbers in the appropriate blanks.

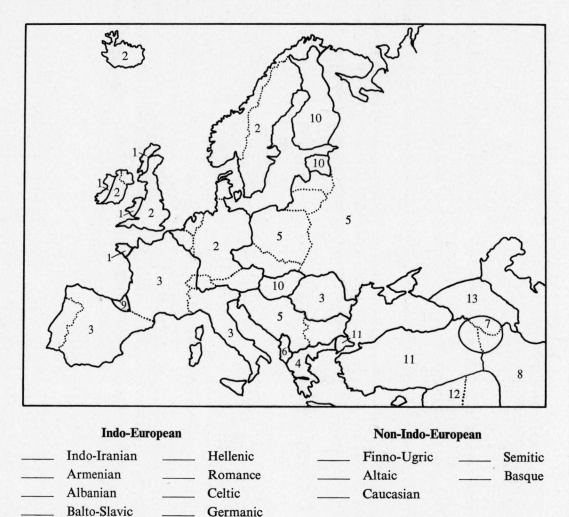

Indo-European

____	Indo-Iranian	____	Hellenic
____	Armenian	____	Romance
____	Albanian	____	Celtic
____	Balto-Slavic	____	Germanic

Non-Indo-European

____	Finno-Ugric	____	Semitic
____	Altaic	____	Basque
____	Caucasian		

4.6 THE MAIN DIVISIONS OF THE INDO-EUROPEAN GROUP (I)

In describing the historical development of a language group we have recourse to various metaphors and "models." One such metaphor is that of the family, by which we speak of the Indo-European *parent* language with its various *descendants*. Another metaphor is the botanical one, by which we speak of the Indo-European *stem* with its several *branches*. These two metaphors are often combined in a family-tree model of language. Use the languages in the following list (which continues on page 86) to complete the family tree on the next page.

Aeolic	Bengali	Cornish	Faroese	Gothic
Afrikaans	Breton	Czech	Flemish	High German
Albanian	Bulgarian	Danish	French	Hindi
Anglo-Norman	Burgundian	Doric	Frisian	Hindustani
Armenian	Byelorussian	Dutch	Galician	Hittite
Avestan	Catalan	English	Gaulish	Icelandic

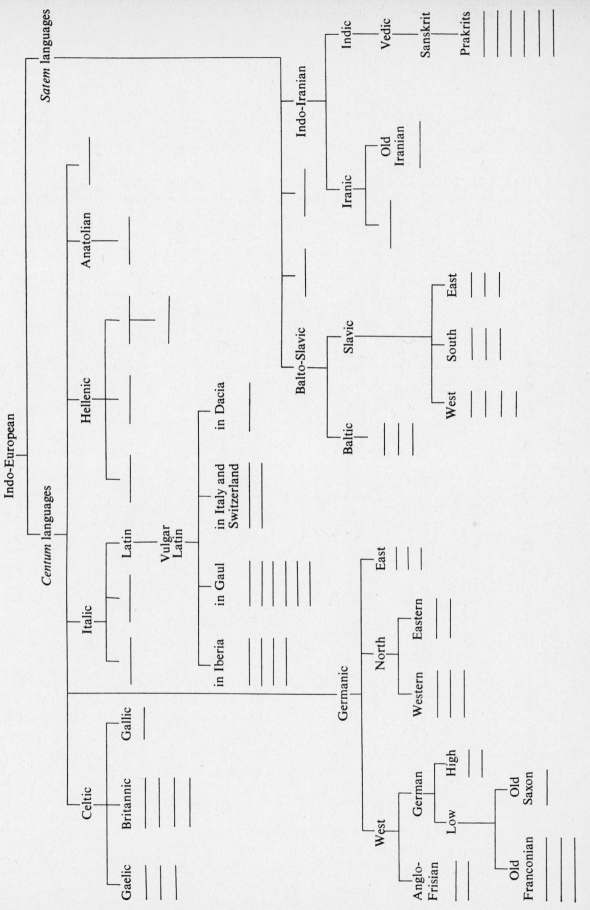

Ionic-Attic	Norman	Portuguese	Serbo-Croatian	Urdu
Irish Gaelic	Norwegian	Provençal	Slovak	Vandalic
Italian	Oscan	Prussian	Slovenian	Walloon
Lettish	Pali	Rhaeto-Romanic	Spanish	Welsh
Lithuanian	Persian	Romany	Swedish	Wendish
Low German	Picard	Rumanian	Tocharian	Yiddish
Manx	Pictish	Russian	Ukrainian	
Modern Greek	Polish	Scots Gaelic	Umbrian	

4.7 *THE MAIN DIVISIONS OF THE INDO-EUROPEAN GROUP (II)*

The circular diagram that follows may, at first sight, look quite different from a family tree, but it is merely a somewhat different way of schematizing the same information. The blocks around the outer rim of the wheel represent important modern Indo-European languages and are so labeled. The interior blocks represent successively larger and older groupings of the various languages. The central point of the circle stands for Proto-Indo-European, the hub from which the linguistic spokes radiate. Complete this wheel diagram by labeling the remaining blocks with the names or numbers of the language groups listed on page 87.

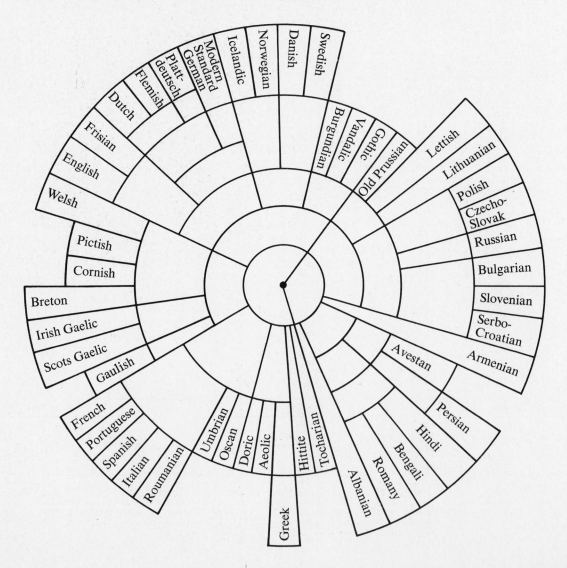

1. *Satem* languages	12. Baltic	23. South Slavic
2. *Centum* languages	13. East Germanic	24. East Slavic
3. Indo-Iranian	14. North Germanic	25. West Slavic
4. Balto-Slavic	15. West Germanic	26. Eastern North Germanic
5. Germanic	16. Britannic	27. Western North Germanic
6. Celtic	17. Gaelic	28. German
7. Italic	18. Gallic	29. Anglo-Frisian
8. Hellenic	19. Latin	30. High German
9. Indic	20. Ionic-Attic	31. Low German
10. Iranic	21. Sanskrit and Prakrits	32. Old Saxon
11. Slavic	22. Old Iranian	33. Old Low Franconian

4.8 *A WAVE MODEL FOR INDO-EUROPEAN*

Another way to look at relationships between languages is the wave model. It recognizes that a linguistic change begins among some speakers and spreads to others, like a wave expanding on the surface of a pond when a pebble has been tossed into the water. When several changes start among different speakers at different times and spread at different rates, the result is the creation of new dialects as speakers are affected by one or another of the changes. It is as though many pebbles were tossed into the water, some waves reinforcing one another, others overlapping. The wave diagram below shows the major dialect groups of Indo-European as the result of wavelike linguistic changes.

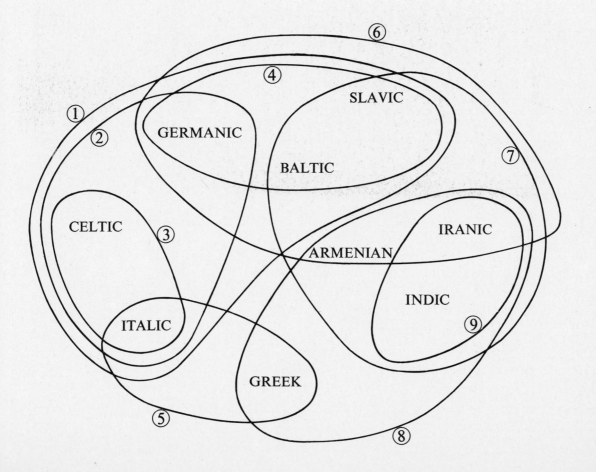

Below are descriptions of the linguistic changes that the wave diagram represents and a list of examples. Match the examples and the changes.

_____ 1. Northern and western languages share a common vocabulary lacking in the other Indo-European dialects.

_____ 2. The western languages share a common vocabulary.

_____ 3. Italo-Celtic dialects have passive forms of the verb in -r.

_____ 4. Northern languages have a dative plural case ending in -m.

_____ 5. Italo-Hellenic dialects have voiceless sounds for the Indo-European voiced aspirates.

_____ 6. In northern and eastern languages (except Indic) medial schwa was lost.

_____ 7. In eastern languages, velars became sibilants in some cases, and labiovelars became velars.

_____ 8. Southeastern languages have a prefixed vowel ("initial augment") in the past tense (aorist) forms of the verb.

_____ 9. In Indo-Iranian, schwa became i.

EXAMPLES:

A.	IE	*dhughətēr-		B.	IE	*porkos 'pig'		C.	Russ.	stol 'table'
	Avest.	duγδar-			Lat.	porcus				stolám 'to tables'
	Armen.	dustr			OIrish	orc			OE	stōl 'chair'
	Goth.	dauhtar			OE	fearh				stōlum 'to chairs'
	Lith.	duktễ			Lith.	paȓšas			Lith.	výras 'man'
	OSlav.	dŭšti			OSlav.	prasę				výrams 'to men'

D.	IE	*wāt-		E.	IE	*é-bherom 'bore'		F.	OIrish	berait 'they bear'
	Lat.	vātēs 'seer'			Armen.	e-ber				bertair 'are borne'
	OIrish	fāith 'poet'			Gk.	é-pheron			Lat.	ferunt 'they bear'
	OE	wōd 'mad, possessed'			Skt.	á-bharam				feruntur 'are borne'
		Wōden 'god of wisdom'			Iran.	a-berem				

G.	IE	*keu/kū/kwā-		*gwei/gwoi-		H.	IE	*pətḗr
	Skt.	śv(áyati) 'be strong'		gáyaḥ 'household'			Skt.	pitár-
	Avest.	sūra 'strong'		gayō 'lifetime'			Avest.	pitar-
	Armen.	sun 'void'		keam 'live'				
	Lith.	šaŭnas 'firm'		gajùs 'healing'				
	OSlav.	sujĭ 'vain'	(Russ.)	goĭ 'peace'				

I.	IE	*gher/ghor-	*bhleg- 'burn'	*dhūmos
	Gk.	khordē 'gut'	phlégō	thūmós 'passion'
	Lat.	hernia	flagrō	fūmus 'smoke'

4.9 THE SOUNDS OF INDO-EUROPEAN

Indo-European had the following sounds:

Consonants: p, t, k, kw; b, d, g, gw; bh, dh, gh, gwh; s; m, n; r; l; y, w

Vowels: i, e, a, o, u; ī, ē, ā, ō, ū; ə

The nasals and liquids [m, n, r, l] could be either syllabic or nonsyllabic. A following *h* indicates that a sound was aspirated. Sounds written with a following *w* were pronounced with rounded lips. The macron over a vowel indicates primarily tenseness and length rather than a qualitative difference. Otherwise, the symbols have their usual phonetic value. Obviously

		+ anterior		− anterior				
		− coronal	+ coronal	− rounded	+ rounded			
− voiced	− aspirated					− continuant	− sonorant	+ consonantal
+ voiced	+ aspirated							
− lateral	+ nasal	———		———	———	+ continuant	+ sonorant	
+ lateral	− nasal	———		———	———			

+ tense / − tense		− back	+ back			
			− rounded	+ rounded		
			———		− syllabic	− consonantal
− low	+ high		———			
	− high				+ syllabic	
+ low		———		———		

the exact pronunciation of Indo-European is a matter of conjecture; thus other reconstructions are possible.

Indo-European at one time had several other phonemes, "laryngeals," the exact number and quality of which are uncertain, although they were presumably nonanterior fricatives of some kind. They were lost early in the Indo-European period; we will take no further note of them.

The chart on page 89 shows the phonetic features of the Indo-European sounds. See exercise 2.26 for a description of the features; then complete the chart by entering the phonetic symbols in the appropriate boxes. The feature "aspirated" refers to the puff of air with which some obstruents were pronounced.

4.10 COGNATE WORDS IN THE INDO-EUROPEAN LANGUAGES (I)

1. All Indo-European languages share some words that are similar in form and meaning. We may confidently suppose that these words are the historical survivals of Indo-European roots. Both form and meaning may, of course, change with time. Thus the Indo-European *oinos 'one' has changed its form in Latin ūnus and Gothic ains; and in Greek oinē 'one-spot on a die,' it has both changed its form and narrowed its meaning.

To illustrate the common Indo-European vocabulary as it appears in the various languages of the group, we may consider the following lists of words, all of which are cited by Pyles on page 91 of *Origins and Development*. Compare the words with one another, observing similarities and differences. The differences are sometimes due to affixes and to vowel alternations in Indo-European; the reconstructed IE forms take into account some, though not all, such variation.

	heart	lung	head	foot
OE	heorte	lungen	hēafod	fōt
Ger.	Herz	Lungen	Haupt	Fuss
ON	hjarta	lunga	höfuð	fótr
Goth.	hairto	leihts 'light'	haubiþ	fotus
Lat.	cordis	levis 'light'	caput	pedis
Gk.	kardia	elachus 'little'		podos
Russ.	serdtse	legkoe		(OSl.) podu 'ground'
Lith.	širdis	lengvas 'light'		pėda 'foot-track'
Ir.	cride	laigiu 'less'		
Skt.	hrd-	laghus 'light'	kapala 'cup, skull'	pad
IE	*kerd-	*le(n)gwh-	*kap-ut-	*ped-/pŏd-

	night	star	snow	sun	moon
OE	niht	steorra	snāw	sunne	mōna
Ger.	Nacht	Stern	Schnee	Sonne	Mond
ON	nátt	stjarna	snjár	sól, sunna	máni
Goth.	nahts	stairno	snaiws	sauil, sunno	mena
Lat.	noctis	stella	nivis	sōl	mēnsis 'month'
Gk.	nuktos	aster	nipha	hēlios	mēn 'month'
Russ.	noch'		sneg	solntse	mesjats 'month'
Lith.	naktis		sniegas	saule	menuo
Ir.	nocht	(Br.) sterenn	snechte	(Br.) heol	mi 'month'
Skt.	naktam	star-	snih- 'sticky'	surya	mas- 'month'
IE	*nokwt-	*ster-	*(s)n(e/o)igwh-	*sāwel-/sun-	*mēn(ōt)-

	wind	*beech*	*corn*	*wolf*	*bear*
OE	wind	bēce	corn	wulf	bera
Ger.	Wind	Buche	Korn 'rye'	Wolf	Bär
ON	vindr	bók	korn	úlfr	björn
Goth.	winds	boka 'letter'	kaurn	wulfs	
Lat.	ventus	fāgus	grānum 'a grain'	lūpus	
Gk.	aēr	phēgos 'oak'	geron 'old man'	lukos	
Russ.	veter		zerno	volk	berloga 'den'
Lith.	vejas		žirnis 'pea'	vilkas	beras 'brown'
Ir.	(Br.) gwent		grān		
Skt.	vatas		jirna- 'worn out'	vrkas	bhallas
IE	*wē-nt-	*bhāgo-	*grno-	*wlkwo-/wlpo-	*bher-

	yoke	*mead*	*weave*	*sew*
OE	geoc	medu	wefan	siwian
Ger.	Joch	Met	weben	(OHG) siuwan
ON	ok	mjöðr	vefa	sýja
Goth.	juk			siujan
Lat.	iugum			suere
Gk.	zugon	methu 'wine'	huphaino	kas-suo 'sew together'
Russ.	igo	med		shit'
Lith.	jungas	medus 'honey'	austi	siuti
Ir.	cuing	mid	figim	
Skt.	yugam	madhu- 'liquor'	urna-vabhi 'spider,' lit. 'wool-weaver'	siv-
IE	*yugo-	*medhu-	*webh-	*syū-

2. Below are lists of words from ten Indo-European languages and a list of their reconstructed Indo-European sources. Use the blank tables that follow to sort the words into cognate lists like the ones in part 1 of this exercise.

Old English: brōþor, dohtor, ēast, eax, fæder, full, hund, mōdor, morðor 'murder,' nama, sunu, sweostor, Tīw, tōþ, widuwe

German: Achse, Bruder, Hund, Mord, Mutter, Name, Osten, Schwester, Sohn, Tochter, Vater, voll, Wittwe, Zahn, (OHG) Zio

Old Norse: austr, bróðir, dóttir, faðir, fullr, hundr, morð, móðir, nafn, öxull, sunr, systir, tönn, Tȳr

Gothic: broþar, dauhtar, fadar, fulls, hunds, maurþr, namo, sunus, swistar, tunþus, widuwo

Latin: aurōra 'dawn,' axis, canis, dens, frāter, Iūppiter, māter, mors, nōmen, pater, plēnus, soror, vidua

Greek: axōn, ēōs 'dawn,' huios, kuōn, mētēr, mortos, odontos, onoma, patēr, phratēr, pleres, thygater, Zeus

Russian: brat, doč', imja, mat', mjortvyǐ, os', polnyǐ, sestra, suka 'bitch,' syn, vdova

Lithuanian: ašis, aušra 'dawn,' brolis, dantis, diẽvas 'god,' dukte, (OPruss.) emmens, mirtìs, mote 'woman,' pilnas, sesuo, sunus, šuns, (OPruss.) widdewu

Irish: (Br.) ahel, ainm, athir, brathir, cū, det, dia 'god,' fedb, lan, marb, mathir, siur

Sanskrit: aksa-, bhrātar-, çvan-, dant-, duhitar-, dyaus-pitar, martaš, mātar-, naman-, pitar-, purna-, sunu-, svasar-, uṣas 'dawn,' vidhava-

Indo-European: *aks-, *aus(t)-, *bhrāter-, *deiwos/dyeu, *dent-/(o)dont-,*dhughǝtēr, *kw(o)n(-to)-/kan-i-, *māter-, *m(e)rt(r)-, *(o)nomen-, *pǝtēr-, *plǝno-, *sunu-, *swesor-, *widhēwo-

	father	*mother*	*brother*	*sister*	*son*
OE					
Ger.					
ON					
Goth.					
Lat.					
Gk.					
Russ.					
Lith.					
Ir.					
Skt.					
IE					

	daughter	*widow*	*name*	*east*	*full*
OE					
Ger.					
ON					
Goth.					
Lat.					
Gk.					
Russ.					
Lith.					
Ir.					
Skt.					
IE					

	hound	*tooth*	*axle*	*Sky-father, god*	*mortal, death*
OE					
Ger.					
ON					
Goth.					
Lat.					
Gk.					
Russ.					
Lith.					
Ir.					
Skt.					
IE					

3. For each of the following English words, find cognates in three or four other Indo-European languages. You can find the cognates in the *Oxford English Dictionary*, C. T. Onions's *Oxford Dictionary of English Etymology* (Oxford, 1966), W. W. Skeat's *An Etymological Dictionary of the English Language* (Oxford, 1879), E. Klein's *Comprehensive Etymological Dictionary of the English Language* (Amsterdam, 1966), C. D. Buck's *Dictionary of Selected Synonyms in the Principal Indo-European Languages* (Chicago, 1949), or J. Pokorny's *Indogermanisches Etymologisches Wörterbuch* (Bern, 1948–1969).

acre _____
birch _____
bleat _____
blue _____
bright _____
comb _____
eat _____
fee _____
for _____
free _____
friend _____
give _____
have _____
mind _____
much _____
numb _____
oak _____
queen _____
right _____
that _____
thatch _____
thunder _____
town _____
tree _____
what _____
wheel _____
wit _____
worth _____

4.11 COGNATE WORDS IN THE INDO-EUROPEAN LANGUAGES (II)

1. The following lists of the numbers 1 to 10 and 100 are from various Indo-European languages. The languages are grouped together according to the branch of the Indo-European family to which they belong. What similarities and differences can you find among the members of each branch? What similarities and differences are there among the various branches?

Reconstructed Indo-European[8]	GERMANIC				ARMENIAN	ALBANIAN
	English	German	Dutch	Danish	Armenian	Albanian
*oinos	one	eins	een	en	mi	nji
*dwo	two	zwei	twee	to	erku	dy
*treies	three	drei	drie	tre	erek	tre
*kwetwor	four	vier	vier	fire	čork	katër
*penkwe	five	fünf	vijf	fem	hing	pesë
*s(w)eks	six	sechs	zes	seks	vec	gjashtë
*septm	seven	sieben	zeven	syv	evtn	shtatë
*oktō	eight	acht	acht	otte	ut	tetë
*neun	nine	neun	negen	ni	inn	nând
*dekm	ten	zehn	tien	ti	tasn	dhiet
*kmtom	hundred	hundert	honderd	hundrede	hariur	qind

ITALIC				CELTIC		HELLENIC
Latin	Italian	French	Spanish	Irish	Welsh	Greek
ūnus	uno	un	uno	aon	un	heis
duo	due	deux	dos	dó	dau	duo
trēs	tre	trois	tres	trí	tri	treis
quattuor	quattro	quatre	cuatro	ceathair	pedwar	tettares
quīnque	cinque	cinq	cinco	cúig	pump	pente
sex	sei	six	seis	sé	chwech	hex
septem	sette	sept	siete	seacht	saith	hepta
octō	otto	huit	ocho	ocht	wyth	oktō
novem	nove	neuf	nueve	naoi	naw	ennea
decem	dieci	dix	diez	deich	deg	deka
centum	cento	cent	ciento	céad	cant	hekaton

SLAVIC				BALTIC	IRANIC	INDIC
Russian	Polish	Bulgarian	Slovak	Lithuanian	Persian	Hindustani
odin	jeden	edin	jeden	vienas	yek	ek
dva	dwa	dva	dva	du	do	do
tri	trzy	tri	tri	trys	se	tin
chetyre	cztery	četiri	štyri	keturi	cahar	char
pyat'	pięć	pet	pät'	penki	panj	panch
shest'	sześć	šest	šest'	šeši	shesh	chha
sem'	siedem	sedem	sedem	septyni	haft	sat
vosem'	osiem	osem	osem	aštuoni	hasht	ath
devyat'	dziewięć	devet	devät'	devyni	noh	nau
desyat'	dziesięć	deset	desat'	dešimt	dah	das
sto	sto	sto	sto	šimtas	sad	sau

[8] The numbers show various "irregularities" in their phonological development. See the entry for *four* in the *Oxford English Dictionary* for the unexpected *f-* in Germanic languages. The number *five* has a similarly unexpected development in Italo-Celtic.

2. The languages from which the following numbers come are also Indo-European. By comparing these lists with those above, you should be able to make a reasonable guess as to which branch of the Indo-European family each of these languages belongs. Write the name of the branch (Germanic, Armenian, Albanian, Italic, Celtic, Hellenic, Slavic, Baltic, Iranic, Indic) over each list.

	A	B	C	D	E	F
1	aon	jedinu	adzin	ains	onen	um
2	dha	duva	dva	twai	deu	dois
3	tri	trije	try	þrija	trȳ	tres
4	ceithir	četyre	čatyry	fidwor	peswar	quatro
5	coig	pęti	piac'	fimf	pymp	cinco
6	sia	šesti	šesc'	saihs	whēgh	seis
7	seachd	sedmi	siem	sibun	seyth	sete
8	ochd	osmi	vosiem	ahtau	ēth	oito
9	naoi	devęti	dzieviac'	niun	naw	nove
10	deich	desęti	dziesiac'	taihun	dēk	dez
100	ceud	suto	sto	taihuntehund	cans	cem

	G	H	I	J	K	L
1	un	ein	yek	un	jedan	ān
2	dos	zwene	du	dos	dva	twēgen
3	tres	dri	se	tres	tri	þrȳ
4	quatre	fior	cwar	quatre	četiri	fēower
5	cinc	finf	penj	cinc	pet	fīf
6	seis	sehs	šest	sis	šest	syx
7	set	sibun	hewt	set	sedam	seofon
8	ueg	ahto	ešt	vuit	osam	eahta
9	nou	niun	no	nou	devet	nigon
10	detz	zehan	de	deu	deset	tȳn
100	cent	zehanzo	sed	cent	sto	hundtēontig

	M	N	O	P	Q	R
1	meg	eden	jeden	en	einn	ek
2	yergu	dva	dva	två	tveir	dui
3	yerek	tri	tři	tre	þrír	tin
4	čors	štiri	čtyři	fyra	fjórir	char
5	hing	pet	pět	fem	fimm	panch
6	vec	šest	šest	sex	sex	chhoe
7	yotə	sedem	sedm	sju	sjau	shat
8	utə	osem	osm	åtta	átta	at
9	innə	devet	devět	nio	níu	noe
10	dasə	deset	deset	tio	tíu	dosh
100	haryur	sto	sto	hundra	tíutigir	sho

3. Ten of the languages from which the following numbers come are Indo-European; the remaining eight are not. Distinguish the Indo-European languages from the non-Indo-European ones by writing *IE* or *non-IE* above each list.

	A	B	C	D	E	F
1	en	un	bir	jedyn	egy	ün
2	twene	doui	iki	dwaj	két	duos
3	thria	trei	üç	tři	három	trais
4	fiuwar	patru	dört	štyri	négy	quatter
5	fif	cinci	beş	pjeć	öt	tschinch
6	sehx	şase	altı	šěsć	hat	ses
7	sibun	şapte	yedi	sedm	hét	set
8	ahto	opt	sekiz	wosm	nyolcz	och
9	nigun	nouă	dokuz	dźewjeć	kilencz	nouv
10	tehan	zice	on	dźesać	tíz	dêsch
100	hunderod	sută	yüz	sto	száz	tschient

	G	H	I	J	K	L
1	nigen	mot	unan	mek	i	aeva
2	khoyar	hai	daou	yerku	liang	dva
3	ghorban	ba	tri	yerek	san	þrayo
4	durben	bon	pevar	čors	ssu	caþwaro
5	tabon	nam	pemp	hing	wu	panca
6	jirghoghan	sau	c'houec'h	vec	liu	xšvaš
7	dologhan	bay	seiz	yot	ch'i	hapta
8	naiman	tam	eiz	ut	pa	ašta
9	yisun	chin	nao	innə	chiu	nava
10	arban	muoi	dek	tas	shih	dasa
100	jaghon	tram	kant	haryur	pai	satem

	M	N	O	P	Q	R
1	ichi	hana	eka	yaw	eden	echad
2	ni	tul	dvau	daw	dva	shnayim
3	san	set	trayas	dree	tri	shlosha
4	shi	net	catur	tsaloor	četiri	arba'a
5	go	tasŏt	pañca	pindze	pet	chamishsha
6	roku	yŏsŏt	şaş	shpazz	šest	shishsha
7	shichi	ilgop	sapta	uwe	sedum	shiv'a
8	hachi	yŏdŏl	aṣṭa	ate	osum	shmona
9	ku	ahop	nava	ne	devet	tish'a
10	ju	yŏl	daça	las	deset	'asara
100	hyaku	paek	çata	sulu	sto	mea

The first six conjugations show the verb 'bear' in varieties of Indo-European, with the thematic vowel, if any, and the ending separated from the base with a slash. These forms are discussed by Pyles on pages 89–90 of *Origins and Development*. The next six conjugations show the same verb in other varieties of Indo-European. Separate the base from the thematic vowel and the ending with a slash. Note how the endings in the various languages are alike and how they differ.

IE	Gothic	early OE	Sanskrit	Greek	Latin
*bher/ō	bair/a	ber/u	bhar/āmi	pher/ō	fer/ō
*bher/esi	bair/is	bir/is	bhar/asi	pher/eis	fer/s
*bher/eti	bair/iþ	bir/iþ	bhar/ati	pher/ei	fer/t
*bher/omes	bair/am	ber/aþ	bhar/āmas	pher/omes	fer/imus
*bher/ete	bair/iþ	ber/aþ	bhar/atha	pher/ete	fer/tis
*bher/onti	bair/and	ber/aþ	bhar/anti	pher/onti	fer/unt

Proto-Germanic	OHG	OIcelandic	OSlavonic	Lithuanian	OIrish
*berō	biru	ber	berǫ	beriù	biru
*berizi	biris	berr	bereši	berì	biri
*beriði	birit	berr	beretŭ	bẽria	berid
*beramiz	beramēs	berom	beremŭ	bẽriame	bermi
*bereðe	beret	bereþ	berete	bẽriate	berthe
*berandi	berant	bera	berǫtŭ	bẽria	berit

4.13 *THE MAJOR CHANGES FROM INDO-EUROPEAN TO GERMANIC*

All Germanic languages, in their oldest forms, share certain characteristics that distinguish them from other Indo-European languages. In *Origins and Development*, Pyles lists seven of these peculiarly Germanic features:

1. a two-tense verbal system
2. a dental suffix for the preterit tense
3. "strong" versus "weak" adjectives
4. a fixed stress accent
5. certain vowel changes
6. the First Sound Shift
7. a common distinctive vocabulary

Here are several examples of these Germanic characteristics. Forms from a Germanic language are listed together with parallel forms from a non-Germanic, but Indo-European, language. Compare the forms with one another and with the discussion in *Origins and Development*; then identify the Germanic characteristic that each example most clearly illustrates by writing the appropriate number, from 1 through 7, in the blank at the left.

_____ *Old English:* micel guma   *Latin:* magnus homo 'a great man'
se micela guma   iste magnus homo 'that great man'
micele guman   magnī homines 'great men'
þā micelan guman   istī magnī homines 'those great men'

_____ *Old English:* þorp 'town'   *Latin:* turba 'crowd'
etan 'eat'   edō 'eat'
īecan 'eke'   augeō 'increase'

_____ *Old English:* brū 'brow'   *Sanskrit:* bhrū 'brow'
rēad 'red'   rudh-ira 'blood'
gangan 'go' (cf. gangway)   jaŋghā⁹ 'heel, lower leg'

_____ *Old English:* mṓdor 'mother'   singular nominative   *Greek:* mḗtēr 'mother'
mṓdor   singular genitive   mētrós
mḗder   singular dative   mētrí
mṓdor   singular accusative   mētéra
mṓdor   plural nominative   mētéres
mṓdra   plural genitive   mētérōn
mṓdrum   plural dative   mētrási
mṓdor   plural accusative   mētéras

_____ *Old English:* brōðor 'brother'   *Latin:* frāter 'brother'
bōc 'beech tree'   fāgus 'beech tree'
mōdor 'mother'   māter 'mother'

_____ *Old English:* ic sēce 'I seek'   *Latin:* sagiō 'I perceive'
ic sōhte 'I sought'   sagīvī 'I perceived'
ic temme 'I tame'   domō 'I tame'
ic temede 'I tamed'   domuī 'I tamed'

_____ *Gothic:* gasts 'stranger'   *Latin:* hostis 'stranger'
nahts 'night'   nox 'night'
gards 'garden'   hortus 'garden'

_____ *Old English:* sǽ 'sea'   *Greek:* thalassa 'sea'
Dutch: zee   *Latin:* mare
Old High German: sēo   *Irish:* muir
Icelandic: sær   *Lithuanian:* jūra
Danish: sö   *Hindustani:* samundar
Gothic: saiws   *Old Persian:* drayah

_____ *Old English:* nefa 'nephew'   *Latin:* nepōs 'grandson'
weorþan 'become'   vertō 'turn'
hōre 'whore'   cāra 'dear one'

_____ *Old English:* ic dō 'I do, am doing, will   *Greek:* tithēmi 'I am placing'
do'   thēsō 'I will place'
ic dyde 'I was doing, did,   etithēn 'I was placing'
have done'   ethēka 'I placed'
    tethēka 'I have placed'

---

⁹ The initial *j* is due to a sound change which is of no importance for Germanic languages.

The Germanic Consonant Shift (also known as the First Sound Shift or Grimm's Law) occurred in five steps. Step 3 is called Verner's Law. Each step was completed before the next began, so there was no overlapping or repetition of the changes.

1. The shift is described here in articulatory terms. Complete the blanks to show the development of each sound.

   STEP 1: All aspirated voiced stops became the corresponding voiced fricatives:
   bh > _____; dh > _____; gh > _____; gwh > _____.

   STEP 2: Voiceless stops became the corresponding voiceless fricatives (except when they followed another voiceless fricative): p > _____; t > _____; k > _____; kw > _____.

   STEP 3: Voiceless fricatives were voiced (when they were in a voiced environment and the Indo-European stress was not on the preceding syllable): f > _____; þ > _____; x > _____; xw > _____; s > _____.

   STEP 4: All voiced stops were unvoiced: b > _____; d > _____; g > _____; gw > _____.

   STEP 5: Voiced fricatives sometimes became the corresponding voiced stops (the exact conditions depended on the sound, the environment, and the dialect): ƀ > _____; ð > _____; ȝ > _____; ȝw > _____. In this same step, the voiced fricative z became an *r*-like sound that was spelled with a distinctive letter (transliterated ʀ) in the early runic inscriptions of North Germanic; it later merged with the *r* inherited from Indo-European.

2. The Consonant Shift can also be described by rules stated in phonetic features, thus:

   STEP 1: $\begin{bmatrix} -\text{ continuant} \\ +\text{ aspirated} \end{bmatrix} \rightarrow [+ \text{ continuant}]$

   That is, any sound that is both noncontinuant and aspirated (an aspirated stop) becomes a continuant (a fricative).

   STEP 2: $\begin{bmatrix} -\text{ continuant} \\ -\text{ voiced} \end{bmatrix} \rightarrow [+ \text{ continuant}]$ *except* / [− voiced] _____

   That is, any sound that is both noncontinuant and nonvoiced (voiceless stop) becomes a continuant (fricative), except following a nonvoiced sound.

   STEP 3: $[+ \text{ continuant}] \rightarrow [+ \text{ voiced}] / [- \text{ stressed}][+ \text{ voiced}] _____ [+ \text{ voiced}]$
   That is, any sound that is a continuant (fricative) is voiced, when between voiced sounds and preceded by a nonstressed syllable.

   STEP 4: $[- \text{ continuant}] \rightarrow [- \text{ voiced}]$
   That is, any noncontinuant (stop) becomes nonvoiced.

   STEP 5: $\begin{bmatrix} -\text{ sonorant} \\ +\text{ voiced} \end{bmatrix} \rightarrow [- \text{ continuant}] / \begin{Bmatrix} \# \\ [+ \text{ nasal}] \end{Bmatrix} _____$

   That is, any voiced nonsonorant (in practice, a voiced fricative) becomes a noncontinuant (stop), in initial position (# indicates word beginning) or after a nasal.

   The foregoing rules state the Consonant Shift in a somewhat different fashion from the more traditional description in part 1, but they account for the same changes. Complete the blanks in the chart on page 100 to show how the IE obstruent system looked after each step in the Shift. (The labiovelars, *kw*, *gw*, *gwh*, have been omitted for simplicity's sake.)

IE SYSTEM	AFTER STEP 1	AFTER STEP 2	AFTER STEP 3	AFTER STEP 4	AFTER STEP 5
		(p t k)*	(p t k)*		
p t k	p t k	— — —	f þ x	f þ x	f þ x
b d g	b d g	b d g	b d g	— — —	p t k
bh dh gh	— — —	ƀ ð ʒ	ƀ ð ʒ	ƀ ð ʒ	— — —
					(ƀ ð ʒ)*
s	s	s	s	s	s
			—	z	r

* Sounds in parentheses occurred in limited environments.

3. In each of the following pairs, the first item is a reconstructed Indo-European root and the second is a related English word. The English word may be based on a form with affixes added to the root or may involve a change in vowel, but the Indo-European consonants you are asked to examine correspond regularly with those in the root of the English word. No exceptions and no examples of Verner's Law (step 3 of the Shift) are involved. Supply the missing letters.

*bha 'speak' / _____an
*dheu- 'flow' / _____ew
*ghans- / _____oose
*bend- 'protruding point' / _____en
*de- / _____o
*gel- / _____ool
*pau- / _____ew
*tr- 'cross over' / _____rough
*kan- 'sing' / _____en
*angh- 'tight' / an_____er
*bher- / _____ear
*koimo- / _____ome
*pā- / _____ood
*swād / swee_____
*gl- 'ball' / _____lue
*dhrēn- / _____rone
*lab- / la_____ 'lick'
*pūlo- 'rotten' / _____oul
*wadh- 'pledge' / we_____
*wāb- / wee_____

*magh- 'can' / (OE) ma_____an 'may'
*wegh- 'go' / (OE) we_____ 'way'
*plōu- / _____low
*aug- 'increase' / e_____e
*kel- 'cover' / _____ell
*leb- / li_____
*dem- 'build' / _____imber
*bhlō- / _____loom
*dhō 'set, put' / _____o
*tum- 'swollen' / _____umb
*tong- 'feel' / _____an_____
*pet- 'fly' / _____ea_____er
*treud- 'squeeze' / _____rea_____
*bhreg- / _____rea_____
*bheid- 'split' / _____i_____e
*dhragh- / _____ra_____
*grebh- 'scratch' / _____ra_____
*porko- / (OE) _____ear_____ 'small pig'
*kwerp- 'turn about' / w_____ar_____
*ghreib- / _____ri_____

4. In the following examples, the Indo-European stress was on some syllable other than the first; consequently Verner's Law (step 3 of the Consonant Shift) applies. Supply the missing letters.

*kaput- / (Goth.) hau____iþ 'head'
*plōtu- / floo____
*konk- / han____
*wes- 'dwell' / we____e

*sep(t)m- / (Goth.) si____un 'seven'
*klūto- / (OE) hlū____ 'loud'
*dukā- / (OE) to____ian 'tow'
*sauso- 'dry' / sea____

5. Examine the following pairs; then list the Indo-European consonants that underwent no change in Germanic: _____

*lem- 'break' / (OE) lama 'lame'
*mā- 'damp' / (OE) mō-r 'moor'
*mel- 'soft' / (OE) mel-tan 'melt'
*mer- 'harm' / (OE) mare 'nightmare'
*nas- 'nose' / (OE) nosu 'nose'

*newo- 'new' / (OE) nēowe 'new'
*wel- 'wish' / (OE) wel 'well'
*wen- 'strive' / (OE) winnan 'win'
*wir- 'man' / (OE) wer 'man'
*yēro- 'year' / (ModE) year

4.15 THE HIGH GERMAN CONSONANT SHIFT

English and the Low German languages—Dutch, Flemish, and Plattdeutsch—differ from modern Standard German partly because Standard German has undergone a second or High German Consonant Shift. English preserves the older common Germanic sounds which were changed in High German between the sixth and the eighth centuries.

Summarize in the following chart those parts of the Second Consonant Shift which Pyles describes on page 111 of *Origins and Development*.[10]

OLDER GERMANIC		p	t	k	d
HIGH GERMAN	*after vowels*				
	otherwise			—	

Below are some English and High German cognates that show sound correspondence according to the Second Consonant Shift. Supply the missing letters.

ENGLISH	GERMAN	ENGLISH	GERMAN	ENGLISH	GERMAN
pan	____anne	boo____	Busse	bite	bei____en
grip	Gri____	sha____e	schaffen	plough	____lug
to	____u	____ath	Pfad	weaponless	wa____enlos
foot	Fu____	ri____e	reiten	heart	Her____
book	Bu____	hol____	Holz	fret	fre____en
door	____ür	re____on	rechnen	alike	glei____
pole	____ahl	ha____e	Hass	deed	____a____
tame	____ahm	o____en	offen	token	____ei____en
make	ma____en	floo____	Flut	plant	____lan____e
dream	____raum	shi____	Schiff	tide	____ei____

[10] A complete statement of the High German Consonant Shift would require some additional remarks about sounds and positions. The chart does, however, include the most important changes.

The following selections are translations of the parable of the prodigal son (Luke 15:11–24) in four early Germanic languages: Gothic, Old English, Old High German, and Old Icelandic. The Latin Vulgate text has been added for comparison. The Gothic, Old English, and Old High German versions are fairly close translations; with the help of a modern English translation and some imagination you should be able to make them out. The Old Icelandic version, however, is an unusually free and prolix rendering; therefore a gloss has been given for it.

Compare the translations with one another to discover similarities and differences among the Germanic languages. Vowel length is marked with macrons in Old English and with acute accents in Old Icelandic.

Gothic

(11) Manne sums aihta twans sununs. (12) Jah qaþ sa juhiza ize du attin: "Atta, gif mis sei undrinnai mik dail aiginis." Jah disdailida im swes sein. (13) Jah afar ni managans dagans, brahta samana allata sa juhiza sunus jah aflaiþ in land fairra wisando, jah jainar distahida þata swes seinata libands usstiuriba. (14) Biþe þan frawas allamma, warþ huhrus abrs and gawi jainata, jah is dugann alaþarba wairþan. (15) Jah gaggands gahaftida sik sumamma baurgjane jainis gaujis. Jah insandida ina haiþjos seinaizos haldan sweina. (16) Jah gairnida sad itan haurne, þoei matidedun sweina, jah manna imma ni gaf. (17) Qimands þan in sis qaþ: "Hwan filu asnje attins meinis ufarassau haband hlaibe, iþ ik huhrau fraqistna! (18) Usstandands gagga du attin meinamma, jah qiþa du imma: 'Atta, frawaurhta mis in himin, jah in andwairþja þeinamma; (19) ju þanaseiþs ni im wairþs ei haitaidau sunus þeins; gatawei mik swe ainana asnje þeinaize.'" (20) Jah usstandands qam at attin seinamma. Nauhþanuh þan fairra wis-andan, gasahw ina atta is, jah infeinoda, jah þragjands draus ana hals is, jah kukida imma. (21) Jah qaþ imma sa sunus: "Atta, frawaurhta in himin, jah in andwairþja þeinamma, ju þanaseiþs ni im wairþs ei haitaidau sunus þeins." (22) Qaþ þan sa atta du skalkam seinaim: "Sprauto bringiþ wastja þo frumiston, jah gawasjiþ ina, jah gibiþ figgragulþ in handu is, jah gaskohi ana fotuns is, (23) jah bringandans stiur þana alidan ufsneiþiþ, jah matjandans wisam waila, (24) unte sa sunus meins dauþs was, jah gaqiunoda, jah fralusans was, jah bigitans warþ."

Old English

(11) Sōðlīce sum man hæfde twēgen suna. (12) Þā cwæð se gingra tō his fæder: "Fæder, syle mē mīnne dæl mīnre æhte þe mē tō gebyreþ." Þā dælde hē him his æhte. (13) Ðā æfter fēawum dagum, ealle his þing gegaderode se gingra sunu, and fērde wræclice on feorlen rīce, and forspilde þār his æhta, lybbende on his gælsan. (14) Ðā hē hīg hæfde ealle āmyrrede, þā wearð mycel hunger on þām rīce, and hē wearð wædla. (15) Þā fērde hē, and folgode ānum burhsittendan men þæs rīces. Ðā sende hē hine tō his tūne þæt hē hēolde his swȳn. (16) Ðā gewilnode hē his wambe gefyllan of þām bēancoddum, þe ðā swȳn æton, and him man ne sealde. (17) Þā beþōhte hē hine, and cwæð: "Ēalā, hū fela hȳrlinga on mīnes fæder hūse hlāf genōhne habbað, and ic hēr on hungre forwurðe! (18) Ic ārīse, and ic fare tō mīnum fæder, and ic secge him: 'Ēalā fæder, ic syngode on heofenas, and beforan þē; (19) nū ic ne eom wyrðe þæt ic bēo þīn sunu nemned; dō mē swā ānne of þīnum hȳrlingum.'" (20) And hē ārās þā, and cōm tō his fæder. And þā gȳt þā hē wæs feorr his fæder, hē hyne geseah, and wearð mid mildheortnesse āstyrod, and agēn hine arn, and hine beclypte, and cyste hine. (21) Ða cwæð his sunu: "Fæder, ic syngode on heofon, and beforan ðē; nū ic ne eom wyrþe þæt ic þīn sunu

bēo genemned." (22) Ða cwæþ se fæder tō his þēowum: "Bringað raðe þone sēlestan gegyre-
lan, and scrȳdað hyne, and syllað him hring on his hand, and gescȳ tō his fōtum, (23) and
bringað ān fætt styric, and ofslēað, and uton etan, and gewistfullian, (24) for þām þēs
mīn sunu wæs dēad, and hē geedcucode, hē forwearð, and hē is gemēt."

Old High German

(11) Sum man habata zuuene suni. (12) Quad tho ther iungoro fon then themo fater:
"Fater, gib mir teil thero hehti, thiu mir gibure." Her tho teilta thia heht. (13) Nalles after
manegen tagon, gisamonoten allen ther iungoro sun elilentes fuor in uerra lantscaf, inti dar
ziuuarf sina heht lebento uirnlustigo. (14) Inti after thiu her iz al forlos, uuard hungar strengi
in thero lantscefi, her bigonda tho armen. (15) Inti gieng, inti zuoclebeta einemo thero burg-
liuto thero lantscefi. Inti santa inan in sin thorf, thaz her fuotriti suuin. (16) Inti girdinota
gifullen sina uuamba fon siliquis, theo thiu suuin azzun, inti nioman imo ni gab. (17) Her tho
in sih giuuorban quad: "Vvuo manege asnere mines fater ginuht habent brotes, ih uoruuirdu
hier hungere! (18) Arstantu, inti faru zi minemo fater, inti quidu imo: 'Fater, ih suntota in
himil, inti fora thir; (19) inti ni bim iu uuirdig ginemnit uuesan thin sun; tuo mih so einan fon
thinen asnerin.'" (20) Inti arstantanti quam zi simemo fater. Mittiu thanne noh ferro uuas,
gisah inan sin fater, inti miltida giruorit uuard, inti ingegin louffenti fiel ubar sinan hals, inti
custa inan. (21) Tho quad imo der sun: "Fater, ih suntota in himil, inti fora thir, iu ni bim
uuirdig ginemnit uuesan thin sun." (22) Tho quad ther fater zi sinen scalcun: "Sliumo bringet
thaz erira giuuati, inti giuuatet inan, inti gebet fingirin in sina hant, inti giscuohiu in fuozi,
(23) inti leitet gifuotrit calb, inti arslahet, inti ezzemes, inti goumumes, (24) uuanta theser
min sun tot uuas, inti arqueketa, foruuard, inti funtan uuard."

Old Icelandic

(11) Einn auðigr maðr átti tvá sunu. (12) En sá hinn yngri sunr hans mælti til föður
  A   rich   man   had two sons.   And he this younger son of his said to father

síns: "Faðir," sagði hann, "fá mér þann hlut fjár míns, er til mín telst í
his Father said   he   give me the portion of possessions my which to me counts in

erfðum millum vár feðganna." Sem faðir hans heyrði þetta, þá skipti hann hánum
inheritance among us father and sons. When father his heard this   then divided he   to him

sínum hlut. (13) En hann varð þegar í brotto ok fór langt í önnor land með sínum
his portion. And he got at once away and went far to other lands with his

hlut, ok lifði þar fólslega, eyddi fénu öllu í fúllífi svá snáplega, at um síðir
portion and lived there foolishly wasted substance all in foul life so brutishly that at last

hafði hann sjálfr alls ekki. (14) Ok fluttist þar fram með mykilli fátœkt, þvíat í
had   he himself at all nothing.   And moved there from with great   poverty because at

þeim tíma var mykit úáran í þvi landi ok mykill sultr. (15) Ok kom hann sér í
that time was great dearth in the land and great hunger.   And came he himself into

fátœka þjónustu með einum ríkum manni, en hann sendi hann til eins kotbœar, at
impoverished service with a   powerful man and he sent him to a farmstead that

hann skyldi gæta svína hans. (16) En hans vesöld vóx svá mjök þar, at hann fystist
he   should watch swine his.   And his misery grew so much there that he desired

fyrir hungrs sakar at fylla kvið sinn af   bauna skálmum ok stiklum, er   svínum var
for hunger's sake to fill belly his with bean pods   and thorns which to swine was

gefit til matar, ok fékk hann sér   þat til fœzlu, þvíat engi vildi gefa hánum
given as meat and took he   himself that as food because no one would give him

annat. (17) Ok hugleíddi hann þá, sjálfr, hversu fólslega er hann hafði farit med sínu
any other. And considered he   then himself how foolishly that he had dealt with his

ráði ok mæltist þá við einn samann þessum orðum: "Faðir minn fœðir hversdaglega
life and spoke then to himself   in these words Father my   feeds commonly

heima með sér   mykinn fjölda leigumanna með gnógu brauði ok annarri vist œrinni,
at home with himself a great multitude of hired men with enough bread and other food enough

en ek svelt her af matleysi! (18) Ok því   skal ek skyndilega fara til föður míns ok
and I die here of starvation!   And therefore shall I quickly   go to father my and

biðja hann miskunnar með þessum orðum: 'Faðir, ek hefi syndgazt ok misgört í móti
beg him for mercy with these words Father I have sinned   and done amiss against

guði himneskum ok svá móti þér; (19) ok firir því em ek eigi verðr heðan ifrá, at
god in heaven and also against thee   and therefore am I not worthy henceforth that

þú haldir mik svá sem þinn sun; nú bið ek, at þú gefir mér slíkan rétt í garði þínum
thou hold me thus as thy son now beg I that thou give me such due in house thy

sem einum leigumanne þínum.'" (20) Ok siðan   fór hann skyngilega ok kom til
as one of hired men thy.   And afterwards went he quickly   and came to

föður síns. Nú þegar sem faðir hans leit hann mjök fjarri komandi, þá sneri hann
father his. Now at once when father his saw him very far off coming then turned he

þegar miskunn sinni til   hans ok rann at hánum ok tók höndum sínum um háls
at once mercy his towards him and ran to him   and held with hands his about neck

hánum ok kysti hann með myklum fagnaði.[11] (22) Ok mælti við þjónustumenn sína, er
his and kissed him with great delight.   And said to servants his who

í hjá   hánum váru: "Skyndið heim ok takit góða gangverju   með fögrum skóm ok
close by him were Hurry home and take good walking cloak with fair shoes and

fœrið syni mínum ok gott fingrgull   dregit á hönd hánum ok sœmið hann,
bring to son my and good gold finger-ring put on hand his and honor him

(23) drepit ok einn feitan oxa; vér skulum hafa, í dag mykla veizlu ok fagnaðar öl í
slay also a fat ox we shall have to day great feast and for rejoicing ale at

heimkomu sunar míns, (24) þvíat ek hugða hann vera dauðan ok er hann nú lífs,
homecoming of son my because I thought him to be dead and is he now alive

þar sem hann hvarf í brott ok er nú aptr kominn."
whereas he vanished away and is now back come.

Latin

(11) Homo quidam habuit duos filios. (12) Et dixit adolescentior ex illis patri: "Pater, da mihi portionem substantiae quae me contingit." Et divisit illis substantiam. (13) Et non post

[11] Verse 21 is lacking.

multos dies, congregatis omnibus, adolescentior filius peregre profectus est in regionem longin-
quam, et ibi dissipavit substantiam suam vivendo luxuriose.   (14) Et postquam omnia consum-
masset, facta est fames valida in regione illa, et ipse coepit egere.   (15) Et abiit, et adhaesit uni
civium regionis illius. Et misit illum in villam suam ut pasceret porcos.   (16) Et cupiebat
implere ventrem suum de siliquis, quas porci manducabant, et nemo illi dabat.   (17) In se
autem reversus, dixit: "Quanti mercenarii in domo patris mei abundant panibus, ego autem
hic fame pereo!   (18) Surgam, et ibo ad patrem meum, et dicam ei: 'Pater, peccavi in caelum,
et coram te;   (19) iam non sum dignus vocari filius tuus; fac me sicut unum de mercenariis
tuis.'"   (20) Et surgens venit ad patrem suum. Cum autem adhuc longe esset, vidit illum pater
ipsius, et misericordia motus est, et accurrens cecidit super collum eius, et osculatus est eum.
(21) Dixitque ei filius: "Pater, peccavi in caelum, et coram te, iam non sum dignus vocari filius
tuus."   (22) Dixit autem pater ad servos suos: "Cito proferte stolam primam, et induite illum,
et date annulum in manum eius, et calceamenta in pedes eius,   (23) et adducite vitulum sagina-
tum, et occidite, et manducemus, et epulemur,   (24) quia hic filius mortuus erat, et revixit,
perierat, et inventus est."

What words in each of the Germanic versions correspond to the Latin (or English) below?

	GOTHIC	OLD ENGLISH	OLD HIGH GERMAN	OLD ICELANDIC
(11) homo 'man'				
duos 'two'				
filios 'sons'				
(12) adolescentior 'younger'				
patri 'to (his) father'				
pater 'father'				
(14) fames 'hunger'				
(15) porcos 'swine'				
(16) cupiebat 'desired'				
(17) panibus 'bread'				
ego 'I'				
fame 'in hunger'				
(18) caelum 'heaven'				
(19) filius 'son'				
(20) venit 'came'				
ad patrem suum 'to his father'				
(22) in manum eius 'on his hand'				
calceamenta 'shoes'				
(23) vitulum 'calf, young steer'				
(24) mortuus 'dead'				

5

The Old English Period (449–1100)

5.1 QUESTIONS FOR REVIEW AND DISCUSSION

1. Define the following terms:

grammatical gender	a-stem	grammatical change
natural gender	n-stem	preterit-present verb
case	ō-stem	anomalous verb
nominative	mutation (umlaut)	enclitic
accusative	gradation (ablaut)	personal endings
genitive	short syllable	indicative
dative	long syllable	subjunctive
instrumental	dual number	imperative
"strong" declension	preterit	finite forms
"weak" declension	principal parts	nonfinite forms

2. What peoples inhabited the British Isles before the coming of the English?

3. According to Bede, what circumstances brought the Germanic tribesmen to Britain, and which tribes participated in the settlement of the island?

4. What was the influence of the Scandinavian settlement on the English language?

5. Which dialect of Old English was the standard language and from which dialect has Modern English descended?

6. What difference between the Old English sound system and that of Modern English is illustrated by the following pairs? *spanan* 'attract, urge,' *spannan* 'join, fasten'; *suga* 'sows,' *sugga* 'a bird'; *fela* 'much, many,' *fella* 'of hides, skins'; *rǣde* '(I) give advice,' *rǣdde* '(I) gave advice'

7. What is the chief difference between the stress patterns of Old English and Modern English, and what historical events help to account for the difference?

8. What are the main differences in word order between Old English and Modern English?

9. From which Old English declension do the living noun inflections of Modern English derive?

10. How do the grammatical devices for indicating plurality in Old English and in Modern English differ?

11. What was the difference in use between the strong and weak forms of an Old English adjective?

12. What Old English adjective inflections have survived as living suffixes in Modern English?

13. What is the origin of Modern English adverbs without endings such as *deep, fast*, and *loud*?

14. What is the difference between mutation (umlaut) and gradation (ablaut)?

15. From what class of Old English verbs are the Modern English modal auxiliaries *shall, should, may, might, can, could, must*, and *ought* derived?

16. What distinctions in form, universal in Old English verbs, are preserved in Modern English only in the verb *to be*?

17. What is the Old English origin of the *y-* in Spenser's "A Gentle Knight was pricking on the plaine, / Ycladd in mightie armes and silver shielde"?

18. Old English differs from Modern English in the amount of inflection for nouns, adjectives, pronouns, and verbs. Name four or five other major differences between the linguistic systems of the two periods.

5.2 ANGLO-SAXON ENGLAND

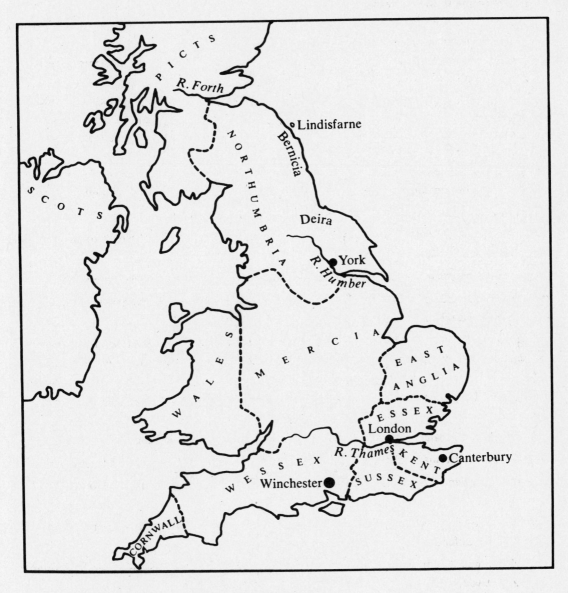

Locate the four main Old English dialects on the map.

ANGLIAN

Northumbrian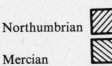

Mercian

West Saxon

Kentish

1. Summarize the rules for Old English stress on

    words without a prefix *Stressed on first syllable*

    words with a prefix *Stressed on the first syllable of the second element*

    compounds *most stressed on first syllable, N-N compounds and N-Adj compounds had secondary stress, be- for- and ge compounds were never stressed on be- for- or ge-*

2. Indicate the primary stress of the following Old English words, all of which are without prefix, by placing a stress mark ( ) over the stressed vowel.

cúman	'to come'	swéotol	'clear'
féngon	'(they) took'	swéotolian	'to reveal'
físcere	'fisherman'	spéllian	'to relate'
déarnunga	'secretly'	lústfullić	'joyful'

3. Indicate the primary stress of the following Old English words by placing a stress mark ( ) over the stressed vowel. Prefixes have been set off with hyphens to call attention to them.

on-fón	'to receive'	be-sprécan	'to talk about'
and-féngness	'reception'	bī-spéll	'proverb'
wið-sprécan	'to contradict'	be-cúman	'to happen'
wiðer-sprǽċ	'contradiction'	be-cýme	'result'
of-þýncan	'to offend'	for-fón	'to take away'
æf-þúnca	'offense'	for-fáng	'seizure'
to-cúman	'to arrive'	ge-réċċan	'to explain'
tō-cýme	'arrival'	ge-réċedness	'interpretation'

4. Indicate the primary stress ( ) and the secondary stress ( ) of the following compounds by writing the appropriate marks over the stressed vowels. Compounds have been divided with hyphens. Some of the words have prefixes which you should recognize from the preceding question.

spéll-bòda	'messenger'	forfáng-fèoh	'reward for rescuing property'
gód-spèllere	'evangelist'	scīr-gerèfa	'shire reeve'
sprǽċ-hùs	'senate house'	bebód-dæ̀ġ	'appointed day'
mán-cynn	'mankind'	ġehát-land	'promised land'
bōc-cræftiġ	'learned'	dǽd-cène	'daring'
lóf-ġèornost	'most eager for praise'	héah-fæ̀der	'patriarch'
héah-burg	'capital city'	léorning-cnìht	'disciple'
túngol-wìtega	'astrologer'	mýnster-mànn	'monk'

Late Old English had the following vowels:[1]

SPELLING	SOUND	SPELLING	SOUND	SPELLING	SOUND
a	[ɑ]	i	[ɪ]	y	[y]
ā	[ɑ̄]	ī	[ī]	ȳ	[ȳ]
æ	[æ]	o	[ə]	ea	[æə]
ǣ	[ǣ]	ō	[ō]	ēa	[ǣə]
e	[ɛ]	u	[ʊ]	eo	[ɛə]
ē	[ē]	ū	[ū]	ēo	[ēə]

1. Complete the following chart by filling in the phonetic symbols listed above to show the articulation of Old English vowels.

2. Complete the following chart to show (1) the phonetic symbol for the Old English vowel, (2) the phonetic symbol for a typical Modern English development of the vowel, and (3) the typical spelling of the Modern English development. Complete columns (2) and (3) according to the Modern English key words.

[1] For the use of macrons in Old English spelling see Pyles, p. 122, n. 11. Other interpretations are possible for some of the sounds listed here; see Pyles, p. 123. To pronounce [ȳ], say [ī] with your lips well-rounded, as though for [ū]; similarly, [y] is like [ɪ] with lip rounding as for [ʊ]. The macron is used in phonetic transcriptions to show that the vowel is long and tense; a colon following the vowel can be used for the same purpose: thus [ū] or [u:].

	OLD ENGLISH			MODERN ENGLISH		
vowel	(1) *phonetic symbol*	*key words*		*key words*		(2) *phonetic symbol*	(3) *typical spelling*

vowel	(1) phonetic symbol	key words		key words		(2) phonetic symbol	(3) typical spelling
a	[ɑ]	habban sadol	batt lamb	have saddle	bat lamb	[æ]	a
ā	[ā]	hām tācen	gād pāl	home token	goad pole	[o]	o oa
æ	[æ]	þæt bæc	pæð mæst	that back	path mast	[æ]	a
ǣ	[ǣ]	dǣl hǣlan	nǣdl mǣne	deal heal	needle mean	[i]	ea ee
e	[ɛ]	settan rest	weddian denn	set rest	wed den	[ɛ]	e
ē	[ē]	fēdan grēne	cēne mētan	feed green	keen meet	[i]	~~ea~~ ee
i	[ɪ]	sittan mist	timber rima	sit mist	timber rim	[ɪ]	i
ī	[ī]	rīdan līf	tīma bī	ride life	time by	[əɪ]	i y
o	[ɔ]	moððe oft	pott botm	moth oft(en)	pot bottom	[a]	o
ō	[ō]	fōda nōn	gōd brōm	food noon	good broom	[u] [ʊ]	oo
u	[ʊ]	sundor þus	wundor pullian	sunder thus	wonder pull	[ə] [ʊ]	u o
ū	[ū]	mūs dūne	nū ūt	mouse down	now out	[aʊ]	ou ow
y	[y]	fyllan mynster	pytt þynne	fill minster	pit thin	[ɪ]	i y
ȳ	[ȳ]	mȳs hȳdan	fȳr hwȳ	mice hide	fire why	[əɪ]	i y
ea	[æə]	ċeaf nearu	sleac fealu	chaff narrow	slack fallow	[æ]	a
ēa	[ǣə]	bēatan lēaf	ēast stēap	beat leaf	east steep	[i]	ea ee
eo	[ɛə]	ġeolu eolh	heofon seofon	yellow elk	heaven seven	[ɛ]	e ea
ēo	[ēə]	crēopan flēon	dēop bēo	creep flee	deep bee	[i]	ee

110

Late Old English had the following consonants:

SPELLING	SOUND	SPELLING	SOUND	SPELLING	SOUND
b	[b]	h	[h], [x], [ç] [2]	s	[s], [z]
c, k	[k]	l	[l]	t	[t]
ċ [3]	[č]	m	[m]	þ, ð	[θ], [ð]
d	[d]	n	[n], [ŋ]	w	[w]
f	[f], [v]	p	[p]	sc	[š]
g	[g], [ʒ] [2]	r	[r]	cg	[ǰ]
ġ [3]	[j]				

Complete the following chart by filling in the symbols listed above so as to show the place and manner of articulation of Old English consonants. A review of the chart of Modern English consonants will help you complete this one. Although [ʒ] is a fricative it should be put with [g] among the stops for a reason we will presently see.

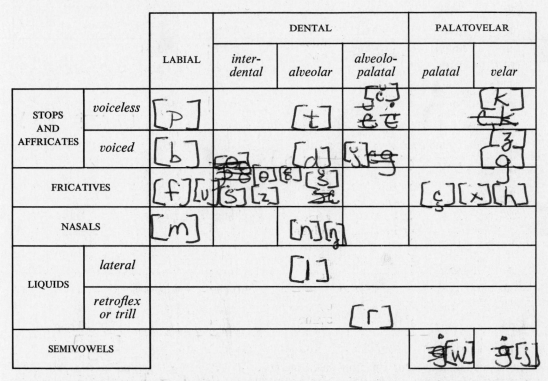

[2] To pronounce [x] and [ç] you may find one or more of the following techniques helpful: (1) Start to make the sound [k], but stop before the back of the tongue actually touches the roof of the mouth, and breathe out strongly; or make a [k] with light contact between the tongue and the roof of the mouth, and with the tongue still in that position, breathe out strongly; or (2) make an [š] sound, and while you are making it, force your tongue as far back in the mouth as it will go, the result being [x]; or (3) make the [hj] sound as in *hew* force-fully so that the [h] and [j] blend into a single sound, which will be [ç]. Palatal [ç] and velar [x] differ from each other much as do the [k] sounds of *keen* and *coon*. Children sometimes use repeated [x]'s or [ç]'s to represent the sound of a train engine. The sound [ʒ] is simply a voiced [x], so the simplest way to make it is to vibrate your vocal cords while making an [x], or try techniques (1) and (2) described above, but using [g] instead of [k] and [ž] instead of [š]. Or make a [w], unround your lips, and concentrate on producing a friction noise by slightly raising the back of your tongue. Children sometimes use a prolonged [ʒ] to represent the sound of an airplane engine.

[3] The dot over the spellings *ċ* and *ġ* is, like the macron over vowel spellings, a modern editorial device to help the reader. It was not used by Old English scribes. In some words the pronunciation of *c* and *g*, especially in medial position, is uncertain; it is likely that there was variation among the Anglo-Saxons themselves.

5.6 THE PRONUNCIATION OF OLD ENGLISH: CONSONANT ALTERNATIONS

Thirteen of the consonant sounds listed in the preceding exercise are grouped thus:

[f] / [v]   [θ] / [ð]   [s] / [z]   [g] / [ʒ]   [h] / [x] / [ç]   [n] / [ŋ]

The sounds in each group alternate in different environments. For example, [f] occurs in one set of positions and [v] occurs in a different set of positions. Neither [f] nor [v] normally turns up in any of the positions belonging to the other sound. Since the two labial fricatives alternate in this way, they are, as far as Old English is concerned, the same sound; that is, they are allophones of the same phoneme.

Examine the following words to determine the positions (environment) in which the sounds of each group occur.

1. [f] / [v], [θ] / [ð], [s] / [z]

folc	[fɔlk]	'folk'	offrian	[ɔffrɪan]	'to offer'
þurh	[θurx]	'through'	moððe	[mɔθθɛ]	'moth'
sōna	[sōna]	'immediately'	mæsse	[mæssɛ]	'mass'
fīf	[fīf]	'five'	fīfel	[fīvɛl]	'sea-monster'
bæð	[bæθ]	'bath'	baðu	[baðu]	'baths'
hūs	[hūs]	'house'	māse	[māzɛ]	'titmouse'
fīfta	[fīfta]	'fifth'	ofnas	[ɔvnas]	'ovens'
hyhþu	[hȳçθu]	'height'	māðmas	[māðmas]	'treasures'
hæpse	[hæpsɛ]	'hasp'	fæsl	[fæzl]	'progeny'

a. Which of the six sounds occur only between two voiced sounds? [z] [ð] [v]

b. Which sounds occur in other positions, such as initially, finally, doubled, or next to a voiceless sound? [f] [θ] [s]

2. [g] / [ʒ]

gōd	[gōd]	'good'	sungen	[suŋgɛn]	'sung'
gēs	[gēs]	'geese'	lagu	[laʒu]	'law'
grund	[grund]	'ground'	āgan	[āʒan]	'to own'
glæd	[glæd]	'glad'	swelgan	[swɛlʒan]	'to swallow'
gnorn	[gnɔrn]	'sad'	fuglas	[fuʒlas]	'fowls'
frogga	[frɔgga]	'frog'	sorg	[sɔrʒ]	'sorrow'
song	[sɔŋg]	'song'	bōg	[bōʒ]	'bough'

a. Which of the two sounds occurs initially, doubled, or after n [ŋ]? [g]

b. Which sound occurs in other positions, such as between vowels, between a consonant other than [ŋ] and a vowel, or finally except after [ŋ]? [ʒ]

3. [h] / [x] / [ç]

hilt	[hɪlt]	'hilt'	riht	[rɪçt]	'right'
hāl	[hāl]	'whole'	nīhsta	[nīçsta]	'next'
hræfn	[hrævn]	'raven'	brōhte	[brōxtɛ]	'brought'
hnutu	[hnutu]	'nut'	neah	[næəx]	'near'
hlāf	[hlāf]	'loaf'	wealh	[wæəlx]	'foreigner'
hwēol	[hwēəl]	'wheel'	rūh	[rūx]	'rough'
eoh	[ɛəx]	'horse'	fāh	[fāx]	'foe'

a. Which of the three sounds occurs initially? [h]

b. Which sound occurs after a front vowel?___[ç]_____

c. Which sound occurs in other positions, such as after a back vowel, diphthong, or consonant?___[x]_____

4. [n] / [ŋ]

singan	[sɪŋɡɑn]	'to sing'	mannes	[mɑnnɛs]	'man's'
drincan	[drɪŋkɑn]	'to drink'	mōna	[mōnɑ]	'moon'
gang	[ɡɑŋɡ]	'journey'	font	[fɔnt]	'font'
þanc	[θɑŋk]	'thought'	ende	[ɛndɛ]	'end'
nōn	[nōn]	'noon'	cylna	[kylnɑ]	'kilns'

a. Which of the two sounds occurs before [g] or [k]?___[ŋ]_____

b. Which sound occurs in other positions, such as initially, finally, or internally before a vowel or consonant other than a velar stop?___[n]_____

5. Supply the missing symbols in these phonetic transcriptions. For some words you must add two symbols.

fæt	[**f**æt]	'vat'	weorð	[wɛr**ð θ**]	'worth'
hæfde	[hæ**v**dɛ]	'had'	weorðan	[wɛr**ð**ɑn]	'to become'
hafoc	[hɑ**v**ɔk]	'hawk'	þorn	[**θ**ɔrn]	'thorn'
of	[ɔ**v**]	'of'	oþþe	[ɔ**ðð**ɛ]	'or'
cræft	[kræ**f**t]	'skill'	wriþan	[wrī**ð**ɑn]	'to twist'
pyffan	[py**f**ɑn]	'to puff'	rīsan	[rī**z**ɑn]	'rise'
ēaster	[ǣ ə**s**tɛr]	'Easter'	hors	[**h**ɔrs]	'horse'
missan	[mɪ**s**ɑn]	'to miss'	cniht	[knɪ**ç**t]	'lad'
miltsian	[mɪlt**s**ɪɑn]	'to pity'	feoh	[fɛə**x**]	'cattle'
sylf	[**s**ylf]	'self'	hnipian	[**h**nɪpɪɑn]	'to droop'
rās	[rā**z**]	'arose'	beorht	[bɛr**x**t]	'bright'
bōsm	[bō**zə**m]	'bosom'	finger	[fɪ**ŋɡ**ɛr]	'finger'
plōg	[plō**ʒ**]	'plow'	findan	[fɪ**n**dɑn]	'to find'
gold	[**ɡ**ɔld]	'gold'	sanc	[sɑ**ŋk**]	'sank'
boga	[bɔ**ʒ**ɑ]	'bow'	sunu	[su**n**ʊ]	'son'
glēo	[**ɡ**lēə]	'mirth'	sunne	[su**n**ɛ]	'sun'
burg	[bur**ʒ**]	'city'	lang	[lɑ**ŋɡ**]	'long'
belgan	[bɛl**ʒ**ɑn]	'to be angry'	scruncen	[šru**ŋk**ɛn]	'shrunken'

5.7   OLD ENGLISH SPELLING AND PRONUNCIATION

A perfectly alphabetical writing system has a distinct symbol for each of its consonant and vowel phonemes; each distinctive sound has only one symbol and each symbol represents only one such sound. Old English comes much closer to that ideal than does Modern English, but even Old English had some irrationalities in its spelling. The most troublesome of these are the letters *c* and *g*. Review in Pyles's *Origins and Development*, pages 124–25, the discussion of the sounds represented by these two spellings; then examine the following words. Each group of words illustrates a typical position of the letters *c* and *g*; if the prehistoric form of the word is relevant, it is given as a reconstruction with the usual asterisk. For each group of words, decide whether *c* represents [k] or [č] and whether *g* represents [g] or [ʒ] or [j]. Write the appropriate phonetic symbol within the brackets. The dots have been omitted from *c* and *g* in this exercise.

c = [k]
clif 'cliff'
cniht 'boy'
crisp 'curly'
cweorn 'mill'

g = [g]
glæs 'glass'
gnorn 'sad'
grimm 'fierce'

c = [k]
catt 'cat'
cōl 'cool'
cū 'cow'

g = [g]
gāt 'goat'
gold 'gold'
guma 'man'

c = [č]
ceaf 'chaff'
ceorl 'churl'
cīdan 'to chide'
cyrran 'to turn'

g = [y]
geard 'yard'
gē 'ye'
geolu 'yellow'
gimm 'gem'
gylp 'boast'

c = [k]
cēlan 'to cool' < *kōljan
cȳ 'kine' < *kūiz

g = [g]
gǣt 'goats' < *gātiz
gylden 'golden' < *guldīn

c = [k]
āc 'oak'
brōc 'breech'
munuc 'monk'

g = [ȝ]
plōg 'plow'
burg 'city'

c = [č]
pic 'pitch'
līc 'body'
brēc 'breeches'

g = [ȝ]
īg 'island'
bodig 'body'
þegnas 'thanes'
sægde 'said'

c = [k]
nacod 'naked'
sūcan 'to suck'
bacan 'to bake'

g = [ȝ]
sagu 'saying'
swōgan 'to sound'
āgan 'to own'

c = [č]
micel 'much'
bēce 'beech'
ræced 'building'

g = [ȝ]
sige 'victory'
drȳge 'dry'
segel 'sail'
nægel 'nail'

a. Which sounds occur initially before a consonant, a back vowel, or a front vowel resulting from mutation? _____ g, k _____

b. Which sounds occur after or between back vowels? _k, ʒ_

c. Which sounds occur initially before an original front vowel and after or between front vowels? _č, y_

5.8 OLD ENGLISH TRANSCRIPTION

Write these Old English words in phonetic transcription:

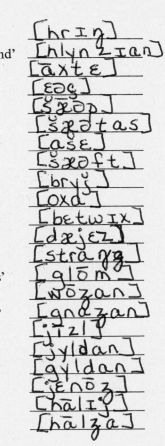

fyxen	'vixen'	[fyxɛn]
wīf	'woman'	[wīf]
wīfes	'woman's'	[wīvɛz]
þēofas	'thieves'	[θēovɑz]
bæð	'bath'	[bæð]
baðian	'to bathe'	[baðian]
sǣs	'seas'	[sǣz]
nosu	'nose'	[nɔsʊ]
lȳs	'lice'	[lȳs]
lūsa	'of lice'	[lūsa]
hām	'home'	[hām]
bazere	'baptist'	[bazɛrɛ]
weorc	'work'	[wɛɔrk]
čēosan	'to choose'	[čēɔzɑn]
čiriče	'church'	[čirīčɛ]
styčče	'piece'	[styčɛ]
cuman	'to come'	[kʊman]
cyčene	'kitchen'	[kyčɛnɛ]
cēpan	'to keep'	[kēpan]
friġnan	'to ask'	[friʲnan]
dæġ	'day'	[dæʒ]
dagas	'days'	[daʒas]

hring	'ring'	[hrɪŋ]
hlynsian	'to resound'	[hlynzian]
āhte	'owned'	[āxtɛ]
eoh	'horse'	[ɛɔç]
scēap	'sheep'	[šǣɔp]
sceattas	'coins'	[šæɑtas]
asce	'ash'	[asɛ]
sceaft	'shaft'	[šæɑft]
brycg	'bridge'	[bryǰ]
oxa	'ox'	[oxa]
betwix	'between'	[betwɪx]
dæġes	'day's'	[dæʒɛz]
strang	'strong'	[straŋg]
glōm	'darkness'	[glōm]
wōgan	'to woo'	[wōʒan]
gnagan	'to gnaw'	[gnɑʒan]
ġīsl	'hostage'	[ʲīzl]
ġyldan	'to yield'	[ʲyldan]
gyldan	'to gild'	[gyldan]
ġenōg	'enough'	[ʲenōʒ]
hāliġ	'holy'	[hālɪʲ]
hālga	'saint'	[hālʒa]

5.9 MUTATION OR UMLAUT

Mutation or umlaut is a change in the quality of a vowel resulting from its assimilation to a neighboring sound. The change took place during the prehistoric period of Old English.

1. The following words and their reconstructed sources will illustrate some mutations. Each historical form shows the result of umlaut in its first syllable.

lengest < *langista 'longest'
gēs < *gōsiz 'geese'
bēċ < *bōki 'book (dat.)'
strengþu < *strangiþu 'strength'
fēdan < *fōdjan 'to feed' (cf. Goth. fōdjan)

trymman < *trumjan 'to fortify'
yfel < *ubil 'evil' (cf. Goth. ubil)
fǣrþ < *fariþ 'goes' (cf. Goth. fariþ)
synn < *sunjō 'sin'
hell < *hælju 'hell' (older haljō, cf. Goth. halja)

What sounds caused mutation? _i, j_

Why is the cause of mutation not clear in recorded Old English? _____
_____

?

2. In the following examples, the first word in each pair has a mutated vowel, and the second word is a related form with unmutated vowel.

ȳtemest 'outmost' / ūte 'outside'   secgan 'to say' / sæġde 'said'
dehter 'daughter (dat.)' / dohtor 'daughter (nom.)'   frȳnd 'friends' / frēond 'friend'
gǣt 'goats' / gāt 'goat'   wyrþe 'worthy' / weorþ 'worth'
bæcþ 'bakes' / bacan 'to bake'   nȳr 'nearer' / nēah 'near'
hilpþ 'helps' / helpan 'to help'   yldra 'elder' / eald 'old'

All the vowels except the high front, *i, ī, y, ȳ* and the front long *ē, ǣ* are subject to mutation. Short *a* has two mutations, depending on whether or not it is followed by a nasal consonant. Indicate the mutation of each of the following vowels.

FRONT VOWELS	DIPHTHONGS	BACK VOWELS
		ŭ _____
ĕ _____	ĕo _____	ð _____
		ă + n _____
ǽ _____	ĕa _____	ă _____

After you have compared these changes with the articulation chart of Old English vowels, describe the general direction in which vowels move when they are mutated.
from low back vowels to high front vowels
_____

?

3. In the following pairs, the first word has a mutated vowel omitted from its spelling, and the second word is a related form without mutation. Supply the missing vowel.

d_____man 'to judge' / dōm 'judgment'   m_____lt 'melts' / meltan 'to melt'
t_____nan 'to close' / tūn 'enclosure'   w_____tt 'goes' / wadan 'to go'
f_____nd 'enemies' / fēond 'enemy'   þ_____ċċan 'to cover' / þæċ 'thatch'
f_____llan 'to fill' / full 'full'   m_____rġen 'morning' / morgen 'morning'
h_____lan 'to heal' / hāl 'whole'   ċ_____pan 'to buy' / ċēap 'price'
sc_____rtest 'shortest' / sceort 'short'   h_____rdan 'to harden' / heard 'hard'
m_____tan 'to meet' / mōt 'meeting'   m_____s 'mice' / mūs 'mouse'
str_____ngest 'strongest' / strang 'strong' m_____st 'most' / mā 'more'

5.10 SOUND CHANGES FROM INDO-EUROPEAN TO OLD ENGLISH

The following charts summarize the Indo-European sources of the Old English sound system. Only the main line of development has been given; there are many conditioned changes not represented here. The charts show which Indo-European sounds fell together in Proto-Germanic (for example, IE *ə, a,* and *o* as PG *a*) and which Proto-Germanic sounds split into more than one Old English sound (as, for example, PG *e* did).

1. VOWELS: Complete the vowel chart by supplying the phonetic symbols for the Old English developments.

INDO-EUROPEAN SOURCE		PROTO-GERMANIC	OLD ENGLISH DEVELOPMENT	
key word	vowel	vowel	phonetic symbol	key word
*pisk-	i	i		fisc 'fish'
*ed-	e	e		etan 'to eat'
*ert-				eorðe 'earth'
*pəter	ə			fæder 'father'
*man-	a	a		mann 'man'
*oktō	o			eahta 'eight'
*hunto-		u		hund 'dog'
*kubi-	u			hyp 'hip'
*ghuto-		o		god 'god'
*swīno-	ī	ī		swīn 'swine'
*steigh-	ei			stīgan 'to rise'
*dhēti-	ē	æ		dǣd 'deed'
*māter-	ā	ō		mōdor 'mother'
*pōd-	ō			fōt 'foot'
*mūs	ū	ū		mūs 'mouse'
*pūri				fȳr 'fire'
*aidh-	ai	ai		ād 'pyre'
*oino-	oi			ān 'one'
*keus-	eu	eu		čēosan 'to choose'
*aug-	au	au		ēacan 'to eke'
*roudh-	ou			rēad 'red'
uncertain		ē		hēr 'here'

2. CONSONANTS: Complete the consonant chart by supplying the phonetic symbols for the Proto-Germanic and Old English developments.

INDO-EUROPEAN SOURCE		PROTO-GERMANIC	OLD ENGLISH DEVELOPMENT	
key word	*consonant*	*consonant*	*consonant*	*key word*
*bend-	b			penn 'pen'
*del-	d			tellan 'to tell'
*gombho-	g			camb 'comb'
*geus-				ċēosan 'to choose'
*bhugo-	bh			buc 'buck'
*ghebh-				ġyfan 'to give'
*dherg-	dh			deorc 'dark'
*ghaido-	gh			gāt 'goat'
*dhragh-				dragan 'to draw'
*ghel				ġellan 'to yell'
*wlpo-	p			wulf 'wolf'
				wulfas 'wolves'
*uperi [4]				ofer 'over'
*bhəto-	t			bæð 'bath'
				baðian 'to bathe'
*dhouto- [4]				dēad 'dead'
*kortu-	k			heard 'hard'
*marko-				mearh 'horse'
*dukā- [4]				togian 'to tow'
*akyā-				ecg 'edge'
*wes-	s			wes 'be!'
				wesan 'to be'
*dheuso- [4]				dēor 'animal'
*skeud-	sk			scēotan 'to shoot'
*med-	m			metan 'to mete'

[4] Step 3 of the Germanic Consonant Shift (Verner's Law) applies.

INDO-EUROPEAN SOURCE		PROTO-GERMANIC	OLD ENGLISH DEVELOPMENT	
key word	consonant	consonant	consonant	key word
*ne-	n			ne 'not'
*loist-	l			lāst 'footprint'
*reidh-	r			rīdan 'to ride'
*wir-	w			wer 'man'
*yuga	y			ġeoc 'yoke'

5.11 GRAMMATICAL GENDER

Examine the following phrases:

MASCULINE	FEMININE	NEUTER
se wīfmann 'the woman'	sēo hlǣfdiġe 'the lady'	þæt wīf 'the woman'
se mete 'the food'	sēo reord 'the meal'	þæt ealu 'the ale'
se mōna 'the moon'	sēo sunne 'the sun'	þæt tungol 'the star'
se grund 'the ground'	sēo eorðe 'the earth'	þæt land 'the land'
se æppel 'the apple'	sēo bēan 'the bean'	þæt ǣġ 'the egg'
se earm 'the arm'	sēo eaxl 'the shoulder'	þæt lim 'the limb'
þes wīfmann 'this woman'	þēos hlǣfdiġe 'this lady'	þis wīf 'this woman'
þes grund	þēos eorðe	þis land
sum æppel 'a certain apple'	sumu bēan 'a certain bean'	sum ǣġ 'a certain egg'
sum earm	sumu eaxl	sum lim
(Ic seah) sumne wīfmann	(Ic seah) sume hlǣfdiġan	(Ic seah) sum wīf
'(I saw) a certain woman'	'(I saw) a certain lady'	'(I saw) a certain woman'
(Ic seah) sumne æppel	(Ic seah) sume bēane	(Ic seah) sum ǣġ
se mōna . . . hē is gōd	sēo sunne . . . hēo is gōd	þæt tungol . . . hit is gōd
'the moon . . . it is good'	'the sun . . . it is good'	'the star . . . it is good'
se mete . . . hē is gōd	sēo reord . . . hēo is gōd	þæt ealu . . . hit is gōd
se wīfmann . . . hēo is gōd	sēo hlǣfdiġe . . . hēo is gōd	þæt wīf . . . hēo is gōd

1. Which of the following is the best indicator of the grammatical gender of an Old English noun? Which is the poorest indicator?

    meaning (sexual gender)
    the ending of the noun
    concord of adjective and noun
    concord of pronoun and noun

2. What is the gender of each of the italicized nouns?

séo *ċeaster* 'the city' _____

þæt *scip* 'the ship' _____

Ic seah sum *fæt* 'I saw a certain vessel.' _____

se *tūn* 'the village' _____

sumu *lūs* 'a certain louse' _____

þes *blōstm* 'this blossom' _____

þis *lēaf* 'this leaf' _____

þēos *costung* 'this temptation' _____

Ic seah sume *bollan* 'I saw a certain bowl.' _____

Ic seah sumne *disc* 'I saw a certain dish.' _____

3. Translate these phrases into Old English:

the blossom _____

this moon _____

this ship _____

this sun _____

a certain meal _____

I saw a certain star. _____

I saw a certain arm. _____

4. What is the basis for determining the "gender" of a noun in Modern English, and how many "genders" do we have? How would you explain the gender relationship between noun and pronoun in these sentences?

"That's a lovely baby. What's its name?"

"You have a visitor in the lounge." "Who is it?"

"Somebody telephoned you." "What did they want?"

"I saw his new boat. She's a beauty."

"My car's nearly out of gas—fill 'er up."

5.12 *INFLECTION OF NOUNS*

Write the declension of these Old English nouns:

	a-DECLENSION, MASCULINE	*a*-DECLENSION, NEUTER	*ō*-DECLENSION, FEMININE
	grund 'ground' (like *hund*)	*ġēar* 'year' (like *dēor*)	*talu* 'tale' (like *lufu*)
sing. nom.	_____	_____	_____
acc.	_____	_____	_____
gen.	_____	_____	_____
dat.	_____	_____	_____
plur. nom.	_____	_____	_____
acc.	_____	_____	_____
gen.	_____	_____	_____
dat.	_____	_____	_____

	n-DECLENSION, MASCULINE	*n*-DECLENSION, FEMININE	*u*-DECLENSION, MASCULINE
	nama 'name' (like *oxa*)	*sunne* 'sun' (like *belle*)	*wudu* 'wood' (like *sunu*)
sing. nom.	_____	_____	_____
acc.	_____	_____	_____
gen.	_____	_____	_____
dat.	_____	_____	_____
plur. nom.	_____	_____	_____
acc.	_____	_____	_____
gen.	_____	_____	_____
dat.	_____	_____	_____

	ATHEMATIC DECLENSION, MASCULINE	ATHEMATIC DECLENSION, FEMININE	*r*-DECLENSION, NEUTER
	fēond 'fiend, foe' (like *fōt*, but with mutation of *ēo* to *ȳ*)	*bōc* 'book' (like *brōc*)	*lamb* 'lamb' (sing. like *dēor*; pl. has *-r-* in all forms)
sing. nom.	_____	_____	_____
acc.	_____	_____	_____
gen.	_____	_____	_____
dat.	_____	_____	_____
plur. nom.	_____	_____	_____
acc.	_____	_____	_____
gen.	_____	_____	_____
dat.	_____	_____	_____

5.13 *INFLECTION OF DEMONSTRATIVES AND ADJECTIVES*

Write the declension of these phrases:

	se tila hlāford 'the good lord' (like *se dola cyning*)	*þæt tile sweord* 'the good sword' (like *þæt dole bearn*)	*sēo tile reord* 'the good meal' (like *sēo dole ides*)
sing. nom.	_____	_____	_____
acc.	_____	_____	_____
gen.	_____	_____	_____
dat.	_____	_____	_____
ins.	_____	_____	_____
plur. nom.	_____	_____	_____
acc.	_____	_____	_____
gen.	_____	_____	_____
dat.	_____	_____	_____

	til hlāford	*til sweord*	*tilu reord*
sing. nom.	_____	_____	_____
acc.	_____	_____	_____
gen.	_____	_____	_____
dat.	_____	_____	_____
ins.	_____	_____	_____
plur. nom.	_____	_____	_____
acc.	_____	_____	_____
gen.	_____	_____	_____
dat.	_____	_____	_____

5.14 *MODERN SURVIVALS OF OLD ENGLISH INFLECTION*

Some Old English inflectional endings have survived into Modern English and have actually increased in importance, that is, in the number of words to which they are added. Other inflections still survive, but only in petrified forms; they survive as dead museum pieces that illustrate earlier living endings. Each italicized word in the phrases below contains a modern survival of an Old English inflection. Match the modern forms with the Old English inflections listed on the right.

NOUNS

_____	The *boats* were floating by the dock.	A. nominative-accusative plural ending *-as*
_____	He found a *raven's* nest.	B. nominative-accusative plural ending *-an*
_____	They took a four-*day* trip.	C. nominative-accusative plural ending *-ru*
_____	The *oxen* follow the plow.	D. nominative-accusative plural with mutation of the stem vowel
_____	The *dormice* are hunting for food.	E. nominative-accusative plural identical in form with nominative-accusative singular
_____	The *sheep* are in the pasture.	
_____	These *kind* are oak trees.	
_____	It *seldom* rains.	F. genitive singular ending *-es*
_____	The feast of the Annunciation is called *Lady* Day.	G. genitive singular without *-s*
		H. genitive plural ending *-a*
_____	Honeybun is five *foot* tall.	I. dative singular ending *-e*
_____	There is hardly a man *alive*.	J. dative plural ending *-um*

(The next four italicized words have double inflection; each preserves two Old English inflectional changes. Identify both.)

_____	_____	a herd of beeves, fair oxen, and fair *kine*
_____	_____	They sewed fig leaves together, and made themselves *breeches*.
_____	_____	Jacob begat Judah and his *brethren*.
_____	_____	Suffer the little *children* to come unto me.

_____ a *colder* day

_____ the *narrowest* margin

_____ an *elder* son

_____ the *eldest* daughter

_____ the *foremost* advocate

_____ *Mondays* they come home early.

_____ And feed *deep*, deep upon her peerless eyes. (Keats)

_____ He drives *slower* in town.

_____ He slept *days*.

_____ She has a lot to do *besides*.

_____ They called *once*.

_____ Why livest thou, dead dog, a *lenger* day? (Spenser)

A. adverb formed with the suffix *-e*

B. genitive singular used adverbially

C. adverb comparative ending *-or*

D. adjective comparative ending *-ra*

E. adjective superlative ending *-est* (from earlier *-ist*) with mutation

F. adjective comparative ending *-ra* (from earlier *-ira*) with mutation

G. adjective superlative ending *-ost*

H. adjective double superlative ending

5.15 *THE SYNTAX OF NOUNS*

The sentences below illustrate some of the common uses of Old English cases. The case of each noun or noun phrase is identified by an abbreviation after it: (*n*) nominative, (*a*) accusative, (*g*) genitive, (*d*) dative, (*i*) instrumental.

Give the number of a sentence that contains an example of each of the following case uses:

NOMINATIVE: as subject _____, subject complement _____, direct address _____

ACCUSATIVE: as object of a verb _____, adverbial of duration _____, object of a preposition _____

GENITIVE: as possessive _____, expression of measure _____, adverbial of time _____, object of a verb _____, object of a preposition _____

DATIVE: as object of a verb _____, object of a preposition _____, expression of means or cause _____

INSTRUMENTAL: as expression of time _____, of accompaniment _____, of comparison _____

1. Gif þēowman[n] wyrċe on Sunnandæġ[a] be his hlāfordes[g] hǣse[d],   sȳ   hē[n]   frēo,

   If   a serf   work on Sunday   by his lord's   command shall be he   free

   and se hlāford[n] ġeselle xxx scillinga[g] tō wīte[d].

   and the lord   pay   30 shillings   as fine

2. Cædmon[n], sing mē[d] hwæthwugu.

   Cadmon,   sing me   something

3. He is ordfrume[n] and ende[n].

   He is beginning   and end

4. He[n] wræc   þone aldorman Cumbran[a].

   He   avenged the   earl   Cumbra

5. Ond þæs[g]   ymb ānne mōnaþ[a] ġefeaht Ælfred cyning[n] wiþ   alne þone
And afterwards about a   month   fought Alfred the king against all   the

here[a].
[Viking] army

6. Cynewulf[n] oft miċlum   ġefeohtum[d] feaht wið   Bretwālum[d].
Cynewulf   often with great battles   fought against the Britons

7. Cynewulf[n] benam Siġebryht[a] his   rīċes[g].
Cynewulf   deprived Sigebryht of his kingdom

8. Iōseph[n] ðā   ārās nihtes[g].
Joseph   then arose at night

9. Ond þȳ ilcan   ġēare[i] mon[n] ofslōg Æþelbald[a].
And in that same year   someone slew   Athelbald

10. Beornræd[n] lȳtle   hwīle[a] hēold.
Beornred   for a little while   ruled

11. And þā ġeāscode hē[n] þone cyning[a]   lȳtle   werode[i] on wīfcȳþþe[d]
And then learned he   the king [to be] with a small troop   in woman's company

on Meran tūne[d].
at Merton

12. And wunodon   þǣr ealne þone winter[a].
And [they] stayed there all   the   winter

13. Hē[n] ne mæġ ǣtes[g] oððe wǣtes[g] brūcan.
He cannot food or   drink   enjoy

14. Þā ġewendon hī[n] wið   þæs ċildes[g].
Then traveled   they toward the child

15. Ne ġedafenað þān   gāstlicum[d] þæt hī[n] ðam flǣsclicum[d] ġeefenlǣċen.
Nor does it befit the   spiritual   that they the fleshly   emulate

16. Se eorl[n] wæs þē[i] blīþra.
The earl   was the happier

17. Wīġend[n] cruncon, wundum[d] wēriġe.
Warriors fell   by wounds wearied

5.16 PRONOUNS

For each of the Modern English pronouns, give the Old English word from which it developed and tell the case of the Old English source pronoun.

MOD-E PRONOUN	OE SOURCE	CASE OF OE PRONOUN	MOD-E PRONOUN	OE SOURCE	CASE OF OE PRONOUN
I	ic	nominative	his		
me			she		
mine			her		
we			it		
us			(you tell) 'em		
our			who		
thou			whom		
thee			whose		
thine			what		
ye			why (adv.)		
you			which		
your			that		
he			this		
him			those		

5.17 *WEAK AND STRONG VERBS*

1. The following verbs are cited in both their infinitive and their preterit singular forms. Mark weak verbs *W* and strong verbs *S*.

   _____ brengan–brōhte 'to bring'   _____ hyngran–hyngrede 'to hunger'
   _____ ġifan–ġeaf 'to give'   _____ lōcian–lōcode 'to look'
   _____ habban–hæfde 'to have'   _____ scīnan–scān 'to shine'
   _____ hȳran–hȳrde 'to hear'   _____ steppan–stōp 'to step'
   _____ hōn–hēng 'to hang'   _____ tǽċan–tāhte 'to teach'

2. Some Modern English verbs come in pairs: *fall* and *fell*, *lie* and *lay*, *sit* and *set*. What difference in meaning is there between the members of each pair? _____

   _____

   _____

   What is the cause of their difference in form? _____

   _____

Which verb in each pair is weak, and which strong? _____
_____

3. Explain why there is a difference between the stem vowel of the infinitive and that of the preterit in these verbs: *sēċan–sōhte* 'seek–sought,' *bycgan–bohte* 'buy–bought,' *þencan–þōhte* 'think–thought.' _____
_____
_____

4. Explain why there is a difference between the stem vowel of the infinitive and that of the preterit in these verbs: *rīdan–rād* 'ride–rode,' *teran–tær* 'tear–tore,' *frēosan–frēas* 'freeze–froze.'_____
_____
_____
_____
_____

5.18 *THE SEVEN CLASSES OF STRONG VERBS*

Strong verbs are characterized by a lack of the dental suffix in their preterit and by an internal vowel change (gradation or ablaut) between their present and preterit forms.

1. Strong verbs are conventionally divided into seven classes on the basis of what vowels occur in each of their four principal parts. List here the typical vowel series found in each of the classes.

CLASS	INFINITIVE	PRETERIT SINGULAR	PRETERIT PLURAL	PAST PARTICIPLE
I	_____	_____	_____	_____
II	_____ or _____	_____	_____	_____
III	_____	_____	_____	_____
	_____ or _____	_____	_____	_____
IV	_____	_____	_____	_____
V	_____	_____	_____	_____
	_____	_____	_____	_____
VI	_____	_____	_____	_____
VII	_____	_____	_____	_____
	_____	_____	_____	_____

2. Identify by number the class of each of these strong verbs. All four principal parts are given.

_6_	bacan	bōc	bōcon	bacen	'to bake'
_7_	bēatan	bēot	bēoton	bēaten	'to beat'
_4_	beran	bær	bæron	boren	'to bear'
_1_	bītan	bāt	biton	biten	'to bite'
_7_	blandan	blēnd	blēndon	blanden	'to blend'
_2_	brūcan	brēac	brucon	brocen	'to enjoy'
_3_	ċeorfan	ċearf	curfon	corfen	'to carve'
_2_	clēofan	clēaf	clufon	clofen	'to cleave'
_5_	cweðan	cwæð	cwædon	cweden	'to say, quoth'
_3_	delfan	dealf	dulfon	dolfen	'to delve'
_3_	drincan	dranc	druncon	druncen	'to drink'
_5_	forġyfan	forġeaf	forġēafon	forġyfen	'to forgive'

3. It is usually possible to recognize the class to which a strong verb belongs from its infinitive alone. Unless there are special irregularities, it is then possible to predict the other principal parts, for all classes except class VII. All of the following verbs belong to classes I through VI and are regular. Write their remaining principal parts.

INFINITIVE	PRETERIT SINGULAR	PRETERIT PLURAL	PAST PARTICIPLE
beġytan 'to get'	beġeat	beġēaton	beġyten
bīdan 'to bide'	_____	_____	_____
bindan 'to bind'	_____	_____	_____
būgan 'to bow'	_____	_____	_____
cnedan 'to knead'	_____	_____	_____
flēotan 'to float'	_____	_____	_____
meltan 'to melt'	_____	_____	_____
scafan 'to shave'	_____	_____	_____
stelan 'to steal'	_____	_____	_____
steorfan 'to die'	_____	_____	_____

5.19 INFLECTION OF VERBS

Hǣlan 'to heal' and *helpan* 'to help' are typical verbs, weak and strong respectively. Conjugate them in full. The imperative singular of both verbs is without ending; the imperative plural ends in *-að*.

PRINCIPAL PARTS	hǣlan, hǣlde, hǣled		helpan, healp, hulpon, holpen	
	PRESENT	PRETERIT	PRESENT	PRETERIT
INDICATIVE				
iċ	_____	_____	helpe	healp
þū	_____	_____	helpest	hulpe
hē	_____	_____	helpeð	healp
wē, ġē, hī	_____	_____	helpað	hulpon
SUBJUNCTIVE				
iċ, þū, hē	_____	_____	helpe	hulpe
wē, ġē, hī	_____	_____	helpen	hulpen
IMPERATIVE				
þū	_____	_____	help	
ġē	_____	_____	helpað	
PARTICIPLE				
	_____	_____		holpen

5.20 SYNTAX: WORD ORDER

Old English word order is, in general, similar to that of Modern English; however, some differences exist. For each of the following examples, describe how the word order departs from that of the present-day language.

1. His ġelēafa hine ġetrymde. _____
   His faith   him strengthened

2. Ōswold him cōm tō. _____
   Oswald him came to

3. And hē nǣfre nǣniġ leoð ġeleornade. _____
   And he never no   poetry learned

4. And hē hine sōna   tō þǣre abbudissan ġelǣdde. _____
   And he him immediately to the abbess   led

5. And þā onġeat   se cyning þæt._____
   And then discovered the king   that

6. Hē ofslōg þone aldorman þe him lengest wunode. _____
   He slew the earl   that him longest had served

7. Hē þǣr wunode oþþæt hine ān swān   ofstang. _____
   He there dwelt   until him a swineherd stabbed

8. Þā   on morgenne ġehȳrdon þæt þæs cyninges þeġnas, þæt se cyning ofslæġen wæs.
   Then in the morning heard   that the king's   thanes that the king slain   was

_____

5.21 OLD ENGLISH ILLUSTRATED

The following passages illustrate Old English. The dialect of all the selections is basically West Saxon. You may notice some spelling variations and some differences in grammatical forms between these passages and the language described in Pyles's *Origins and Development*. Such differences may be due to slight dialect variation, time lapse, or simply the predilections of different writers.

The glosses which accompany the selections are generally word-for-word renderings of the Old English. They are inadequate as translations, but will help in reading the original.

Compare the passages with the description of Old English in Pyles. Note the distinctive features of Old English spelling, inflections, syntax, and vocabulary.

THE GOOD SAMARITAN

This version of the parable of the good Samaritan (Luke 10:30–36) is from a late West Saxon translation of the Gospels.[5]

Sum   man fērde fram Hiērūsalem tō Hiēricho, and becōm on   ðā sceaðan; þā hine
A certain man went from Jerusalem to Jericho, and came upon the thieves; they him

berēafodon and tintregodon hine, and forlēton hine sāmcucene. Þā   ġebyrode hit þæt
robbed   and tormented him, and left   him half-alive. Then happened it that

sum   sāċerd fērde on þām ylcan weġe, and þā   hē þæt ġeseah, hē hine forbēah. And
a certain priest went on the same way, and when he that saw   he him passed by. And

eall swā se dīacon, þā   hē wæs wið þā stōwe and þæt ġeseah, hē hyne ēac forbēah. Ðā
also   this deacon when he was at the place and that saw   he him also passed by. Then

⁵ James W. Bright, *The Gospel of Saint Luke in Anglo-Saxon* (Oxford, 1893).

fērde sum   Samaritanisc man wið hine; þā   hē hine ġeseah, þā   wearð hē mid
went a certain Samaritan   man by him; when he him saw   then became he with

mildheortnesse ofer hine āstyred.   Þā   ġenēalǣhte hē, and wrāð his wunda and on āġēat
compassion   for him stirred up. Then drew near he, and bound his wounds and poured on

ele and wīn, and hine on hys nȳten sette, and ġelǣdde on his lǣċehūs and hine lācnode; and
oil and wine, and him on his beast set, and led   to his hospital and him medicated; and

brōhte ōðrum   dæġe twēġen peneġas, and sealde þām lǣċe,   and þus cwæð,
brought on the second day two   pennies, and gave to the doctor, and thus said,

"Beġȳm   hys, and swā hwæt swā þū māre tō   ġedēst, þonne iċ cume, iċ hit forġylde
"Take care of him and whatsoever thou more besides dost, when I come, I it will repay

þē." Hwylċ þāra þrēora þynċð þē   þæt sȳ   þæs   mæġ þe on ðā
thee." Which of the three seems to thee that may be that one's neighbor who among the

sceaðan befēoll?
thieves fell?

THE COMING OF THE ENGLISH

St. Bede describes the coming of the English to Britain in his *Historia Ecclesiastica Gentis Anglorum* (A.D. 731). Although it was written in Latin, the *History* was translated into Old English during the reign of King Alfred. The passage below is taken from that Old English version.[6]

Þā ġesomnedon hī   ġemōt   and þeahtedon and rǣddon, hwæt him   to dōnne
Then gathered   they[7] an assembly and deliberated and counseled, what for them to do

wǣre, hwǣr him   wǣre   fultum tō sēċanne tō ġewearnienne and tō wiðscūfanne
might be, where for them might be help to be sought to avoid   and to shove back

swā rēðre hergunge and swā ġelōmlīcre   þāra norðþēoda. And þā ġelīcode him
such fiercer raids and such more frequent ones of the north people. And then it pleased them

eallum mid   heora cynínge, Wyrtġeorn wæs hāten, þæt hī Seaxna   þēode
all together with their king (Vortigern he was called) that they the Saxons' people

ofer þām sǣlīcum dǣlum him on fultum ġeċȳġdon and ġelaðedon. Þæt cūð is þæt
beyond the sea   parts to them in aid should call and invite.   It known is that

þæt mid Drihtnes mihte ġestihtad wæs, þæt yfell wrǣc   cōme   ofer ðā wiþcorenan,
that by God's might arranged was, that evil punishment should come upon the rejected ones,

swā on þām ende þāra wīsena sweotolīċe ætȳwed is.
as in the end of the events clearly   shown is.

Ðā wæs ymb fēower hund wintra and nigon and fēowertiġ fram ūres Drihtnes
Then it was about four hundred years and nine and forty   after our Lord's

menniscnysse, þæt Martiānus cāsere rīċe   onfēng and VII ġēar hæfde. Sē wæs
incarnation, that Marcian Caesar the kingdom[8] received and seven years held. He was

---

6 Thomas Miller, ed., *The Old English Version of Bede's Ecclesiastical History of the English People* (EETS OS 95; London, 1890).

7 The Britons.

8 The Roman Empire.

syxta   ēac fēowertiġum fram Agusto þām cāsere. Đā Angel þēod and Seaxna   wæs
the sixth and forty   from Augustus the   Caesar. The Angle people and the Saxons' was

ġelaðod fram þām foresprecenan cyninge, and on Breotone cōm on þrim myċlum scypum;
invited by   the foresaid   king,   and into Britain   came in three great   ships;

and on ēastdǣle   þyses ēalondes eardungstōwe onfēng þurh   ðæs ylcan cyninges
and in the east part of this island   a dwelling place received through the same king's

bebod, þe hī   hider ġelaðode, þæt hī   sceoldan for heora ēðle   compian and
decree, who them hither invited,   that they should for their native land strive   and

feohtan. And hī   sōna   compedon wið heora ġewinnan, þe hī   oft ǣr
fight.   And they immediately fought   with their enemies, who them[9] often before

norðan   onhergedon; and Seaxan   þā siġe ġeslōgan. Þā   sendan hī hām
from the north had harassed; and the Saxons the victory won.   Then sent   they home

ǣrenddracan and hēton   secgan þysses landes wæstmbǣrnysse, and Brytta
a messenger and commanded [him] to report this   land's fruitfulness,   and the Britons'

yrġþo.   And hī þā sōna   hider sendon māran sciphere strengran wiġhena; and
cowardice. And they then immediately hither sent   a larger fleet   of stronger warriors; and

wæs unoferswiðendlīċ weorud, þā hī tōgædere ġeþēodde wǣron. And him Bryttas
it was an invincible   host,   when they together joined   were.   And them the Britons

sealdan and ġēafan eardungstōwe betwih him þæt hī   for sibbe   and hǣlo heora
granted and gave   a dwelling place among them that they for the peace and safety of their

ēðles   campodon and wunnon wið heora fēondum, and hī   him andlyfne and āre
native land might fight and struggle with their enemies, and they them sustenance and revenue

forġēafen for heora ġewinne. Cōmon hī   of þrim folcum, ðām strangestan Germanie,   þæt
allowed   for their labor.   Came   they of three peoples, the strongest of Germania, that

of Seaxum and of Angle and of Ġēatum. Of Ġēata fruman syndon Cantware, and
of Saxons and of Angles and of Jutes.   Of Jutish origin are   Kent-men, and

Wihtsǣtan;   þæt is sēo ðēod þe Wiht þæt ēalond oneardað. Of Seaxum, þæt is of
Wight-settlers; that is the people that Wight the island inhabit.   Of Saxons, that is from

ðām lande þe mon hāteð Ealdseaxan, cōman Ēastseaxan and Sūðseaxan   and
the land that one calls Old Saxons, come East Saxons and South Saxons and

Westseaxan. And of Engle cōman Ēastengle and Middelengle and Myrċe   and eall
West Saxons. And of Angles come   East Angles and Middle Angles and Mercians and all

Norðhembra   cynn; is   þæt land ðe Angulus is nemned, betwyh Ġēatum and
the Northumbrians' race; [it] is the land that Angeln is named, between Jutes   and

Seaxum; is   sǣd of þǣre tīde þe hī ðanon ġewiton oð tō dæġe, þæt hit wēste
Saxons; [it] is said from the   time that they thence departed until today,   that it deserted

wuniġe. Wǣron ðā ǣrest heora   lāttēowas and heretogan twēġen ġebrōðra Hengest and
remains. Were the first of their leaders   and war-chiefs two   brothers Hengest and

---

9 The Britons.

130

Horsa. Hī wǣron Wihtġylses suna, þæs fæder wæs Witta hāten, þæs fæder wæs Wihta
Horsa. They were Wihtgils' sons, whose father was Witta called, whose father was Wihta

hāten, and þæs Wihta fæder wæs Wōden nemned; of ðæs strȳnde moniġra mǣġða
called, and of that Wihta the father was Woden named; of that stock many tribes'

cyningcynn fruman lǣdde. Ne wæs ðā ylding tō þon þæt hī hēapmǣlum cōman māran
royal family [its] origin takes. Nor was then delay before they in droves came, more

weorod of þām ðēodum, þe wē ǣr ġemynegodon. And þæt folc, ðe hider cōm, ongan
bands of those peoples that we before mentioned. And that people that hither came, began

weaxan and myċlian tō þan swīðe, þæt hī wǣron on myċlum eġe þām sylfan
to wax and multiply so much that they were a great terror to the very

landbīgenġan ðe hī ǣr hider laðedon and ċȳġdon.
natives that them before hither had invited and called.

Æfter þissum hī þā ġeweredon tō sumre tīde wið Pehtum, þā hī ǣr
After this they then were allied for a certain time with the Picts, whom they before

þurh ġefeoht feor ādrifan. And þā wǣron Seaxan sēċende intingan and
through battle far away had driven. And then were the Saxons seeking cause and

tōwyrde heora ġedāles wið Bryttas. Cȳðdon him openlīċe and sǣdon, būtan
opportunity for their breaking with the Britons. They informed them openly and said unless

hī him māran andlyfne sealdon, þæt hī woldan him sylfe niman and herġian,
they them more sustenance gave, that they would for themselves take and plunder

þǣr hī hit findan mihton. And sōna ðā bēotunge dǣdum ġefyldon: bærndon
where they it find might. And immediately the threat with deeds fulfilled: they burned

and hergedon and slōgan fram ēastsǣ oð westsǣ; and him nǣniġ wiðstōd. Ne wæs
and harried and slew from the east sea to the west sea; and them none withstood. Nor was

ungelīċ wrǣcc þām ðe iū Chaldēas bærndon Hiērūsaleme weallas and ðā
unlike the vengeance to that when formerly the Chaldees burned Jerusalem's walls and the

cynelīċan ġetimbro mid fȳre fornāman for ðæs Godes folces synnum.
royal building with fire destroyed for God's people's sins.

ST. GREGORY AND THE ENGLISH

St. Gregory the Great began the conversion of the English when he sent St. Augustine to them, thus fulfilling a long-standing ambition. The following account, from Ælfric's homily on St. Gregory,[10] tells how he, in his younger years, first became acquainted with Englishmen and determined to convert them. Gregory was following a popular medieval custom of word-play when he made the three puns recorded here.

Ðā ġelamp hit æt sumum sǣle, swā swā ġȳt for oft dēð, þæt Englisce ċypmenn
Then happened it at a certain time as [it] still very often does that English merchants

brōhton heora ware tō Rōmānabyriġ, and Grēgōrius ēode be þǣre strǣt tō ðām Engliscum
brought their wares to Rome, and Gregory went along the street to the English

[10] As printed in James W. Bright's *Anglo-Saxon Reader* (New York, 1917), pp. 88–89.

mannum, heora ðing sćēawiġende. Þā ġeseah hē betwux ðām warum ċȳpecnihtas ġesette,
men, their things looking at. Then saw he among the wares slaves placed,

þā wǣron hwītes līċhaman and fæġeres andwlitan menn, and æðellīċe ġefeaxode.
who were of white body and of fair countenance men and nobly haired.

Grēgōrius ðā behēold þǣra cnapena wlite, and befrān of hwilċere þēod hī ġebrōhte
Gregory then noticed the boys' fairness, and asked from which nation they brought

wǣron. Þā sǣde him man þæt hī of Englalande wǣron, and þæt ðǣre ðēode
had been. Then told him someone that they from England were and that that nation's

mennisc swā wlitiġ wǣre. Eft ðā Grēgōrius befrān, hwæðer þæs landes folc crīsten
people so fair were. Again then Gregory asked whether that land's people Christian

wǣre ðe hǣðen. Him man sǣde þæt hī hǣðene wǣron. Grēgōrius ðā of innweardre
were or heathen. Him someone told that they heathen were. Gregory then from his inward

heortan langsume sićċetunge tēah, and cwæð, "Wālāwā, þæt swā fæġeres hīwes menn sindon
heart a long sigh drew and said, "Alas, that so fairly hued men should be

ðām sweartan dēofle underðēodde!" Eft hē āxode, hū ðǣre ðēode nama wǣre þe hī
to the dark devil subject!" Again he asked what the nation's name was that they

of cōmon. Him wæs ġeandwyrd, þæt hī Angle ġenemnode wǣron. Þā cwæð hē,
from came. To him it was answered that they Angles named were. Then said he,

"Rihtlīċe hī sind Angle ġehaten, forðan ðe hī engla wlite habbað, and swilcum
"Rightly they are Angles called for they angels' fairness have and for such

ġedafenað þæt hī on heofonum engla ġefēran bēon." Ġȳt ðā Grēgōrius befrān, hū
it is fitting that they in heaven angels' companions be." Still then Gregory asked how

ðǣre scīre nama wǣre þe ðā cnapan of ālǣdde wǣron. Him man sǣde, þæt ðā
the district named was that the boys from brought had been. To him one said that the

scīrmen wǣron Dēre ġehātene. Grēgōrius andwyrde, "Wel hī sind Dēre ġehātene,
district men were Deirans called. Gregory answered, "Well they are Deirans called

forðan ðe hī sind fram graman[11] ġenerode, and tō Crīstes mildheortnysse ġeċȳġede." Ġȳt
because they are from wrath delivered and to Christ's mercy called." Yet

ðā hē befrān, "Hū is ðǣre lēode cyning ġehāten?" Him wæs ġeandswarod þæt se
again he asked, "How is the people's king called?" To him it was answered that the

cyning Ælle ġehāten wǣre. Hwæt, ða Grēgōrius gamenode mid his wordum tō ðām naman,
king Alle called was. Well, then Gregory played with his words on the name

and cwæð, "Hit ġedafenað þæt Allēlūia sȳ ġesungen on ðām lande tō lofe þæs ælmihtiġan
and said, "It is fitting that Alleluia be sung in that land as praise of the almighty

scyppendes."
creator."

THE ANGLO-SAXON CHRONICLE

The *Anglo-Saxon Chronicle* was an annual record of important events. The exact date of its origin is unknown, but it was probably first compiled during the reign of King Alfred. There-

---

[11] The pun is on the name of the district, Deira, and the Latin *de ira* 'from wrath.'

after it was continued at various monasteries so that there are several different versions of the *Chronicle*. The last entry, describing the death of King Stephen and the election of a new Abbot of Peterborough, is for the year 1154. The most remarkable thing about the *Chronicle* is that it was written in English at a time when other historical writings throughout Europe were composed exclusively in Latin. The extracts printed below are all taken from the Peterborough Chronicle (Bodleian MS. Laud. 636).[12]

Brittene īġland is ehta hund   mīla lang and twā hund   brād, and hēr sind
[PROLOGUE] *Britain   island is eight hundred miles long and two hundred broad, and here are*

on þis īġlande fīf ġeþēode: Englisc and Brytwylsc   and Scyttisc and Pyhtisc and
in this island   five languages: English and British-Welsh[13] and Scottish[14] and Pictish and

Bōclēden.   Ērest wēron būgend   þises landes Brittes; þā cōman of   Armēnia and
book-Latin.[15] First were   inhabitants of this land   Britons; they came   from Armenia[16] and

ġesǣtan sūðewearde Bryttene ǣrost . . . .
settled   southern   Britain   first.

An. CCCC.XLIX.   Hēr   Martiānus and Ualentīnus onfēngon rīċe   and rīxadon VII.
A.D. *449*   *Here[17] Marcian   and Valentinian received the kingdom and ruled   7*

winter, and on heora dagum ġelaðode Wyrtġeorn Angelcin   hider, and hī   þā   cōmon
years, and in their days   invited Vortigern English people hither, and they then came

on þrim ċēolum hider to Brytene . . . .
in three ships   hither to Britain.

An. D.XCVI.   Hēr Grēgōrius pāpa   sende to Brytene Augustīnum mid wel maneġum
A.D. *596[18]   Here Gregory   the Pope sent to Britain Augustine   with very many*

munucum, þe   Godes word Engla   þēoda godspellodon.
monks,   who God's word to English people preached.

An. DCC.LXXXVII.   Hēr . . . cōmon ǣrest III. scipu Norðmanna of   Hereðalande, and
A.D. *787 [789][19]   Here   came first 3 ships of Northmen from Hörthaland,   and*

þā se ġerēfa þǣr tō rād, and hī   wolde drīfan tō þēs cininges tūne, þȳ hē nyste
then the reeve there to rode, and them wished to force to the king's   manor, for he knew not

hwæt hī   wǣron, and hine man ofslōh þā. Đæt wǣron þā ērestan scipu Deniscra manna
what they were,   and him one slew then. Those were   the first   ships of Danish men

þe Angelcynnes   land ġesōhton.
that English people's land sought.

[12] Benjamin Thorpe, ed., *The Anglo-Saxon Chronicle, According to the Several Original Authorities* (London, 1861).

[13] The Peterborough Chronicle has *Brittisc* and *Wilsc*; the scribe mistook the compound noun as two words, thus increasing the language names to six. The correct *Brytwylsc* is found in the Worcester Chronicle.

[14] That is, 'Erse.'

[15] That is, 'Latin as a learned tongue.'

[16] An error resulting from a misreading of Bede, who says *fram Armoricano* 'Armorica or Brittany.'

[17] That is, 'now, in this year.'

[18] Augustine left Rome in 596 and arrived in England in 597.

[19] The dates in the *Chronicle* are occasionally mistaken; they are corrected in brackets.

An. DCC.XCIII. Hēr wǣron rēðe forebēcna cumene ofer Norðanhymbra land, and þæt
A.D. 793 *Here were terrible foresigns come over Northumbrians' land, and the*

folc earmlīċe brēġdon; þæt wǣron ormēte līġræscas, and wǣron ġeseowene fȳrene
people wretchedly terrified; they were intense lightnings and were seen fiery

dracan on þām lyfte flēogende. Ðām tācnum sōna fyliġde myċel hunger, and lītel
dragons in the air flying. On the tokens immediately followed great hunger, and a little

æfter þām þæs ilcan ġēares on VI Id. Ianr. earmlīċe hēþenra manna hergung ādiligode
after that in the same year on January 8 wretchedly the heathen men's harrying destroyed

Godes ċyriċan in Lindisfarena ēe þurh rēaflāc and mansleht . . . .
God's church in Lindisfarne island[20] through plunder and manslaughter.

An. DCC.XCIIII. Hēr . . . þā hǣðenan on Norðhymbrum hergodon, and Ecgferðes
A.D. 794 *Here the heathens among the Northumbrians harried, and Ecgferth's*

mynster æt Donemūðe berēfodon . . . .
monastery at Donmouth [Jarrow] plundered.

An. DCCC.LXV. Hēr sæt se hæþene here on Tenet and ġenam frið wið
A.D. 865 *Here camped the heathen army in Thanet and made peace with*

Cantwarum, and Cantware heom feoh behēton wið þām friðe, and on þām feohbehāte
Kentmen, and Kentmen them money promised for the peace, and for the money-promise

se here hine on niht up bestæl, and oferhergode ealle Cent ēastewarde.
the army itself at night up stole, and overran all Kent eastward.

An. DCCC.LXXI. Hēr . . . fēng Ælfrēd Æþelwulfing . . . tō West Seaxna rīċe,
A.D. 871 *Here succeeded Alfred Ethelwulf's son to the West Saxons' kingdom,*

and þæs ymb I. mōnað ġefeaht Ælfrēd cining wið ealne þone here lītle werede
and after that 1 month fought Alfred the king against all the army with a little force

æt Wiltūne, and hine lange on dæġ ġeflȳmde, and þā Deniscan āhton
at Wilton, and it far into the day put to flight, and the Danish owned

wælstōwe ġeweald . . . .
the slaughter-place's control.[21]

An. DCCC.LXXVIII. Hēr . . . Ælfrēd cyning . . . ġefeaht wið ealne here, and hine
A.D. 878 *Here Alfred the king fought with the whole army, and it*

ġeflȳmde, and him æfter rād oð þet ġeweorc, and þǣr sæt XIIII niht, and þā
put to flight, and after it rode to the fortress, and there camped 14 nights, and then

sealde se here him ġīslas and myċċle āðas, þet hī of his rīċe woldon, and him
gave the army him hostages and great oaths, that they from his kingdom would [go], and him

ēac ġehēton þet heora cyng fulwihte onfōn wolde, and hī þæt ġelāston . . . .
also they promised that their king baptism receive would, and they that did.

[20] *Lindisfarena ēa* 'Lindisfarne,' lit. 'Lindisfare people's water.'
[21] That is, 'Alfred's small force repelled the Danish army throughout the day, but the Danes finally won the battle.'

An. DCCCC.I.   Hēr   ġefōr   Ælfrēd cyning,   VII Kl. Nouembris, and hē hēold þet
A.D. *901 [899]*   *Here passed away Alfred the king, October 26,   and he held the*

rīċe   XXVIII wintra and healf ġēar . . . .
kingdom 28   winters and a half year.

An. DCCCC.XCI.   Hēr wæs Ġypeswiċ ġehergod, and æfter þām swȳðe raðe   wæs
A.D. *991*   *Here was Ipswich   harried,   and after that very   quickly was*

Brihtnōð ealdorman   ofslæġen æt Mældune, and on þām ġēare man ġerǣdde þæt man
Byrhtnoth the ealdorman slain   at Maldon,   and in this year one decided that one

ġeald ǣrest gafol   Deniscum mannum for þām myċċlan brōgan þe hī   worhton be
yielded first tribute[22] *to Danish men   for the great   terror that they caused   along*

þām sǣriman; þæt wæs ǣrest X. þūsend   pūnda . . . .
the seacoast; it   was first 10 thousand pounds.

An. DCCCC.XCIIII.   Hēr on þisum ġēare cōm Ānlāf and Sweġen to Lundenbyriġ on
A.D. *994*   *Here in this   year came Olaf and Svein   to London town on*

Nātīuitas   Sancte Mārīe mid IIII and hundniġontiġum scipum, and hī   þā on þā burh
the Nativity of St. Mary with 4 and ninety   ships, and they then the town

festlīċe   feohtende wǣron . . . .
continuously attacking were.

Millēsimo. XVII.   Hēr on þisum ġēare fēng   Cnut cyning to eall Angelcynnes
1017   *Here in this   year succeeded Cnut the king to all the English people's*

rīċe . . . and þā   tōforan Kl. Aug. hēt   se cyng feċċan   him Æðelrēdes lāfe
kingdom and then before August 1 commanded the king to be brought him Ethelred's widow

þēs ōðres cynges him   to cwēne, Ricardes dōhtor.
(this other king's) for him as queen   (Richard's daughter).

Millēsimo. XLI.   Hēr forðfērde   Hardacnut cyng   æt Lambhyðe on VI. Idus Iun. and
1041 [1042]   *Here passed away Harthacnut the king at Lambeth   on June 8,   and*

hē wæs cyng ofer eall Englaland twā ġēar buton X. nihtum, and hē is bebyrġed on ealdan
he was king over all England   two years less 10 nights, and he is buried   in the old

mynstre on Winċeastre mid Cnute cynge   his fæder; and ēar þan þe hē bebyrġed wǣre, eall
minster at Winchester with Cnut the king his father; and before   he buried   was, all

folc   ġeċēas Ēadward to cynge on Lundene, healde   þā hwīle þe him God
the people chose Edward as king at London,   may he rule the while that him God

unne . . . .
grants.

Millēsimo. XLII.   Hēr wæs Æðward gehālgod   to cyng on Winċeastre on Æster dæġ mid
1042 [1043]   *Here was Edward   consecrated as king at Winchester on Easter day with*

myċċlum wurðscipe . . . and raðe   þæs   se cyng lēt   ġerīdan   ealle þā land þe
great   honor   and quickly after that the king caused to be seized all   the lands that

[22] That is, 'it was first decided to pay tribute.'

his mōdor āhte   him to handa,   and nam of   hire eall þæt hēo āhte   on golde and on
his mother owned into his own hands, and took from her all that she owned in gold and in

seolfre and on unāsecgendlīcum þingum forþan hēo hit hēold tō feste wið hine.
silver and in indescribable   things   because she it held   too firmly from him.

Millēsimo. LXVI.   On þissum ġeare man hālgode   þet mynster   æt Westmynstre on
   1066   In this   year they consecrated the monastery at Westminster on

Ċyldamæsse dæġ, and se cyng Ēadward forðfērde   on Twelfta mæsse æfen, and hine mann
Childermas day, and the king Edward   passed away on Epiphany   eve,   and him they

bebyrġede on Twelftan mæssedæġ innan þære nīwa hālgodre   ċirċean on Westmynstre, and
buried   on Epiphany day   within the newly consecrated church at Westminster, and

Harold eorl   fēng   to Englalandes cynerīċe swā swā se cyng hit him ġeūðe,   and ēac
Harold the earl succeeded to England's   realm   as   the king it him promised, and also

men hine þærtō ġecuron . . . and þā hwīle cōm Willelm eorl   upp æt Hestingan, on
men him thereto chose   and meanwhile came William the earl up at Hastings   on

Sancte Mīchaeles mæssedæġ, and Harold cōm norðan,   and him wið ġefeaht ēar þan þe
St.   Michael's massday,   and Harold came from the north, and with him fought   before

his here cōme eall,   and þær hē fēoll, and his twæġen ġebrōðra, Gyrð and Lēofwine, and
his army came entirely, and there he fell, and his two   brothers Gurth and Leofwine, and

Willelm þis land ġeēode and cōm to Westmynstre, and Ealdrēd arċebiscop   hine to
William this land occupied and came to Westminster, and Ealdred the Archbishop him as

cynge gehālgode . . . .
king   consecrated.

THE FORMER AGE

One of the most enduringly popular works in the history of European literature is Boethius's
Consolation of Philosophy. Cast into prison for suspected treason, the Roman nobleman
Boethius wrote his *Consolation* to explore man's relationship to the order of the universe.
The Latin original, which alternates prose passages with metrical stanzas, has been repeatedly
translated into English, for example by Alfred the Great, by Chaucer, and by Queen Elizabeth
I. The passage that follows (Book 2, Meter 5) is a short poem that looks back from the
complexities of contemporary—that is, sixth-century—life to the simplicity and goodness of
an earlier time when commerce, war, and greed had not corrupted mankind. This prose
translation is by King Alfred.[23]

Ēalā hū ġesǣliġ sēo forme eld wæs þises middanġeardes, þā   ælċum men þūhte ġenōg
Oh how happy the first   age was of this world   when to each man seemed enough

on þære eorþan wæstmum. Nǣron   þā weliġe hāmas, ne mistliċe swōtmettas, ne
on the   earth   in fruits. There were not then rich   houses nor various sweetmeats nor

[23] Based on Samuel Fox, ed., *King Alfred's Anglo-Saxon Version of Boethius' De Consolatione Philosophiae* (London, 1895).

drincas; ne dīorwyrþra hrægla hī ne ġirndan, forþam hī þā ġit næran,
drinks and expensive clothing they did not yearn for because those things then yet were not

ne hīo nānwuht ne ġesāwon, ne ne ġehērdon. Ne ġēmdon hīe nānes fyrenlustes, būton
and they none such saw nor heard of. Nor cared they for any luxury but

swīþe ġemetlīċe þā ġecynd beēodan; ealne weġ hī ǣton ǣne on dæġ, and þæt wæs tō
very moderately nature followed; always they ate once a day and that was at

ǣfennes. Trēowa wæstmas hī ǣton and wyrta; nalles scīr wīn hī ne druncan; ne
evening. Trees' fruits they ate and vegetables; not at all clear wine they drank; nor

nānne wætan hī ne cūþon wið huniġe mengan; ne seolocenra hrægla mid mistliċum
any liquor they did not know with honey to mix; nor silken clothing of various

blēowum hī ne ġimdon. Ealne weġ hī slēpon ūte on trīowa sceadum; hlūterra wella
colors they did not care for. Always they slept out in trees' shade; pure wells'

wæter hī druncon; ne ġeseah nān ċēpa ēaland, ne weroþ; ne ġehērde nān mon þā
water they drank; nor saw any merchant an island or shore; nor heard any man then

ġet nānne sciphere, ne furþon ymbe nān ġefeoht sprecan; ne sēo eorþe þā ġet
yet of any ship-army nor indeed about any fight to speak; nor [was] the earth then yet

besmiten mid ofsleġenes monnes blōde, ne mon furðum ġewundod; ne monn ne ġeseah ðā
polluted with slain man's blood nor one even wounded; and no one saw then

ġet yfel willende men, nænne weorþscipe næfdon, ne hī nān mon ne lufude. Ēalā þæt ūre
yet ill-willed men no honor [such] had and them no man loved. Alas that our

tīda nū ne mihtan weorðan swilċe. Ac nū manna ġītsung is swā byrnende, swā þæt fȳr on
times now cannot be thus. But now men's greed is as burning as the fire in

þǣre helle, sēo is on þām munte ðe Ætne hātte, on þām īeġlande þe Sīċīlia hātte,
that hell which is in the mountain that Etna is called on the island that Sicily is called

se munt bið simle swefle birnende, and ealla þā nēah stōwa þǣr ymbūtan
which mountain is ever with sulphur burning and all the near places there about

forbærnð. Ēalā hwæt se forma ġītsere wære, þe ǣrest þā eorþan ongan delfan æfter golde,
burns up. Oh what the first miser was who first the earth began to dig after gold

and æfter ġimmum, and þā frēcnan dēorwurþnessa funde ðe ǣr behȳd wæs and behelod
and after gems and the perilous riches found that before hidden was and covered

mid ðǣre eorþan?
with the earth?

CÆDMON'S HYMN

The following poem, "Cædmon's Hymn," is the oldest known example of Old English religious poetry. Although Cædmon was an early northern poet, the hymn is given here in a West Saxon version, in keeping with the most common form of Old English. Since the position of stress is especially important in Old English poetry, accent marks have been added. The story of Cædmon and his poem can be found in Bede's *Ecclesiastical History of the English People*, 4, xxiv.

Nú sculon hérigean   héofonrìces Wéard,
Now shall [we][24] *praise*   *heaven-kingdom's Guardian,*

Métodes méahte   and his mŏdġeþánc,
[the] Creator's might   *and his heart-thought,*

wéorc Wúldorfæ̆der: swā hē wúndra ġehwæ̆s,
[the] works [of the] Glory-father: *how he [of] wonders [of] each*

éċe Drýhten,   ŏr onstéalde.
[the] eternal Lord,   *[the] beginning established.*[25]

Hē æ̆rest sceŏp   éorðan béarnum
He first shaped   *[for] earth's children*

héofon tō hrŏfe,   hă̆liġ Scýppend;
heaven as [a] roof,   *[the] holy Creator;*

þā míddanġéard,   mónncỳnnes Wéard,
then [a] middle-dwelling[26]   *mankind's Guardian,*

éċe Drýhten,   æfter tŏ̆ede
[the] eternal Lord,   *afterwards prepared*

fírum fóldan,   Frŏ̆a æ̆lmìhtiġ.
[for the] men [of] earth,   *[the] Lord almighty.*

THE FALL OF MAN

The following passage (Genesis 3:1–13) is from a translation of the first books of the Bible by Ælfric, the chief prose writer of the later Old English period. This text is slightly regularized in spelling; the full version can be found in S. J. Crawford's edition for the Early English Text Society (OS 160, 1922). Although most of the words are easily recognizable or can be guessed, more difficult forms are glossed below.

1. Ēac swylċe sēo næddre wæs ġēapre ðonne ealle ðā ōðre nȳtenu ðe God ġeworhte ofer eorðan, and sēo næddre cwæð tō ðām wīfe: "Hwī forbēad God ēow ðæt ġē ne æten of ælċum trēowe binnan Paradīsum?"

2. Þæt wīf andwyrde: "Of ðæra trēowa wæstme ðe synd on Paradīsum wē etað;

3. And of ðæs trēowes wæstme þe is on middan neorxnawange, God bebēad ūs, ðæt wē ne æten, ne wē ðæt trēow ne hrepoden ðȳ læs ðe wē swelten."

4. Ðā cwæð sēo nædre eft tō ðām wīfe: "Ne bēo ġē nāteshwōn dēade, ðeah ðe ġē of ðām trēowe eten.

5. Ac God wāt sōðlīċe ðæt ēowre ēagan bēoð ġeopenode on swā hwylċum dæġe swā ġē etað of ðām trēowe, and ġē bēoð ðonne englum ġelīċe, witende æ̆ġðer ġe gōd ġe yfel."

[24] That is, 'we are bound to.'
[25] That is, 'how he, the eternal Lord, established the beginning of every wonder.'
[26] That is, 'the earth.'

6. Ðā ġeseah ðæt wīf ðæt ðæt trēow wæs gōd tō etenne, be ðām ðe hyre ðūhte, and wlitiġ on ēagum and lustbǣre on ġesyhðe, and ġenam ðā of ðæs trēowes wæstme and ġeǣt and sealde hyre were: he ǣt ðā.

7. And heora bēġra ēagan wurdon ġeopenode; hī oncnēowon ðā ðæt hī nacode wǣron, and sӯwodon him ficlēaf, and worhton him wǣdbrēċ.

8. Eft ðā ðā God cōm, and hī ġehӯrdon his stemne ðǣr he ēode on neorxnawange ofer midne dæġ, ðā behӯdde Ādām hine, and his wīf ēac swā dyde, fram Godes ġesihðe on middan ðām trēowe neorxnanwonges.

9. God clypode ðā Ādām, and cwæð: "Ādām, hwǣr eart ðū?"

10. Hē cwæð: "Ðīne stemne iċ ġehӯre, lēof, on neorxnawange, and iċ ondrǣde mē, for ðām ðe iċ eom nacod, and iċ behӯde mē."

11. God cwæð: "Hwā sǣde ðē ðæt ðū nacod wǣre, ġyf ðū ne ǣte of ðām trēowe ðe iċ ðē bebēad ðæt ðū ne ǣte?"

12. Ādām cwæð: "Ðæt wīf ðe ðū mē forġēafe tō ġefēran, sealde mē of ðām trēowe, and iċ ǣtt."

13. God cwæð to ðām wīfe: "Hwī dydestū ðæt?" Hēo cwæð: "Sēo nǣdre bepǣhte mē and iċ ǣtt."

GLOSSES

ēac swylċe 'and furthermore'	*wlitiġ* 'fair'
ġēapre 'more cunning'	*lustbǣre* 'desirable'
nӯtenu 'beasts'	*were* dat. 'husband'
ǣlċum dat. 'each, every'	*heora bēġra* 'both of their'
neorxnawange dat. 'Paradise'	*wǣdbrēċ* 'breeches'
hrepoden 'should touch'	*stemne* 'voice'
ðī lǣs ðe 'lest'	*clypode* 'called'
nāteshwōn 'by no means'	*lēof* 'Sir'
swā hwylċum dat. 'whatsoever'	*dydestū* = dydest þū
ǣġðer ġe . . . ġe 'both . . . and'	*bepǣhte* 'tricked'
be ðām ðe 'as'	

PARABLES

The following parables, which have been slightly regularized in spelling, are from James W. Bright's edition of *The Gospel of Saint Luke in Anglo-Saxon* (Oxford, 1893).

Ðā sǣde hē him sum bīspell, Sæġst þū, mæġ se blinda þone blindan lǣdan? hū ne feallaþ hī bēġen on þone pytt?

Nis se leorning-cniht ofer þone lārēow; ǣlċ bið fulfremed, ġif hē is swylċe his lārēow.

Hwӯ ġesyhst þū þā eġle on þīnes brōþor ēagan, and ne ġesyhst þone bēam on þīnum ēagan?

And hū miht þū secgan þīnum brēþer, Brōþor, lǣt þæt iċ ātēo þā eġle of þīnum ēagan, and þū sylf ne ġesyhst þone bēam on þīnum āgenum ēagan? Ēalā liċetere, tēoh ǣrest þone bēam of þīnum ēagan, and þonne þū ġesyhst þæt ðū ātēo þā eġle of þīnes brōðor ēagan.

Nis gōd trēow þe yfelne wæstm dēð; nē nis yfel trēow gōdne wæstm dōnde.

Ǣlċ trēow is be his wæstme oncnāwen; nē hī of þornum fīc-æppla ne gaderiaþ, nē wīn-berian on gorste ne nimað.

Gōd man of gōdum gold-horde his heortan gōd forðbringð; and yfel man of yfelum gold-horde yfel forðbringþ: sōðlīċe se mūð spicð swā sēo heorte þencð.

Hwȳ clypie ġē mē Drihten, Drihten, and ne dōð þæt iċ ēow secge?

bēġen 'both'
nis, contraction of ne and is
lārēow 'teacher'
fulfremed 'fulfilled, perfected'
swylċe 'as, like'
eġle 'mote'

(a)tēo(h) 'draw out'
līċetere 'hypocrite'
dēð, dōnde 'produces, producing'
fīc 'fig'
berian 'berries'
nimað 'take'

6

The Middle English Period
(1100–1500)

6.1 QUESTIONS FOR REVIEW AND DISCUSSION

1. Define the following terms:

Norman	vocalization	leveling (merging)
Anglo-Norman	off-glide	inorganic -*e*
elision	lengthening	scribal -*e*
unrounding	shortening	syncope (syncopation)
monophthongization (smoothing)	open syllable	analogy (analogical form)
diphthongization	closed syllable	verbal noun

2. Summarize the historical events of the Norman Conquest.

3. What was the chief influence of the Conquest on the English language?

4. Which variety of Middle English became the standard dialect and when did it become the literary standard?

5. Compare the vowel system of Old English with that of Middle English as they are shown in the two vowel charts. What additions, losses, and rearrangements took place between the two periods?

6. Make a similar comparison of the consonant systems of the two periods.

7. Which sound change between Old and Middle English had the most far-reaching effect on the language?

8. What is the chief difference between Old and Middle English grammar?

9. Did word order and function words increase or decrease in importance during the Middle English period?

10. What factors contributed to the loss of grammatical gender in Middle English?

11. How did English acquire a device for indicating plurality independent of case?

12. What grammatical category of number was lost from the Middle English personal pronouns?

13. The traditional seven classes of strong verbs survived in Middle English, but what factors began to disturb their orderly arrangement?

14. What was the origin of the verbal ending -*ing*?

15. What is the chief difference in word order between Middle and Modern English?

16. What caused the decline of French as the language of the governing classes in England?

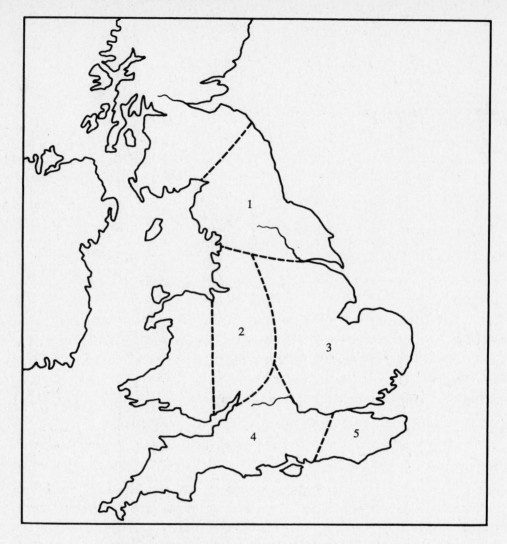

1. List the main Middle English dialect areas according to the numbers on the map.

1 *Northern*   4 *Southern*

2 *West Midland*   5 *Kentish*

3 *East Midland*

2. In the *Reeve's Tale* Chaucer has two clerics—university students—who had come originally from the north of England. Their dialogue is full of northernisms, which Chaucer's London audience doubtlessly found highly comic. In the blanks write the standard London or East Midland forms of the italicized words. You will find it easier to identify the forms if you have read all of Chapter VI in Pyles's *Origins and Development*.

_____ "Hou *fares* thy faire doghter and thy wyf?" (4023)

"By God, right by the hopur wil I stand,"

_____ Quod John, "and se howgates [how] the corn *gas* in.

Yet saugh I never, by my fader kyn,

_____ How that the hopur wagges *til* and *fra*." (4036–39)

_____ "I is as ille a millere as *ar* ye." (4045)

_____ "What, *whilk* way is he geen [gone]?" he gan to crie. (4078)

_____ "A wilde fyr upon *thair* bodyes falle!" (4172)

"I is thyn awen clerk, *swa* have I seel [bliss]!" (4239)

"Myn heed is toty [dizzy] of my swynk [work] to nyght,

That *makes* me that I ga nat aright." (4253–54)

6.3 *THE PRONUNCIATION OF MIDDLE ENGLISH: CONSONANTS*

Middle English had the following consonants:[1]

COMMON SPELLING	SOUND	COMMON SPELLING	SOUND	COMMON SPELLING	SOUND
b	[b]	m	[m]	y, з	[j]
d	[d]	n	[n], [ŋ]	z, s	[z]
f	[f]	p	[p]	ch	[č]
g	[g]	r	[r]	gh, з, h	[x], [ç]
h	[h]	s, c	[s]	sh, sch	[š]
ʝ (i), g	[j]	t	[t]	th, þ	[θ]
k, c, q	[k]	v (u)	[v]	th, þ	[ð]
l	[l]	w, u	[w]		

Complete the following chart by filling in the symbols listed above to show the place and manner of articulation of the Middle English consonants. In spite of the customary spelling differences between [h] on the one hand and [x] and [ç] on the other, they were probably still variants of the same phoneme; put [h] in the spot appropriate for the other two.

		LABIAL	DENTAL			PALATOVELAR	
			inter-dental	*alveolar*	*aveolo-palatal*	*palatal*	*velar*
STOPS AND AFFRICATES	*voiceless*	[p]		[t] [č]			[k] [h]
	voiced	[b] [d]		[ǰ]			[g] [x]
FRICATIVES	*voiceless*	[f] [s]	[θ]	[s] [š]			
	voiced	[v] [	[ð]	[z]			
NASALS		[m]		[n]			[ŋ]
LIQUIDS	*lateral*			[l]			
	retroflex or trill					[r]	
SEMIVOWELS						[j]	[w]

[1] There were a good many other spellings less common than those cited here; for example, [š] could also be spelled *ssh, ss,* or *s* in various parts of England. In the writing system, *x* was also used in its modern value [ks]. Do not confuse it with the same letter used as a phonetic symbol.

6.4 THE PRINCIPAL CONSONANTAL CHANGES

In *Origins and Development*, pages 158–60, Pyles lists nine consonantal changes which occurred during the Middle English period:

1. loss of [h] before [l], [n], and [r]
2. [ʒ] > [w] after [l] or [r]
3. loss of [w] between consonant and back vowel
4. loss of final [č] in unstressed syllables
5. loss of medial [v]
6. prefix [jɛ] (*ge-*) > [ɪ] (*i-, y-*)
7. Southern voicing of initial [f], [s], and [θ]
8. loss of final [n] in many unstressed syllables
9. appearance of [v], [z], and [ð] in initial position because of word-borrowing or voicing due to lack of stress

Identify the change which each of these Middle English words illustrates by writing the appropriate number, from 1 through 9, before the word. For many of the words you will find it necessary to compare the Middle English with the corresponding Old English form to determine what change has occurred. You can find the Old English form in the etymology given for the word in any good dictionary. The modern form of the word is given in parentheses whenever it differs from the Middle English spelling.

_3_	also	_8_	lothely (loathly)	_7_	then
_8_	eve	_8_	maide (maid)	_3_	thong
_3_	ho (who)	_1_	neyen (neigh)	_7_	vane
_4_	I	_8_	o (a)	_9_	very
_8_	icleped (yclept)	_1_	raven	_6_	ynogh (enough)
_1_	lady	_2_	sorwe (sorrow)	_7_	zenith
_1_	laughen (laugh)	_2_	swelwen (swallow)	_7_	zinne (sin)

6.5 MINOR CONSONANTAL CHANGES

The preceding exercise was concerned with nine of the more important consonantal changes of the Middle English period, but there were other changes affecting Middle English consonants. You can discover some of these additional changes by examining the words listed here. (1) Determine the pre-Middle English form of each word (Old English, Old French, Old Norse). (2) Describe the consonantal change which seems to have affected each group of words. Each group is intended to illustrate a single consonantal change.

MIDDLE ENGLISH	PRE-MIDDLE ENGLISH	DESCRIPTION OF THE CONSONANTAL CHANGE
A. elle 'ell'	_____	
kill 'kiln'	_____	_____
mille 'mill'	_____	
B. kindred	_____	
thunder	_____	
jaundice	_____	_____
spindle	_____	

C. glistnen 'glisten' _____
   listnen 'listen'   _____
   against   _____ _____
   biheste 'behest'   _____

D. hemp   _____
   noumpere 'umpire'   _____ _____
   comfort   _____

E. strenkth 'strength' _____
   lenkth 'length'   _____ _____

F. shambles   _____
   slumbren 'slumber' _____
   thimble   _____ _____
   empty   _____

G. lemman 'leman'   _____
   wimman 'woman'   _____ _____
   Lammasse 'Lammas'   _____

H. wurshipe 'worship' _____
   Sussex   _____ _____
   Norfolk   _____

I. best   _____
   laste 'last'   _____
   Wessex   _____ _____
   blosme 'blossom'   _____

J. answerien 'answer' _____
   gospelle 'gospel'   _____ _____
   gossib 'gossip'   _____

K. eech 'each'   _____
   suche 'such'   _____ _____
   which   _____

L. coom 'comb'   _____
   dum 'dumb'   _____ _____
   lam 'lamb'   _____

M. bird   _____
   thirde 'third'   _____
   bright   _____ _____
   through   _____
   wrighte 'wright'   _____

N. adder   _____
   apron   _____
   auger   _____ _____
   neute 'newt'   _____
   nones 'nonce'   _____

The changes illustrated above are typical of some general tendencies which have operated at various times in the history of our language. These tendencies are described by the following five terms. Match the terms with the changes A through N by writing the appropriate letters in the blank before each term.

_____ ARTICULATIVE INTRUSION: the addition of a new sound produced by the speech organs as they move from the position for one sound to that for another or to silence (for example, *once* [wəns] pronounced as [wənts] or [wənst]; *film* pronounced [fɪləm]).

_____ PARTIAL ASSIMILATION: a change in pronunciation such that one sound becomes more like a neighboring sound (for example, *have to* pronounced [hæftu]).

_____ CONSONANT LOSS: the disappearance of a consonant sound from a word (for example, *cupboard* pronounced [kəbərd]); the loss is often the result of a complete assimilation by which two sounds become identical and reduce to one.

_____ METATHESIS: the inversion of two sounds (for example, *apron* pronounced either [eprən] or [epərn]).

_____ JUNCTURE LOSS OR DISPLACEMENT: a shift in the boundary between syllables so that a sound formerly in one syllable comes to be in another (for example, *at all* pronounced like *a tall*).

6.6 *THE PRONUNCIATION OF MIDDLE ENGLISH: VOWELS*

Because the Middle English period lasted for some four hundred years and included several strikingly different dialects of our language, no single description of the sounds of Middle English can cover all the varieties of the language which the student may encounter. The treatment of Middle English sounds in this exercise concerns itself with Chaucer's language, since he is the Middle English writer who is most read. In his dialect, these vowels occur:

SPELLING	SOUND	SPELLING	SOUND	SPELLING	SOUND
a	[a][2]	o	[ɔ]	au, aw	[au]
a, aa	[ā]	o, oo	[ɔ̄]	ai, ay, ei, ey	[æɪ][3]
e	[ɛ], [ə]	o, oo	[ō] *(oʌts)*	eu, ew	[ɛu]
e, ee	[ɛ̄]	u, o	[u] *(bull)*	eu, ew, u	[ɪu]
e, ee, ie	[ē] *(ape)*	ou, ow	[ū] *(ooze)*	oi, oy	[ɔɪ]
i, y	[ɪ] *(sit)*			ou, ow	[ɔu]
i, y	[ī] *(eat)*			oi, oy	[uɪ]

Notice that Middle English spelling was a less accurate record of pronunciation than Old English spelling had been. Complete the following charts by filling in the symbols listed above to show the articulation of Middle English vowels.

[2] The exact sound of this vowel is uncertain; it may have been [ɑ] or [æ]. The symbol [a] is used here as a compromise. The same uncertainty exists for the corresponding long vowel.

[3] The exact quality of this diphthong is doubtful; it represents a combination of two older diphthongs, [aɪ] and [ɛɪ]. Many modern Chaucerians pronounce it [æɪ], the symbol used here. There are some similar doubts about the quality of several other diphthongs.

SIMPLE VOWELS

			FRONT	CENTRAL	BACK
HIGH	long			—	
	short			—	
MID	long	close		—	
		open		—	
	short			—	
LOW	long		—		—
	short		—		—

DIPHTHONGS

Classify the diphthongs according to the position of their initial element. The arrows indicate the direction of the second element in the diphthong.

	FRONT	CENTRAL	BACK	
HIGH	→	—	←	
MID	↗	—	↖	↑
LOW	↑	↗	—	

Complete the following chart to show (1) the phonetic symbols for the Old English sounds from which the Middle English vowel developed, (2) the phonetic symbol for the corresponding Modern English vowel, and (3) the typical spelling of the Modern English development of the vowel. You can get all of this information from the key words.

The complete history of the Middle English vowels is quite complex because it involves many minor sound changes and borrowings between dialects. However, when you have completed this chart, you will have a list of the Middle English vowels with their main sources and future developments.

OLD ENGLISH SOURCES		MIDDLE ENGLISH		MODERN ENGLISH DEVELOPMENT		
key words	(1) *phonetic symbol*	*vowel*	*key words*	*key words*	(2) *phonetic symbol*	(3) *typical spelling*
sacc bæc sceal		[a]	sak bak shal	sack back shall	[sak] [bæk] [šæl]	a
talu æcer		[ā]	tale aker	tale acre	[tel] [ekər]	ai a—e a
bedd seofon		[ɛ]	bed seven	bed seven	[bɛd] [sɛvən]	e ea ai
clǣne[4] dǣl[4] bēam stelan		[ɛ̄]	clene deel beem stelen	clean deal beam steal	[klin] [dɨl] [bɨm] [stɪl]	ea ie e—e ee
gēs slǣp[4] sēoþan		[ē]	gees sleep sethen	geese sleep seethe	[gɨs] [slɨp] [sɨð]	ea ee—e ie ee
fisc lim hyll cynn		[ɪ]	fish lym hil kyn	fish limb hill kin	[fɪsh]	i e ee
hrīm wīf hȳdan mȳs		[ī]	rim wyf hiden mys	rime wife hide mice		i—e y—e ei
frogga cocc		[ɔ]	frogge cok	frog cock		o
hām bāt wā þrote		[ɔ̄]	hoom boot wo throte	home boat woe throat		oa o—e o
mōna gōd flōd		[ō]	mone good flood	moon good flood		oo, u oo—e u—e ou
full bucca sunne cuman		[ʊ]	ful bukke sonne comen	full buck sun come		u oo o—e o
mūs brū		[ū]	mous brow	mouse brow		ou—e ou ow
lagu clawu aht		[au]	lawe clawe aught	law claw aught		au aw ou

4 See Pyles, pp. 161–62.

148

OLD ENGLISH SOURCES		MIDDLE ENGLISH		MODERN ENGLISH DEVELOPMENT		
key words	(1) *phonetic symbol*	*vowel*	*key words*	*key words*	(2) *phonetic symbol*	(3) *typical spelling*
hæġl dæġ seġl weġ eahta		[æɪ]	hail day seil wey eighte	hail day sail way eight		ai a_e ei <del>ae</del> ey ay
lǣwede fēawe		[ɛʊ]	lewed fewe	lewd few		oo ew u_e ue ie
nīwe Tīwesdæġ cnēow		[ɪu]	newe Tuesdai knew	new Tuesday knew		oo ue o wo
No OE source; from OF development of Lat. [au]: OF joie < Lat. gaudia OF cloistre < Lat. claustra		[ɔɪ]	joy cloistre	joy cloister		oy oi
snāw āgan dāh grōwan boga dohtor brohte		[ɔu]	snow owen dough growen bowe doughter broughte	snow owe dough grow bow daughter brought		ow ou oe o ew
No OE source; from OF development of Lat. [u] and [ō]: OF joindre < Lat. jungere OF poison < Lat. pōtio		[ʊɪ]	joinen poysen	join poison		oi

6.7 *THE LENGTHENING AND SHORTENING OF VOWELS*

Vowels were lengthened during the late Old English period or in early Middle English times

1. before certain consonant sequences (especially *mb*, *nd*, *ld*) and
2. in open syllables.

They were shortened

3. in closed syllables before two or more consonants (other than those above),
4. in unstressed syllables, and
5. in a syllable followed by two unaccented syllables.

Which of the five conditions listed above accounts for the vowel length of the first syllable in each of the following words? Vowel length is indicated by macrons. Write the appropriate number before the word.

5 2	abīden 'to abide'	4	dōre 'door'	5	stiropes 'stirrups'
2	āker 'acre'	3	evere 'ever'	5	sutherne 'southern'
5 2	arīsen 'to arise'	5	fedde 'fed'	2	tāle
2 3	asken 'to ask'	1	feeld 'field'	4	the
2	bēren 'to bear'	1	ground	5	today
2	bētel 'beetle'	1	hōlden 'to hold'	3	us
2	bēver 'beaver'	2	hōpe	5	wepenes 'weapons'
3	blosme 'blossom'	1	kīnde 'kind'	2	wimmen 'women'
1	cōld	3	naddre 'adder'	1	wōmb

The results of the lengthening and shortening of vowels in Middle English words like *hīden–hidde* or *wīs–wisdom* can still be seen in their Modern English developments, although now the vowels differ primarily in quality or tenseness rather than in length. For each of the following Modern English words, which have developed from Middle English forms with long vowels, supply a related word which has developed from a form with a short vowel. For example, *five* might be matched with *fifty*, *fifteen*, or *fifth*.

bathe	bath	dear 'beloved'	darling	lead 'guide'	led
bleed	bled	deep	depth	mead 'grassland'	meadow
break	brick (breakfast)	glaze	glass	shade	shadow
clean	cleanse	goose	gosling	shoe	shod
creep	crept	heal	hell	white	whit

6.8 MIDDLE ENGLISH TRANSCRIPTION

Write these Middle English words in phonetic transcription. Unstressed *e* at the end of a word is phonetically [ə]. The modern development is given as a gloss when there is possible ambiguity.

flat	[flæt]	now	[nʊw]	ye 'ye'	
glad	[glɑd]	boot 'boot'	[bɔt]	ye 'eye'	
nest	[nɛst]	boot 'boat'	[bōt]	gyse 'guise'	
shin	[šɪn] [šīn]	cook	[kōk]	shoo 'shoe'	
top	[tɔp]	hoom 'home'	[hōm]	doute 'doubt'	
broth	[brɔth]	dool 'dole'	[dōl]	wood 'wood'	
cuppe	[kʊppə]	doten 'to dote'	[dōtən]	wood 'woad'	
love	[lɔvə]	fode 'food'	[fōde]	theme	
wolf	[wɔlf]	strete 'street'	[strētə]	gaude	
synne	[sɪnnə]	lene 'lean'	[lēnə]	grey	
fable	[fabl]	felen 'to feel'	[fēlən]	main	
caas 'case'	[kɑs]	dreem 'dream'	[drēm]	towen 'to tow'	
pipe	[pɪpə]	wreken 'to wreak'		sought	
hyden 'to hide'	[hīdən]	weep		lawe	
cloud	[klūd]	sete 'seat'		rein 'rain'	

150

Middle English spelling was less perfectly alphabetical than Old English spelling had been. The letter *o* alone could be used to spell four different vowels—[ɔ], [ɔ̄], [ō], [ʊ]—and as part of a digraph it could help to spell four more—[ū], [ɔu], [ɔɪ], [ʊɪ]. Yet Middle English orthography can be pronounced with reasonable accuracy on the basis of four clues:

1. the spelling of the Middle English word,
2. the pronunciation of the modern development (provided the word still exists),
3. the spelling of the modern development (with the same obvious provision), and
4. the etymology of the Middle English word.

The four clues are listed in the order of their usefulness, but to apply them you must have a firm mastery of the information on pages 158–63 of Pyles's *Origins and Development* and in exercises 6.3 and 6.6. For example, to pronounce the word *boon* as in the line "We stryve as dide the houndes for the boon," we can note first that the *oo* spelling indicates a long vowel, either [ɔ̄] or [ō]. The modern development *bone* [bon] indicates by both its sound and its spelling that the Middle English vowel must have been [ɔ̄]. Finally, if we happen to know that the Old English source of the word was *bān*, we can be confident that the Middle English was [bɔ̄n]. If the reason for these observations is not clear to you, review the discussions mentioned above.

There will, of course, still be much uncertainty. Some words, like *halwes* 'shrines' have not survived into Modern English. Others, like *seeke* 'sick' have survived, but in a different form. Also the diphthongs [ɔɪ] and [ʊɪ] were usually spelled alike in Middle English, and their modern developments are both spelled and pronounced alike; they can be distinguished only by their etymology, which a beginning student is unlikely to know. The same difficulty exists for the diphthongs [ɛu] and [ɪu]. Nevertheless, a mastery of the pronunciation and spelling correspondences between Middle and Modern English will allow you to read Chaucer's language with a fair degree of accuracy.

1. Write each of these phonetically transcribed words in one possible Middle English spelling:

[parfit] 'perfect'	*parfyt, parfit*	[mētə]	*mete, meete, miete*
[māt] 'dead'	*mat, maat*	[mētə]	*mete, meete*
[bɛllə]	*belle*	[fōl]	*fol, fool*
[krūdən]	*krouden, krowden*	[grɔ̄pən]	*gropen, groopen*
[dɔggə]	*dogge*	[wrīðən]	*writhen, urython, writhen*
[rudɪ]	*rudi, rodi, rudy, rody*	[wæɪvən]	*waiven*
[gnauən]	*gnauen, gnawen*	[nɔɪzə]	*noise*
[θɔux]	*þouჳ*	[pʊɪnt]	*point*
[hwɪč]	*which*	[hɪu] 'hue'	*heu*
[knɪçt]	*knight, cnyჳt*	[hɛuən] 'to hew'	*hewen, heuen*

2. An examination of the following passages from the *Canterbury Tales* will make apparent both the uses and the limitations of pronunciation clues. The phonetic transcriptions represent a fairly conservative pronunciation of Middle English; some of the words might have been written differently because there is not complete agreement among scholars about Chaucer's pronunciation.[5]

---

[5] Unstressed syllables and words are particularly susceptible to changes. For example, final *s* and *th* in unstressed syllables may have been voiced; initial *h* in unstressed words like *him, hem, hir* was probably silent; unstressed words like *I* and *to* probably had short vowels. For the pronunciation of schwa in final syllables, see Pyles, p. 170.

Whan that Aprille with hise shoures soote | hwan ðat āprıl wıθ hıs šūrəs sōtə
The droghte of March hath perced to the roote | ðə drūxt əf marč haθ pērsəd tō ðə rōtə
And bathed euery veyne in swich licour | and bāðəd ɛv(ə)rı væın ın swıč lıkūr
Of which vertu engendred is the flour; | əf hwıč vɛrtıu ɛnǰendrəd ıs ðə flūr
Whan Zephirus eek wᵗ his sweete breeth | hwan zɛfırus ēk wıθ hıs swētə brēθ
Inspired hath in euery holt and heeth | ınspīrəd haθ ın ɛv(ə)rı hɔlt and hēθ
The tendre croppes, and the yonge sonne | ðə tɛndrə krɔppəs and ðə juŋgə sunnə
Hath in the Ram his half cours yronne, | haθ ın ðə ram hıs halvə kūrs ırunnə
And smale foweles maken melodye, | and smalə fūləs mākən mɛlɔdīə
That slepen al the nyght with open eye— | ðat slēpən al ðə nıxt wıθ ōpən īə
So priketh hem nature in hir corages— | sō prıkəθ hɛm natıur ın hır kurāǰəs
Thanne longen folk to goon on pilgrimages, | ðan lɔŋgən fɔlk tō gōn ɔn pılgrımāǰəs
And Palmeres for to seken straunge strondes, | and palm(ə)rəs fər tō sēkən straunǰə strɔndəs
To ferne halwes kowthe in sondry londes | tō fɛrnə halwəs kūθ ın sundrı lɔndəs
And specially fram euery shires ende | and spɛsjallı frəm ɛv(ə)rı šīrəs ɛndə
Of Engelond to Caunterbury they wende | əf ɛŋgələnd tō kauntərbrī ðæı wɛndə
The hooly blisful martir for to seke | ðə hōlı blısful martır fər tō sēkə
That hem hath holpen whan þᵗ they were seeke. | ðat hɛm haθ hɔlpən hwan ðat ðæı wēr sēkə
Bifil that in that seson on a day, | bıfıl ðat ın ðat sēzun ɔn ə dæı
In Southwerk at the Tabard as I lay | ın suðərk at ðə tabard as ī læı
Redy to wenden on my pilgrymage | rēdı tō wɛndən ɔn mī pılgrımāǰə
To Caunterbury with ful deuout corage, | tō kauntərbrī wıθ ful dəvūt kurāǰə
At nyght were come in to that hostelrye | at nıçt wēr kum ın tō ðat əstəlrīə
Wel nyne and twenty in a compaignye | wɛl nīn and twɛntı ın ə kumpæınīə
Of sondry folk by auenture yfalle | əf sundrı fɔlk bī avəntıur ıfallə
In felaweshipe, and pilgrimes were they alle | ın fɛlaušıp and pılgrım(ə)s wēr ðæı allə
That toward Caunterbury wolden ryde. | ðat tōward kauntərburı wōldən rīdə

But first I pray yow, of youre curteisye, | but fırst ī præı jū əf jūr kurtæızīə
That ye narette it nat my vileynye, | ðat jē narɛt ıt nat mī vılæınīə
Thogh that I pleynly speke in this mateere, | ðoux ðat ī plæınlı spēk ın ðıs matērə
To telle yow hir wordes and hir cheere, | tō tɛllə jū hır wərdəs and hır čērə
Ne thogh I speke hir wordes proprely. | nə ðoux ī spēk hır wərdəs prɔprəlī
For this ye knowen al so wel as I, | fər ðıs jē knɔuən al sō wɛl as ī
Who so shal telle a tale after a man, | hwō sō šal tɛl a tāl aftər a man
He moote reherce as ny as euere he kan | hē mōt rəhērs as nī as ɛvər hē kan
Euerich a word, if it be in his charge, | ɛv(ə)rıč a wərd ıf ıt bē ın hız čarǰə
Al speke he neuer so rudeliche or large, | al spēk hē nɛvər sō rıudəlıč ər larǰə
Or ellis he moot telle his tale vntrewe, | ər ɛllıs hē mōt tɛl hıs tāl untrıuə
Or feyne thyng, or fynde wordes newe. | ər fæınə θıŋg ər fīndə wərdəs nıuə
He may nat spare, al thogh he were his brother; | hē mæı nat spār al ðoux hē wēr hıs brōðər
He moot as wel seye o word as another. | hē mōt as wɛl sæı ō wərd as anōðər
Crist spak hym self ful brode in hooly writ, | krīst spak hımsɛlf ful brōd ın hōlı wrıt

And wel ye woot no viieynye is it.
Eek Plato seith, who so kan hym rede,
"The wordes moote be cosyn to the dede."

and wɛl jē wōt nō vɪlæɪnī ɪs ɪt
ēk plātə sæɪθ hwō sō kan hɪm rēdə
ðə wordəs mōt bē kuzɪn tō ðə dēdə

THE WIFE OF BATH'S PROLOGUE, ll. 469–80

But, lord crist! whan that it remembreth me
Vpon my yowthe, and on my Iolitee,
It tikleth me aboute myn herte roote.
Vnto this day it dooth myn herte boote
That I haue had my world as in my tyme.
But Age, allas! that al wole enuenyme,
Hath me biraft my beautee and my pith.
Lat go, fare wel! the deuel go therwith!
The flour is goon, ther is namoore to telle;
The bren, as I best kan, now moste I selle;
But yet to be right myrie wol I fonde.
Now wol I tellen of my fourthe housbonde.

but lōrd krīst hwan ðat ɪt rəmɛmbrəθ mē
upən mī jūθ and ən mī jɔlɪtē
ɪt tɪkləθ mē abūt mīn hɛrtə rōtə
untō ðɪs dæɪ ɪt dōθ mīn hɛrtə bōtə
ðat ī hav had mī wurld as ɪn mī tīmə
but āǰ allas ðat al wəl ɛnvənīmə
haθ mē bɪraft mī bɛutē and mī pɪθ
lat gō fār wɛl ðə dɛvəl gō ðēr wɪθ
ðə flūr ɪs gōn θēr ɪs namōr tō tɛllə
ðə brɛn as ī bɛst kan nū mōst ī sɛllə
but jɛt tō bē rɪçt mɪrɪ wəl ī fōndə
nū wəl ī tɛllən əf mī fourθ huzbōndə

CHAUCER'S RETRACTION

Now preye I to hem alle that herkne this litel tretys or rede, that if ther be any thyng in it that liketh hem, that therof they thanken oure lord Ihesu crist, of whom procedeth al wit and al goodnesse. And if ther be any thyng that displese hem, I preye hem also that they arrette it to the defaute of myn vnkonnynge, and nat to my wyl, that wolde ful fayn haue seyd bettre if I hadde had konnynge. For oure boke seith, "al that is writen is writen for oure doctrine," and that is myn entente. Wherfore I biseke yow mekely for the mercy of god, that ye preye for me that crist haue mercy on me and foryeue me my giltes, and namely of my translacions and enditynges of worldly vanitees, the whiche I reuoke in my retraccions.

nū præɪ ī tō hɛm al ðat hɛrknə ðɪs lɪtəl trētɪs ər rēd ðat ɪf ðēr bē anɪ θɪŋg ɪn ɪt ðat līkəθ əm ðat ðērəf ðæɪ θaŋkən ūr lōrd jēzu krīst əf hwōm prəsēdəθ al wɪt and al gōdnɛs and ɪf ðēr bē anɪ θɪŋg ðat dɪsplēz əm ī præɪ əm alsō ðat ðæɪ arɛt ɪt tō ðə dəfaut əf mīn unkunnɪŋg and nat tō mī wɪl ðat wəld ful fæɪn hav sæɪd bɛttrə ɪf ī had had kunnɪŋg fər ūr bōk sæɪθ al ðat ɪs wrɪtən ɪs wrɪtən fər ūr dɔktrīn and ðat ɪs mīn ɛntent hwērfər ī bɪsēk jū mēkəlɪ fər ðə mɛrsɪ əf gɔd ðat jē præɪ fər mē ðat krīst hav mɛrsɪ ən mē and fərjēv mē mī gɪltəs and nāməlɪ əf mī tranzlāsɪənz and ɛndītɪŋgəs əf wurldlɪ vanɪtēs ðə hwɪč ī rəvōk ɪn mī rətraksɪənz

6.10 *THE REDUCTION OF INFLECTIONS*

The number of inflectional distinctions which had existed in Old English was strikingly diminished in Middle English. The decrease in endings was due partly to the merger of unstressed vowels and partly to the operation of analogy. The declension of the adjective in Old and Middle English is illustrated below. Write *S* before each Old English form that developed into the corresponding Middle English form by regular sound change, and *A* before each form that was lost through analogy.

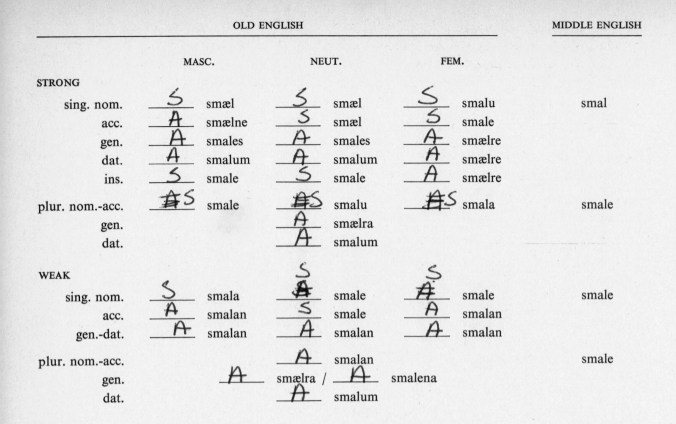

	MASC.	NEUT.	FEM.	
STRONG				
sing. nom.	smæl	smæl	smalu	smal
acc.	smælne	smæl	smale	
gen.	smales	smales	smælre	
dat.	smalum	smalum	smælre	
ins.	smale	smale	smælre	
plur. nom.-acc.	smale	smalu	smala	smale
gen.		smælra		
dat.		smalum		
WEAK				
sing. nom.	smala	smale	smale	smale
acc.	smalan	smale	smalan	
gen.-dat.	smalan	smalan	smalan	
plur. nom.-acc.		smalan		smale
gen.	smælra /	smalena		
dat.		smalum		

NOTE: The loss of final nasals in unstressed syllables must have been the result of both sound change and analogy. First a sound change began to operate whereby nasals were lost when they were followed by a consonant but were retained when they were followed by a vowel; the resulting fluctuation can be seen in the two forms of the indefinite article, *a bird* but *an owl*. Almost immediately, however, analogy came into play to eliminate the final nasal completely in adjective endings and to restore it generally in the endings of strong past participles like *eaten* and of noun plurals like *oxen*. The result is a phonological rule that is sensitive to the grammatical identity of the forms to which it applies.

The effect of leveling, whether phonological or analogical, was to eliminate all differences of case and gender from the adjective and to eliminate the distinction of number from the weak forms of the adjective. What effects did leveling have on the Middle English noun and verb?

6.11 THE INFLECTION OF NOUNS AND ADJECTIVES

1. Write the following phrases in Middle English. All of the nouns are declined alike according to the usual Middle English pattern. The adjectives, however, vary; see Pyles's *Origins and Development*, page 166.

VOCABULARY

the 'the'	*free* 'noble'	*lord* 'lord'
oold 'old'	*long* 'long'	*wyf* 'wife'
hethen 'heathen'	*feend* 'fiend'	*yeer* 'year'

~~oolde fiende~~ *feende*	old fiend	_____	the old fiend
oolde feendes	old fiend's	_____	the old fiend's
oolde feendes	old fiends	_____	the old fiends
_____	heathen lord	_____	the heathen lord
_____	heathen lord's	_____	the heathen lord's
_____	heathen lords	_____	the heathen lords
_____	noble wife	_____	the noble wife
_____	noble wife's	_____	the noble wife's
_____	noble wives	_____	the noble wives

2. Explain the origin of each of the following doublets:

brothers _____

brethren _____

latter _____

later _____

older _____

elder _____

3. Explain the vowel difference between the singular *child* and the plural *children*.

_____

_____

4. In his description of the Knight in the *Canterbury Tales*, Chaucer wrote, "His hors were goode." Did the Knight have one horse or more than one, and how can you tell? (The verb is no help; it might be either a plural or a subjunctive singular. And the noun *hors* had a plural that was identical with its singular, like Modern English *deer*.) _____

_____

6.12 *PERSONAL PRONOUNS*

Write the declensions of the Middle English personal pronouns. The four cases of the personal pronoun are the nominative, the objective, the adjectival genitive (as in "That is *my* book"), and the pronominal genitive (as in "That is *mine*"). Mark forms which are not East Midland (Chaucerian) with an asterisk (*). Mark forms borrowed from Scandinavian with a dagger (†). Mark new analogical forms with a double dagger (‡). The first person singular has been done.

FIRST PERSON SINGULAR		FIRST PERSON PLURAL	
nom.	I, ich, ik*	nom.	wē
obj.	me	obj.	ūs
adj. gen.	mi, min	adj. gen.	our, oure, oures
pron. gen.	min	pron. gen.	oure, oures

SECOND PERSON SINGULAR		SECOND PERSON PLURAL	
nom.	thou	nom.	yē
obj.	thee	obj.	you
adj. gen.	thī, thīn	adj. gen.	youre, youres
pron. gen.	thīn	pron. gen.	your, youres

<table>
<tr><td colspan="2" align="center">THIRD PERSON SINGULAR
MASCULINE</td><td colspan="2" align="center">THIRD PERSON PLURAL</td></tr>
</table>

nom.	*he*	nom.	*they, thei, thay, thai*
obj.	*hem*	obj.	*heom*
adj. gen.	*his*	adj. gen.	*theire, theires*
pron. gen.	*his*	pron. gen.	*theire, theires*

THIRD PERSON SINGULAR FEMININE		**THIRD PERSON SINGULAR NEUTER**	
nom.	*shē*	nom.	~~they, thei, thay, thai~~ *hit*
obj.	*hīre*	obj.	~~heom~~ *him*
adj. gen.	*here s*	adj. gen.	~~theire, theires~~ *his*
pron. gen.	*heres*	pron. gen.	~~theire, theires~~ *his*

6.13 DEMONSTRATIVE PRONOUNS

The Old English demonstratives consisted in part of these forms:

NOMINATIVE SINGULAR		NOMINATIVE PLURAL	INSTRUMENTAL SINGULAR
masc.	*sē* 'the, that'; *þes* 'this'	*þā* 'the, those'; *þās* 'these'	*þē* 'by the, that'
fem.	*sēo* *þēos*		
neut.	*þæt* *þis*		

Middle English had the following forms. Indicate which Old English form each developed from, and explain any irregularities in the development.

singular and plural	*the*	Dev. from sē
singular	*that*	
plural	*tho*	
	thos	
singular	*this*	
plural	*these*	
	thise	

6.14 INTERROGATIVE AND RELATIVE PRONOUNS

Notice how the italicized pronouns are used in the following quotations from Chaucer.[6]

Who herd euer of swich a thyng or now? (D 2229)

Who hath no wyf he is no cokewold. (A 3152)

Who so first cometh to the mille first grynt [grinds]. (D 389)

Who that is moost vertuous alway . . . . Taak hym for the grettest gentil man. (D 1113)

"To *whom*?" quod he. (G 304)

My lady, *whom* I loue and serue. (A 1143)

The sighte of hire, *whom that* I serue. (A 1231)

---

[6] Following each quotation the source is identified by the customary abbreviation.

Whos is that faire child that stondeth yonder? (B 1018)

Of him *whos* I am all, whil I may dure. (Venus 6)

Syk lay the goode man *whos that* the place is. (D 1768)

What is bettre than a good womman? (B 2298)

Whan folk in chirche had yeue [given] him *what* hem leste [pleased them], He wente his wey.
   (D 1735)

Ne euery appul that is fair at eye Ne is nat good, *what so* men clappe [chatter] or crye. (G 965)

But God woot [knows] *what that* May thoughte in hire herte. (E 1851)

Which was the mooste fre [noble], as thynketh yow? (F 1622)

Thise riotoures thre, of *which* I telle. (C 661)

He *which that* hath no wyf, I hold hym shent [ruined]. (E 1320)

Taak heede of euery word *that* I you seye. (E 475)

To me, *that* am thy cosyn and thy brother. (A 1131)

Thou hast nat doon *that* I comanded thee. (D 2041)

1. What pronouns, simple and compound, does Middle English use as

   interrogatives _who, whom, whos, what, which_
   indefinite relatives (introducing noun clauses) _who, who so, whom,_
   whos, whos that, what so, what that, ~~that~~
   relatives (introducing adjective clauses) _who that, whom that, what,_
   which, which that, that

2. Describe one difference between Middle English and contemporary English in their use of
   which. _____
   _____

3. Describe three differences between Middle English and contemporary English in their use of
   that. _____
   _____
   _____
   _____
   _____

6.15   *VERBS*

The principal parts of many Old English strong verbs survived in Middle English with no
changes other than those resulting from the regular sound shifts affecting all words. The
following Old English verbs, typical of the seven strong classes, had such regular development.
By applying what you have already studied about sound and spelling changes you should be
able to predict their Middle English forms. Write the Middle English developments; mark all
long vowels with a macron and use the hook to show open ę [ɛ] and ǫ [ɔ].

	OLD ENGLISH	MIDDLE ENGLISH		OLD ENGLISH	MIDDLE ENGLISH	
CLASS I	'to write'		CLASS II	'to cleave'	clēven	clēve
$\bar{a} \to \bar{o}$	wrītan	wrīte		clēofan	clēfen	Dipthongs >
	wrāt	wrǭt		clēaf	clęf	single
	writon	writen		clufon	cluven	
	writen	writen		clofen	clǭven	

157

CLASS III	'to bind'		CLASS V	'to knead'	
	bindan	_____		cnedan	_____
	band	_____		cnæd	_____
	bundon	_____		cnǣdon [7]	_____
	bunden	_____		cneden	_____
	'to melt'		CLASS VI	'to shake'	
	meltan	_____		scacan	_____
	mealt	_____		scōc	_____
	multon	_____		scōcon	_____
	molten	_____		scacen	_____
	'to warp'		CLASS VII	'to know'	
	weorpan	_____		cnāwan	_____
	wearp	_____		cnēow	_____
	wurpon	_____		cnēowon	_____
	worpen	_____		cnāwen	_____
CLASS IV	'to bear'			'to let'	
	beran	_____		lǣtan [7]	_____
	bær	_____		lēt	_____
	bǣron [7]	_____		lēton	_____
	boren	_____		lǣten	_____

6.16 INFLECTION OF VERBS

The Middle English weak verb *hēlen* 'to heal' and strong verb *helpen* 'to help' are typical developments of their Old English counterparts. Conjugate them in full, using the endings characteristic of the Midland dialects. The imperative endings are regular developments of the Old English forms.

PRINCIPAL PARTS	hēlen, hēlde, hēled		helpen, halp, hulpen, holpen	
	PRESENT	PRETERIT	PRESENT	PRETERIT
INDICATIVE				
I	_____	_____	_____	_____
thou	_____	_____	_____	_____
he	_____	_____	_____	_____
we, ye, they	_____	_____	_____	_____
SUBJUNCTIVE				
I, thou, he	_____	_____	_____	_____
we, ye, they	_____	_____	_____	_____
IMPERATIVE				
thou	_____		_____	
ye	_____			
PARTICIPLE				
	_____	_____	_____	_____

[7] The stem vowel was *ā* in West Germanic, so we would expect the spelling *ee* if the word had survived into Modern English.

Although the word order of Middle English is basically the same as that of the modern language, the sentences below exemplify some minor differences. The first five, which are from the *Peterborough Chronicle*, were written in the first half of the twelfth century. The second five, from Chaucer's "Tale of Melibee," were written in the last half of the fourteenth century. For each sentence, describe how the syntax, and particularly the word order, differs from present-day use.

1. Ðis gear heald se kyng Heanri his hird æt Cristesmæsse on Windlesoure.
   This year King Henry held his court at Christmas in Windsor.

   _____

2. And him com togænes Willelm eorl of Albamar.
   And William, Earl of Aumale, came against him.

   _____

3. Þerefter com þe kinges dohter Henries, þe hefde ben emperice in Alamanie.
   Thereafter came King Henry's daughter, who had been empress in Germany.

   _____

4. Þe King him sithen nam in Hamtun.
   The King afterwards captured him in Hampton.

   _____

5. Sume he iaf up, and sume ne iaf he noht.
   Some he gave up, and some he did not give.

   _____

6. Thre of his olde foes han it espyed.
   Three of his old foes have noticed it.

   _____

7. Wepyng is no thing deffended to hym that sorweful is.
   Weeping is by no means forbidden to him that is sorrowful.

   _____

8. And whan this wise man saugh that hym wanted audience, al shamefast he sette hym down agayn.
   And when this wise man saw that audience was lacking for him, all ashamed he sat down again.

   _____

9. My lord, I you biseche as hertely as I dar and kan, ne haste yow nat to faste.
   My lord, I beseech you as heartily as I dare and can, don't move too fast.

   _____

10. But seyeth and conseileth me as you liketh.
    But tell and counsel me as it pleases you.

    _____

The following passages illustrate Middle English through a period of some three hundred years. The first selection preserves many of the inflections characteristic of Old English; the last selection is hardly distinguishable from early Modern English. Some dialect variation is also represented in the passages. The translations which accompany most of the texts scarcely do literary justice to their originals, but they will serve as glosses.

Compare the passages with one another. Note significant differences among them and any characteristics which help to date them as early or late Middle English.

Observe the spelling, inflections, word order, and vocabulary.

THE PETERBOROUGH CHRONICLE

The *Anglo-Saxon Chronicle* was continued at Peterborough for almost a century after the Norman Conquest. The passage reproduced here was written about the middle of the twelfth century. The text is based on Benjamin Thorpe's *The Anglo-Saxon Chronicle, According to the Several Original Authorities* (London, 1861), corrected by readings from Dorothy Whitelock's *The Peterborough Chronicle: The Bodleian Manuscript Laud Misc. 636* ("Early English Manuscripts in Facsimile," Vol. IV [Copenhagen, 1954]). Abbreviations have been silently expanded.

Millesimo. C.XXXV.   On þis gære for   se king Henri ouer sæ æt te Lammasse. and ðat
   1135   *In this year went the King Henry over sea at the Lammas,   and that*

oþer dei þa   he lai an slep in   scip. þa þestrede þe dæi ouer al landes. and
second day while he lay asleep in [the] ship then darkened the day over all lands, and

uuard þe sunne suilc als it uuare   thre niht ald mone. an sterres abuten him at middæi.
became the sun   such as it were [a] three night old moon and stars   about   him at midday.

Wurþen men suiðe ofuundred   and ofdred. and sæden ðat   micel þing sculde
Became men greatly filled with wonder and afraid,   and said   that [a] great thing should

cumen herefter. sua   dide. for þat ilc   gær warth þe king ded. ðat oþer   dæi efter
come   hereafter; so [it] did, for that same year was   the King dead the second day after

Sanct Andreas massedæi on Normandi. Þa   þestre[den] sona   þas landes. for æuric
Saint Andrew's mass-day in Normandy. Then darkened   immediately these lands, for every

man sone   ræuede oþer   þe mihte. Þa   namen his sune and his frend. and brohten
man immediately robbed another who might.[8] Then took   his son and his friends and brought

his lic   to Engleland. and bebiriend in Redinge. God   man he wes. and micel æie wes of
his body to England   and burying   at Reading. [A] good man he was, and much awe was of

him. durste nan man misdon wið   oðer   on his time. Pais he makede   men and dær.
him; durst no man misdo against another in his time. Peace he made [for] man and beast.

Wua sua bare his byrthen   gold and sylure. durste nan man sei to him naht   bute god.
Who so   bore his burden [of] gold and silver, durst   no man say of him naught but   good.

Enmang þis   was his nefe   cumen to Engleland. Stephne de blais. and com to lundene.
Among this[9] was his nephew come   to England,   Stephen de Blois, and came to London,

[8] That is, 'every man who might immediately robbed another.'
[9] That is, 'at this time.'

and te   lundenisce folc him underfeng. and senden efter þe   ærcebiscop Willelm curbuil. and
and the London   folk him received   and sent   after the archbishop William Corbeil, and

halechede   him to kinge on midewintre dæi. On þis kinges time wes al unfrið. and yfel. and
consecrated him as king on midwinter   day. In this king's time was all strife   and evil and

ræflac. for agenes him risen sona   þa   rice   men þe   wæron swikes.
robbery, for against him rose at once those powerful men that were   traitors.

THE CHRONICLE OF ROBERT OF GLOUCESTER

Histories enjoyed a great popularity during the Middle Ages; the so-called *Metrical Chronicle of Robert of Gloucester*, edited by William Aldis Wright (London, 1887), was written about 1300 by three men, only one of whom has been identified by name. Wright said of this chronicle, "As literature, it is as worthless as twelve thousand lines of verse without one spark of poetry can be." Although it is rimed in an undistinguished doggerel, the work is linguistically interesting. The eleven lines printed here express an oft repeated sentiment.

Þus com   lo engelond in to normandies hond
Thus came, lo, England   into   Normandy's hand,

& þe normans ne couþe speke þo bote hor owe speche
and the Normans   could speak then only their own speech,

& speke french as hii dude atom   & hor children   dude also teche
and spoke French as they did   at home and their children [they] did   also teach,

So þat heiemen of þis lond þat of hor blod come
so that nobles   of this land, who of their blood come,

Holdeþ alle þulke   speche þat hii of   hom nome
keep   all that same speech that they from them took.[10]

Vor bote   a man conne frenss me telþ of him lute
For unless a man knows French, one accounts him little.

Ac lowe   men holdeþ to engliss & to hor owe speche ȝute
But humble men hold   to English and to their own speech yet.

Ich wene   þer ne beþ in al þe world contreyes none
I   believe there are in all the world countries none

Þat   ne holdeþ to hor owe speche bote engelond one
that [do] not hold   to their own speech but England   alone;

Ac wel me wot uor to conne boþe wel it is
but well one knows, to know both, well it is;[11]

Vor þe more þat a mon can   þe more wurþe he is.
for the more that a man knows, the more worth he is.

THE ANCRENE RIWLE

The *Ancrene Riwle* (rule for anchoresses) is a guide to the religious life written for three sisters of good family, who had determined to retire from the world and to lead lives of holy

10 That is, 'which they inherited from them.'
11 That is, 'but it is well-known that it is good to know both.'

solitude. The book gives them advice about their devotions, about moral questions, temptations, penance, and about numerous small domestic matters. The subject is hardly a promising one, but the treatment is so refreshingly unorthodox that readers continue to discover the *Riwle* with pleasure and surprise. The selection printed here is based on James Morton's *The Ancren Riwle* (London, 1853); more recent editions have been published by the Early English Text Society. In West Midland dialect, it was composed probably in the late twelfth century.

Eue heold ine parais   longe tale mid te neddre, and told hire   al þat lescun þat
Eve held in paradise [a] long talk with the serpent, and told him[12] all that lesson that

God hire hefde ilered, and Adam, of þen epple; and so þe ueond þurh   hire word,
God her had taught and Adam of the apple; and so the fiend through her words

understond anonriht hire wocnesse, and ivond   wei touward hire of hire uorlorenesse.
understood at once her weakness and found [a] way toward her for her ruin.

Vre lefdi, Seinte Marie, dude al anoðer wise: ne tolde heo þen engle none tale; auh askede
Our lady, Saint Mary, did all another way: told she the angel no   tale, but asked

him   þing scheortliche þat heo   ne kuðe. Ye, mine leoue sustren, uoleweð ure
him [the] thing briefly   that she [did] not know. Ye, my dear sisters, follow   our

lefdi and nout þe kakele Eue. Vorþi   ancre,   hwat se heo beo, alse muchel ase
lady and not the cackling Eve. Therefore [an] anchoress, what so she be, as   much as

heo euer con and mei, holde   hire   stille: nabbe heo   nout henne kunde. Þe
she ever can and may, [should] keep her[self] still: [let]   her have not [a] hen's nature. The

hen hwon heo haueð ileid, ne con buten kakelen. And hwat biyit heo þerof?   Kumeð þe
hen when she has   laid, cannot but   cackle. And what gets she from that? Comes the

coue   anonriht and reueð hire   hire eiren, and fret   al þat of hwat heo schulde
chough at once and robs her [of] her eggs and devours all that from which she should

uorð bringen hire cwike briddes: and riht also þe luðere coue   deouel   berð awei
bring forth   her live birds; and just so the evil   chough, [the] devil, bears away

urom þe kakelinde ancren, and uorswoluweð al þat god þat heo istreoned   habbeð,
from the cackling anchoress and swallows up all that good that she has brought forth,

þat schulden ase briddes beren ham   up touward heouene, yif hit nere   icakeled.
that should   as birds bear them[selves] up toward heaven, if it were not cackled.[13]

Þe wreche peoddare more noise he makeð to yeien his sope, þen a riche mercer
The wretched peddler more noise he makes to hawk his soap, than a rich mercer [does for]

al his deorewurðe ware. To sum gostliche monne þat ye beoð strusti uppen ase ye
all his expensive   wares. Of some spiritual man   that ye are trustful upon as ye

muwen beon of hit, god is   þat ye asken   red, and salue þat he teche ou
may   be   of it,[14] good is [it] that ye ask [for] advice and remedy that he teach you

to yeines fondunges, and ine schrifte   scheaweð him gif he wule iheren ower greste, and
against   temptations, and in confession show   him, if he will hear, your greatest and

[12] Literally, 'her'; a survival of grammatical gender from Old English, in which adders were feminine.
[13] That is, 'if it had not been for the cackling.'
[14] That is, 'in such matters.'

ower lodlukeste   sunnen; uor þi þat him areowe   ou;   and þurh   þe bireaunesse
your most loathsome sins   in order that it may pity him you[15] *and through the pity*

crie   Crist inwarliche merci   uor ou, and habbe ou ine munde, and in his bonen.
cry [to] Christ inwardly   [for] mercy for you and have   you in   mind   and in his prayers.

"Auh witeð ou and beoð iwarre," he seið, ure Louerd, "uor monie cumeð   to ou
"But know you and beware,"   he said, our Lord,   "for many [will] come to you

ischrud mid lombes fleose, and beoð wode wulues." Worldliche men ileueð lut;   religuise
clothed with lamb's fleece, and are   mad wolves." Worldly   men believe little; religious

yet lesse. Ne wilnie ye nout to muchel hore kuðlechunge. Eue wiðute drede spec mit
still less.[16] *Nor desire ye not   too much   their acquaintance. Eve without dread spoke with*

te   neddre. Vre lefdi was of drede of Gabrieles speche.
the serpent. Our lady was afraid   of Gabriel's speech.

THE FORMER AGE

Chaucer, like King Alfred before him, made a translation of Boethius's *Consolation of Philosophy*.[17] Compare his version of Book 2, Meter 5, with the Old English one given in Chapter 5. The parenthesized material is explanatory comment rather than translation of the original. For a modern translation see the footnote on pages 197-98.

Blysful was þe first age of men. Þei helden hem apaied [content] wiþ þe metes þat þe trewe erþes brouȝten furþe. Þei ne destroyed ne desceyued not hem self wiþ outerage [excess]. Þei weren wont lyȝtly to slaken her hunger at euene wiþ acornes of okes. Þei ne couþe nat medle þe ȝift of bacus to þe clere hony (þat is to seyn, þei couþe make no piment of clarre), ne þei couþe nat medle þe briȝt flies of þe contre of siriens wiþ þe venym of tirie (þis is to seyne, þei couþe nat dien white flies of sirien contre wiþ þe blode of a manar shelfysshe þat men fynden in tyrie, wiþ whiche blode men deien purper). Þei slepen holesom slepes vpon þe gras, and dronken of þe rynnyng watres, *and* laien vndir þe shadowe of þe heyȝe pyne trees. Ne no gest ne no straunger karf [sailed] ȝit þe heye see wiþ oores or wiþ shippes, ne þei ne hadden seyne ȝitte none newe strondes to leden merchaundyse in to dyuerse contres. Þo weren þe cruel clariouns ful whist [quiet] *and* ful stille, ne blode yshed by egre hate ne hadde nat deied ȝit armurers, for wherto or whiche woodenesse of enmys wolde first moeuen armes, whan þei seien cruel woundes ne none medes ben of blood yshad. I wolde þat oure tymes sholde turne aȝeyne to þe oolde maneres. But þe anguissous loue of hauyng brenneþ in folke moore cruely þan þe fijr of þe Mountaigne of Ethna þat euer brenneþ. Allas what was he þat first dalf [dug] vp þe gobets or þe weyȝtys of gold couered vndir erþe, *and* þe precious stones þat wolden han ben hid, he dalf vp precious perils (þat is to seyne þat he þat hem first vp dalf, he dalf vp a precious peril, for-whi, for þe preciousnesse of swyche haþ many man ben in peril).

JOHN OF TREVISA'S POLYCHRONICON

The *Polychronicon*, written in Latin by Ralph Higden and translated into English in the 1380's by John of Trevisa, is a compendium of universal history. It begins with a geographical

[15] That is, 'he may pity you'; an impersonal construction.
[16] That is, 'Believe worldly men' and so forth; the construction is a command, not a statement.
[17] Richard Morris, ed. (EETS ES 5; London, 1868).

survey of the known world and traces human history from the creation to the fourteenth century.

The following selection concerning the languages of the British Isles is Chapter 59 of Book I. Trevisa sometimes felt it necessary to correct his source; his additions are indicated by parentheses. The complete work has been edited by Churchill Babington, *Polychronicon Ranulphi Higden Monachi Cestrensis; together with the English Translations of John Trevisa and of an Unknown Writer of the Fifteenth Century* (London, 1869).

As it is i-knowe how meny manere   peple beeþ in þis ilond, þere beeþ also so many
As it is known   how many kinds [of] people are   in this island, there are   also as many

dyuers longages and tonges; noþeles   Walsche men and Scottes, þat beeþ nouȝt
diverse languages and tongues; nevertheless Welshmen   and Scots,   who are not

i-medled wiþ oþer naciouns, holdeþ wel nyh   hir firste   longage and speche; but
mixed   with other nations,   keep   very nearly their original language and speech; except

ȝif the Scottes þat were somtyme confederat and wonede wiþ þe Pictes drawe
that the Scots   that were formerly confederate and dwelt   with the Picts follow

somwhat after hir   speche; but þe Flemmynges þat woneþ in þe weste side of Wales
somewhat   their speech; but the Flemings   that dwell in the west   part of Wales

haueþ i-left her   straunge speche and spekeþ Saxonliche i-now. Also Englische men, þey
have   left their foreign speech and speak Saxonly   enough. Also Englishmen,   they

hadde from the bygynnynge þre   manere   speche, norþerne, sowþerne, and middel speche
had   from the beginning   three kinds [of] speech, northern, southern,   and midland speech

in þe myddel of þe lond, as þey come of   þre   manere   peple of Germania,
in the middle of the land, as they came from three kinds [of] people of Germania;

noþeles   by comyxtioun and mellynge firste wiþ Danes and afterward wiþ Normans, in
nevertheless by mixture   and mingling first with Danes and afterward with Normans, in

meny   þe contray longage is apayred, and som vseþ strong wlafferynge, chiterynge,
many [ways] the native   language is debased and some use   harsh stammering, chattering,

harrynge, and garrynge grisbayting.   This apayrynge of þe burþe tunge is bycause of
snarling, and scolding gnashing of teeth. This abasement of the birth-tongue is because of

tweie þinges; oon is for children in scole aȝenst þe vsage and manere of alle oþere
two   things; one is that children in school against the usage and custom of all other

naciouns beeþ compelled for to leue hire owne langage, and for to construe hir   lessouns
nations   are compelled   to leave their own language and   to construe their lessons

and here þynges in Frensche, and so þey haueþ seþ þe Normans come first in to
and their subjects in French,   and so they have   since the Normans came first into

Engelond. Also gentil men children beeþ i-tauȝt to speke Frensche from þe tyme þat þey
England.   Also gentlemen's children are   taught to speak French   from the time that they

beeþ i-rokked in here cradel, and kunneþ   speke and playe wiþ a childes broche; and
are rocked   in their cradle and are able to speak and play with a child's bauble; and

vplondisshe men wil likne hym self to gentil men, and fondeþ wiþ greet besynesse for to
country men will liken himself[18] *to gentlemen and strive with great labor to*

speke Frensce, for to be i-tolde of. (Þis manere was moche i-vsed
speak French in order to be taken account of.[19] *(This practice was much followed*

to for firste deth and is siþþe sumdel i-chaunged; for Iohn Cornwaile, a maister
before [the] first plague and is since somewhat changed; for John Cornwall, a teacher

of grammer, chaunged þe lore in gramer scole and construccioun of Frensche
of grammar, changed the instruction in grammar school and interpretation from French

in to Englische; and Richard Pencriche lerned þe manere techynge of hym and
into English;[20] *and Richard Pencritch learned the manner [of] teaching from him and*

oþere men of Pencrich; so þat now, þe ȝere of oure Lorde a þowsand þre hundred
other men from Pencritch so that now, the year of our Lord a thousand three hundred

and foure score and fyue, and of þe secounde kyng Richard after þe conquest nyne, in alle
and four score and five, and of the second King Richard after the conquest nine, in all

þe gramere scoles of Engelond, children leueþ Frensche and construeþ and lerneþ an
the grammar schools of England children leave French and interpret and learn in

Englische, and haueþ þerby auauntage in oon side and disauauntage in anoþer
English and have thereby [an] advantage in one way and [a] disadvantage in another

side; here auauntage is, þat þey lerneþ her gramer in lasse tyme þan children were
way; their advantage is that they learn their grammar in less time than children were

i-woned to doo; disauauntage is þat now children of gramer scole conneþ na
accustomed to do; [the] disadvantage is that now children in grammar school know no

more Frensche þan can hir lift heele, and þat is harme for hem and þey schulle
more French than knows their left heel, and that is harm[ful] for them if they shall

passe þe see and trauaille in straunge landes and in many oþer places. Also gentil men
cross the sea and travel in foreign lands and in many other places. Also gentlemen

haueþ now moche i-left for to teche here children Frensche.) Hit semeþ a greet wonder
have now much neglected to teach their children French.) It seems a great wonder

how Englische, þat is þe burþe tonge of Englisshe men and her owne langage and
that English, which is the birth-tongue of Englishmen and their own language and

tonge, is so dyuerse of sown in þis oon ilond, and þe langage of Normandie is
tongue, is so diverse in sound in this one island, and the language of Normandy is [a]

comlynge of anoþer londe, and hath oon manere soun among alle men þat spekeþ hit
newcomer from another land, and has one kind [of] sound among all men that speak it

ariȝt in Engelond. (Neuerþeles þere is as many dyuers manere Frensche in þe
properly in England. (Nevertheless there are as many diverse kinds [of] French in the

[18] That is, 'wish to make themselves like.'
[19] That is, 'in order to be thought important.'
[20] Whereas French had been the language in which classes were held and into which school children translated their Latin, English was becoming the language of instruction. The change was doubtlessly regarded as a milestone in progressive education.

reem of Fraunce as is   dyuers manere   Englische in þe reem of Engelond.) Also of þe
realm of France   as are diverse kinds [of] English   in the realm of England.)   Also of the

forsaide Saxon tonge   þat   is i-deled aþre,   and is abide scarsliche wiþ   fewe
aforesaid Saxon tongue, which is divided in three and remains scarcely   among [a] few

vplondisshe men is   greet wonder; for men of þe est wiþ men of þe west, as it
rustic   men [there] is great wonder; for men of the east with men of the west, as it

were vndir þe same partie of heuene, acordeþ more in sownynge of speche þan men of þe
were under the same part of heaven, agree   more in pronunciation   than men of the

norþ wiþ men of þe souþ; þerfore it is þat Mercii,   þat beeþ men of myddel Engelond,
north with men of the south; therefore it is that Mercians, who are   men of middle England,

as it were parteners of þe endes,   vnderstondeþ bettre þe side   langages, norþerne
as it were partners of the extremes, understand   better the adjacent languages, northern

and souþerne, þan norþerne and souþerne vnderstondeþ eiþer oþer. Al þe longage of þe
and southern, than northern and southern understand   each other. All the language of the

Norþhumbres, and specialliche at ȝork, is so scharp, slitting, and frotynge and vnschape,
Northumbrians, and especially   at York, is so shrill,   cutting, and grating   and ill-formed,

þat we souþerne men may þat longage vnneþe vnderstonde. I trowe þat þat is bycause
that we southern men can that language barely understand.   I believe that that is because

þat þey beeþ nyh to straunge men and naciouns þat spekeþ strongliche, and also
they are near to foreign men and nations   that speak harshly   and also

bycause þat þe kynges of Engelond woneþ alwey fer from þat cuntrey; for þey beeþ
because   the kings of England dwell always far from that country; for they are

more i-torned to þe souþ contray, and ȝif þey gooþ to þe norþ contray þey gooþ wiþ
more turned to the south country, and if they go   to the north country, they go   with

greet help and strengþe. Þe cause why þey beeþ more in þe souþ contrey þan in þe
great force and strength. The cause that they are more in the south country than in the

norþ, is for hit may be   better corne londe, more peple, more noble citees, and more
north is that it may have better grain land, more people, more noble cities, and more

profitable hauenes.
profitable harbors.

ANOTHER ENGLISH POLYCHRONICON

Ralph Higden's *Polychronicon* was translated again in the mid-fifteenth century. This second translation, which might be called late Middle English or early Modern English, will illustrate the considerable changes in the language wrought by the intervening years. The passage reprinted here from Babington's edition corresponds to the earlier translation but of course lacks Trevisa's comments. In some ways, it corresponds rather more closely to the Latin original.

Hit may be schewede clerely to the wytte that there were so mony diuersites of langages in that londe as were diuersites of nacions. But Scottes and men of Wales kepe theire propre langage, as men inpermixte with other naciones; but perauenture Scottes haue taken somme parte in theire communicacion of the langage of Pictes, with whom thei dwellede somme tyme, and were confederate with theyme. Men of Flaundres that inhabite the weste partes of Wales levenge the speche of barbre speke after the Saxones. And thauȝhe men of Englonde hade in the begynnenge a langage tripartite, as of the sowthe parte of Englond, of the myddelle parte of Englonde, and of the northe parte of Englonde, procedenge as of thre peple of Germanye, bor-owe moche in theire speche now, thro the commixtion with the Danes and after that with the Normannes. The corrupcion of that natife langage is causede moche of ij. thynges, that is to say, childer sette to schole after the commenge of Normannes in to Englonde were compellede to constru in Frenche ageyne the consuetude of oþer naciones. In so moche that the childer of nowble men, after that thei were taken from the cradelle, were sette to lerne the speche of Frenche men. Wherefore churles seenge that, willenge to be like to theyme, laborede to speke Frenche with alle theire myȝhte. Where hit is to be hade in meruayle that the propur langage of Englische men scholde be made so diuerse in oon lytelle yle in pronunciacion, sythe the langage of Normannes is oon and vniuocate allemoste amonge theyme alle. But as of the tripartite langage of Saxones, whiche remaynethe now but amonge fewe men, the weste men of Englonde sownde and acorde more with the men of the este of that londe as vnder the same clyme of heuyn, then the men of the northe with men of the sowthe. Wherefore hit is that Englishe men of þe Marches of the mydelle partes of Englonde, takenge as by participacion the nature of bothe extremities, vnderstonde the langages collateralle arthike and anthartike better then the extremites vnderstonde theyme selfe to geder. Alle the langage of men of Northumbrelonde, and specially in Yorke, sowndethe so that men of the sowthe cuntre may vnnethe vnderstonde the langage of theyme, whiche thynge may be causede for the nye langage of men of barbre to theyme, and also for the grete distaunce of kynges of Englonde from hyt, whiche vse moste the southe partes of that londe, returnenge not in to the costes of the northe but with a grete multitude. Also an other cause may be assignede, for the sowthe partes be more habundante in fertilite then the northe partes, moo peple in nowmbre, hauenge also more plesaunte portes.

7

The Modern English Period to 1800:
Sounds and Spellings

7.1 QUESTIONS FOR REVIEW AND DISCUSSION

1. Define the following terms:

Great Vowel Shift	rising and falling diphthongs	inverse spelling
apocopation	hypercorrect pronunciation	assibilation

2. Explain the significance of the following typographical devices sometimes used in early Modern English printing: the letter *y* with a small superscript *e*, a line or tilde over a vowel, final *e*'s other than those used to show length of the preceding vowel, the distinction between the letters *u* and *v*.

3. Compare the vowel system of Middle English with that of early Modern English as they are shown in the vowel charts of Chapter 6 and of this chapter. What additions, losses, or rearrangements took place between the two periods?

4. Make a similar comparison of the consonant system of Middle English with that of Modern English as it is described in Chapter 2.

5. From what kinds of evidence do we gain our knowledge of the pronunciation of earlier periods?

6. The phonetic transcription from *1 Henry IV* on pages 193–94 of Pyles's *Origins and Development* records a pronunciation that is somewhat earlier than the one described in the following exercises. Read it aloud and note which sounds differ from your own pronunciation. Explain the cause of as many of the differences as you can.

7.2 THE EARLY MODERN ENGLISH VOWELS

Like those of all other historical periods, speakers of early Modern English employed no single, uniform pronunciation. Sounds varied from place to place and from social group to social group. Moreover, they continued to change during the period. Only with these important qualifications can we speak of a typical early Modern English phonology. Such a typical sound system in the later seventeenth century might have included the vowels listed at the top of page 169.

By the early Modern period, spelling had reached its present state of complexity although it differed from contemporary practice in many details. The common spellings listed below are only samples; additional spellings can be cited for every vowel. The spellings *a-e, e-e, i-e, o-e, u-e* represent the use of silent *e* after a consonant as in *name, mete, fine, cope, tune.*

COMMON SPELLING	SOUND	COMMON SPELLING	SOUND	COMMON SPELLING	SOUND
a	[æ]	a, al	[ǣ]	ir, ur, er, ear	[ər]
e, ea	[ɛ]	a, a-e, ay, ai, ey, ei	[ɛ̄] or [ē][1]	oy, oi	[ɔɪ]
		ea, e-e	[ē]	i, i-e, ie, y, oy, oi	[əɪ] or [aɪ][1]
i, y	[ɪ]	e, ee, e-e, ie, ea	[ī]	ow, ou	[əʊ] or [aʊ][1]
o	[ɔ] or [ɑ]	aw, au, a, al, ough, o	[ɔ̄]	ew, eu, ue, u-e, u	[jū]
u, o	[ə]	oa, o, o-e, oe, ow, ou, ol	[ō]		
u, oo	[ʊ]	oo, o, oe	[ū]		

Complete the following charts by filling in the phonetic symbols listed above to show the articulation of early Modern English vowels.

SIMPLE VOWELS

		FRONT	BACK— UNROUNDED	BACK— ROUNDED
HIGH	long		—	
	short			
MID	long		—	
	short			—
LOW	long		—	
	short			

DIPHTHONGS

Classify the diphthongs [ɔɪ], [aɪ], and [aʊ], and the sequence [jū] according to the position of their initial element. The arrows indicate the direction of the second element in the diphthong.

	FRONT	CENTRAL	BACK
HIGH	→		
MID			
LOW		↖ ↗	↖

[1] The second pronunciation was in existence by the seventeenth century, although as Pyles observes in *Origins and Development*, pp. 184–85, it did not become normal in Standard English until the eighteenth century.

Complete the following chart to show (1) the phonetic symbols for the Middle English sounds from which the early Modern English vowels developed and (2) the phonetic symbol for the current English vowel. This information can be found in Pyles's *Origins and Development* and in the key words, the spellings of which have varied only slightly since Middle English times.

(1) MIDDLE ENGLISH SOUNDS	EARLY MODERN ENGLISH VOWEL	(2) CURRENT ENGLISH VOWEL	KEY WORDS
	[æ]		lamp, fat, back, flax, sad
	[ǣ]		staff, glass, path half, salve, psalm [2]
	[ɛ]		edge, bless, bed, set head, death, deaf
	[ɛ̄] or [ē]		lady, lane, face, take, name day, tail, they, vein
	[ē]		great, steak, break, yea [3] east, mean, peace, bead, theme [3]
	[ɪ]		in, sit, lid, king, hill
	[ī]		she, sweet, these, grief east, mean, peace, bead, theme [3]
	[ə] or [ɑ] [4]		mock, lodge, odd, pot, fop
	[ɔ̄]		law, claw, aught, cause call, hall, small, wall talk, walk, chalk, stalk brought, ought, sought soft, lost, cloth, cross dog, log, frog, bog
	[ō]		boat, throat, go, home, toe snow, soul, grow, dough folk, yolk, holm
	[ʊ]		full, pull, bull, put, push foot, good, wood, look, hook [5]
	[ū]		goose, moon, boot, do, shoe
	[ə]		but, sun, son, come

[2] Current English has more than one vowel in these words because the early Modern sound has developed differently in different dialects.

[3] In the standard dialect of early Modern English, these words were pronounced with [ē]; but in some nonstandard regional or social dialects, with [ī]. During the eighteenth century, speakers of the nonstandard [ī]-dialects began to set the fashion for pronunciation. The standard changed, and as a result the older elegant pronunciation with [ē] was generally displaced. Except for dialects like Irish where it is more common, the [ē] survives in only a handful of words. See Pyles, pp. 185–86.

[4] In various dialects.

[5] On the fluctuation of [ū], [ʊ], and [ə], see Pyles, p. 184.

(1) MIDDLE ENGLISH SOUNDS	EARLY MODERN ENGLISH VOWEL	(2) CURRENT ENGLISH VOWEL	KEY WORDS
	[ər]		stir, bird, dirt spur, burn, hurt
	[ɔɪ]		joy, boy, noise join, boil, point, spoil[6]
	[əɪ] or [aɪ]		child, hide, mice, die, why join, boil, point, spoil[6]
	[əʊ] or [aʊ]		mouse, brow, town, pound
	[jū]		few, cue, hue, mute deuce, new, tune, lewd

7.3 THE GREAT VOWEL SHIFT

Although a good many changes of various kinds affected the English vowel system as it developed from Middle to Modern English, those changes to which the long vowels were subject are especially worthy of note. The seven Middle English long vowels underwent a remarkably systematic shift in their place of articulation, a shift for which there was no cause that we can discover.

1. Show the changes effected by the Great Vowel Shift by writing the appropriate phonetic symbols in the brackets:

   [   ] > [   ] as in *mice*: ME [mīs] > ModE [   ]
   [   ] > [   ] as in *mouse*: ME [mūs] > ModE [   ]
   [   ] > [   ] as in *geese*: ME [gēs] > ModE [   ]
   [   ] > [   ] as in *goose*: ME [gōs] > ModE [   ]
   [   ] > [   ] as in *break*: ME [brɛ̄kən] > ModE [   ]
   [   ] > [   ] as in *broke*: ME [brɔ̄kən] > ModE [   ]
   [   ] > [   ] as in *name*: ME [nāmə] > ModE [   ]

2. The following are phonetic transcriptions of Middle English words. Write their present-day developments (1) in phonetic transcription and (2) in normal orthography.

	CURRENT SOUND	CURRENT SPELLING		CURRENT SOUND	CURRENT SPELLING
[bɔ̄st	_____	_____	mīn	_____	_____
brōd	_____	_____	pās	_____	_____
dēm	_____	_____	pōl	_____	_____
grɛ̄t	_____	_____	pɔ̄l	_____	_____
gūn	_____	_____	rēd	_____	_____
jɛ̄	_____	_____	rɔ̄st	_____	_____
kās	_____	_____	rōst	_____	_____
līs	_____	_____	sāf	_____	_____
lūd	_____	_____	ūt	_____	_____
mēt	_____	_____	wīd]	_____	_____

6 For the development of these words, see Pyles, p. 187.

7.4 *THE GREAT VOWEL SHIFT: PHONETIC FEATURES*

By the end of the Middle English period a system of long vowels had developed whose phonetic features can be described as follows:

	− back	+ back	
		− rounded	+ rounded
+ high − low	ī		ū
− high − low	ē		ō
− high + low	ɛ̄	ā	ɔ̄

These vowels underwent a series of phonetic changes whose exact nature we cannot be sure of. A description of the changes is given by Pyles in *Origins and Development*, pages 183–88. The Great Vowel Shift can also be described as having taken place in a series of steps somewhat like the following:

1a. ī > īy,   ū > ūw
1b. īy > ɨy,   ūw > ɨw

That is, (a) each of the high vowels was diphthongized by developing a following semivowel; and (b) the vowel itself was centralized (or, in terms of the features, made unrounded and back—the phonetic symbol [ɨ] can be used for such a vowel). Although the formal statement of the rule describing this change is of no intrinsic importance, it will be given here and also for the changes below without further comment. Unless the reader has a special interest in such matters, he can ignore the formal rules:

$$\begin{bmatrix} +\text{ high} \\ \alpha \text{ back} \end{bmatrix} \rightarrow \begin{bmatrix} -\text{ rounded} \\ +\text{ back} \end{bmatrix} \begin{bmatrix} -\text{ syllabic} \\ \alpha \text{ back} \end{bmatrix}$$

2a. ɨy > ə̄y,   ɨw > ə̄w
2b. ē > ī,   ō > ū

That is, (a) the high vowels in the diphthongs were lowered to mid vowels; and (b) the mid vowels were raised to the high region. In effect, the high and mid vowels simply reversed height, each moving onto the other's level:

$$\begin{bmatrix} \alpha \text{ high} \\ -\text{ low} \end{bmatrix} \rightarrow [-\ \alpha \text{ high}]$$

3. ā > ɛ̄

That is, the vowel [ā] fronted, thus falling together with [ɛ̄]:

$$\begin{bmatrix} +\text{ back} \\ -\text{ rounded} \\ +\text{ low} \end{bmatrix} \rightarrow [-\text{ back}]$$

4a. $\bar{\mathrm{ə}}y > \bar{a}y$, $\bar{\mathrm{ə}}w > \bar{a}w$
4b. $\bar{ɛ} > \bar{e}$, $\bar{ɔ} > \bar{o}$

That is, (a) the mid vowels in the diphthongs were made low vowels; and (b) the low vowels were raised to the mid region. In effect, the mid and low vowels reversed height by moving onto each other's level:

$$\begin{bmatrix} - \text{ high} \\ \alpha \text{ low} \end{bmatrix} \rightarrow [- \alpha \text{ low}]$$

As a result of these changes, a new distribution of vowels among the phonetic features emerged. Complete the following chart to show it:

	− back	+ back	
		− rounded	+ rounded
+ high − low			
− high − low			
− high + low			

Each of the sets below represents the long vowel system at some stage in the Great Vowel Shift. Number them 1 through 4 according to their chronological order as products of the four rules given above.

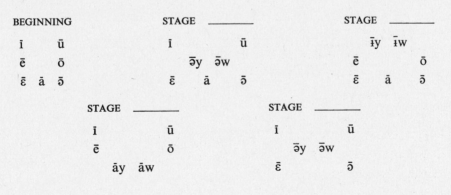

BEGINNING

ī ū
ē ō
ɛ̄ ā ɔ̄

STAGE _____

ī   ū
   ə̄y ə̄w
ɛ̄   ā   ɔ̄

STAGE _____

      ɨ̄y ɨ̄w
ē   ō
ɛ̄   ā   ɔ̄

STAGE _____

ī   ū
ē   ō
   āy āw

STAGE _____

ī   ū
   ə̄y ə̄w
ɛ̄   ɔ̄

7.5 MINOR VOWEL CHANGES

1. The following words contained the vowel [a] in Middle English.

   lap, crab, at, add, back, bag
   staff, craft, path, bath, glass, class
   ash, crash, flash, rash
   all, call, hall, stall, tall

also, halt, bald, salt

balk, calk (n.), chalk, walk

calf, half, halve, salve

alms, calm, palm, psalm

What vowel developed from Middle English [a] before a stop? _____

before a voiceless fricative? _____

before final [l] or [l] plus a dental?_____

before [l] plus [k] (what happened to the [l])? _____

before [l] plus a labial fricative (what happened to the [l])?_____

before [l] plus a nasal (what happened to the [l])?_____

How do typical British and American usage differ in their developments of [a] in these words?_____
_____
_____

2. The following words contained the vowel [ɔ] in Middle English.

hop, cob, pot, odd, dock

dog, bog, frog, log, hog

soft, off, lost, cross, cloth, moth

boll or bowl, roll, toll, bolt, bolster, folk, yolk

What vowel developed from Middle English [ɔ] before most stops? _____

before the voiced velar stop?_____

before a voiceless fricative? _____

before [l]? _____

How do current British and American usage differ in their developments of this vowel?
_____
_____

3. The following words all had [ʊ] in Middle English.

bud, buck, puff, gull, dull, skull, blush, rush, cut, nut, but, putt, mull

bull, full, pull, bush, push, put

What is the usual development of Middle English [ʊ]?_____

In what environments did it remain unchanged?_____
_____
_____

Which of the words above is an exception to the second generalization? _____
_____

4. The following words contained the vowel [ɛ̄] in standard Middle English.

great, break, steak, yea

sweat, threat, head, bread, death, breath

In the second group of words the long vowel was shortened to [ɛ]. Before what kind of consonants did the shortening occur? _____

Was [ɛ] always shortened before those consonants? Give an example. _____
_____

5. After Middle English [ō] as in *food, good, flood* had changed to [ū] during the Great Vowel Shift, it went on to be shortened in some words like *good* and unrounded in others like *flood*.

The rimes in early Modern English poetry suggest divided usage in the vowels of these words. List some words which still vary between [u] and [ʊ]. _____

_____

6. The following words had [jū] in early Modern English.
   pew, beauty, few, view, mew, cue, argue, hue, ewe
   tune, due, sue, zeugma, new, rue, lute, thew

   In what environments has it been retained, and in what environments has it become [ū]? Name classes of sounds, not individual sounds.
   [jū] retained _____
   [ū] developed _____

7. The following words had in Middle English the sounds indicated at the beginning of each group. Write the phonetic symbols for the modern development of the short vowels before [r]. There is some dialect variation for several of these vowels, as there is also for the long vowels of the next question.

MIDDLE ENGLISH	MODERN ENGLISH	
[ɪr]	_____	spirit, pyramid
	_____	bird, first, shirt, sir
[ʊr]	_____	courage, furrow
	_____	hurt, spur, turn, worth
[ɛr]	_____	merry, very
	_____	person, vermin, clerk, serve
	_____	parson, varmint, Clark, starve
[ar]	_____	marry, narrow
	_____	large, park, sharp, stark
[ɔr]	_____	foreign, sorry
	_____	horse, morn, short

   Describe the environmental conditions which determine the two possible developments of each vowel. (Ignore the *person/parson* difference in answering this question.)
   _____
   _____

   _____

   What pronunciations does the name *Derby* have? Cite any other names you know which have similar alternate pronunciations. _____

   _____

8. The following words had in Middle English the sounds indicated at the beginning of each group. Write the phonetic symbols for the modern development of the long vowels before [r]. You may not pronounce the same vowel in all the words of every group.

MIDDLE ENGLISH	MODERN ENGLISH	
[īr]	_____	desire, mire, fire, hire, iron
[ūr]	_____	our, devour, hour, shower, tower, bower, flour/flower
[ēr]	_____	here, mere, peer, deer, beer, bier, hear, dear, clear

MIDDLE ENGLISH	MODERN ENGLISH	
[ɛ̄r]	_____	near, rear, shear, smear, spear, beard, ear
	_____	pear, swear, tear (v.), wear, bear
[ār]	_____	mare, hare, spare, bare, care, fare, declare, Mary
[ōr]	_____	door, floor, moor, poor
[ɔ̄r]	_____	more, sore, boar, port, hoarse, force, story
[ɪur]	_____	(im)mure, cure, (en)dure
[æɪr]	_____	mayor, their, air, heir, fair, despair

7.6 *THE EARLY MODERN ENGLISH CONSONANTS*

Because the inventory of consonants in early Modern English is identical with that for contemporary English, there is no need for a complete list. The chart from Chapter 2 can serve for the seventeenth century as well as for the twentieth. Here we will be concerned with some of the changes which have affected consonants since Middle English times.

1. Middle English [x] and [ç] were either lost or became [f], depending partly on dialect and partly on the kind of vowel or diphthong which they followed. Modern Standard English has preserved, somewhat haphazardly, the developments characteristic of several dialects.

    Describe the development of the palatovelar fricatives in each of the following groups of words by comparing the Middle English forms given here with the current pronunciation of the words.

    ME [īç]   hīgh, nīgh, thīgh _____
    ME [ɪç]   night, light, right _____
    ME [ūx]   drōughte, plōugh _____
                    rōugh, ynōugh, tōugh _____
    ME [æɪç] eighte, straight _____
    ME [aux] aught, slaughter, taught _____
                    laughen, draught _____
    ME [ɔux] boughte, ought, thoughte _____
                    dough, though _____
                    coughen, trough _____

What effect did the loss of [ç] have on a preceding short vowel? _____

_____

Did it have that effect before or after the operation of the Great Vowel Shift? How can you tell? _____

_____

What effect did the change of [x] to [f] have on a preceding long vowel? _____

_____

Did it have that effect before or after the operation of the Great Vowel Shift? How can you tell? _____

_____

When [aʊx] became [aʊf], what was the subsequent development of the diphthong?

_____

Which of these two sound changes occurred first? How can you tell?
  (1) [x] either became [f] or was lost altogether.
  (2) [ɔu] followed by a consonant became [ɔ̄]; not followed by a consonant, it became [ō].

_____

_____

Which allophone, [ç] or [x], sometimes became [f]? _____
Explain the existence in modern Standard English of a doublet like *enough–enow*.

_____

_____

Look up the etymology of *delight*, *haughty*, and *spright*, and explain the presence of *gh* in their spelling. _____

_____

2. Assibilation is a process of mutual assimilation whereby an alveolar [t], [d], [s], or [z] combines with a following palatal [j] to produce a single alveolopalatal consonant. Assibilation did not occur in all dialects of English or in all positions within a word. For each of the following groups, write the phonetic symbol for the contemporary sound which has developed from the older sequence.

  _____ from [tj] in *stew, tune, Tuesday*
  _____ from [tj] in *future, Christian, fortune*
  _____ from [dj] in *dew, duke, dune, dupe*
  _____ from [dj] in *educate, graduate, soldier*
  _____ from [sj] in *sue, consume, suit*
  _____ from [sj] in *mission, vicious, social*
  _____ from [zj] in *vision, measure, pleasure*

In what position within a word is assibilation most likely to occur? _____

_____

Sure appears to be an exception to that generalization. Can you think of any others?

_____

_____

Explain why [ž] is the rarest of English phonemes and the most limited in the positions in which it occurs. _____

_____

_____

What is the usual pronunciation of these phrases in conversation?

(I'll) hit you. _____
Did you (go)? _____
(I'll) miss you. _____
Where's your (hat)? _____
Supply additional examples of assibilation, either within a word or between words.
[tj]_____
[dj] _____
[sj]_____
[zj] _____

3. In late Middle English or very early Modern English, [g] was lost from the sequence [ŋg] under certain conditions. This loss of [g] is parallel to the earlier loss of [b] in [mb] and the less regular loss of [d] in [nd]. Consider the following examples.

king [kɪŋ]	sling [slɪŋ]	singer [síŋər]
rang [ræŋ]	sting [stɪŋ]	ringer [ríŋər]
sung [səŋ]	thing [θɪŋ]	hanger [hǽŋər]
finger [fíŋgər]	anger [ǽŋgər]	whistling [wíslɪn]
linger [líŋgər]	tangle [tǽŋgəl]	nesting [nɛ́stɪn]
hunger [hə́ŋgər]	language [lǽŋgwɪ̆j]	nothing [nə́θɪn]

What effect did the change of [ŋg] to [ŋ] have upon the phonemic system of English? (Compare *king, rang, sung* with *kin, ran, sun*.) _____

_____

In what position in a word was [g] lost and in what position was it retained? (Ignore *singer, ringer, hanger* in answering this question.) _____

_____

Explain the apparent irregularity in *singer, ringer, hanger*. _____

_____

Under what condition did [ŋg] become [ŋ] and under what condition did it become [n]?

_____

_____

_____

4. In certain positions [l] was lost. Consider the modern pronunciation of the following words. In some of them [l] has always been pronounced; in others it has been lost, but is sometimes restored as a spelling pronunciation. Indicate whether [l] was retained or lost in each group, but disregard spelling pronunciations in reaching your decision.

FROM MIDDLE ENGLISH [al]   FROM MIDDLE ENGLISH [ɔl]

_____	ball, fall, wall, gall	_____	boll, roll, stroll, toll
_____	malt, bald, salt, scald	_____	bolt, molten, bolster
_____	chalk, stalk, talk, walk	_____	folk, yolk
_____	calf, half, calve, halve	_____	holp (dialectal: [hōp])
_____	calm, palm, psalm, alms	_____	holm, Holmes

Describe the phonetic environments in which [l] was lost. _____

_____

_____

_____

5. Look up the etymology of *cuss* and describe the sound change which has affected the word.

_____

_____

What is the traditional pronunciation of *worsted*?_____
What other words are examples of this change? _____

_____

6. Compare the earlier forms of *groin* and *woodbine* with those of *to pound* and *horehound*.

What consonant changes have occurred in these words? _____

_____

If you are familiar with any words that show a similar fluctuation in current English, cite them. _____

_____

7. Explain the *b* in the spellings of *crumb, numb,* and *thumb* by comparing these words with *dumb* and *plumb*. _____

_____

_____

8. In some of the following words the pronunciation with [h] is the result of the spelling rather than a historical sound development. Write *S* before the words that have such a spelling pronunciation, and *H* before the words that had [h] historically.

_____ habit   _____ honey   _____ humble

_____ health   _____ hospital   _____ humor

_____ heart   _____ host

_____ herb   _____ hue

9. In some of the following words the pronunciation with [θ] is the result of the spelling rather than a historical sound development. Write *S* before the words that have a such spelling pronunciation and *H* before the words that had [θ] historically.

_____ apothecary   _____ hearth   _____ thing

_____ authority   _____ panther   _____ throng

_____ breath   _____ theater

_____ catholic   _____ theme

10. Changes in pronunciation do not happen instantaneously or uniformly for all speakers of a language. Helge Kökeritz has suggested that *gn* and *kn*, which were certainly [gn] and [kn] for Chaucer, may have been pronounced simply [n] about 1600.[7] He bases his conclusion partly on the evidence of puns in Shakespeare's plays. Another kind of evidence is the testimony of the orthoëpists. Here are statements from three such writers on pronunciation during the century following Shakespeare.

Simon Daines, Orthoepia Anglicana (1640)[8]

Gnat, gnaw, gne, A-gnes, gnit, gno, gnu. *G* in this combination inclines to the force of *N*. **Knub, knuckle.** Pronounce *kn*, as the Latines doe their **Cn**, a little in the nose, or upper palat.

The Writing Scholar's Companion (1695)[9]

(g) Must be written (in these words) though it is not sounded . . . . Nor can (g) well be sounded in *gnaw, gnash, gnat*.

(k) Cannot well be sounded in such Words as begin with (kn), as *knife, knot, know,* &c.

John Jones, Practical Phonography (1701)[10]

When is the *Sound* of *n written gn*? Wherein the *g* is not sounded, as it is not also in *gnar, gnarl, gnash, gnat, gnaw, gnibble, gnomon*.

[7] *Shakespeare's Pronunciation* (New Haven, Conn., 1953), p. 304 f.
[8] M. Rösler and R. Brotanek, eds. (Halle, Germany, 1908).
[9] Eilert Ekwall, ed. (Halle, Germany, 1911).
[10] Eilert Ekwall, ed. (Halle, Germany, 1907).

When is the *Sound* of *n* written *kn*? When it may be sounded *kn*, as in *knack, knacker, knag, knap, knapple, knapsack* . . . .

When is the *Sound* of *k* written *k*? Always before *n* except in *Cnidos*.

Such comments are sometimes difficult to interpret, but what would you conclude from these three sources about the sound sequences [gn] and [kn] in the seventeenth century?

_____

_____

_____

_____

_____

7.7 STRESS

What stress does the meter suggest for the italicized words in these passages from Shakespeare? Circle the stressed syllables.

Oh good old man, how well in thee appeares
The constant seruice of the *antique* world,
When seruice sweate for dutie, not for meede.　　(*As You Like It*, II.iv)

　　　　　　　. . . but how the feare of vs
May *Ciment* their diuisions, and binde vp
The petty difference, we yet not know.　　(*Antony and Cleopatra*, II.i)

No, not to be so odde, and from all fashions,
As Beatrice is, cannot be *commendable*,
But who dare tell her so?　　(*Much Ado About Nothing*, III.i)

Therefore take with thee my most greeuous Curse,
Which in the day of Battell tyre thee more
Then all the *compleat* Armour that thou wear'st.　　(*Richard III*, IV.iii)

No, I protest, I know not the *contents*.　　(*As You Like It*, IV.iii)

Care is no cure, but rather *corrosive*,
For things that are not to be remedy'd.　　(*1 Henry VI*, III.iii)

The nimble-footed Mad-Cap, Prince of Wales,
And his *Cumrades*, that daft [thrust] the World aside.　　(*1 Henry VI*, IV.i)

And I will kisse thy *detestable* bones.　　(*King John*, III.iii)

When I was dry with Rage, and *extreame* Toyle,
Breathlesse, and Faint, leaning vpon my Sword,
Came there a certaine Lord, neat and trimly drest.　　(*1 Henry IV*, I.iii)

　　　　　　　. . . I
Do come with words, as *medicinall*, as true.　　(*The Winter's Tale*, II.iii)

If he outliue the enuy of this day,
England did neuer owe so sweet a hope,
So much *misconstrued* in his Wantonnesse.　　(*1 Henry IV*, V.ii)

I [aye], and peruersly, she *perseuers* so.　　(*The Two Gentlemen of Verona*, III.ii)

For what aduancement may I hope from thee,
That no *Reuennew* [revenue] hast, but thy good spirits
To feed & cloath thee.   (*Hamlet*, III.ii)

Take heed you dally not before your King,
Lest he that is the *supreme* King of Kings
Confound your hidden falshood.   (*Richard III*, II.i)

7.8   *THE DEVELOPMENT OF THE MODERN VOWELS: A REVIEW*

Trace the chief sources of the present-day vowels by adding the phonetic symbols appropriate
to the key words in the following chart. The vowel [i] has been done as a sample. Because
there is dialect variation in current English as well as in the older periods, all the key words
in the first column for a given vowel may not have the same phoneme in your speech. Note any
such variations.

MODERN ENGLISH		MIDDLE ENGLISH		OLD ENGLISH	
[i]	geese	[ē]	gees	[ē]	gēs
	sleep		sleep	[ē], [æ]	slēp (WS slǣp)
	deep		deep	[ēə]	dēop
	field		feeld	[ɛ] before *ld*	feld
	beetle		betel	[ɪ] in open syllable	bitula
	evil		evil	[y] in open syllable	yvel
	clean	[ē]; in most dialects and earlier in all dialects: [ɛ̄]	clene	[ǣ]	clǣne
	leaf		leef	[ǣə]	lēaf
	steal		stelen	[ɛ] in open syllable	stelan
	mead		mede	[ɛə] in open syllable	meodu
[e]	tale		tale		talu
	acre		aker		æcer
	day		day		dæġ
	way		wey		weġ

MODERN ENGLISH	MIDDLE ENGLISH	OLD ENGLISH
[ē] eight	eighte	ehta (WS eahta)
neigh	neyen	hnǣġan
great	greet	grēat
break	breken	brecan
[o] boat	boot	bāt
old	oold	ald (WS eald)
throat	throte	þrote
snow	snow	snāw
own	owen	āgen
dough	dough	dāh
grow	growen	grōwan
bow	bowe	boga
folk	folk	folc
[u] goose	goos	gōs
Gould	goold	gold
[(j)u] new	newe	nīwe
knew	knew	cnēow
few	fewe	fēawe
lewd	lewede	lǣwede
[aɪ] wife	wyf	wīf
mice	mys	mȳs
child	child	ċild
bridle	bridel	briġdel
night	night	niht
thigh	thigh	þēh (WS þēoh)
high	high	hēh (WS hēah)
lie	lien	lēġan (WS lēogan)
eye	ye	ēġe (WS ēage)

MODERN ENGLISH		MIDDLE ENGLISH	OLD ENGLISH
[aʊ]	mouse	mous	mūs
	hound	hound	hund
	sow	sowe	sugu
	bough	bough	bōh
[ɔɪ]	joy	joy	OF joie (Lat. gaudia)
	join	joinen	OF joindre (Lat. jungere)
	poison	poison, puisun	OF poison, puisun (Lat. pōtiōnem)
[ʊ]	full	ful	full
	good	good	gōd
	wood	wode	wudu
[ə]	sun	sonne	sunne
	hussy	huswif	hūswīf
	southern	sutherne	sūþerne
	blood	blood	blōd
[ər]	bird	bird	bird, brid
	shirt	shirte	scyrte
	herd	herd	heord
	spurn	spurnen	spurnan
[ɪ]	fish	fish	fisc
	kin	kyn	cynn
	fifth	fifte	fīfta
	filth	filthe	fȳlþu
[ɛ]	edge	egge	ecg
	seven	seven	seofon
	kept	kepte	cēpte
	theft	theft	þēoft (WS þȳfþ)
	sweat	swete	swǣtan
	dead	deed	dēad

MODERN ENGLISH	MIDDLE ENGLISH	OLD ENGLISH
[æ] lamb	lamb	lamb
back	bak	bæc
narrow	narwe	nearwe
hallow	halwen	hālgian
bladder	bladdre	blǣdre
chapman	chapman	ċēapman
bath	bath	bæð
half	half	healf
ask	asken	āscian
[ɑ] pot	pot	pott
holiday	holiday	hāligdæġ
palm	palm	palm
psalm	psalm	sealm
far	fer	feor
[ɔ] claw	clawe	clawu
law	lawe	lagu
fought	faught	feaht
ought	oughte	āhte
bought	boughte	bohte
hall	hall	heall
walk	walken	wealcan
warm	warm	wearm
wash	wash	wascan
dog	dogge	dogga
broth	broth	broþ
soft	softe	sōfte

Trace the phonological history of these words by transcribing their pronunciation during each of the three periods. The first word has been done as an example.

	OLD ENGLISH	MIDDLE ENGLISH	MODERN ENGLISH	
tīma	[tīmɑ]	[tīmə]	[taɪm]	time
ribb				rib
ynċe				inch
ebba				ebb
seofon				seven
crabba				crab
cæppe				cap
sceaft				shaft
hnutu				nut
pott				pot
blīþe				blithe
hȳdan				hide
ċēse				cheese
hwēol				wheel
dǣd				deed
sǣ				sea
hēap				heap
fūl				foul
fōda				food
gāt				goat
hām				home
ġung				young
cnēo				knee
cyssan				kiss
ēast				east
fæst				fast
fisc				fish
fox				fox
henn				hen
hlūd				loud
lǣċe				leech
lǣfan				leave
pāpa				pope
rīsan				rise
brȳd				bride
sāpe				soap
sōna				soon
standan				stand
sunne				sun
tēþ				teeth
dæġ				day
pleġa				play

OLD ENGLISH	MIDDLE ENGLISH	MODERN ENGLISH	
grǣġ	_____	_____	_____ gray
rāw	_____	_____	_____ row
glōwan	_____	_____	_____ glow
āgan	_____	_____	_____ owe
spīwan	_____	_____	_____ spew
flēos	_____	_____	_____ fleece
dēaw	_____	_____	_____ dew
mǣw	_____	_____	_____ mew
clawe	_____	_____	_____ claw
gnagan	_____	_____	_____ gnaw
apa	_____	_____	_____ ape
hræfn	_____	_____	_____ raven
melu	_____	_____	_____ meal
open	_____	_____	_____ open
wicu	_____	_____	_____ week
wudu	_____	_____	_____ wood
yfel	_____	_____	_____ evil
sceadu	_____	_____	_____ shade
sceadwe	_____	_____	_____ shadow

7.10 PRONUNCIATION AND RIME

One kind of evidence which is used in reconstructing the older pronunciation of a language is that afforded by poetry, especially rimes. Rime-evidence, however, must be used with some discretion. Poets may deliberately use various kinds of imperfect rimes, like Emily Dickinson's

> I taste a liquor never brewed—
> From Tankards scooped in Pearl—
> Not all the Vats upon the Rhine
> Yield such an Alcohol![11]

The off-rime *pearl/alcohol* lends a delicate dryness to the verse; it is unnecessary to assume that an exact rime was intended. Similarly, when Swift writes, in "To Mr. Congreve,"

> Thus prostitute my Congreve's name is grown
> To ev'ry lewd pretender of the town,

an investigation of the riming words will show that Old English *grōwen* became Middle English [grəuən], Modern English [gron], whereas Old English *tūn* became Middle English [tūn], Modern English [taʊn]. The words do not rime today and never have. Swift must have used them as off-rimes or as eye-rimes since the spelling looks like a rime. This couplet tells us very little about Swift's pronunciation.

Nevertheless, with appropriate caution we can use rime as evidence for pronunciation, especially when other evidence supports it. Examine the following rimes from Swift. (1) Decide in each case whether the rimes are probably true or false. (2) Write the riming sounds in phonetic transcription. Be prepared to explain your decision.

[11] Reprinted by permission of the publishers and the Trustees of Amherst College from Thomas H. Johnson, ed., *The Poems of Emily Dickinson* (Cambridge, Mass., The Belknap Press of Harvard University Press). Copyright 1951, 1955, by The President and Fellows of Harvard College.

1. Yet want your criticks no just cause to rail,
   Since knaves are ne'er obliged for what they steal.

   Other similar rimes used by Swift are *ease/Bays*, *please/bays*, *dreams/names*, *dream/same*. You may consider these rimes as additional evidence in reaching a decision about the couplet.

---

(2) Contented he—but Fate ordains,
    He now shall shine in nobler scenes.

    Similarly, *scenes/entertains*, *scene/vein*, *scene/vain*, *scene/dean*.

---

(3) In ready counters never pays,
    But pawns her snuff-box, rings, and keys.

    Similarly, *key/sway*, *key/day*, *key/tea*.

---

(4) Unhappy ship, thou art returned in vain;
    New waves shall drive thee to the deep again.

    Similarly, *again/unclean*,
    but also, *again/then*, *again/ten*, *agen/pen*.

---

(5) Why, there's my landlord now, the squire, who all in money wallows,
    He would not give a groat to save his father from the gallows.

    Similarly, *watch/scratch*, *watch/match*, *wand/land*, *wand/hand*, *squabble/rabble*, *want/grant*, *wanting/planting*, *wanting/canting*, *water/matter*, *wander/by-stander*, *squat/mat*.

---

(6) In velvet cap his head lies warm;
    His hat for show, beneath his arm.

    Similarly, *war/far*, *war/star/tar*.

---

(7) A passage may be found, I've heard,
    In some old Greek or Latin bard

    Similarly, *search/arch*, *learn/darn*, *served/starved*, *unheard/guard*, *clerk/mark*, *herbage/garbage*, *deserve it/starve it*, *verse/farce*, *clergy/charge ye*, (*thou*) *wert/*(*Faustus'*) *art*.

---

(8) Would you rise in the church? Be stupid and dull;
    Be empty of learning, of insolence full.

    Similarly, *skull/full*, *blush/bush*, *thrush/bush*, *cut/put*, *guts/puts*, *touch her/butcher*. In the contemporary Irish dialect, Middle English [ʊ] is still a rounded vowel in all positions. How is this information apposite to Swift's rimes?

---

(9) Corinna in the morning dizen'd,
    Who sees will spew; who smells, be poison'd.

    Similarly, *wild/spoil'd*, *child/spoil'd*, *malign/join*, *surprise one* [ən]*/poison*.

---

(10) An act for laying down the plough—
      England will send you corn enough.

                    but also

      Tomorrow will be time enough
      To hear such mortifying stuff.

---

(11) The cold conceits, the chilling thoughts,
      Went down like stupifying draughts.

      Similarly, *draught/bought, draught/caught.*

---

(12) Next, for encouragement of spinning,
      A duty might be laid on linen.

      Similarly, *loving/sloven, teazing/treason, brewing/ruin, picking/chicken, barking/hearken, trimming/women, breathing/heathen, bubbling/Dublin, smelling/dwell in, building/skill'd in.*

---

(13) Who makes the best figure,
      The Dean or the digger?

      Similarly, *figure/vigour/bigger, venture/centre, ventures/representers, lecture/hector, volumes/columns.*

---

(14) For my friends have always thought
      Tenderness my greatest fault.

      Similarly, *brought/fault, haughty/faulty, thought/vault.*

---

(15) Within an hour and eke a half,
      I preached three congregations deaf.

      Similarly, *half/safe, halves/knaves.* Compare the Standard British pronunciation of *halfpenny.*

---

(16) Then Mrs. Johnson gave her verdict,
      And every one was pleased, that heard it.

---

(17) Soon repent, or put to slaughter
      Every Greek and Roman author.

---

(18) Proud Baronet of Nova Scotia,
      The Dean and Spaniard must reproach ye.

      Compare *charge ye/clergy.*

The following passages exemplify English from the late fifteenth century to the early seventeenth. The spelling, capitalization, and punctuation are typical of the bewildering variety that characterizes the early Modern period. In the earlier passages look for spelling evidence of the sound changes that characterize Modern English. For example, in the opening sentence of the first selection *write* is spelled *wryght* and *out* is spelled *ought*; what do these spellings indicate about the writer's pronunciation of *gh* in words like *night* and *thought*, in which the digraph represented a velar fricative in Middle English? Look for grammatical differences between early Modern and present-day English with regard to inflections, function words, and word order. Rewrite one of the passages in contemporary idiom and note the points at which you must rephrase to avoid an archaic flavor.

THE PASTON LETTERS

The Pastons were a Norfolk family of substance whose voluminous correspondence reflects the political and social life of fifteenth-century England.[12] Although the letters were written during a century that is usually though of as ending the Middle English period, they show many of the linguistic changes that are characteristic of the early Modern period. There are no sharp breaks in the historical development of a language, and therefore the Paston letters may be taken as examples of the transition from Middle to Modern English.

The first letter printed here is a proposal, or at least a declaration of honorable intentions. That it was favorably received by the lady is apparent in the second letter, although some disagreement had arisen between her father and her suitor over the dowry. The disagreement was eventually resolved, and in the third letter the wife, who is preoccupied with her first pregnancy, writes her husband various requests and bits of gossip.

From John Paston to Margery Brews, 1476

Mastresse, thow so be that I, unaqweyntyd with yow as yet, tak up on me to be thus bold as to wryght on to yow with ought your knowlage and leve, yet, mastress, for syche pore servyse as I now in my mynd owe yow, purposyng, ye not dyspleasyd, duryng my lyff to contenu the same, I beseche yow to pardon my boldnes, and not to dysdeyn, but to accepte thys sympyll byll to recomand me to yow in syche wyse as I best can or may imagyn to your most plesure. And, mastress, for sych report as I have herd of yow by many and dyverse persones, and specyally by my ryght trusty frend, Rychard Stratton, berer her of, to whom I beseche yow to geve credence in syche maters as he shall on my behalve comon with yow of, if it lyke you to lystyn hym, and that report causythe me to be the more bold to wryght on to yow, so as I do; for I have herd oft tymys Rychard Stratton sey that ye can and wyll take every thyng well that is well ment, whom I beleve and trust as myche as fewe men leveing, I ensuer yow by my trowthe. And, mastress, I beseche yow to thynk non other wyse in me but that I wyll and shall at all seasons be redy wythe Godes grace to accomplyshe all syche thynges as I have enformyd and desyerd the seyd Rychard on my behalve to geve yow knowlage of, but if it so be that a geyn my wyll it come of yow that I be cast off fro yowr servyse and not wyllyngly by my desert, and that I am and wylbe yours and at your comandmen in every wyse dwryng my lyff. Her I send yow thys bylle wretyn with my lewd hand and sealyd with my sygnet to remayn with yow for a wyttnesse ayenste me, and to my shame and dyshonour if I contrary it. And, mastress, I

---

[12] James Gairdner, ed., *The Paston Letters*, A.D. *1422–1509*. 6 vols. (London, 1904).

beseche yow, in easyng of the poore hert that somtyme was at my rewle, whyche now is at yours, that in as short tyme as can be that I may have knowlage of your entent and hough ye wyll have me demeanyd in thys mater, and I wylbe at all seasons redy to performe in thys mater and all others your plesure, as ferforth as lythe in my poore power to do or in all thers that ought wyll do for me, with Godes grace, Whom I beseche to send yow the accomplyshement of your most worchepfull desyers, myn owne fayer lady, for I wyll no ferther labore but to yow, on to the tyme ye geve me leve, and tyll I be suer that ye shall take no dysplesur with my ferther labore.

From Margery Brews to John Paston, Feb., 1477

Ryght reverent and wurschypfull, and my ryght welebeloved Voluntyne, I recomande me unto yowe, ffull hertely desyring to here of yowr welefare, whech I beseche Almyghty God long for to preserve un to Hys plesur, and yowr herts desyre. And yf it please yowe to here of my welefar, I am not in good heele of body, nor of herte, nor schall be tyll I her ffrom yowe;

> For there wottys no creature what peyn that I endure,
> And for to be deede, I dare it not dyscure [discover].

And my lady my moder hath labored the mater to my ffadur full delygently, but sche can no mor gete then ye knowe of, for the whech God knowyth I am full sory. But yf that ye loffe me, as I tryste verely that ye do, ye will not leffe me therefor; for if that ye hade not halfe the lyve-lode that ye hafe, for to do the grettest labur that any woman on lyve myght, I wold not forsake yowe.

> And yf ye commande me to kepe me true wherever I go,
> I wyse I will do all my myght yowe to love and never no mo.
> And yf my freends say, that I do amys,
> Thei schal not me let so for to do,
> Myne herte me bydds ever more to love yowe
> Truly over all erthely thing,
> And yf thei be never so wroth,
> I tryst it schall be better in tyme commyng.

No more to yowe at this tyme, but the Holy Trinite hafe yowe in kepyng. And I besech yowe that this bill be not seyn of none erthely creatur safe only your selffe, &c.

And thys letter was indyte at Topcroft, with full hevy herte, &c.

> By your own,   Margery Brews.

From Margery Brews Paston to John Paston, Dec., 1477

Ryth reverent and worscheful husbond, I recomaunde me to yow, desyryng hertyly to here of yowr wylfare, thankyng yow for the tokyn that ye sent me be Edmunde Perys, preyng yow to wete that my modyr sent to my fadyr to London for a goune cloth of mustyrddevyllers [gray woolen cloth] to make of a goune for me; and he tolde my modyr and me wanne he was comme home, that he cargeyt yow to beyit, aftyr that he were come oute of London.

I pre yow, yf it be not bowt, that ye wyl wechesaf to byit, and sendyt home as sone as ye may, for I have no goune to weyre this wyntyr but my blake and my grene a lyer [a shade of green], and that is so comerus that I ham wery to weryt.

As for the gyrdyl that my fadyr be hestyt me, I spake to hym ther of a lytyl before he ȝede to London last, and he seyde to me that the faute was in yow, that ȝe wolde not thynk ther uppe on to do makyt [to have it made]; but I sopose that ys not so; he seydyt but for a skwsacion. I pre yow, yf ye dor takyt uppe on yow, that ye wyl weche safe to do makyt a yens ye come home, for I hadde never more nede ther of than I have now, for I ham waxse so fetys [well-proportioned, handsome] that I may not be gyrte in no barre [band] of no gyrdyl that I have but of one. Elisabet Peverel hath leye sek xv. or xvj. wekys of the seyetyka, but sche sent my modyr word be Kate, that sche xuld come hedyr wanne God sent tyme, thoow sche xuld be crod [trundled] in a barwe.

Jon of Damm was here, and my modyr dyskevwyrd me to hym, and he seyed, be hys trouth that he was not gladder of no thyng that he harde thys towlmonyth, than he was ther of.

I may no lenger leve be my crafte, I am dysscevwyrd of alle men that se me.

Of alle odyr thyngys that ye deseyreyd that I xuld sende yow word of, I have sent yow word of in a letter that I dede wryte on Ouwyr Ladyis Day laste was. The Holy Trenyte have yow in Hese kepyng.

Wretyn at Oxnede, in ryth gret hast, on the Thrusday next be fore Seynt Tomas Day.

I pre yow that ye wyl were the reyng with the emage of Seynt Margrete, that I sent yow for a rememraunse, tyl ye come home; ye have lefte me sweche a rememraunse, that makyth me to thynke uppe on yow bothe day and nyth wanne I wold sclepe.

Your ys,   M. P.

CAXTON'S PREFACE TO THE ENEYDOS

In several of his prefaces Caxton discusses the problems he has encountered as a translator. The best known of these discussions is the one printed below.[13] Caxton has just described how he came upon a French version of the *Aeneid*.

And whan I had aduysed me in this sayd boke, I delybered and concluded to translate it in to englysshe, And forthwyth toke a penne & ynke, and wrote a leef or tweyne / whyche I ouersawe agayn to corecte it / And whā I sawe the fayr & straunge termes therin / I doubted that it sholde not please some gentylmen whiche late blamed me, sayeng yᵗ in my translacyons I had ouer curyous termes whiche coude not be vnderstande of comyn peple / and desired me to vse olde and homely termes in my translacyons. and fayn wolde I satysfye euery man / and so to doo, toke an olde boke and redde therin / and certaynly the englysshe was so rude and brood that I coude not wele vnderstande it. And also my lorde abbot of west-mynster ded do shewe to me late, certayn euydences wryton in olde englysshe, for to reduce it in to our englysshe now vsid / And certaynly it was wreton in suche wyse that it was more lyke to dutche than englysshe: I coude not reduce ne brynge it to be vnderstonden / And certaynly our langage now vsed varyeth ferre from that whiche was vsed and spoken whan I was borne / For we englysshe men / ben borne vnder the domynacyon of the mone, whiche is neuer stedfaste / but euer wauerynge / wexynge one season / and waneth & dyscreaseth another season / And that comyn englysshe that is spoken in one shyre varyeth from a nother. In so moche that in my dayes happened that certayn marchaūtes were in a shippe in tamyse for to haue sayled ouer the see into zelande / and for lacke of wynde, thei taryed atte forlond, and wente to lande for to refreshe them: And one of theym named sheffelde, a mercer, cam in to an hows and axed for mete: and specyally he axyd after eggys: And the goode wyf answerde, that she coude speke no frenshe. And the marchaūt was angry, for he also coude speke no frenshe, but wolde haue hadde egges / and she vnderstode hym not / And thenne at laste a nother sayd that he wolde haue eyren / then the good wyf sayd that she vnderstod hym wel / Loo, what sholde a man in thyse dayes now wryte, egges or eyren / certaynly it is

13 From W. T. Culley and F. J. Furnivall, eds., *Caxton's Eneydos, 1490* (EETS ES 57; London, 1890).

harde to playse euery man / by cause of dyuersite & chaūge of langage. For in these dayes euery man that is in ony reputacyon in his coūtre, wyll vtter his cōmynycacyon and maters in suche maners & termes / that fewe men shall vnderstonde theym / And som honest and grete clerkes haue ben wyth me, and desired me to wryte the moste curyous termes that I coude fynde / And thus bytwene playn rude / & curyous, I stande abasshed. but in my Iudgemente / the comyn termes that be dayli vsed, ben lyghter to be vnderstonde than the olde and aūcyent englysshe / And for as moche as this present booke is not for a rude vplondyssh man to laboure therin / ne rede it / but onely for a clerke & a noble gentylman that feleth and vnderstondeth in faytes of armes in loue & in noble chyualrye / Therfor in a meane bytwene bothe I haue reduced & translated this sayd booke in to our englysshe, not ouer rude ne curyous, but in suche termes as shall be vnderstanden, by goddys grace, accordynge to my copye. And yf ony man wyll enter mete in redyng of hit, and fyndeth suche termes that he can not vnderstande, late hym goo rede and lerne vyrgyll / or the pystles of ouyde / and ther he shall see and vnderstonde lyghtly all / Yf he haue a good redar & enformer / For this booke is not for euery rude and vnconnynge man to see / but to clerkys and very gentylmen that vnderstande gentylnes and scyence.

ELYOT'S CASTEL OF HELTH

Sir Thomas Elyot is best known today as the author of *The Governor,* but in his own time his most popular work was *The Castel of Helth Gathered and Made by Syr Thomas Elyot knyghte, out of the chiefe Authors of Physyke, wherby euery manne may knowe the state of his owne body, the preseruatiō of helth, and how to instructe welle his physytion in syckenes that he be not deceyued* (1539). The purpose of this work is adequately stated in its title: It is a handbook of physiology, hygiene, and diagnostics. Of the extracts printed here, the first two deal with the constitution of the body according to physiological theories inherited from the Middle Ages, the third is one of several exercises designed to preserve and promote health, and the fourth describes one common means of letting blood, a widely practiced therapeutic technique.

Of humours

In the body of Man be foure pryncipal humours, which continuynge in the proporcion, that nature hath lymitted, the body is free frome all syckenesse. Contrary wise by the increase or diminution of any of theym in quantitie or qualitie, ouer or vnder theyr naturall assignement, inequall temperature commeth into the bodye, whiche sickenesse foloweth more or lasse, accordyng to the lapse or decaye of the temperatures of the sayd humours, whiche be these folowynge.

Bloudde,	Choler,
Fleume,	Melancholy

[Of spirits]

Spirite is an ayry substance subtyll, styryng the powers of the body to perfourme their operations, whiche is dyuyded into

Naturalle, whiche taketh his begynnynge of the lyuer, and by the vaynes whiche haue no pulse, spredeth into all the hole body.

Vitall, whiche procedeth from the hart, and by the arteries or pulses is sent into all the body.

Animalle, whiche is ingendred in the brayne, and is sente by the senewes throughout the body, & maketh sence or feelynge.

Of vociferation

The chiefe exercyse of the brest and instrumentes of the voyce, is vociferation, whiche is synging, redyng, or crienge, wherof is the propertie, that it purgeth naturall heate, and maketh it also subtyll and stable, and maketh the membres of the body substancyall and stronge, resystynge diseases. This exercyse wold be vsed, of persones shorte wynded, and theym, whiche can not fetche theyr brethe, but holdyng their necke streight vpright. Also of them, whose fleshe is consumed, speciallye about the breaste and shoulders, also which haue had apostumes broken in theyr breastes : moreouer of them that are hoorse by the moche moysture, and to them, whiche haue quartene feuers, it is conuenient, it louseth the humour, that stycketh in the brest, and dryeth vp the moystenesse of the stomacke, whiche properly the course of the quartayne is wont to brynge with hym, it also profiteth them whiche haue feble stomakes, or do vomyte contynually, or do breake vp sowrenesse out of the stomake. It is good also for grefes of the heed. He that intendeth to attempt this exercise, after that he hath ben at the stoole, and softly rubbed the lower partes, and washed his handes. Lette hym speake with as base a voyce as he can, and walkynge, begynne to synge lowder & lowder, but styll in a base voyce, and to take no hede of sweete tunes or armonye. For that nothynge dothe profyte vnto helthe of the body, but to inforce hym selfe to synge greatte, for therby moche ayre drawen in by fetchyng of breath, thrustyth forth the breast and stomacke, and openeth and inlargeth the poores. By hygh crienge and lowde readynge, are expellyd superfluouse humours. Therfore menne and women, hauynge theyr bodyes feeble, and theyr flesshe lowse, and not fyrme, muste reade oftentymes lowde, and in a baase voyce, extendynge oute the wynde pype, and other passages of the breathe.

But notwithstandying, this exercyse is not vsed alway, and of all persons. For they in whome is abundance of humours corrupted, or be moche diseased with crudite in the stomak and vaines, those doo I counsayle, to abstayne from the exercyse of the voyce, leste moche corrupteth iuyce or vapours, may therby be into all the body dystrybuted. And here I conclude to speake of exercyse, whiche of them, that desyre to remayne longe in helth, is most diligently, & as I mought say, moste scrupulousely to be obserued.

Of bloude suckers or leaches

There is also an other fourme of euacuation by wormes, founde in waters callyd bloude suckers or leaches, whiche beinge put vnto the body or member, do draw out blode. And their drawynge is more conuenient for fulnesse of bloudde than scarifyenge is, forasmoche as they fetche bloud more deper, and is more of the substance of bloud, yet the opinion of some men is, that they do drawe no bloude but that, which is corrupted, and not proporcionable vnto our body. And therfore in griefes, whiche happen betwene the skynne and the flesshe of blode corrupted, these are more conuenient than scarifienge. But before that they be putte vnto any parte of the body, they muste be fyrste kepte all one day before, gyuyng vnto them a lyttel blode in freshe flesshe. And than putte theym in a cleane water, somwhat warme, and with a spounge wype awaye the slyme, whiche is about theym, and than laye a lyttell bloudde on the place greued, and putte theym thanne to it, and laye on theym a spounge, that whan they be fulle, they may falle awaye, or yf ye wyll sooner haue them of, put a horse heare bytweene theyr mouthes, and the place, and drawe them awaye, or putte to theyr mouthes salte or ashes, or vyneger, and forthwith they shall falle, and than wasshe the place with a spounge : and if there doo yssue moche bloudde, laye on the place the poulder of a spounge, and pytche bourned, or lynnen clothe bourned, or galles bourned, or the herbe callyd *Bursa pastoris* bruysed. And this suffyseth concernyng bloud suckers.

Sir Thomas More's *Utopia*, which has lent its name to an entire genre of imaginative social commentary, was written in Latin but was translated into English by Raphe Robinson some fifteen years after More's execution. The title page of the first English edition reads as follows:

> A fruteful and pleasaunt worke of the beste state of a publyque weale, and of the newe yle called Utopia: written in Latine by Syr Thomas More knyght, and translated into Englyshe by Raphe Robynson Citizein and Goldsmythe of London, at the procurement, and earnest request of George Tadlowe Citezein & Haberdassher of the same Citie. Imprinted at London by Abraham Vele, dwelling in Pauls churcheyarde at the sygne of the Lambe. Anno. 1551.

The selection printed here is the beginning of Robinson's Preface, or Epistle Dedicatory, in which he explains why he translated the *Utopia*.

To the right honourable, and his verie singuler good maister, maister William Cecylle esquiere, one of the twoo principal secretaries to the kyng his moste excellent maiestie, Raphe Robynson wissheth cōtinuaunce of health, with dayly increase of vertue, and honoure.

Vpon a tyme, when tidynges came too the citie of Corinthe that kyng Philippe father to Alexander surnamed yᵉ Great, was comming thetherwarde with an armie royall to lay siege to the citie. The Corinthiãs being forth with stryken with greate feare, beganne busilie, and earnestly to looke aboute them, and to falle to worke of all handes. Some to skowre & trymme vp harneis, some to carry stones, some to amende and buylde hygher the walles, some to rampiere and fortyfie the bulwarkes, and fortresses, some one thynge, and some an other for the defendinge, and strengthenynge of the citie. The whiche busie labour, and toyle of theires when Diogenes the phylosopher sawe, hauing no profitable busines wherupō to sette himself on worke (neither any man required his labour, and helpe as expedient for the commē wealth in that necessitie) immediatly girded about him his phylosophicall cloke, & began to rolle, and tumble vp and downe hether & thether vpon the hille syde, that lieth adioyninge to the citie, his great barrel or tunne, wherein he dwelled: for other dwellynge place wold he haue none. This seing one of his frendes, and not alitell musynge therat, came to hym: And I praye the Diogenes (quod he) whie doest thou thus, or what meanest thou hereby? Forsothe I am tumblyng my tubbe to (quod he) bycause it were no reason yᵗ I only should be ydell, where so many be workīg. In semblable maner, right honorable sir, though I be, as I am in dede, of muche lesse habilitie then Diogenes was to do any thinge, that shall or may be for the auauncement & commoditie of the publique wealth of my natiue countrey: yet I seing euery sort, and kynde of people in theire vocatiō, & degree busilie occupied about the cōmō wealthes affaires: & especially learned mē dayly putting forth in writing newe inuentions, & deuises to the furtheraūce of thē same: thought it my boūden duetie to God, & to my countrey so to tūble my tubbe, I meane so to occupie, & exercise meself in bestowing such spare houres, as I beinge at yᵉ becke, & cōmaundement of others, cold conueniently winne to me self: yᵗ though no cōmoditie of that my labour, & trauaile to the publique weale should arise, yet it myght by this appeare, yᵗ myne endeuoire, & good wille hereunto was not lacking. To the accōplishemēt therfore, & fulfyllyng of this my mynde, & purpose: I toke vpō me to tourne, and translate out of Latine into oure Englishe tonge the frutefull, & profitable boke, which sir Thomas more knight compiled, & made of the new yle Utopia, cōteining & setting forth yᵉ best state, and fourme of a publique weale: A worke (as it appeareth) writtē almost fourtie yeres ago by the said sir Thomas More yᵉ authour therof.

A renaissance successor to medieval histories like the *Polychronicon* was Raphael Holinshed's *The Chronicles of England, Scotland, and Ireland* (1587), which is remembered today as one of Shakespeare's sources.

The first passage printed here is from the geographical survey with which such chronicles usually begin. In it the author expresses a proper Englishman's opinion of the superiority of his birth tongue.

The second passage is an account of the British king, Leir, whose story is better known from Shakespeare's play.

Of the languages spoken in this Iland

What language came first with *Samothes* and afterward with *Albion*,[14] and the giants of his companie, it is hard for me to determine, sith nothing of sound credit remaineth in writing, which may resolue vs in the truth hereof. Yet of so much are we certeine, that the speach of the ancient Britons, and of the Celts, had great affinitie one with another, so that they were either all one, or at leastwise such as either nation with small helpe of interpretors might vnderstand other, and readilie discerne what the speaker meant. Some are of the opinion that the Celts spake Greeke, and how the British toong resembled the same, which was spoken in Grecia before *Homer* did reforme it: but I see that these men doo speake without authoritie and therefore I reiect them, for if the Celts which were properlie called Galles did speake Greeke, why did Cesar in his letters sent to Rome vse that language, because that if they should be intercepted they might not vnderstand them, or why did he not vnderstand the Galles, he being so skilfull in the language without an interpretor? Yet I denie not but that the Celtish and British speaches might haue great affinitie one with another, and the British aboue all other with the Greeke, for both doo appeere by certeine words, as first in *tri* for three . . . .

Next vnto the British speach, the Latine toong was brought in by the Romans, and in maner generallie planted through the whole region, as the French was after by the Normans. Of this toong I will not say much, bicause there are few which be not skilfull in the same . . . .

The third language apparantlie knowne is the Scithian or high Dutch, induced at the first by the Saxons (which the Britons call *Saysonaec*, as they doo the speakers *Sayson*) an hard and rough kind of speach, God wot, when our nation was brought first into acquaintance withall, but now changed with vs into a farre more fine and easie kind of vtterance, and so polished and helped with new and milder words, that it is to be aduouched how there is no one speach vnder the sunne spoken in our time, that hath or can haue more varietie of words, copie of phrases, or figures and floures of eloquence, than hath our English toong, although some haue affirmed vs rather to barke as dogs, than talke like men, bicause the most of our words (as they doo indeed) incline vnto one syllable . . . .

After the Saxon toong, came the Norman or French language ouer into our countrie, and therein were our lawes written for a long time. Our children also were by an especiall decree taught first to speake the same, and therevnto inforced to learne their constructions in the French, whensoeuer they were set to the Grammar schoole . . . .

Afterward also, by diligent trauell of *Geffray Chaucer*, and *Iohn Gowre*, in the time of Richard the second, and after them of *Iohn Scogan*, and *Iohn Lydgate* monke of Berrie, our said toong was brought to an excellent passe, notwithstanding that it neuer came vnto the type of perfection, vntill the time of Queene Elizabeth . . . .

[14] Two legendary settlers of Britain.

This also is proper to vs Englishmen, that sith ours is a meane language, and neither too rough nor too smooth in vtterance, we may with much facilitie learne any other language, beside Hebrue, Greeke & Latine, and speake it naturallie, as if we were home-borne in those countries; & yet on the other side it falleth out, I wot not by what other meanes, that few forren nations can rightlie pronounce ours, without some and that great note of imperfection, especiallie the French men, who also seldome write any thing that sauoreth of English trulie.

Leir the Ruler

Leir the sonne of Baldud was admitted ruler ouer the Britaines, in the yeare of the world 3105, at what time Ioas reigned in Iuda. This Leir was a prince of right noble demeanor, gouerning his land and subiects in great wealth. He made the towne of Caerleir now called Leicester, which standeth vpon the riuer of Sore. It is written that he had by his wife three daughters without other issue, whose names were Gonorilla, Regan, and Cordeilla, which daughters he greatly loued, but specially Cordeilla the yoongest farre aboue the two elder. When this Leir therefore was come to great yeres, & began to waxe vnweldie through age, he thought to vnderstand the affections of his daughters towards him, and preferre hir whome he best loued, to the succession ouer the kingdome. Wherupon he first asked Gonorilla the eldest, how well she loued him: who calling hir gods to record, protested that she loued him more than hir owne life, which by right and reason should be most deere vnto hir. With which answer the father being well pleased, turned to the second, and demanded of hir how well she loued him: who answered (confirming hir saiengs with great othes) that she loued him more than toong could expresse, and farre aboue all other creatures of the world.

Then called he his yoongest daughter Cordeilla before him, and asked of hir what account she made of him, vnto whome she made this answer as followeth: Knowing the great loue and fatherlie zeale that you haue alwaies borne towards me (for the which I maie not answere you otherwise than I thinke, and as my conscience leadeth me) I protest vnto you, that I haue loued you euer, and will continuallie (while I live) loue you as my naturall father. And if you would more vnderstand of the loue that I beare you, assertaine your selfe, that so much as you haue, so much you are worth, and so much I loue you, and no more. The father being nothing content with this answer, married his two eldest daughters, the one vnto Henninus the duke of Cornewall, and the other vnto Maglanus the duke of Albania, betwixt whome he willed and ordeined that his land should be diuided after his death, and the one halfe thereof immediatlie should be assigned to them in hand: but for the third daughter Cordeilla he reserued nothing.

Neuertheles it fortuned that one of the princes of Gallia (which now is called France) whose name was Aganippus, hearing of the beautie, womanhood, and good conditions of the said Cordeilla, desired to haue hir in mariage, and sent ouer to hir father, requiring that he might haue hir to wife: to whome answer was made, that he might haue his daughter, but as for anie dower he could haue none, for all was promised and assured to hir other sisters alreadie. Aganippus notwithstanding this answer of deniall to receiue anie thing by way of dower with Cordeilla, tooke hir to wife, onlie moued thereto (I saie) for respect of hir person and amiable vertues. This Aganippus was one of the twelue kings that ruled Gallia in those daies, as in the British historie it is recorded. But to proceed.

After that Leir was fallen into age, the two dukes that had married his two eldest daughters, thinking it long yer the gouernment of the land did come to their hands, arose against him in armour, and rest from him the gouernance of the land, vpon conditions to be continued for terme of life: by the which he was put to his portion, that is, to liue after a rate assigned to him for the maintenance of his estate, which in processe of time was diminished as well by Maglanus as by Henninus. But the greatest griefe that Leir tooke, was to see the vnkindnesse of his daughters, which seemed to thinke that all was too much which their father had, the same being neuer so little: in so much that going from the one to the other, he was brought to that miserie, that scarslie they would allow him one seruant to wait vpon him.

In the end, such was the vnkindnesse, or (as I maie saie) the vnnaturalnesse which he found in his two daughters, notwithstanding their faire and pleasant words vttered in time past, that being constreined of necessitie, he fled the land, & sailed into Gallia, there to seeke some comfort of his yongest daughter Cordeilla, whom before time he hated. The ladie Cordeilla hearing that he was arriued in poore estate, she first sent to him priuilie a certeine summe of monie to apparell himselfe withall, and to reteine a certeine number of seruants that might attend vpon him in honorable wise, as apperteined to the estate which he had borne: and then so accompanied, she appointed him to come to the court, which he did, and was so ioifullie, honorablie, and louinglie receiued, both by his sonne in law Aganippus, and also by his daughter Cordeilla, that his hart was greatlie comforted: for he was no lesse honored, than if he had beene king of the whole countrie himselfe.

Now when he had informed his sonne in law and his daughter in what sort he had beene vsed by his other daughters, Aganippus caused a mightie armie to be put in a readinesse, and likewise a great nauie of ships to be rigged, to passe ouer into Britaine with Leir his father in law, to see him againe restored to his kingdome. It was accorded, that Cordeilla should also go with him to take possession of the land, the which he promised to leaue vnto hir, as the rightfull inheritour after his decesse, notwithstanding any former grant made to hir sisters or to their husbands in anie maner of wise.

Herevpon, when this armie and nauie of ships were readie, Leir and his daughter Cordeilla with hir husband tooke the sea, and arriuing in Britaine, fought with their enimies, and discomfited them in battell, in the which Maglanus and Henninus were slaine: and then was Leir restored to his kingdome, which he ruled after this by the space of two yeeres, and then died, fortie yeeres after he first began to reigne. His bodie was buried at Leicester in a vaut vnder the chanell of the river of Sore beneath the towne.

THE FORMER AGE

Queen Elizabeth I, like her distinguished ancestor, King Alfred, also put *The Consolation of Philosophy* into English. Elizabeth's translation is, however, less successful than either Alfred's or Chaucer's. It is indeed hardly more than a school exercise, suffering from the double faults of a word-by-word rendering and occasional mistranslations. It follows the Latin original in assuming verse form.[15]

[15] Caroline Pemberton, ed. (EETS OS 113; London, 1899). For comparison and assistance in reading Elizabeth's English, a more idiomatic version of the Latin is given here:

> The former age of men was very happy;
> Content with the faithful field
> And not ruined by slothful lust,
> They used to break their long fasts
> With easily gotten acorns.
> They did not know Bacchic gifts [wine]
> Mixed with clear honey,
> Nor the shining fleece [silk] of the Chinese
> Stained with Tyrian dye.
> Herbs gave healthful sleep,

Happy to muche the formar Age
    With faithful fild content,
Not Lost by sluggy Lust,
    that wontz the Long fastz
To Louse by son-got Acorne.
    that knew not Baccus giftz
With molten hony mixed
    Nor Serike shining flise
With tirius venom[16] die.
    Sound slipes Gaue the grasse
ther drink the running streme
    Shades gaue the hiest pine.
The depth of sea they fadomd not
    Nor wares chosen from fur
Made Stranger find new shores.
    Than wer Navies[17] Stil,
Nor bloudshed by Cruel hate
    Had fearful weapons[18] staned.
What first fury to foes shuld
    any armes rayse,
Whan Cruel woundz he Saw
    and no reward for bloude?
Wold God agane Our formar time
    to wonted maners fel!
But Gridy getting Loue burnes
    Sorar than Etna with her flames.
O who the first man was
    of hiden Gold the waight
Or Gemmes that willing lurkt
    The deare danger digd?

And smooth streams, drink,
The highest pines, shade;
They did not yet sail the deep seas;
Nor with merchandise gathered from everywhere
Did the stranger seek new shores.
Then the raging calls of the trumpet were stilled;
And with cruel hate, extensive
Bloodshed did not stain the fearful fields,
For why should inimical fury first
Draw any weapons to wage war
When they saw severe wounds
And no profit in blood?
Oh that our times might
Only return to the former customs.
But more fierce than the fires of Etna
Blazes the burning love of getting.
Oh, who first was it
Who dug the weight of hidden gold
And gems wishing to lie hidden,
The precious peril?

[16] The Latin word *venēnum* can mean either 'poison, venom' or 'dye, coloring matter.'
[17] Elizabeth translated *classis* 'navy' instead of *classicum* 'trumpet call.'
[18] Elizabeth translated *arma* 'weapons' instead of *arva* 'fields.'

SIR WALTER RALEIGH'S INSTRUCTIONS
TO HIS SON

During the last fifteen years of his life, while imprisoned in the Tower of London, Sir Walter Raleigh wrote his major prose work, *The History of the World*. He also found time to compose a short handbook of practical advice for his son. Wat, the son for whom the book was probably written, stood in need of it. Ben Jonson was his tutor during a trip to France and described the twenty-year-old's fondness for women and practical jokes, one of which had Jonson himself as its butt.

Instructions to his Sonne: and to Posteritie was published in 1632, fourteen years after Raleigh's execution. The selection printed here gives advice on choosing and not choosing a wife.

The next, and greatest care ought to be in choice of a Wife, and the onely danger therein is Beauty, by which all men in all Ages, wise and foolish, have beene betrayed. And though I know it vain to use Reasons, or Arguments to disswade thee from being captiuated therewith, there being few or none that ever resisted that Witcherie; yet I cannot omit to warne thee, as of other things, which may be thy ruine and destruction. For the present time, it is true, that every man preferres his fantasie in that Appetite before all other worldly desires, leaving the care of Honour, credit, and safety in respect thereof; But remēber, that though these affections doe not last, yet the bond of Marriage dureth to the end of thy life; and therefore better to be borne withall in a Mistris, then in a wife; for when thy humour shal change thou art yet free to chuse again (if thou give thy selfe that vaine liberty.) Remember, secondly, that if thou marry for Beauty, thou bindest thy selfe for all thy life for that which perchance will neither last nor please thee one yeer; and when thou hast it, it will bee unto thee of no price at all, for the desire dyeth when it is attayned, and the affection perisheth, when it is satisfied. Remember when thou wert a sucking Child, that then thou diddest love thy Nurse, and that thou wert fond of her, after a while thou didst love thy dry Nurse, and didst forget the other, after that thou didst also despise her; so will it be with thee in thy liking in elder yeeres; and therefore, though thou canst not forbeare to love, yet forbeare to linke, and after a while thou shalt find an alteration in thy selfe, and see another far more pleasing then the first, second, or third love. . . . Let thy time of marriage bee in thy young, and strong yeeres; for beleeve it, ever the young Wife betrayeth the old Husband, and shee that had thee not in thy flower, will despise thee in thy fall, and thou shalt bee unto her, but a captivity and sorrow. Thy best time will be towards thirty, for as the younger times are unfit, either to chuse or to governe a Wife and family; so if thou stay long, thou shalt hardly see the education of thy Children, which being left to strangers, are in effect lost, and better were it to bee unborne then ill bred; for thereby thy posterity shall either perish, or remaine a shame to thy name, and family.

The Modern English Period to 1800: Forms and Syntax

8.1 *QUESTIONS FOR REVIEW AND DISCUSSION*

1. Define the following terms:

Overgeneralization — uniform (handwritten)

his-genitive	leveling (leveled form)	reflexive construction
group-genitive	eye dialect	purism
uninflected genitive	expanded verb form	prescriptive grammar
analytical comparison	impersonal construction	contraction

2. What are the living inflections of present-day English, that is, the inflectional endings that we might add to newly created nouns, adjectives, and verbs?

3. What is the historical source of each of those inflections?

4. What additional inflections were freely used in early Modern English?

5. How do early Modern and present-day English differ in the form and use of pronouns?

6. How do early Modern and present-day English differ with respect to contractions?

7. What criteria, other than the observation of actual use, guided the eighteenth-century grammarians in their making of rules for English?

8. Identify Robert Cawdrey, Henry Cockeram, Nathan Bailey, Samuel Johnson, John Wallis, Robert Lowth, Joseph Priestley, George Campbell, Lindley Murray.

8.2 *NOUNS*

1. Describe the history of the Modern English regular noun plural ending -*s*, using the forms cited below as illustrations. Consider the history of (1) the pronunciation, (2) the meaning, and (3) the domain (that is, the number and kinds of nouns that take the ending).

OLD ENGLISH

hundas 'dogs'	ċyriċan 'churches'	gatu 'gates'
hunda 'of dogs'	ċyriċena 'of churches'	gata 'of gates'
hundum 'to, with dogs'	ċyriċum 'to, with churches'	gatum 'to, with gates'

MIDDLE ENGLISH

houndes '(of, to, with) dogs'	chirches '(of, to, with) churches'	gates '(of, to, with) gates'

MODERN ENGLISH

hounds	churches	gates

(1) pronunciation: _____

_____

(2) meaning: _____

_____

(3) domain: _____

_____

2. A number of Modern English irregular noun plurals are survivals of inflectional patterns that once had much wider domains. Describe the origin of the following plurals, and list other words that have a similar plural form in Modern English.

thief–thieves: _____

_____

foot–feet: _____

_____

ox–oxen: _____

_____

deer–deer: _____

_____

3. *Woman* and its plural, *women*, have had a complex history. The forms cited below illustrate some of the most important changes the word has undergone (the Middle English rounding of [wɪ] to [wʊ] was a dialect variation).

   Describe the development of the Old English forms into the current singular and plural; explain each step of the development as due to sound changes you have already studied or to such factors as dialect borrowing and analogy.

	SINGULAR	PLURAL
OLD ENGLISH	wīfman (nom.-acc. sing.)	wīfmen (nom.-acc. pl.)
MIDDLE ENGLISH	wimman, wumman, womman, wiman, woman	wimmen, wummen, wommen, wimen, women
MODERN ENGLISH	woman [wʊmən]	women [wɪmɪn], [-ən]

_____

_____

_____

_____

_____

_____

_____

_____

_____

_____

4. As English has borrowed words, it has sometimes borrowed the foreign plural as well as the singular. Among such loan-words are the following. For each, give the foreign plural, specify the language from which it derives, and list some other words with the same plural formation.

vertebra _____

_____

nucleus _____

stratum _____

index _____

matrix _____

analysis _____

species _____

criterion _____

stigma _____

cherub _____

5. List some loan-words that have foreign plurals other than those cited above.

_____

_____

6. Explain the function and the apparent origin of the following italicized pronouns:

by Mars *his* gauntlet (Shakespeare, *Troilus and Cressida*, IV.v)

Tamburlaine the Great . . . shewed vpon Stages in the Citie of London, By the right honorable the Lord Admyrall, *his* seruants. (title page of the 1590 edition)

Ben: Ionson *his* Volpone or The Foxe. (title page of the 1607 edition)

_____

_____

_____

7. The sign of the genitive (-'s) is traditionally called an inflectional affix. How does it differ from other inflections in its position, and why might it more accurately be called a grammatical particle in Modern English? _____

_____

_____

_____

8. Explain the origin of the *s*-less genitives in these expressions:

ladyfinger _____

by my fatherkin _____

Ulysses' voyage _____

for heaven sake _____

1. What caused the Middle English distinction between strong and weak and between singular and plural adjectives to disappear from our language? _____

   _____

2. Cite an early Modern English example for each of the following:
   polysyllabic adjective with inflectional comparison _____
   monosyllabic adjective with analytical comparison _____
   adjective with double comparison _____
   adverb without ending that would now require *-ly* _____

3. Cite a few adjectives that still fluctuate between inflectional and analytical comparison in current English. _____

   _____

4. Cite a few adverbs like *deep–deeply* that have two forms in current English.

   _____

   _____

5. What is the origin of the adverb without *-ly*? _____

   _____

   _____

8.4 *PRONOUNS*

1. How does current English differ from early Modern in its use of the genitives *my* and *mine*? The difference is illustrated in this quotation from Shakespeare:

   Falstaff ... Shall I not take mine ease in mine inn, but I shall have my pocket picked? I have lost a seal ring of my grandfather's worth forty mark.   (*1 Henry IV*, III.iii)

   _____

   _____

2. What nuances of meaning are implied by the choice between *y*-forms and *th*-forms of the second person pronoun in the following passages from Shakespeare?

   [Miranda questions her father about the tempest which has apparently wrecked a ship.]

   Miranda If by *your* Art (my deerest father) *you* haue
   Put the wild waters in this Rore; alay them.

   · · · · · ·

   Prospero I haue done nothing, but in care of *thee*
   (Of *thee* my deere one; *thee* my daughter) who
   Art ignorant of what *thou* art.   (*The Tempest*, I.ii)

   _____

   _____

   [King Henry doubts his son's loyalty and is reassured by Hal.]

   King But wherefore doe I tell these Newes to *thee*?
   Why, Harry, doe I tell *thee* of my Foes,
   Which art my neer'st and dearest Enemie?
   Thou, that art like enough, through Vassal Feare,

Base Inclination, and the start of Spleene,
To fight against me vnder Percies pay,
To dogge his heeles, and curtsie at his frownes,
To shew how much *thou* art degenerate.

Prince Doe not thinke so, *you* shall not finde it so:
And Heauen forgiue them, that so much haue sway'd
Your Maiesties good thoughts away from me:
I will redeeme all this on Percies head,
And in the closing of some glorious day,
Be bold to tell *you*, that I am *your* Sonne.   (*1 Henry IV*, III.ii)

[King Claudius and Queen Gertrude urge Hamlet to forgo his mourning and to remain at the Danish court.]

King How is it that the Clouds still hang on *you*?
Hamlet Not so my Lord, I am too much i'th'Sun.
Queen Good Hamlet cast *thy* nightly colour off,
And let *thine* eye looke like a Friend on Denmarke.
Do not for euer with *thy* veyled lids
Seeke for *thy* Noble Father in the dust;
Thou know'st 'tis common, all that liues must dye,
Passing through Nature, to Eternity.

. . . . .

King 'Tis sweet and commendable
In *your* Nature Hamlet,
To giue these mourning duties to *your* Father:
But *you* must know, *your* Father lost a Father.

. . . . .

And we beseech *you*, bend *you* to remaine
Heere in the cheere and comfort of our eye,
Our cheefest Courtier Cosin, and our Sonne.
Queen Let not *thy* Mother lose her Prayers Hamlet:
I pry*thee* stay with vs, go not to Wittenberg.
Hamlet I shall in all my best
Obey *you* Madam.
King Why 'tis a louing, and a faire Reply.   (*Hamlet*, I.ii)

[Harry Percy, Northumberland's son, has defended his brother-in-law, Mortimer, against the charge of treason. King Henry still refuses to ransom Mortimer, who was captured in battle by Owen Glendower.]

King *Thou* do'st bely him Percy, *thou* dost bely him;
He neuer did encounter with Glendower:
I tell *thee*, he durst as well haue met the diuell alone,
As Owen Glendower for an enemy.
Art *thou* not asham'd? But, Sirrah, henceforth
Let me not heare *you* speake of Mortimer.

Send me *your* Prisoners with the speediest meanes,
Or *you* shall heare in suche a kinde from me
As will displease *ye*. My Lord Northumberland,
We License *your* departure with *your* sonne,
Send vs *your* Prisoners, or *you*'l heare of it.   (*1 Henry IV*, I.iii)

[Hotspur (Harry Percy) is secretly planning to join a revolt against King Henry IV; his wife has questioned him about his mysterious activities.]

Hotspur   Come, wilt *thou* see me ride?
  And when I am a horsebacke, I will sweare
  I loue *thee* infinitely. But hearke *you* Kate,
  I must not haue *you* henceforth, question me,
  Whether I go: nor reason whereabout
  Whether I must, I must: and to conclude,
  This Euening must I leaue *thee*, gentle Kate.
  I know *you* wise, but yet no further wise
  Than Harry Percies wife. Constant *you* are,
  But yet a woman: and for secrecie,
  No lady closer. For I will beleeue
  Thou wilt not vtter what *thou* do'st not know,
  And so farre wilt I trust *thee*, gentle Kate.   (*1 Henry IV*, II.iii)

[Lear has just disinherited his youngest daughter, Cordelia, and Kent speaks in her defense.]

Kent   Royall Lear,
  Whom I haue euer honor'd as my King,
  Lou'd as my Father, as my Master follow'd,
  As my great Patron thought on in my praiers.
Lear   The bow is bent & drawne, make from the shaft.
Kent   Let it fall rather, though the forke inuade
  The region of my heart, be Kent vnmannerly,
  When Lear is mad, what wouldest *thou* do old man?
  Think'st *thou* that dutie shall haue dread to speake,
  When power to flattery bowes?
  To plainnesse honour's bound,
  When Maiesty falls to folly, reserue *thy* state,
  And in *thy* best consideration checke
  This hideous rashnesse, answere my life, my iudgement:
  Thy yongest Daughter do's not loue *thee* least.   (*King Lear*, I.i)

[Lady Anne is on her way to the funeral of her father-in-law, King Henry VI, when she meets Richard, who has murdered both the old King and Lady Anne's husband.]

Anne   *Thou* was't prouoked by *thy* bloody minde,

	That neuer dream'st on ought but Butcheries:
	Did'st *thou* not kill this King?
Richard	I graunt *ye*.

. . . . .

Anne	He is in heauen, where *thou* shalt neuer come.
Richard	Let him thank me, that holpe to send him thither:
	For he was fitter for that place then earth.
Anne	And *thou* vnfit for any place, but hell.
Richard	Yes one place else, if *you* will heare me name it.
Anne	Some dungeon.
Richard	*Your* Bed-chamber.
Anne	Ill rest betide the chamber where *thou* lyest.
Richard	So will it Madam, till I lye with *you*.

. . . . .

Anne	*Thou* was't the cause, and most accurst effect.
Richard	*Your* beauty was the cause of that effect:
	Your beauty that did haunt me in my sleepe,
	To vndertake the death of all the world,
	So I might liue one houre in *your* sweet bosome.
Anne	If I thought that, I tell *thee* Homicide,
	These Nailes should rent that beauty from my Cheekes.
Richard	These eyes could not endure y^t beauties wrack,
	You should not blemish it, if I stood by;
	As all the world is cheared by the Sunne,
	So I by that: It is my day, my life.
Anne	Blacke night ore-shade *thy* day, & death *thy* life.
Richard	Curse not *thy* selfe faire Creature,
	Thou art both.
Anne	I would I were, to be reueng'd on *thee*.
Richard	It is a quarrell most vnnaturall,
	To be reueng'd on him that loueth *thee*.

. . . . .

[After Richard has offered to kill himself, Anne relents.]

Richard	Looke how my Ring incompasseth *thy* Finger,
	Euen so *thy* Brest incloseth my poore heart:
	Weare both of them, for both of them are *thine*.
	And if *thy* poore deuoted Seruant may
	But beg one fauour at *thy* gracious hand,
	Thou dost confirme his happinesse for euer.
Anne	What is it?
Richard	That it may please *you* leaue these sad designes,
	To him that hath most cause to be a Mourner,
	And presently repayre to Crosbie House:
	Where (after I haue solemnly interr'd
	At Chertsey Monast'ry this Noble King,
	And wet his Graue with my Repentant Teares)
	I will with all expedient duty see *you*,

For diuers vnknowne Reasons, I beseech *you*,

Grant me this Boon.

Anne   With all my heart, and much it ioyes me too,

To see *you* are become so penitent.

Tressel and Barkley, go along with me.

Richard   Bid me farwell.

Anne   'Tis more than *you* deserue:

But since *you* teach me how to flatter *you*,

Imagine I haue saide farewell already.   (*Richard III*, I.ii)

---

3. Some of the *ye*'s and *you*'s in the following quotations from Shakespeare are used "correctly" according to the case distinctions of Old and Middle English, and some show a confusion of the older forms. Circle the pronouns that confuse the older nominative and objective functions.

Antony   I do beseech *yee*, if *you* beare me hard,

Now whil'st your purpled hands do reeke and smoake,

Fulfill your pleasure.   (*Julius Caesar*, III.i)

Poet   For shame *you* Generals; what do *you* meane?

Loue, and be Friends, as two such men should bee,

For I haue seene more yeeres I'me sure then *yee*.   (*Julius Caesar*, IV.iii)

Porter   *You*'l leaue your noyse anon *ye* Rascals: doe *you* take the Court for Parish Garden:

ye rude Slaues, leaue your gaping.   (*Henry VIII*, V.iii)

King   As I haue made *ye* one Lords, one remaine:

So I grow stronger, *you* more Honour gaine.   (*Henry VIII*, V.ii)

Banquo   Are *ye* fantasticall, or that indeed

Which outwardly *ye* shew? My Noble Partner

You greet with present Grace, and great prediction

Of Noble hauing, and of Royall hope.   (*Macbeth*, I.iii)

4. Can you think of any reason why nominative *ye* and objective *you* should have been widely confused whereas other nominative-objective distinctions like *he–him*, *she–her*, *I–me*, *we–us*, *they–them* were not so confused? Suggestion: consider the influence of lack of stress.

---

5. Identify the origin of the italicized forms as

        S—regular stressed development of the Middle English pronoun,

        U—unstressed development of the Middle English pronoun, or

        A—analogical form.

_____   *A* toke me to him and ast how my suster dede, and I answeryd wyll, never better. (*Paston Letters*, no. 260)

_____   *Hit* was at Ierusalem the feaste of the dedication. (Tindale's Gospel of John, 10:22)

_____   I shall report *it* so. (*All's Well That Ends Well*, II.v)

_____   It lifted vp *it* head. (*Hamlet*, I.ii)

_____   Heauen grant vs *its* peace. (*Measure for Measure*, I.ii)

_____ And the earth brought forth grass, and herb yielding seed after *his* kind. (Genesis 1:12)

_____ Were our Teares wanting to this Funerall,
These Tidings would call forth *her* flowing Tides. (*1 Henry VI*, I.i)

_____ *Lear* Be my Horsses ready?
Fool Thy Asses are gone about '*em*.   (*King Lear*, I.v)

6. What is the first citation in the *Oxford English Dictionary* for each of the following pronouns used as a simple relative? Give the quotation and the date.

the_____

that_____

which _____

who_____

7. Circle the pronouns that have "improper" case forms according to the rules of school grammar.

   Oliver Know you before whom [you are] sir?
Orlando I, better then him I am before knowes mee.   (*As You Like It*, I.i)

We are alone, here's none but thee, & I.   (*2 Henry VI*, I.ii)

Is she as tall as me?   (*Antony and Cleopatra*, III.iii)

Consider who the King your father sends,
To whom he sends, and what's his Embassie.   (*Love's Labor's Lost*, II.i)

Oh, the dogge is me, and I am my selfe.   (*The Two Gentlemen of Verona*, II.iii)

            The King,
His Brother, and yours, abide all three distracted,
And the remainder mourning ouer them,
Brim full of sorrow, and dismay: but chiefly
Him that you term'd Sir, the good old Lord Gonzallo.   (*The Tempest*, V.i)

Yes, you haue seene Cassio, and she together.   (*Othello*, IV.ii)

For this, from stiller Seats we came, our Parents, and vs twaine.   (*Cymbeline*, V.iv)

Who ioyn'st thou with, but with a Lordly Nation,
That will not trust thee, but for profits sake?   (*1 Henry VI*, III.iii)

Now could I (Caska) name to thee a man,

            · · · · ·

A man no mightier then thy selfe, or me,
In personall action; yet prodigious growne.   (*Julius Caesar*, I.iii)

8.5 *VERBS: THE SEVEN STRONG CLASSES*

Verbs from all of the seven strong classes have survived in Modern English, but sound change and analogy have played such havoc with the vowels which once marked their principal parts that the traditional classification into seven groups has only historical validity.

The most common strong verbs in Modern English, arranged according to the traditional class to which they most nearly conform, are these:

CLASS I   abide, bite, chide, dive, drive, hide, ride, rise, shine, slide, smite, stride, strike, strive, thrive, write

CLASS II   choose, cleave, fly, freeze

CLASS III   begin, bind, cling, dig, drink, fight, find, fling, grind, ring, run, shrink, sing, sink, sling, slink, spin, spring, stick, sting, stink, string, swim, swing, win, wind, wring

CLASS IV   bear, break, come, get, heave, shear, speak, steal, swear, tear, tread, weave

CLASS V   bid, eat, give, lie, see, sit

CLASS VI   draw, forsake, shake, slay, stand, take

CLASS VII   beat, blow, crow, fall, grow, hang, hold, know, throw

Some of these verbs were originally weak or were loan-words but acquired strong inflection by analogy. Their history is discussed in Pyles's *Origins and Development*, pages 208–18, and is summarized in the following outline. For each class, the typical vowels of the Middle English principal parts are listed, the development of the principal parts of modern Standard English is summarized, and the vowels of the three modern parts (infinitive, preterit, past participle) are given in phonetic notation. Complete the outline by writing all three parts of each verb in an appropriate blank. Thus *abide, abode, abode* would go under IC; *bite, bit, bitten,* under IB; and so forth.

CLASS I   (ME ī ǭ i i)

A. Normal development with Modern English preterit from Middle English preterit singular: [aɪ o ɪ-n]

_____   _____

_____   _____

_____   _____

B. Normal development with Modern English preterit from Middle English preterit plural and past participle: [aɪ ɪ ɪ(-n)]

_____   _____

_____   _____

C. Modern English preterit and past participle from Middle English preterit singular: [aɪ o o]

_____   _____

D. Modern English preterit of uncertain origin; normal development of the past participle is now used only metaphorically: [aɪ ə ɪ-n]

_____

E. Originally a weak verb; strong preterit acquired by analogy: [aɪ o aɪ-d]

_____

CLASS II   (ME ē,ō ę̄ u ǭ)

A. Modern English preterit from Middle English past participle: [i,u o o-n]

_____   _____

B. Modern English preterit perhaps by analogy with Class VII: [aɪ u o-n]

_____

209

CLASS III   (ME i,ī a u,ōu u,ōu)

A. Normal development with Modern English preterit from Middle English preterit singular: [ɪ æ ə(-n)]

_____   _____
_____   _____
_____   _____
_____   _____
_____

B. Normal development with Modern English preterit from Middle English preterit plural and past participle: [ɪ,aɪ ə,aʊ ə,aʊ]

_____   _____
_____   _____
_____   _____
_____   _____
_____   _____
_____   _____

C. Modern English present from Middle English past participle: [ə æ ə]

_____

D. Normal development, allowing for the influence of Middle English _h_ [ç,x] on a preceding vowel: [aɪ ɔ ɔ]

_____

CLASS IV   (ME ẹ̄ a ē ǭ)

A. Modern English preterit from Middle English past participle: [i,e o o(-n)]

_____   _____
_____   _____
_____   _____

B. Modern English preterit from Middle English past participle; variation in the vowels is due to the influence of [r]:   [ɛr,ɪr or,ɔr or,ɔr-n]

_____   _____

C. Modern English preterit from Middle English past participle; shortened vowels in all parts: [ɛ ɑ ɑ(-n)]

_____   _____

D. Normal development of the forms _cumen_, _cām_, _cumen_, which were irregular in Middle English: [ə e ə]

_____

CLASS V   (ME ẹ̄ a ē ẹ̄)

A. Modern English preterit from a lengthened form of Middle English preterit singular: [i e i-n]

_____

B. Present stem with irregular [ɪ] since Old English times; three Modern English preterits from the Middle English preterit singular by normal development, from a lengthened form of the

210

Middle English preterit singular, and from the irregular past participle; past participle vowel perhaps from the present by analogy with other verbs which had the same vowel in the present and past participle:　[ɪ æ,e,ɪ ɪ(-n)]

_____

C. Not a continuation of the native English verb (Chaucer's *yeven*, *yaf*, *yaven*, *yeven*), but of a related Scandinavian verb:　[ɪ e ɪ-n]

_____

D. Modern English preterit and past participle from Middle English preterit singular; the present has had an irregular [ɪ] since Old English times:　[ɪ æ æ]

_____

E. Normal development, allowing for influence of [j] on the preceding vowel, except in present stem (for which see Pyles's *Origins and Development*, p. 214, n. 65):　[aɪ e e-n]

_____

F. Normal development of Middle English irregular forms with the vowels [ē aʊ ē]:　[i ɔ i-n]

_____

CLASS VI　　(ME ă̄ ō ō ă̄)

A. Normal development with Modern shortening of the preterit vowel:　[e ʊ e-n]

_____　　　_____

_____

B. Modern English past participle from Middle English preterit:　[æ ʊ ʊ]

_____

C. Present stem vowel from the past participle; preterit vowel by analogy with Class VII verbs:　[e u e-n]

_____

D. Preterit vowel by analogy with Class VII verbs; present and past participle are normal developments of Middle English [aʊ]:　[ɔ u ɔ-n]

_____

CLASS VII　　(ME:　several different vowels in the present and part participle;
　　　　　　　preterit singular and plural:　ĕ or iu)

A. Normal development:　[o u o-n]

_____　　　_____

B. Normal development of the preterit; only the weak past participle now exists:　[o u o-d]

_____

C. Normal development, with spelling of the preterit from the other forms:　[i i i-n]

_____

D. Normal development:　[ɔ ɛ ɔ-n]

_____

E. Modern English past participle from Middle English preterit:　[o ɛ ɛ]

_____

F. Modern English forms are a mixture of three Middle English verbs (*hōn*, Class VII; *hangen*, weak; *hengen*, a Scandinavian loan):　[æ ɔ ɔ]

_____

8.6 VERB ENDINGS AND CONSTRUCTIONS

1. Explain the inflectional form of the italicized verbs.

Thou hotly *lusts* to vse her in that kind, for which thou *whip'st* her.   (*King Lear*, IV.vi)

Sometime she *driueth* ore a Souldiers necke, & then *dreames* he of cutting Forraine throats.
     (*Romeo and Juliet*, I.iv)

His teares *runs* downe his beard like winters drops
From eaues of reeds: your charm so strongly works 'em
That if you now beheld them, your affections
Would become tender.   (*The Tempest*, V.i)

Where is thy Husband now? Where *be* thy Brothers?
Where *be* thy two Sonnes? Wherin dost thou Ioy?   (*Richard III*, IV.iv)

I suppose you *was* in a dream.   (Bunyan, *Pilgrim's Progress*)

For all the Welchmen hearing thou *wert* dead,
Are gone to Bullingbrooke, disperst, and fled.   (*Richard II*, III.ii)

Thou *was't* borne of woman.   (*Macbeth*, V.vii)

2. Paraphrase the italicized expressions in current idiom, and comment on the grammar of the early Modern constructions.

Yet hold I off. Women are Angels *wooing*,
Things won are done, ioyes soule lyes in the dooing.   (*Troilus and Cressida*, I.ii)

The clocke strook nine, when I *did send* the Nurse.   (*Romeo and Juliet*, II.v)

What *saies he* of our marriage? What of that?   (*Romeo and Juliet*, II.v)

I *care not*.   (*Romeo and Juliet*, III.i)

Tis knowne to you he is mine enemy:
Nay more, an enemy vnto you all,
And no great friend, *I feare me* to the King.   (*2 Henry VI*, I.i)

But *me list* not here to make comparison.   (Peele, *The Arraignment of Paris*, prologue)

          The common executioner
Whose heart th'accustom'd sight of death makes hard
Falls not the axe vpon the humbled neck,
But first begs pardon.   (*As You Like It*, III.v)

His Lordship *is walk'd* forth into the Orchard.　　(*2 Henry IV*, I.i)

3. More than one twentieth-century grammar lists forms like these as the "future tense" of English:

I shall go	we shall go
thou wilt go	you will go
he will go	they will go

Comment on the historical validity and the contemporary reality of such a paradigm.

_____

_____

_____

4. The present-day verbal system includes a number of phrases that combine the auxiliaries *be* and *have* with a main verb to produce periphrastic tenses. By consulting the *Oxford English Dictionary* entries for *be* and *have*, determine the earliest date for each of the following constructions.

passive (for example, *is sung*) _____

progressive (for example, *is singing*) _____

progressive passive (for example, *is being sung*) _____

perfect (for example, *has sung*) _____

perfect passive (for example, *has been sung*) _____

8.7　*THE IMPORTANCE OF PREPOSITIONS*

As the inflections of English nouns disappeared, prepositions became more important as grammatical signals, and their number increased.

1. Prepositions have been created from phrases (*because of* from *by cause of*), adapted from inflectional forms (*during* from the archaic *to dure*) or borrowed from other languages (*per* from Latin). Describe the origin of the following prepositions.

amidst _____

among _____

between _____

despite _____

down _____

instead of _____

near _____

past _____

pending _____

plus _____

since _____

via _____

2. The idiomatic use of prepositions has changed somewhat since the early Modern period. What expressions would current English prefer in place of the italicized prepositions in the following quotations?

Antony　Thou can'st not feare [frighten] *vs* Pompey *with* thy sailes.

Weele speake with thee at Sea. *At* land thou know'st
How much we do o're-count [outnumber] thee.　　(*Antony and Cleopatra*, II.vi)

Marcellus　Some sayes, that euer *'gainst* that Season comes
　　　　　Wherein our Sauiours Birth is celebrated,
　　　　　The Bird of Dawning singeth all night long.　　(*Hamlet*, I.i)

Rivers　Then is my Soueraigne slaine?
Queen　I [aye] almost slaine, for he is taken prisoner,
　　　　　　・　・　・　・　・
　　　　And as I further haue to vnderstand,
　　　　Is new committed to the Bishop of Yorke,
　　　　Fell Warwickes Brother, and *by* that our Foe.　　(*3 Henry VI*, IV.iv)

Helena　That you may well perceiue I haue not wrong'd you,
　　　　One of the greatest in the Christian world
　　　　Shall be my suretie: *for* whose throne 'tis needfull
　　　　Ere I can perfect mine intents, to kneele.　　(*All's Well That Ends Well*, IV.iv)

Hamlet　For any thing so ouer-done, if *frō* the
　　　　purpose of Playing, whose end both at the
　　　　first and now, was and is, to hold as 'twer
　　　　the Mirrour vp to Nature.　　(*Hamlet*, III.ii)

Salisbury　And charge, that no man should disturbe your rest,
　　　　　In paine of your dislike, or paine of death.　　(*2 Henry VI*, III.ii)

Portia　And yet I am sure you are not satisfied
　　　　Of these euents at full. Let vs goe in,
　　　　And charge vs there vpon intergatories,
　　　　And we will answer all things faithfully.　　(*The Merchant of Venice*, V.i)

Fool　Why this fellow ha's banish'd two
　　　on's Daughters, and did the third a blessing
　　　against his will, if thou follow him,
　　　thou must needs weare my Coxcombe.　　(*King Lear*, I.iv)

King　. . . he which hath no stomack *to* this fight,
　　　Let him depart, his Pasport shall be made,
　　　And Crownes for Conuoy put into his Purse:
　　　We would not dye in that mans companie.　　(*Henry V*, IV.iii)

---

2 Gent.　What, pray you, became of Antigonus,
　　　　that carryed hence the Child?
3 Gent.　Like an old Tale still, which will haue
　　　　matter to rehearse, though Credit be asleepe,

214

And not an eare open; he was torne to pieces
with a Beare.   (*The Winter's Tale*, V.ii)

8.8 SUBJECTS AND COMPLEMENTS

The italicized portions of the following sentences illustrate constructions that have been used at various times in the history of English. Whenever possible, examples from Old, Middle, and Modern English have been cited.[1] For each group of sentences, describe the construction that is illustrated and indicate whether or not you believe it to be a living part of present-day English.

1. *Sigon* þā tō slǣpe. '[*They*] *sank* then into sleep.' (*Beowulf*)
   Quen he had his broiþer slan, *Began* to hid his corse o-nan. 'When he had slain his brother, [*he*] *began* to hide his corpse anon.' (*Cursor Mundi*)
   This is my Son belov'd, in him *am pleas'd*. (Milton, *Paradise Regained*)

2. Weard maþelode, *ðǣr on wicge sæt*. 'The watchman spoke, *sat there on horseback*.' (*Beowulf*)
   He hadde founde a corn *lay in the yerd*. (Chaucer, *Canterbury Tales*)
   I had it all planned out to go there this summer with a friend of mine *lives in Winnipeg*. (Sinclair Lewis, "Mantrap")

3. *Hit* is weliġ þis ēalond. '*It* is rich, *this island*.' (Bede, *Ecclesiastical History*)
   It stondeth written in thy face *Thyn errour*. (Chaucer, *Parlement of Fowles*)
   What may *it* be, *the heavy sound*? (Scott, "The Lay of the Last Minstrel")

4. *Moyse* ǣrest *and Helias hī* fæston. '*Moses* first *and Elias, they* fasted.' (*St. Guthlac*)
   His sonnes & þe barons Sone þei rised strif. '*His sons and the baron's son, they* raised strife.' (*Langtoft's Chronicle*)
   Her father he couldn't come. (Galsworthy, "Freelands")

5. Cnut *wende him* ūt. 'Cnut *went* out.' (*Anglo-Saxon Chronicle*)
   She *went her* out to pley. (Gower, *Confessio Amantis*)
   The good manne *goeth him* home. (St. Thomas More)

6. Þū ġenōh wel understentst þæt iċ *þē tō* sprece. 'You understand well enough what I speak *to you*.' (Alfred, *Consolation of Philosophy*)
   We aske the leve to speke *the wyth*. 'We ask you leave to speak *with you*.' (Robert of Brunne, *Chronicle*)

[1] The examples are taken from F. Th. Visser, *An Historical Syntax of the English Language* (Leiden, 1963).

7. Ġife iċ *hit ðē*. 'I give *you it*.' (Genesis)

  Þei wyll tele *it yow*. 'They will tell *you it*.' (*Book of Margery Kempe*)

  Your father would never have given *it you*. (Robert Graves, *I, Claudius*)

---

8. Describe the historical development of the italicized construction from the examples in the following sentences:

  Hē cwæþ sōþlīċe, *Iċ hit eom*. (Gospel of John)

  Our Lord answered, *I it am*. (*Book of Margery Kempe*)

  Now speke to me, for *it am I*, Crisseyde. (Chaucer, *Troilus & Crisseyde*)

  Ya soth, said David, *it es I*. (*Cursor Mundi*)

  It is I who should be consulted. (Wilde, *The Ideal Husband*)

  It is not *me* you are in love with. (Steele, *Spectator*)

  "*It's me*," he answered her. (Aldous Huxley, *Antic Hay*)

8.9 *THE EARLY DICTIONARIES*

The first English dictionaries were lists of "hard words" with simple and very concise glosses. As the tradition of lexicography developed, dictionaries increased their scope both in the number of entries and in the amount of information given for each word. Below are sample entries from a number of early works ranging from Henry Cockeram's *English Dictionarie*, the first to use the word *dictionary* in its title, to Samuel Johnson's *Dictionary of the English Language*, in which lexicographical technique approaches contemporary standards. The complete entry for the word *mother*, its compounds, and its derivatives has been quoted from each dictionary.

1623. Henry Cockeram, *The English Dictionarie: or, An Interpreter of hard English Words*.

  Mother. A disease in women when the wombe riseth with paine upwards: sweet smelles are ill for it, but loathsome savors good.

1656. Thomas Blount, *Glossographia: or a Dictionary, Interpreting all such Hard Words Whether Hebrew, Greek, Latin, Italian, Spanish, Teutonick, Belgick, British or Saxon, as are now used in our refined English Tongue*.

  Mother, a disease in women, when the womb riseth with pain, for which the smelling to all sweet savors is harmful; as contrarily, to all strong and loathsom, good.

1676. Elisha Coles, *An English Dictionary, Explaining the Difficult Terms that are used in Divinity, Husbandry, Physick, Philosophy, Law, Navigation, Mathematicks, and other Arts and Sciences*.

  Mother, *a painful rising of the womb, for which all sweet smells are bad, and stinking ones good.*
  Motherwort, Cardiaca, *A cleasing* [sic] *Astringent herb.*
  Mother-tongues, *having no Affinity with one another.*

1689. Anonymous, *Gazophylacium Anglicanum*.

  Mother, from the AS **Moðor**, the Fr. Th. **Mudder**, the Belg. **Moeder**, or the Teut. **Mutter**, the same; all from the Lat. *Mater*, or the Gr. *Mḗtēr, idem.*
  The **Mother** *of Wine*, from the Belg. **Moeder**, lees, thickning; this again from **Modder, Moder**, mud.

1702. John Kersey, *A New English Dictionary*.

A Mother.
A Mother-in-law.
A God-mother.
A Grand-mother.
A Step-mother.
A Mother-city, or *chief City.*
A Mother-tongue.
Mother of Pearl, *a shellfish.*
Mother of time *an herb.*
The Mother, or *dregs of Oil, Wine,* &c.
The Mother, or *womb*; also *a disease in that part.*
Fits of the Mother.
Mother-wort, *an herb.*
Mother-hood, *the quality* or *functions of a* mother.
Motherless, *bereft of a* mother.

1706. John Kersey, revision of Edward Phillips's *The New World of Words: or, Universal English Dictionary.*

Mother, a Woman that has brought forth a Child; also the Womb in which the Child is form'd, or a Disease in that Part; also the Dregs of Ale, B er [sic], Oil, &c.
Mother of Pearl, the Shell that contains the Pearl-fish.
Mother of Time, a kind of Herb.
Mother-Tongues, such Languages as seem to have no Dependence upon, Derivation from, or Relation one to another.
Mother-wort, an Herb, of a cleansing and binding Quality.

1707. *Glossographia Anglicana Nova: or, A Dictionary, Interpreting Such Hard Words of whatever Language, as are at present used in the* English *Tongue, with their* Etymologies, Definitions, *&c.*

Mother, the Womb, or a Disease in that part; also Dregs of Ale, Beer, Oil, &c.
Mother-Tongues, are such Languages as seem to have no dependence upon, derivation from, or affinity with one another; of which *Scaliger* affirms there are eleven only in *Europe*. The *Greek*, the *Latin*, the *Teutonick* or *German*, the *Sclavonick*, the *Albanese* or *Epirotick*. The *European Tartar* or *Scythian*, the *Hungarian*, the *Finnick*, the *Cantrabrian*, the *Irish*, and the old *Gaulish* or *British*; to this number some add Four others, the *Arabick*, the *Cauchian*, the *Illyrian*, and the *Jazygian*.

1708. John Kersey, *Dictionarium Anglo-Britannicum: Or, a General English Dictionary.*

Mother, a Woman that has brought forth a Child; also the Womb in which the Child is form'd, or a Disease in that Part; also the Dregs of Ale, Beer, Oil, &c.
Mother of Pearl, the Shell that contains the Pearl-fish.
Mother of Time, a kind of Herb.
Mother-Tongues, such Languages as seem to have no Derivation from, or Relation to another.
Mother-wort, an Herb.

1730. Nathan Bailey, *Dictionarium Britannicum: Or a more Compleat Universal Etymological English Dictionary Than any Extant.*

Mo′ther [moðor, *Sax.* moder, *Dan.* and *Su.* moeder, *Du.* and L.G. **mutter,** H.G. **modder,** Goth. mader, Pers. *mere,* F. *madre,* It. and Sp. *may,* Port. *mater,* L.] of a child; also the womb itself; also a disease peculiar to that part; also a white substance on stale liquours.
Mother *of Pearl,* the shell which contains the pearl fish.
Mother *of time,* an herb.
Mother *of Wine, Beer,* &c. [**moeder,** lees,] thickening the mouldiness or dregs of wine, beer, &c.
Mother-*Wort,* an herb.

Diffidence is the Mother of Safety

F. *La defiance est la mere de sureté.* It. *La diffidenza è la madre della Sicurtà,*
Mother *Tongues,* are such languages as seem to have no dependance upon, derivation from, or

affinity with one another. Some have been of opinion, that at the confusion of languages, at the building of *Bable*, there were formed 70 or 72 languages. But bishop *Wilkins* and others are of opinion that there were not so many, nor that men did then disperse into so many colonies.

There have been, and at this time there are in the world a far greater number. *Pliny* and *Strabo* relate that in *Dioscuria*, a town of *Colchos*, there were men of 300 nations, and of so many distinct languages, who did resort thither on account of traffick.

Some historians relate, that in every 80 miles of that vast continent, and almost in every particular valley of *Peru*, a distinct language or mother tongue to them was spoken.

And *Purchase* speaks of a 1000 distinct languages spoken by the inhabitants of north *America*, about *Florida*.

Julius Scaliger asserts, that there are no more than eleven mother tongues used in *Europe*, of which four are of more general use and large extent, and the other seven of a narrower extent and use. Those of the larger extent are.

1. The *Greek*, which in antient times was used in *Europe*, *Asia*, and *Africa*, which also did by dispersion and mixture with other people, degenerate into several dialects. As, the *Attick*, *Dorick*, *Æolick*, *Ionick*.

The *Latin*, which, tho' it is much of it derived from the *Greek*, had antiently four dialects, as *Petrus Crinitus* shews out of *Varro*. From the *Latin* are derived the *Italian*, *Spanish* and *French*.

The *Teutonick* or *German*, which is distinguished into two notable dialects. 1. The *Danish*, *Scandian*, and *Gothick*; to which the languages used in *Denmark*, *Sweden*, *Norway* and *Island* do appertain. 2. The *Saxon*, from which much of the *English* and *Scotch* are derived, and also the *Frizian* language, and those languages on the north of the *Elve*; which of all the modern *German* dialects come the nearest to the ancient *German*, and in this work are called L.G.

The *Sclavonick*, which extends itself thro' many large territories, tho' not without some variation, as *Bohemia*, *Croatia*, *Dalmatia*, *Lithuania*, *Muscovia*, *Poland*, and *Vandalia*, this is said to be a language used by 60 several nations.

The languages of lesser extent are.

1. The *Albanese* or old *Epirotick*, now in use in the mountainous parts of *Epirus*.

2. The *European*, *Tartar* or *Scythian*, from which some suppose the *Irish* took its original.

3. As for the *Turkish* tongue, that originally is no other but the *Asiatick Tartarian* tongue mixed with *Armenian*, *Persian*, much *Arabick*, and some *Greek*.

4. The *Hungarian*, used in the greatest part of that kingdom.

5. The *Finnick*, used in *Finland*, and *Lapland*.

6. The *Cantabrian*, in use with the *Biscainers*, who live near the ocean on the *Pyrenean* hills, which border both on *Spain* and *France*.

7. The *Irish* from thence brought over into some parts of *Scotland*, which, Mr. *Camden* supposes to be derived from the *Welsh*.

8. The old *Gaulish* or *British*, still preserved in *Wales*, *Cornwal* and *Britain* in *France*.

To these Mr. *Brerewood* adds 4 more.

1. The *Arabick* that is now used in the steep mountains of *Granada*, which however is no mother tongue, being a dialect of the *Hebrew*.

2. The *Cauchian*, used in east *Friezland*.

3. The *Illyrian*, in the island *Veggia*.

4. The *Jazygian*, on the north-side of *Hungary*.

MOTHER-*Hood* [of **moðerhod**, *Sax.*] the state or relation of a mother.

MOTHER *Churches*, are such as have founded or erected others.

MOTHER [with *Physicians*] a disease in that part where the child is formed; also the womb it self.

MO'THERING, a custom still retained in many places of *England*, of visiting parents on *Midlent Sunday*; and it seems to be called *Mothering*, from the respect in old time paid to the *Mother Church*. It being the custom for people in old popish times to visit their mother church on *Midlent-Sunday*, and to make their offerings at the high-altar.

MO'THERLESS [of **moðor-leas**, *Sax.*] having no mother.

MO'THERLINESS, [**moðer** and **gelicnesse**, *Sax.*] motherly affection, behaviour, &c.

MOTHERLY, tenderly, affectionately, gravely, soberly.

MOTHERY [of **moðer**, *Sax.*] having a white substance on it by reason of age; as liquors.

1735. Thomas Dyche and William Pardon, *A New General English Dictionary; Peculiarly calculated for the Use and Improvement Of such as are unacquainted with the Learned Languages.*

MO'THER (S.) any female that has or does bring forth young, though it is commonly applied only to women; sometimes it is applied in an ill sense, to an elderly woman who follows the detestable trade of keeping and encouraging young women to prostitute themselves to any body for money, who is vulgarly called a bawd; sometimes it is applied to inanimate things, as the *mother*-church, *mother* of pearl, &c. sometimes the white films or mouldiness that generates upon beer, wine, vinegar, &c. goes by this name.

Fits of the Mother, called also hysterick disorders, is a convulsion of the nerves of the *par vagum* and intercostal in the abdomen, proceeding from a pricking irritation or explosion of spirits; some imagine this distemper wholly depends upon, and flows from the womb, which is a mistake, though it often does, yet sometimes it does not, because men are affected with it as well as women.

MO′THER-CHURCH (S.) such an one within whose district or jurisdiction other churches have been built, as *Stepney* church near *London*, from whose jurisdiction, upon building new churches, the parishes of St. *Paul's Shadwell*, St. *John's Wapping*, *Christ-Church Spittlefields*, &c. have been taken.

MO′THERLESS (A.) the state of one whose mother is dead.

MO′THERLINESS (S.) the kind affectionate care of a mother over her young children; also the sedate and wise behaviour of a matron, or other discreet woman.

MO′THER-TONGUE (S.) the common, living, or vulgar tongue, spoke by any nation or people whatever.

MO′THERY (A.) the state of liquors that are wasting, perishing, or spoiling, by being kept too long, and the air getting to them, and which is perceived by a whitish, musty film or skin that grows over the upper surface.

1755.   Samuel Johnson, *A Dictionary of the English Language: in which the Words are deduced from their Originals, and Illustrated in their Different Significations by Examples from the best Writers.*

MO′THER.   *n. s.* [*moðor*, Saxon; *moder*, Danish; *moeder*, Dutch.]
1. A woman that has born a child, correlative to son or daughter.

> Let thy *mother* rather feel thy pride, than fear
> Thy dangerous stoutness.   *Shakespeare's Coriolanus.*
>
> Come sit down every *mother's* son,
> And rehearse your parts.   *Shakespeare.*
>
> I had not so much of man in me,
> But all my *mother* came into mine eyes,
> And gave me up to tears.   *Shakesp. Henry V.*

2. That which has produced any thing.

> Alas, poor country! It cannot
> Be call'd our *mother*, but our grave.   *Shakespeare.*
>
> The resemblance of the constitution and diet of the inhabitants to those of their *mother* country, occasion a great affinity in the popular diseases.   *Arbuthnot on Air.*
>
> The strongest branch leave for a standard, cutting off the rest close to the body of the *mother* plant.   *Mortimer's Husb.*

3. That which has preceded in time: as, a *mother* church to chapels.
4. That which requires reverence and obedience.

> The good of *mother* church, as well as that of civil society, renders a judicial practice necessary.   *Ayliffe's Parergon.*

5. Hysterical passion; so called, as being imagined peculiar to women.

> This stopping of the stomach might be the *mother*; forasmuch as many were troubled with *mother* fits, although few returned to have died of them.   *Graunt's Bills.*

6. A familiar term of address to an old woman; or to a woman dedicated to religious austerities.
7. MOTHER *in law*. A husband's or wife's mother.   *Ains.*

> I am come to set at variance the daughter in law against the *mother in law*.   *Matth.* x.35.

8. [*Moeder*, Dutch, from *modder*, mud.] A thick substance concreting in liquors; the lees or scum concreted.

> If the body be liquid, and not apt to putrefy totally, it will cast up a *mother*, as the *mothers* of distilled waters.   *Bacon.*
>
> Potted fowl, and fish come in so fast,
> That ere the first is out the second stinks,
> And mouldy *mother* gathers on the brinks.   *Dryden.*

9. [More properly *modder*; *modde*, Dutch.] A young girl. Now totally obsolete.

> A sling for a *mother*, a bow for a boy,
> A whip for a carter.   *Tusser's Husbandry.*

MO'THER. *adj.* Had at the birth; native.

        For whatsoever *mother* wit or art

Could work, he put in proof.   *Hubberd's Tale.*

        Where did you study all this goodly speech?

—It is extempore, from my *mother* wit.   *Shakespeare.*

Boccace, living in the same age with Chaucer, had the same genius, and followed the same studies: both writ novels, and each of them cultivated his *mother* tongue.   *Dryden.*

                   Cecilia came,

Inventress of the vocal frame,

Enlarg'd the former narrow bounds,

And added length to solemn sounds,

With nature's *mother* wit, and arts unknown before.   *Dryd.*

To MO'THER. *v. n.* To gather concretion.

They oint their naked limbs with *mother'd* oil.   *Dryden.*

MO'THER *of pearl.* A kind of coarse pearl; the shell in which pearls are generated.

               His mortal blade

In ivory sheath, ycarv'd with curious slights,

Whose hilt was burnish'd gold, and handle strong

Of *mother-pearl.*   *Fairy Qu. b.* i.

They were made of onyx, sometimes of *mother of pearl.*   *Hakewill on Providence.*

MO'THERHOOD. *n. s.* [from *mother.*] The office or character of a mother.

    Thou shalt see the blessed mother-maid

Exalted more for being good,

Than for her interest of *motherhood.*   *Donne.*

MO'THERLESS. *adj.* [from *mother.*] Destitute of a mother; orphan of a mother.

I might shew you my children, whom the rigour of your justice would make complete orphans, being already *motherless.*   *Waller's Speech to the House of Commons.*

My concern for the three poor *motherless* children obliges me to give you this advice.   *Arbuthnot's Hist. of J. Bull.*

MO'THERLY. *adj.* [from *mother* and *like.*] Belonging to a mother; suitable to a mother.

They can owe no less than child-like obedience to her that hath more than *motherly* power.   *Hooker, b.* v.

They termed her the great mother, for her *motherly* care in cherishing her brethren whilst young.   *Raleigh.*

    Within her breast though calm, her breast though pure,

Motherly cares and fears got head, and rais'd

Some troubled thoughts.   *Milton's Par. Reg. b.* ii.

When I see the *motherly* airs of my little daughters when playing with their puppets, I cannot but flatter myself that their husbands and children will be happy in the possession of such wives and mothers.   *Addison's Spect.* No. 500.

Though she was a truly good woman, and had a sincere *motherly* love for her son John, yet there wanted not those who endeavoured to create a misunderstanding between them.   *Arb.*

MO'THERLY. *adv.* [from *mother.*] In manner of a mother.

    Th' air doth not *motherly* sit on the earth,

To hatch her seasons, and give all things birth.   *Donne.*

MOTHER *of thyme. n. s.* [*serpyllum,* Latin.] It hath trailing branches, which are not so woody and hard as those of thyme, but in every other respect is the same.   *Miller.*

MO'THERWORT. *n. s.* [*cardiaca,* Latin.] A plant.

The flower of the *motherwort* consists of one leaf, and is of the lip kind, whose upper lip is imbricated and much longer than the under one, which is cut into three parts; from the flower-cup arises the pointal, fixed like a nail in the hinder part of the flower, attended by four embrios which become angular seeds, occupying the flower-cup.   *Miller.*

MO'THERY. *adj.* [from *mother.*] Concreted; full of concretions; dreggy; feculent: used of liquors.

1780.   Thomas Sheridan, *A General Dictionary of the English Language,* 2 vols.[2]

MOTHER, mŭth'-thŭr. *s.* A woman that has borne a child, correlative to son or daughter; that which has produced any thing; that which has preceded in time, as, a Mother church to chapels;

2 The numbers over the vowels are diacritics: ŭ as in *but,* ŭ as in *bush,* ŏ as in *not,* and so forth.

hysterical passion; a familiar term of address to an old woman; Mother-in-Law, a husband's or wife's mother; a thick substance concreting in liquors, the lees or scum concreted.

MOTHER, mŭth'-thŭr. a. Had at a birth, native.

To MOTHER, mŭth'-thŭr. v. a. To gather concretion.

MOTHER OF PEARL, mŭth'-thŭr-ŏv-pĕrl'. A kind of coarse pearl, the shell in which pearls are generated.

MOTHERHOOD, mŭth'-thŭr-hŭd. s. The office, state, or character, of a mother.

MOTHERLESS, mŭth'-thŭr-lĭs. a. Destitute of a mother.

MOTHERLY, mŭth'-thŭr-lў. a. Belonging to a mother, suitable to a mother.

MOTHERWORT, mŭth'-thŭr-wŭrt. s. A plant.

MOTHERY, mŭth'-thŭr-ў. a. Concreted, full of concretions, dreggy, feculent: used of liquors.

1. From the beginning, English dictionaries have shown the spelling of a word by its very entry and have given a definition of some sort. We, however, have come to expect a good deal more of our dictionaries. Which of the dictionaries illustrated above was the first to include each of the following kinds of information?

   entries for common words _____

   word-stress _____

   pronunciation _____

   part-of-speech labels _____

   etymology _____

   definitions of everyday as well as of "hard" meanings _____

   illustrative quotations _____

2. Examine the entries for *mother* and related words in a recent dictionary. What are the chief differences between them and the entries cited above? _____

   _____

   _____

   _____

3. What kinds of comments or information in the early dictionaries would seem out of place in a modern work? _____

   _____

   _____

   _____

4. What weakness is apparent in the etymologies of all these early dictionaries? _____

   _____

   _____

5. Suggest several corrections a modern linguist would make to Scaliger's classification of languages given in Bailey's dictionary under the entry *mother tongues.* _____

   _____

   _____

6. Find a quotation used by Johnson that does not illustrate the definition for which it is cited.

   _____

   _____

7. DeWitt T. Starnes and Gertrude E. Noyes maintain that in the early Modern period, "lexicography progressed by plagiarism" and "the best lexicographer was often the most discriminating plagiarist."[3] Discuss these two conclusions in the light of the entries cited above.

[3] *The English Dictionary from Cawdrey to Johnson* (Chapel Hill, N.C., 1946), p. 183.

8.10 *EIGHTEENTH-CENTURY ATTITUDES TOWARD LANGUAGE*

During the eighteenth century, many men tried their hands at writing English grammars, men as diverse as Robert Lowth, Bishop of London, and Joseph Priestley, the discoverer of oxygen. George Campbell, a typical grammarian of the period, was neither as authoritarian as Lowth nor as scientifically objective as Priestley. The theory of use that he set forth in the *Philosophy of Rhetoric* (1776) is one that present-day grammarians can still accept, but his application of that theory abounded with inconsistencies. Campbell's self-contradictory *via media* illustrates well both what is best and what is worst in eighteenth-century attitudes toward language. The following extracts from Chapters I, II, and III of Book II of the *Philosophy of Rhetoric* illustrate Campbell's theory and practice.

CHAPTER I

The Nature and Characters of the Use which gives Law to Language

Every tongue whatever is founded in use or custom,
——————————— Whose arbitrary sway
Words and the forms of language must obey.   Francis.

Language is purely a species of fashion (for this holds equally of every tongue) in which, by the general but tacit consent of the people of a particular state or country, certain sounds come to be appropriated to certain things, as their signs, and certain ways of inflecting and combining those sounds come to be established, as denoting the relations which subsist among the things signified.

It is not the business of grammar, as some critics seem preposterously to imagine, to give law to the fashions which regulate our speech. On the contrary, from its conformity to these, and from that alone, it derives all its authority and value. For, what is the grammar of any language? It is no other than a collection of general observations methodically digested, and comprising all the modes previously and independently established, by which the significations, derivations, and combinations of words in that language are ascertained. It is of no consequence here to what causes originally these modes or fashions owe their existence—to imitation, to reflection, to affectation, or to caprice; they no sooner obtain and become general, than they are laws of the language, and the grammarian's only business is, to note, collect, and methodise them. Nor does this truth concern only those more comprehensive analogies or rules which affect whole classes of words; such as nouns, verbs, and the other parts of speech; but it concerns every individual word, in the inflecting or the combining of which a particular mode hath prevailed. Every single anomaly, therefore, though departing from the rule assigned to the other words of the same class, and on that account called an exception, stands on the same basis, on which the rules of the tongue are founded, custom having prescribed for it a separate rule. . . .

Only let us rest in these as fixed principles, that use, or the custom of speaking, is the sole original standard of conversation, as far as regards the expression, and the custom of writing is the sole standard of style; that the latter comprehends the former, and something more; that to the tribunal of use, as to the supreme authority, and, consequently, in every grammatical controversy, the last resort, we are entitled to appeal from the laws and the decisions of grammarians; and that this order of subordination ought never, on any account, to be reversed.

But if use be here a matter of such consequence, it will be necessary, before advancing any farther, to ascertain precisely what it is. We shall otherwise be in danger, though we agree about the name, of differing widely in the notion that we assign to it. . . .

In what extent then must the word be understood? It is sometimes called *general use*; yet is it not manifest that the generality of people speak and write very badly? Nay, is not this a truth that will be even generally acknowledged? It will be so; and this very acknowledgment shows that many terms and idioms may be common, which, nevertheless, have not the general sanction, no, nor even the suffrage of those that use them. The use here spoken of implies not only *currency*, but *vogue*. It is properly *reputable custom*. . . .

Agreeably then to this first qualification of the term, we must understand to be comprehended under general use, *whatever modes of speech are authorized as good by the writings of a great number, if not the majority, of celebrated authors*. . . .

Another qualification of the term *use* which deserves our attention is, that it must be *national*. This I consider in a twofold view, as it stands opposed both to *provincial* and *foreign*. . . .

But there will naturally arise here another question, 'Is not use, even good and national use, in the same country, different in different periods? And if so, to the usage of what period shall we attach ourselves, as the proper rule? If you say *the present*, as it may reasonably be expected that you will, the difficulty is not entirely removed. In what extent of signification must we understand the word *present*? How far may we safely range in quest of authorities? or, at what distance backwards from this moment are authors still to be accounted as possessing a legislative voice in language?' . . .

As use, therefore, implies duration, and as even a few years are not sufficient for ascertaining the characters of authors, I have, for the most part, in the following sheets, taken my prose examples, neither from living authors, nor from those who wrote before the Revolution; not from the first, because an author's fame is not so firmly established in his lifetime; nor from the last, that there may be no suspicion that the style is superannuated.

CHAPTER II

The Nature and Use of Verbal Criticism, with its Principal Canons

. . . But on this subject of use, there arise two eminent questions, . . . The first question is this, 'Is reputable, national, and present use, which, for brevity's sake, I shall hereafter simply denominate good use, always uniform in her decisions?' The second is, 'As no term, idiom, or application, that is totally unsupported by her, can be admitted to be good, is every term, idiom, and application that is countenanced by her, to be esteemed good, and therefore worthy to be retained?'

In answer to the former of these questions, I acknowledge, that in every case there is not a perfect uniformity in the determinations, even of such use as may justly be denominated good. Wherever a considerable number of authorities can be produced in support of two different, though resembling modes of expression for the same thing, there is always a divided use, and one cannot be said to speak barbarously, or to oppose the usage of the language, who conforms to either side. . . .

In those instances, therefore, of divided use, which give scope for option, the following canons are humbly proposed, in order to assist us in assigning the preference. Let it, in the mean time, be remembered, as a point always presupposed, that the authorities on the opposite sides are equal, or nearly so. . . .

The first canon, then, shall be, When use is divided as to any particular word or phrase, and the expression used by one part hath been pre-occupied, or is in any instance susceptible of a different signification, and the expression employed by the other part never admits a different sense, both perspicuity and variety require that the form of expression which is in every instance strictly univocal be preferred. . . .

In the preposition *toward* and *towards*, and the adverbs *forward* and *forwards*, *backward* and *backwards*, the two forms are used indiscriminately. But as the first form in all these is also an adjective, it is better to confine the particles to the second. Custom, too, seems at present to lean this way. *Besides* and *beside* serve both as conjunctions and as prepositions. There appears some tendency at present to assign to each a separate province. This tendency ought to be humoured by employing only the former as the conjunction, the latter as the preposition. . . .

The second canon is, In doubtful cases regard ought to be had in our decisions to the analogy of the language. . . .

If by the former canon the adverbs *backwards* and *forwards* are preferable to *backward* and *forward*; by this canon, from the principle of analogy, *afterwards* and *homewards* should be preferred to *afterward* and *homeward*. Of the two adverbs *thereabout* and *thereabouts*, compounded of the particle *there* and the preposition, the former alone is analogical, there being no such word in the language as *abouts*. The same holds of *hereabout* and *whereabout*. . . .

The third canon is, When the terms or expressions are in other respects equal, that ought to be preferred which is most agreeable to the ear. . . .

Of this we have many examples. *Delicateness* hath very properly given way to *delicacy*; and for a like reason *authenticity* will probably soon displace *authenticalness*, and *vindictive* dispossess *vindicative* altogether. . . .

The fourth canon is, In cases wherein none of the foregoing rules gives either side a ground of preference, a regard to simplicity (in which I include etymology when manifest) ought to determine our choice.

Under the name simplicity I must be understood to comprehend also brevity; for that expression is always the simplest which, with equal purity and perspicuity, is the briefest. We have, for instance, several active verbs which are used either with or without a preposition indiscriminately. Thus we say either *accept* or *accept of*, *admit* or *admit of*, *approve* or *approve of*; in like manner *address* or *address to*, *attain* or *attain to*. In such instances it will hold, I suppose, pretty generally, that the simple form is preferable. . . .

The fifth and only other canon that occurs to me on the subject of divided use is, In the few cases wherein neither perspicuity nor analogy, neither sound nor simplicity, assists us in fixing our choice, it is safest to prefer that manner which is most conformable to ancient usage.

This is founded on a very plain maxim, that in language, as in several other things, change itself, unless when it is clearly advantageous, is ineligible. This affords another reason for preferring that usage which distinguishes *ye* as the nominative plural of *thou*, when more than one are addressed, from *you* the accusative. . . .

I come now to the second question for ascertaining both the extent of the authority claimed by custom, and the rightful prerogatives of criticism. As no term, idiom, or application, that is totally unsupported by use, can be admitted to be good; is every term, idiom, and application, that is countenanced by use, to be esteemed good, and therefore worthy to be retained? I answer, that though nothing in language can be good from which use withholds her approbation, there may be many things to which she gives it, that are not in all respects good, or such as are worthy to be retained and imitated. . . .

It is therefore, I acknowledge, not without meaning, that Swift affirms, that, "there are many gross improprieties, which, though authorized by practice, ought to be discarded." Now, in order to discard them, nothing more is necessary than to disuse them. And to bring us to disuse them, both the example and the arguments of the critic will have their weight. . . .

The first canon on this subject is, All words and phrases which are remarkably harsh and unharmonious, and not absolutely necessary, may justly be judged worthy of this fate. . . .

Such are the words *bare-faced-ness*, *shame-faced-ness*, *un-success-ful-ness*, *dis-interest-ed-ness*, *wrong-headed-ness, tender-hearted-ness.* They are so heavy and drawling, and withal so ill compacted, that they have not more vivacity than a periphrasis, to compensate for the defect of harmony. . . .

The second canon on this subject is, When etymology plainly points to a signification different from that which the word commonly bears, propriety and simplicity both require its dismission. . . .

The verb *to unloose*, should analogically signify *to tie*, in like manner as *to untie* signifies *to loose*. To what purpose is it, then, to retain a term, without any necessity, in a signification the reverse of that which its etymology manifestly suggests? In the same way, *to annul*, and *to disannul*, ought by analogy to be contraries, though irregularly used as synonymous. . . .

The third canon is, When any words become obsolete, or at least are never used, except as constituting part of particular phrases, it is better to dispense with their service entirely, and give up the phrases. . . .

Examples of this we have in the words *lief, dint, whit, moot, pro,* and *con*, as, 'I had as lief go myself,' for 'I should like as well to go myself.' 'He convinced his antagonist *by dint of argument*,' that is, 'by strength of argument.' 'He made them yield *by dint of arms*,'—'by force of arms.' 'He is *not a whit better*,'—'no better.' 'The case you mention is *a moot point*,'—'a disputable point.' 'The question was strenuously debated *pro and con*,'—'on both sides.'

The fourth and last canon I propose is, All those phrases, which, when analysed grammatically, include a solecism, and all those to which use hath affixed a particular sense, but which, when explained by the general and established rules of the language, are susceptible either of a different sense, or of no sense, ought to be discarded altogether.

It is this kind of phraseology which is distinguished by the epithet *idiomatical*, and hath been originally the spawn, partly of ignorance, and partly of affectation. Of the first sort, which includes a solecism, is the phrase, 'I *had* rather *do* such a thing,' for 'I would rather do it.' The auxiliary *had*, joined to the infinitive active *do*, is a gross violation of the rules of conjugation in our language. . . .

Of the second sort, which, when explained grammatically, leads to a different sense from what the words in conjunction commonly bear, is, 'He sings a good song,' for 'he sings well.' The plain meaning of the words as they stand connected is very different, for who sees not that a good song may be ill sung? . . .

CHAPTER III

Of Grammatical Purity

[Chapter III discusses various barbarisms, solecisms, and improprieties "which writers of great name, and even of critical skill in the language, have slidden into through inattention." Among these offenses against grammatical purity are the following. The italics are Campbell's.]

"The zeal of the *seraphim* breaks forth in a becoming warmth of sentiments and expressions, as the character which is given us of *him* denotes that generous scorn and intrepidity which attends heroic virtue." (Addison)

"This noble nation hath *of all others* admitted *fewer* corruptions." (Swift)

"Such notions would be avowed at this time by none but rosicrucians, and fanatics as mad as them." (Bolingbroke)

"Tell the Cardinal, that I understand poetry better than him." (Smollet)

"My christian and surname begin and end with the same letters." (Addison)

"*Each* of the sexes should keep within *its* particular bounds, and content *themselves* to exult within *their* respective districts." (Addison)

"*If* thou *bring* thy gift to the altar, and there *rememberest* that thy brother hath ought against thee . . ." (Matt. 5:23)

"I shall do all I can to persuade others to *take* the same measures for their cure which I *have*."

(*Guardian*, No. 1)

"Will it be urged, that the four gospels are *as old*, or even *older than* tradition?" (Bolingbroke)

"The greatest masters of critical learning differ *among one another*." (*Spectator*, No. 321)

"A petty constable will *neither* act cheerfully *or* wisely." (Swift)

"I may say, without vanity, that there is not a gentleman in England better read in tomb-stones than myself, my studies having *laid* very much in church-yards." (*Spectator*, No. 518)

"The exercise of reason appears as little in them, as in the beasts they sometimes hunt, and by *whom* they are sometimes hunted." (Bolingbroke)

Adam,

The comeliest man of men *since born*

His sons. The fairest of *her daughters* Eve. (Milton)

1. What does Campbell say is the "supreme authority" in language? _____

_____

2. What does he conceive the task of the grammarian to be? _____

_____

3. What should be the grammarian's attitude toward anomalies, that is, words or constructions that follow no general pattern? _____

_____

4. How does Campbell apparently conceive of the relationship between speech and writing?

_____

_____

5. Campbell's three qualifications of use are that it be *reputable*, *national*, and *present*. Explain what he means by these three terms. _____

_____

_____

_____

_____

6. Would Campbell be willing to settle a question of use by polling a representative cross section of the English population? Explain. _____

_____

_____

7. When use is divided between two different expressions for the same idea, what view does Campbell take of the correctness of the two expressions? _____

_____

_____

8. For choosing between divided use, Campbell proposes five canons. Explain each of them briefly. _____

_____

_____

_____

_____

_____

9. What does Campbell mean when he says that change in language is "ineligible"?

_____

_____

10. How does Campbell answer the question "Is all use good?"_____

_____

_____

11. Whose precept and example is to guide us among the pitfalls of use? _____

_____

12. Briefly explain the four canons Campbell proposes for determining what uses should be discarded. _____

_____

_____

_____

_____

13. List several specific contradictions or inconsistencies in Campbell's discussion of correctness in language._____

_____

_____

_____

_____

14. Identify the "errors" in the quotations from Chapter III of *The Philosophy of Rhetoric*.

15. Look up one of the "errors" in several recent school grammars or guides to usage to see whether there has been any change in attitude toward it.

9

Recent British and American English

9.1 *QUESTIONS FOR REVIEW AND DISCUSSION*

1. Define the following terms:

a language	edited English
a dialect	prescriptive grammar
Americanisms	purism
Britishisms	shibboleths
RP (received pronunciation)	"*ask*" words
collective noun	dialect or linguistic geography
caste dialect	settlement history

2. What justification is there for the claim that one type of English, such as Standard British English, is superior to all others? On what fallacy are such claims based?

3. What accounts for the fact that British English generally has greater prestige than other types, such as American or Australian?

4. In what respects is American English more conservative than British English and in what respects is it less so?

5. Is the Englishman who is concerned about speaking correctly likely to worry more about pronunciation or about syntax? How does the linguistically insecure American differ from his British counterpart?

6. Are there any types of American pronunciation, regional or social, against which prejudice is so great that they would debar a speaker from the learned professions?

7. Katharine Whitehorn observed, "In America, where it is grammar, not accent, that places you, anyone can learn the grammar; maybe Bostonians don't accept it, but Bostonians only impress other Bostonians." ("What Makyth Manners?" *Spectator*, March 9, 1962, p. 317). Which is easier, changing the phonetic patterns of one's speech or avoiding what are thought of as grammatical errors? Why? Is there any regional form of speech that is high in prestige throughout the United States?

8. After determining whether Dorothy Parker is English or American and checking with the *Oxford English Dictionary* and Fowler's *Modern English Usage*, comment on the linguistic pronouncement by Miss Parker that "anyone who, as does [Henry] Miller, follows 'none' with a plural verb . . . should assuredly not be called a writer." (*Esquire*, September 1961, p. 34). Would Miss Parker approve of the number of the verb in this sentence? "As yet none of my characters has been industrialists, economists, trade union leaders." (*New Statesman*, July 17, 1954; cited in Brian Foster, *The Changing English Language*, London, 1968, p. 208).

9. In the preface to *Pygmalion*, George Bernard Shaw insists that all art should be didactic; what is he trying to teach in the play? What actual person did Shaw have in mind when he created the character of Henry Higgins?

228

10. List the important differences between British English and American English. Which of the differences is most significant?

11. Americans have been charged with a tendency to exaggerate. Supply some further examples of "the American love of grandiloquence" referred to on page 243, footnote 32, of Pyles's *Origins and Development*.

12. What are the main scholarly organizations and publications devoted to the study of American English?

13. What importance has the study of British dialects for an understanding of American English?

14. Which are more important, the differences or the similarities between British and American English?

15. What are the chances that English will split up into a number of mutually unintelligible dialects—that is, into separate languages?

9.2   AMERICANISMS

1. Among the words that are in some way peculiar to the United States are the following. Describe the origin of each word, as it is shown in the *Dictionary of American English* (*DAE*) or the *Dictionary of Americanisms* (*DA*).

blue laws _____
bushwhacker _____
carpetbagger _____
charley horse _____
cinch _____
civil rights _____
clambake _____
conniption _____
cybernetics _____
dicker _____
dude _____
ghost writer _____
hex _____
hoodlum _____
law-abiding _____
parlay _____
ranch _____
semester _____
sideburns _____
stoop 'porch' _____

2. By consulting the *DAE* or the *DA*, list ten additional examples of Americanisms.

_____
_____
_____

_____
_____
_____
_____
_____
_____
_____
_____
_____

9.3 NATIONAL DIFFERENCES IN WORD CHOICE

1. Give the distinctively British English equivalents of the following American terms. Most of the words are in Pyles's *Origins and Development*.

baby carriage	_____	(cream) pitcher	_____
billion	_____	prep school	_____
bookkeeper	_____	principal editorial	_____
chain stores	_____	public school	_____
cuffs	_____	raise (in salary)	_____
gasoline	_____	second story	_____
gas water-heater	_____	sedan	_____
hood (of a car)	_____	sneakers	_____
installment buying	_____	spool	_____
intermission	_____	suspenders	_____
(to) mail	_____	trailer	_____
mailbox	_____	trillion	_____
molasses	_____	truck	_____
muffler (on a car)	_____	two weeks	_____
orchestra seat	_____	vest	_____

2. The following terms either are exclusively British English or have at least one special sense that is predominantly British. Give the American English equivalents of the British senses. The terms can be found in a desk dictionary.

accumulator	_____	gangway	_____
bespoke	_____	hoarding	_____
biscuit	_____	holidays	_____
boot (of a car)	_____	minerals	_____
bowler	_____	public house	_____
bug	_____	(to) queue up	_____
chemist	_____	rates	_____
chips	_____	roundabout	_____
costermonger	_____	sleeping partner	_____
cotton wool	_____	suspender	_____
draughts	_____	sweet (n.)	_____
drawing pin	_____	switchback	_____
dustbin	_____	tart	_____
fanlight	_____	underground	_____
form	_____	wing	_____

3. An American reporter who interviewed G. K. Chesterton described him as a "regular guy." What reason had Chesterton, an Englishman, for being or pretending to be offended? What is the probable etymology of *guy*? _____

_____

_____

_____

9.4 *NATIONAL DIFFERENCES IN GRAMMAR AND IDIOM*

1. What constructions in the following quotations from British writers would an American be likely to phrase in a different manner? Underline the constructions and rephrase them.

(1) It is hard to think of a writer of high class who really stretched his imaginative sympathy. . . . Some of the nineteenth-century Russian novelists might have done; their natures were broad enough. (C. P. Snow, *The Two Cultures: and a Second Look*, 1963, pp. 29–30) _____

_____

(2) I thank Mr. Watson Taylor for his compliments and suggest he has another look at what I actually wrote. (*The Times Literary Supplement*, June 27, 1968, p. 679)

_____

(3) When Mr. Macmillan has dispersed the last miasma of the Profumo affair . . . it may be that he will hand over. But to whom? (*Spectator*, October 4, 1963, p. 403)

_____

(4) Investment Notes . . . International Tea are near the bottom with 13.7 per cent. (*Ibid.*, p. 434) _____

_____

(5) A number of London stock-broking firms are recommending their clients to buy Australian ordinary shares. (*Punch*, March 13, 1963, p. 384) _____

_____

(6) I used often to find myself successful in teaching subjects not my own. (*Punch*, April 24, 1963, p. 596) _____

(7) It must be getting a bit of a strain on our public figures, always being called from conferences or rehearsals or typewriters to encounter these extraordinary questions on the telephone. (*Punch*, May 15, 1963, p. 688) _____

_____

(8) The Government have set up the agency to help the industry. (*Time & Tide*, July 8, 1964, p. 38) _____

(9) The Welsh centre Dawes was concussed in the third minute of the game . . . but Ireland were slow to exploit this weakness of manpower. (*The Illustrated London News*, March 20, 1965, p. 12) _____

(10) He omits to mention the far more far-reaching difficulty that there are differences in status between poets, and between individual poems. (*The Times Literary Supplement*, September 2, 1965, p. 755) _____

(11) Pied-à-terre, or bachelor flat, to let in modern block in Sloane Avenue. (*The Times*, August 27, 1965, p. 1)_____

(12) There was a slight bump as the aircraft entered cloud, and the pilot's hands tightened on the controls. (*Blackwood's Magazine*, July 1964, p. 4) _____

_____

(13) "Have you not a father?" I asked. (*Blackwood's Magazine*, September 1964, p. 240)

_____

(14) I began to say, "What will your wife feel about that?" (*Ibid.*, p. 241) _____

_____

2. In British use the past participle *gotten* has been generally replaced by *got*, except for set expressions and derivatives like *forgotten*. In America both past participles remain in use, but with a specialization in meaning. Describe the American difference between *got* and *gotten* as it appears in the following examples.

(1) He doesn't have much hair, but he's got a full beard.
(2) So far he's gotten most of his ideas about ecology from the *Reader's Digest*.
(3) She's got a neurosis.
(4) She's gotten a neurosis.
(5) Whether he wants to or not, he's got to take the exam.
(6) As a result of his petitions, he's finally gotten to take the exam.
(7) Everybody's got to do it.
(8) Everybody's gotten to do it.

_____
_____
_____
_____

The following examples are more characteristic of British than of American use. Rephrase them in the form most common in the United States.

(9) We haven't got a chance._____
(10) The waiter had got a towel over his arm. _____
(11) We've just got ready to eat._____

3. By skimming a British publication, find an example of a grammatical construction or idiom which differs from American usage. _____

_____
_____
_____
_____
_____
_____

9.5   *BRITISH AND AMERICAN PURISM*

Among the constructions that are disapproved by one purist or another are those italicized in the sentences below. Investigate the status of one of these constructions, using the following techniques:

1. Ascertain the earlier history of the construction as it is revealed by the citations in the *Oxford English Dictionary*.

2. Compare the opinions of such widely used contemporary guides to usage as H. W. Fowler's *Dictionary of Modern English Usage*, 2nd ed., rev. and ed. by Sir Ernest Gowers (1965), Margaret Nicholson's *Dictionary of American-English Usage* (1957), Bergen and Cornelia Evans's *Dictionary of Contemporary American Usage* (1957), Porter G. Perrin's *Writer's Guide and Index to English*, 3rd ed. (1959), Margaret M. Bryant's *Current American Usage* (1962), Wilson Follett's *Modern American Usage* (1966), and the usage notes in recent dictionaries, of which perhaps the most self-consciously authoritarian is *The American Heritage Dictionary* (1969). All such guides must be used critically—some aim at objective reporting, others indulge the prejudices of their authors.

3. Survey contemporary use of the construction by finding examples of it or of its alternatives. Skim recent newspapers, magazines, novels, and other printed material. Listen for its use in conversation, over the radio or television, in speeches, or in other forms of oral communication. For each occurrence you observe prepare a note card with the following information:

> CITATION: quotation illustrating the construction or alternative.
> SOURCE: bibliographical data for a printed source; speaker, occasion, and date for an oral source.
> CIRCUMSTANCES: any information which may help to determine the status of the construction (for example, occurs in dialogue, speaker is rustic, used in a formal situation, and so forth).

Write the results of your investigation in the form of an article for a usage dictionary. Describe the usage you have observed, including any apparent social, regional, or functional limitations, and summarize the information in the *OED* and the usage guides you have consulted.

What was he asking *about*? (similarly, other final prepositions)

I'm ready, *aren't I*?

It is *not as* late as we thought.

She felt *badly* about it.

The second is the *best* of the two books. (similarly, other superlatives used for one of two)

There were no secrets *between* the three brothers.

You can't judge a *book's* content by its cover. (similarly, genitives of other inanimate nouns)

Philip wants to leave. *But* he can't. (similarly, *and, or, nor*)

I don't doubt *but what* they will agree.

Can I have another, please?

Houston *contacted* the astronauts on their second orbit.

The *data is* available now. (similarly, *criteria*)

The answer was *different than* what we expected.

It *don't* make any difference.

Due to a power failure, the flight was canceled.

The members of the senate supported *each other* in the election.

Everybody finished *their* work. (similarly, *everyone*, *nobody*, *no one*, *someone*, and so forth with plural pronouns)

Drive three miles *further* south and turn right.

I'll come when I'm *good and* ready.

Have you *gotten* the answer yet?

She *graduated* from Vassar.

You *had better* go. (similarly, *had rather*, *had sooner*, *had best*, and so forth)

We heard about *him* winning the contest. (similarly, other nongenitives before gerunds)

I wonder *if* there's time.

The reason she's late *is because* she ran out of gas.

A finesse *is where* declarer plays the queen instead of the ace while the king is out against him. (similarly, *is when*)

Lay down and take your nap.

We have *less* problems this year than last.

The weather looks *like* it will be clearing soon.

It's *me*. (similarly, objective forms of other pronouns after *to be*)

It is the *most perfect* play ever written. (similarly, comparative and superlative forms of *unique*, *round*, *square*, *white*, and so forth)

They sent separate invitations to my wife and *myself*. (similarly, other *self*-forms without antecedent)

Make the dog get *off of* the bed.

You *only* live once.

James had a *pretty* good reason for asking.

He *raised* his children according to the newest theories.

A switch is not functioning. *This* is enough to cancel the flight. (similarly, *that* and *which* with broad reference)

Vesper didn't like *those kind* of tactics. (similarly, *kind* and *sort* with plural modifiers or verb)

It is necessary *to actively resist* oppression. (similarly, other split infinitives)

You ought to *try and* see the Little Theater's new play.

They were *very* pleased by the public response. (similarly, other qualifiers before past participles)

If the test *was* held on Sunday, more people could take it. (similarly, *was* in other subjunctive clauses)

Who did you see? (similarly, *who* in other object functions)

We *will* probably sing "We *Shall* Overcome."

You never know when your time will come.

9.6 *NATIONAL DIFFERENCES IN PRONUNCIATION*

1. Identify the following pronunciations as typically British (*B*) or typically American (*A*) by writing the appropriate letter in the blanks.

ate	_____	[et]	_____	[ɛt]
been	_____	[bin]	_____	[bɪn]
chagrin	_____	[šǽgrɪn]	_____	[šəgrín]
clerk	_____	[klɑk]	_____	[klərk]

corollary	_____	[kərɔ́lərɪ]	_____	[kɔ́rəlèri]
dynasty	_____	[dínəstɪ]	_____	[dáɪnəsti]
evolution	_____	[ìvəlúšən]	_____	[èvəlúšən]
figure	_____	[fígə]	_____	[fígjər]
fragile	_____	[fræǰɪl]	_____	[fræǰaɪl]
half	_____	[hæf]	_____	[hɑf]
laboratory	_____	[lǽbrətòri]	_____	[ləbɔ́rət(ə)rɪ]
latter	_____	[lǽdər]	_____	[lǽtə]
lieutenant	_____	[luténənt]	_____	[lɛfténənt]
medicine	_____	[médəsən]	_____	[médsɪn]
military	_____	[mílɪt(ə)rɪ]	_____	[mílətèri]
nephew	_____	[néfju]	_____	[névju]
pass	_____	[pæs]	_____	[pɑs]
premier	_____	[prémjə]	_____	[prəmír]
quinine	_____	[kwɪnín]	_____	[kwáɪnàɪn]
schedule	_____	[skéǰəl]	_____	[šédjul]
squirrel	_____	[skwírəl]	_____	[skwɔ́rəl]
trait	_____	[tre]	_____	[tret]
tryst	_____	[trɪst]	_____	[traɪst]
valet	_____	[vælé]	_____	[vǽlɪt]
vase	_____	[vɑz]	_____	[ves]
zenith	_____	[zínɪθ]	_____	[zénɪθ]
Are you there?	_____	Are you there?	_____	Are you there?
What did he tell you?	_____	What did he tell you?	_____	What did he tell you?

2. Describe five of the most important general differences between American and British pronunciation. _____

_____

_____

_____

_____

3. What was the usual quality of *a* before such consonants as [f], [θ], [ð], [s], and [ns] in Standard British English at the beginning of the nineteenth century? _____

_____

4. In what sections of the United States is [r] more or less regularly lost finally and before consonants? _____

_____

5. In what sections of the United States do words like *stop*, *cot*, and *lock* generally have a rounded vowel? _____

_____

6. Some Americans who regularly pronounce [r] where it is spelled do not have it in the middle syllable of *governor*, although they may have it in *governing* and *government*. Can you suggest any reason for the loss of [r] in the one word when it is retained in the other two?

_____

_____

An [r] is sometimes lost even by normally *r*-ish speakers in the following words. Circle the spelling for any [r] that is lost in your speech. Then describe the circumstances under which the loss occurs; note the position of the stress and other [r]'s in the words.

surpríse	Cánterbùry	bòmbardíer	sóutherner
mercúrochròme	réservòir	gùbernatórial	témperature
thermómeter	wíntergrèen	Fébruàry	fórmerly
vernácular	élderbèrry	spéctrogràph	pàraphernália
survívor	répertòry	cáterpìllar	mírror

_____
_____
_____

7. Which of the following pronunciations possess greater clarity? Explain your answer. *Sunday* [sə́ndè] or [sə́ndi]; *to* [tu] or [tə]; *educator* [édjukètər] or [éjəkètər]. _____
_____

9.7   BRITISH AND AMERICAN SPELLING

1. Give typically British spellings of the following words. Some of the "typically British spellings" are becoming less common in England, but they are still British as opposed to American in flavor.

anemic	_____	jail	_____
ax	_____	labor	_____
center	_____	mold 'fungus'	_____
(bank) check	_____	mustache	_____
cipher	_____	omelet	_____
civilize	_____	pajamas	_____
(street) curb	_____	plow	_____
defense	_____	program	_____
esophagus	_____	show (v.) 'display'	_____
gray	_____	story 'floor'	_____
inflection	_____	traveler	_____
install	_____	wagon	_____

2. Some of the spelling differences illustrated above are systematic in that the same difference appears in a large number of words. Describe the more important systematic differences and cite some additional examples. _____
_____
_____
_____
_____
_____
_____
_____
_____

9.8   THE REGIONAL DIALECTS OF AMERICAN ENGLISH

The regional dialects of American English are described by Raven I. McDavid, Jr., in W. Nelson Francis's *The Structure of American English* (New York, 1958), by Charles K. Thomas in *An Introduction to the Phonetics of American English*, 2nd ed. (New York, 1958), and more briefly in the *Standard College Dictionary* (New York, 1963, pp. xix–xxi), by Hans Kurath in *A Word Geography of the Eastern United States* (Ann Arbor, Mich., 1949), by Kurath and McDavid in *The Pronunciation of English in the Atlantic States* (Ann Arbor, Mich., 1961), and by Jean Malmstrom and Annabel Ashley in *Dialects—U.S.A.* (Champaign, Ill., 1963), a work designed for secondary schools and based on McDavid's chapter in Francis's book.

1. After reading one or more of these descriptions, which agree on general facts but not on all details, draw on the map the boundaries of the main regional dialects of the United States.

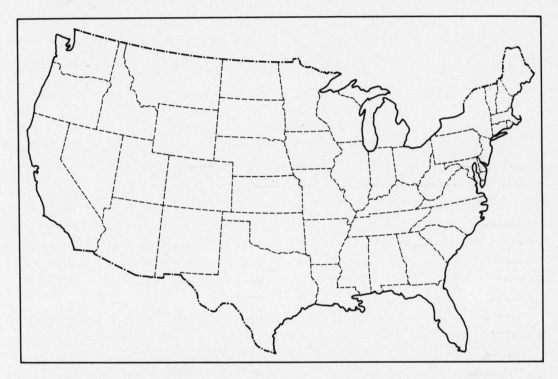

2. Below are some pronunciation features that vary from one regional dialect to another. For each feature indicate what main variations occur. You may not find all these items discussed in any one of the works cited above, but do as many of them as you can.

THE STRESSED VOWEL IN:

crop, top, cot, rot _____

law, caught, wrought _____

dog, fog, log _____

ask, half, path, glass, dance _____

coat, road, home, stone _____

new, tune, due _____

out, house _____

loud, houses _____

nice, white, rice _____

time, tide, ride _____

boil, oil _____

third, bird _____

bar, farm, hard _____

car, garden _____

forest, horrid, orange _____

morning, horse, forty _____

mourning, hoarse, four _____

marry, carry, barren _____

Mary, dairy, vary, area _____

THE PRONUNCIATION OF *r* IN:

fear, beard, poor, more, start, word _____

_____

far away, lore of the jungle, paper and ink _____

_____

THE MEDIAL CONSONANT OF:

greasy _____

THE FINAL CONSONANT OF:

with _____

3. What synonyms exist in regional dialects for the following vocabulary items? All of them can be found in Kurath's *Word Geography* and most of them in McDavid's chapter in Francis's book.

porch _____

pail _____

frying pan _____

faucet _____

kerosene _____

creek _____

sidewalk _____

pancake _____

string beans _____

lima beans _____

dragon fly _____

you (plural) _____

quarter *to* eleven _____

sick *to* the stomach _____

9.9 *LITERARY REPRESENTATIONS OF AMERICAN DIALECTS*

A fiction writer who wants to represent the regional speech of his characters must choose those lexical items, grammatical constructions, turns of phrase, and spellings (to stand for pronunciation) that will give a reader the flavor of the speech without putting too many obstacles in the way of easy comprehension. A literary dialect is not scientific description, but artistic impression and suggestion. Examine the following passages, and then point out how the authors have sought to communicate the flavor of a region's speech. Do literary dialects usually represent standard or nonstandard speech? Why? Some unconventional spellings represent the same pronunciation as the standard spellings and thus give no real information about dialect. Examples of such "eye-dialect" (so called because it appeals to the eye rather than the ear) are *sez* for *says*, *cas'le* for *castle*, *oughta* for *ought to*.[1] Cite some examples from the following passages.

[1] See Paul Hull Bowdre, Jr., "Eye Dialect as a Literary Device," in Juanita V. Williamson and Virginia M. Burke, eds., *A Various Language* (New York, 1971), pp. 178–86.

1. New England (Sarah Orne Jewett, "Andrew's Fortune")

"We was dreadful concerned to hear o' cousin Stephen's death," said the poor man. "He went very sudden, didn't he? Gre't loss he is."

"Yes," said Betsey, "he was very much looked up to;" and it was some time before the heir plucked up courage to speak again.

"Wife and me was lotting on getting over to the funeral; but it's a gre't ways for her to ride, and it was a perishin' day that day. She's be'n troubled more than common with her phthisic since cold weather come. I was all crippled up with the rheumatism; we wa'n't neither of us fit to be out" (plaintively). "'T was all I could do to get out to the barn to feed the stock while Jonas and Tim was gone. My boys was over, I s'pose ye know? I don' know's they come to speak with ye; they're backward with strangers, but they're good stiddy fellows."

"Them was the louts that was hanging round the barn, I guess," said Betsey to herself.

"They're the main-stay now; they're ahead of poor me a'ready. Jonas, he's got risin' a hundred dollars laid up, and I believe Tim's got something too,—he's younger, ye know?"

2. New York City (Damon Runyon, "Pick the Winner")

Well, anyway, when Hot Horse Herbie and his everloving fiancée come into Mindy's, he gives me a large hello, and so does Miss Cutie Singleton, so I hello them right back, and Hot Horse Herbie speaks to me as follows:

"Well," Herbie says, "we have some wonderful news for you. We are going to Miami," he says, "and soon we will be among the waving palms, and reveling in the warm waters of the Gulf Stream."

Now of course this is a lie, because while Hot Horse Herbie is in Miami many times, he never revels in the warm waters of the Gulf Stream, because he never has time for such a thing, what with hustling around the race tracks in the daytime, and around the dog tracks and the gambling joints at night, and in fact I will lay plenty of six to five Hot Horse Herbie cannot even point in the direction of the Gulf Stream when he is in Miami, and I will give him three points, at that.

3. Midwest (Ring Lardner, "Gullible's Travels")

I promised the Wife that if anybody ast me what kind of a time did I have at Palm Beach I'd say I had a swell time. And if they ast me who did we meet I'd tell 'em everybody that was worth meetin'. And if they ast me didn't the trip cost a lot I'd say Yes; but it was worth the money. I promised her I wouldn't spill none o' the real details. But if you can't break a promise you made to your own wife what kind of a promise can you break? Answer me that, Edgar.

I'm not one o' these kind o' people that'd keep a joke to themself just because the joke was on them. But they's plenty of our friends that I wouldn't have 'em hear about it for the world. I wouldn't tell you, only I know you're not the village gossip and won't crack it to anybody. Not even to your own Missus, see? I don't trust no women.

4. Missouri (Samuel L. Clemens, *The Adventures of Huckleberry Finn*)

So Tom says: "I know how to fix it. We got to have a rock for the coat of arms and mournful inscriptions, and we can kill two birds with that same rock. There's a gaudy big grindstone down at the mill, and we'll smouch it, and carve the thing on it, and file out the pens and the saw on it, too."

It warn't no slouch of an idea; and it warn't no slouch of a grindstone nuther; but we allowed we'd tackle it. It warn't quite midnight, yet, so we cleared out for the mill, leaving Jim at work. We smouched the grindstone, and set out to roll her home, but it was a most nation tough job. Sometimes, do what we could, we couldn't keep her from falling over, and she come mighty near mashing us, every time. Tom said she was going to get one of us, sure, before we got through. We got her half way; and then we was plumb played out, and most drownded with sweat. We see it warn't no use, we got to go and fetch Jim. So he raised up his bed and slid the chain off of the bed-leg, and wrapt it round and round his neck, and we crawled out through our hole and down there, and Jim and me laid into that grindstone and walked her along like nothing; and Tom superintended. He could out-superintend any boy I ever see. He knowed how to do everything.

5. Kentucky (Jesse Stuart, *Taps for Private Tussie*)

Watt Tussie was one man that I didn't get around. He didn't look right outten his eyes and I was afraid of him. I think Uncle George was afraid of him too. He didn't belong to either clan of Tussies. He just heard about the big house where all the Tussies were a-comin, so he brought his family to jine the rest in peace, rest and comfortable livin. Grandpa figured for hours to find out if he was any kin to Watt Tussie and he finally figured he was a son of his second cousin, Trueman Tussie. Watt Tussie wore brogan shoes laced with groundhog-hide strings.

6. Georgia (Joel Chandler Harris, "A Run of Luck")

"Well, suh," he said, after a while, "I come mighty nigh gwine off wid my young marster. I 'speck I'd 'a' gone ef he'd 'a' had any chillun, but he ain't had a blessed one. En it look like ter me, such, dat ef de Lord gwine ter stan' by a man, He gwine ter gi' 'im chillun. But dat ain't all, suh. I done been out dar ter Massysip wid my young marster, en dat one time wuz too much fer me. Fust dar wuz de rippit on de steamboat, en den dar wuz de burnin' er de boat, en den come de swamps, en de canebrakes; en I tell you right now, suh, I dunner which wuz de wuss—de rippit on de boat, er de fier, er de swamps, er de canebrakes. Dat ain't no country like our'n, suh. Dey's nuff water in de State er Massysip fer ter float Noah's ark. Hit's in de ve'y lan' what dey plant der cotton in, suh. De groun' is mushy. En black! You may n't b'lieve me, suh, but dey wuz times when I wuz out dar, dat I'd 'a' paid a sev'mpunce fer ter git a whiff er dish yer red dus' up my nose. When you come to farmin', suh, gi' me de red lan' er de gray. Hit may not make ez much cotton in one season, but it las's longer, en hit's lots mo' whole-some."

7. Florida (Marjorie Kinnan Rawlings, "My Friend Moe")

As he worked, he noticed a row of glass jars of huckleberries that I had canned. His grave face brightened.

"Now that's the way to live," he said. "All the good things we got here in Florida, blueberries and blackberries and beans and cow-peas, all them things had ought to be canned and put up on a clean cupboard shelf with white paper on it. That's the way my Ma did. She lived fine, not the way you live, but just as good when it come to cannin' things and keepin' things clean."

His face darkened. "I've tried and I've done tried to get my wife to do that-a-way but it just ain't no use. One time I bought two dozen glass jars and I went out by myself and I picked about a bushel o' blackberries and I went to the store and bought a twenty-five pound sack o' sugar and I takened it home, and I said, 'Wife, here's a bait o' blackberries to put up for us for jam and jelly for the winter.'" He hesitated, his loyalty pricking him.

"She probably didn't have time to do it," I suggested.

"She had time. She let the blackberries spoil, and the antses got in the sugar, and I found the jars throwed out in the back yard."

10

New Words from Old:
Coinages and Adaptations

10.1 QUESTIONS FOR REVIEW AND DISCUSSION

1. Define each of these terms and, when it is appropriate, illustrate the term with an example.

etymology	compound word stress
root creation	amalgamated compound
echoic word (onomatopoeia)	clipped form
sound symbolism	aphetic form (aphesis)
phonestheme	back formation
conventional ejaculation	blend
reduplication	acronym
affix	folk etymology
prefix	common derivative of a proper name
suffix	slang
lexicon	argot
hybrid creation	literary coinage
compound	converted form (conversion)
phrase stress	verb-adverb combination

2. Which of the processes of word-making described in this chapter seem from what you know to have been the most productive in English?

3. Your answer to the preceding question was intuitive, based on your general familiarity with the English vocabulary, but you can substantiate it by making a random sampling from the *Oxford English Dictionary*. Arbitrarily select one or more pages from each volume of the *OED*. Determine the process involved in the making of every word, not merely main entries, on each page you have selected. Many of the words will be loans from other languages. Loan-words will be considered in Chapter 11; for the present, group them together as a separate category, with which you are not concerned. When you have determined the process of word-making responsible for all the words that are not direct loans, tabulate your results and determine whether your intuitions accord with the sample you investigated.

10.2 ROOT CREATIONS

Genuine root creations are rare. *Blurb*, *gas*, *paraffin*, and *rayon* are sometimes suggested as examples. Although it is hardly in general use, *googol* is another candidate. Investigate the histories of these five words and decide which one is the best example of root creation. Explain your decision. _____

_____

_____

_____

_____

_____

10.3 *TRADE NAMES*

These trade names were suggested by already existing words or word elements. Identify the earlier forms which underlie the trade names.

automat	_____	Pepsodent	_____
Band-aid	_____	Pulmotor	_____
Coca-Cola	_____	Quonset	_____
escalator	_____	Sanforized	_____
Frigidaire	_____	Tabasco	_____
Levis	_____	Technicolor	_____
Linotype	_____	Victrola	_____
mimeograph	_____	Windbreaker	_____
Novocain	_____	Xerox	_____
ouija	_____	zipper	_____

10.4 *ECHOIC WORDS*

1. Many words that name sounds, or actions that produce sounds, are echoic in origin, for example, *buzz*, *chatter*, *gag*, *gurgle*, *hawk* 'clear the throat,' *heehaw*, *hiccup*, *honk*, *jingle*, *yak* 'talk volubly,' and *zoom*. Select a particular area of meaning, such as animal noises, noises produced by falling objects, nonspeech sounds made by man, noises made by machines, water noises, noises of rapid motion, and so forth, and list as many echoic words for that area as you can think of. _____

_____

_____

_____

_____

2. Some words of various origins, imitative or not, share a common meaning and a common sound. When meaning and sound thus coincide in several words, it is inevitable that speakers should feel that the sound somehow represents the meaning. Thus, *swagger*, *swash*, *swat*, *sway*, *sweep*, *swerve*, *swig*, *swill*, *swing*, *swipe*, *swirl*, *swish*, *swivel*, *swoop*, and *swoosh* all have the initial sound combination [sw] and are vaguely similar to one another in meaning. The shared meaning, something like 'free-wheeling movement in an arc,' seems to be represented by the sound [sw], which is therefore called a "phonestheme." The phenomenon is known as sound symbolism.

   Here are some short lists of symbolic words. For each list, identify the phonestheme, describe the meaning that is characteristic of it, and add any appropriate words you can find.

tweak, twiddle, twine, twinkle, twirl, twist, twitch

---

glare, gleam, glimmer, glint, glisten, glitter, gloss, glow

---

crack, cramp, cripple, crooked, crouch, crumple, crunch, crush

---

draggle, drain, dredge, dregs, drip, droop, drop, dross

---

bladder, blaze, blimp, blister, bloat, blow, blubber, blurt

---

track, trail, trample, travel, tread, trip, trot, trudge

---

crash, dash, flash, gush, rush, smash, swish, whoosh

---

bangle, dangle, jangle, jingle, jungle, spangle, tangle, tingle

---

bump, chump, dump, hump, lump, plump, rump, slump

---

amble, jumble, mumble, ramble, rumble, scramble, shamble, tremble

---

10.5 *EJACULATIONS*

Phffft, the name of a 1954 motion picture, is an exclamation denoting the sudden collapse of a marriage or some other deflatable thing. The sound, which suggests air escaping from a balloon, is represented well enough by the spelling and is familiar to most English speakers. The critic Bosley Crowther was too pessimistic when he advised, "Don't try to pronounce the title." Crowther's additional comment, "'Phffft' is a skkkt that runs an hour and a half," suggests that he had in mind a conventional pronunciation for the ejaculation, one that rimed with *skit*. When such a noise is pronounced not as the noise it originally symbolized, but rather as a permissible sequence of English phonemes, it has become a word like any other in the lexicon. At first an interjection, the word may come to function as a noun a, verb, or other part of speech.

Here are some ejaculations that have become words through a spelling pronunciation of their written symbols, although not all of them have achieved the honor of a dictionary entry. Describe or produce the noise that each of the spellings originally symbolized.

LAUGHTER: yuk-yuk, yak, hardy-har
ATTENTION-GETTING NOISE: ahem, psst
DELAYING NOISE: hem and haw
EXPRESSION OF CONTEMPT OR DISGUST: humph, piff (cf. piffle), ptui (pronounced [pətúi]), braak, chee(z)

CRY OF HORROR: a(u)gh
EXPRESSION OF RELIEF: whew
SIGNAL FOR SILENCE: shush, hush, ssst
AUTOMATIC NOISES: kerchoo, burp, hack
NEGATION: uh-uh

10.6 *MORPHEMES: PREFIXES, SUFFIXES, AND BASES*

The morpheme is the smallest meaningful unit in a language. *Card, act, moron, random, cardigan*, and *asparagus* are words that consist of a single morpheme each. *Discard, action, moronic, randomly, cardigans*, and *aspáragus plànt* are made of two morphemes each. A morpheme may be a base like *card, asparagus*, and *plant*, a prefix like *dis-*, or a suffix like *-ion*. Words like *refer, defer, confer, receive, deceive, conceive, reduce, deduce*, and *conduce* are made of two morphemes each, a prefix and a base, although the bases *fer, ceive*, and *duce* do not occur as separate words.

Divide each of the following words into its constituent morphemes by rewriting the word with hyphens between the morphemes. For example, *activistic* can be divided into *act-iv-ist-ic*. Note that morphemes are properly represented by sounds, but for convenience we can use conventional spellings.

postage	_____	prepare	_____
impressment	_____	repair	_____
trial	_____	disparity	_____
early	_____	disparage	_____
holistic	_____	repel	_____
worthily	_____	propellant	_____
definite	_____	produce	_____
favoritism	_____	seduce	_____
demarcation	_____	secede	_____
finalization	_____	proceed	_____
unequivocal	_____	placate	_____
palmistry	_____	implacable	_____

10.7 *PREFIXES*

1. From what language was the prefix in each of these words originally derived? Label each word *G* (Greek), *L* (Latin), or *OE* (Old English) according to the source of the prefix.

_____ archenemy	_____ microorganism	_____ stepchild
_____ circumnavigate	_____ midday	_____ surname
_____ cis-Alpine	_____ misfit	_____ transoceanic
_____ counterbalance	_____ monomania	_____ tricolor
_____ crypto-Communist	_____ panhellenic	_____ twilight
_____ demigod	_____ parapsychology	_____ ultraliberal
_____ diacid	_____ polyvalent	_____ unilingual
_____ epicycle	_____ preternatural	_____ vice-regent
_____ malformed	_____ proto-Germanic	
_____ metalanguage	_____ retroactive	

2. Two affixes may be pronounced and spelled alike, yet be two independent elements because they have different functions in the language. Thus the *-ly* of *manly* and the *-ly* of *slowly* are not the same suffix. The first *-ly* forms adjectives; the second *-ly* forms adverbs. The two endings have different meanings and therefore are different suffixes.

On the other hand, an affix may be pronounced and spelled variously in different words, yet remain a single affix. Although the past tense ending is [d] in *said*, [t] in *thought*, and [əd] in *waited*, we say that these three pronunciations are only variants of one affix because their meaning or function is the same.

In each of the following pairs, if both words have the same prefix, mark them *S*; if they have different prefixes, mark them *D*.

	amoral		embed		income
_____	aside	_____	encase	_____	invalid
	autobiography		foreword		intermix
_____	autocar	_____	forswear	_____	intramural
	bemoan		extraordinary		pro-British
_____	besmirch	_____	extrasensory	_____	prologue
	biannual		hypertension		supernatural
_____	bypass	_____	hypotension	_____	supranational
	coeternal		illegal		
_____	copilot	_____	immoral		

10.8 SUFFIXES

Are the suffixes in each pair of words the same morpheme or different morphemes? Use the symbols *S* and *D*.

	absorbent		density		rested
_____	triumphant	_____	chastity	_____	bigoted
	accountable		hyphenate		smithy
_____	responsible	_____	temperate	_____	sleepy
	coastal		occurrence		taller
_____	withdrawal	_____	appearance	_____	teller
	cupful		offing		wooden
_____	careful	_____	scoffing	_____	shorten

10.9 NEW AFFIXES AND NEW USES OF OLD ONES

The *Britannica Book of the Year*, an annual supplement to the *Encyclopaedia Britannica*, lists additions to the English vocabulary under the heading "Words and Meanings, New." The journal *American Speech* also has a department "Among the New Words." Recent years have seen the increased popularity of affixes like *-ology*, *-ism*, *-nik*, *-ery*, *-ify*, *-oree*, *para-*, and *non-* in such specimens as *Saxonology* 'the study of the policies and motives of the British and American governments; the counterpart of Russian Kremlinology,' *Pekingology*, *comitology* 'the study of committees,' *tokenism* 'the practice of token integration,' *oathism* 'the practice of requiring loyalty oaths,' *spacenik* 'an astronaut,' *peacenik* 'a pacifist,' *neatnik* 'a nonbeatnik,' *scrollery* 'the search for documents like the Dead Sea scrolls,' *massified* 'made massive,' *freezoree* 'a winter camporee,' *paralanguage* 'a system of communication that accompanies language,' *nonevent* 'an event arranged by the news media for the purpose of reporting it,' and *nonbook* 'a book conceived as a piece of salable merchandise rather than as an artistic undertaking.'

Consult any five consecutive years of the *Britannica Book of the Year* or *American Speech* to find what affixes have appeared most frequently in the new words recorded for those years. List the more popular affixes and the words containing them. Gloss any word the meaning of which is not apparent. _____

_____

_____

_____

_____

_____

_____

_____

10.10 *THE SPELLING OF COMPOUNDS*

1. Are the following compounds spelled as one word, as two words, or with a hyphen? First decide how you would spell each compound and then check the spelling in a dictionary or, better, in several dictionaries.

half cocked	_____	second story (adj.)	_____
half hour	_____	side band	_____
high chair	_____	side kick	_____
high grade	_____	side light	_____
high light	_____	side step (v.)	_____
prize fighter	_____	side whiskers	_____

2. What conclusion can you draw about the spelling of compounds? _____

_____

3. Read Robert A. Hall, Jr., "To Hyphenate or Not to Hyphenate," *English Journal*, LIII (1964), 662–65, or Dwight L. Bolinger, "Damned Hyphen," *American Speech*, XLII (1967), 297–99, and summarize their conclusions.

_____

_____

_____

10.11 *THE STRESSING OF COMPOUNDS*

1. Write the stresses of these items. Put the accent marks over the stressed vowel, as in *hótbèd* versus *hôt béd*.

redwood	red wood	shorthand	short hand
bluebeard	blue beard	graybeard	gray beard
greenroom	green room	safeguard	safe guard
strongbox	strong box	Stonewall	stone wall
mainland	main land	paperback	paper back

2. Write the stresses.

madhouse keeper	mad housekeeper
new-math teacher	new math-teacher
second-hand cart	second handcart
used-car salesman	used car-salesman
White House lights	white houselights

3. Write the stresses of the italicized words. There is a variation among English speakers for some of these items.

The pot is only *silver plate*.	He ate from a *silver plate*.
They live on *Main Street*.	It is the *main street*.
Hamlet met the *gravedigger*.	He was a serious and *grave digger*.
What is the *subject matter*?	What does the *subject matter*?
She added *baking powder*.	Why is she *baking powder*?

4. Write the stresses of the italicized words.

Who ever asked?	*Whoever* asked?
He found a *new haven*.	He lived in *New Haven*.
It is not a *good morning*.	I wish you *good morning*.
He met an *old lady*.	Here comes your *old lady*.
The river has *grand rapids*.	They eloped to *Grand Rapids*.

5. Each of these compounds has a pronunciation that shows phonetic change due to the complete loss of stress from the second element. Each also has an analytical pronunciation. Transcribe the words phonetically to show both pronunciations.

	WITH PRIMARY STRESS ONLY	WITH PRIMARY-SECONDARY STRESS
blackguard	_____	_____
boatswain	_____	_____
somebody	_____	_____
starboard	_____	_____
topsail	_____	_____

10.12 *THE CONSTRUCTION OF COMPOUNDS*

Compounds are formed according to many patterns, of which the following are only a few:

1. *Bluegrass* is from "the grass is blue."
2. *Bloodthirsty* is from "thirsty for blood."
3. *Daredevil* is from "he dares the devil."
4. *Pale-face* is from "he has a pale face."
5. *Pin-up* is from "it is pinned up."
6. *Overland* is from "over the land."
7. *Typeset* is from "to set the type." [1]

Identify the patterns of these compounds by writing the appropriate number, from 1 through 7, in front of each.

[1] Historically, *typeset* is a back formation from *typesetter*, but in Modern English the construction has become a new type of compound.

_____	backbite	_____	highbrow	_____	proofread
_____	battle-ready	_____	highway	_____	redbird
_____	blowout	_____	homesick	_____	redcap
_____	boy-crazy	_____	hotfoot	_____	redhead
_____	breakdown	_____	kickback	_____	sightsee
_____	downstairs	_____	longbow	_____	spoilsport
_____	gentleman	_____	longhorn	_____	underhand

10.13   AMALGAMATED COMPOUNDS

1. These words are historically compounds. Identify the elements from which each word was formed.

among	_____	halibut	_____
ampersand	_____	hatred	_____
bailiwick	_____	ingot	_____
doff	_____	Lammas	_____
don	_____	neighbor	_____
elbow	_____	no	_____
every	_____	offal	_____
furlong	_____	rigmarole	_____
gamut	_____	shelter	_____
gossip	_____	woof 'thread'	_____

2. Most speakers would be aware that these words are compounds, but at least one part of each compound is semantically obscure. Identify the obscure elements.

backgammon	_____	mildew	_____
bonfire	_____	nickname	_____
cobweb	_____	walnut	_____
good-by	_____	wedlock	_____
midriff	_____	werewolf	_____
midwife	_____	worship	_____

3. These reduplicating compounds are also amalgamated. Identify their original elements.

hob-nob	_____
shilly-shally	_____
willy-nilly	_____

10.14   CLIPPED FORMS

Identify the full forms from which these words were abbreviated:

ad lib	_____	mitt	_____
chap	_____	mutt	_____
chat	_____	pep	_____
chum	_____	prom	_____
cinema	_____	radio	_____
fan 'admirer'	_____	scram	_____
fib 'lie'	_____	sleuth	_____
limey	_____	toady	_____

10.15 *APHETIC FORMS*

Identify the long form from which each of these words was produced by aphesis:

cense	_____	raiment	_____
drawing room	_____	spite	_____
fend	_____	splay	_____
lone	_____	squint	_____
mend	_____	stogie	_____
mien	_____	stress	_____
neath	_____	tend 'serve'	_____
pall 'satiate'	_____	tiring-room	_____
pert	_____	varsity	_____
ply 'use diligently'	_____	venture	_____

10.16 *BACK FORMATION*

These words are the result of back formation. Give the original words from which they were back-formed.

1. BACK FORMATIONS INVOLVING AN INFLECTIONAL ENDING

asset	_____	pry 'lever'	_____
burial	_____	riddle 'puzzle'	_____
hush	_____	(window) sash	_____
inkle 'hint'	_____	shimmy	_____
marquee	_____	sidle	_____

2. BACK FORMATIONS INVOLVING AN AGENT SUFFIX

edit	_____	panhandle	_____
escalate	_____	peddle	_____
hawk 'vend'	_____	scavenge	_____
interlope	_____	(to) swab	_____
mug 'assault'	_____	swindle	_____

3. MISCELLANEOUS BACK FORMATIONS

(to) char	_____	peeve	_____
diagnose	_____	preempt	_____
donate	_____	reminisce	_____
greed	_____	resurrect	_____
homesick	_____	unit	_____

4. Some words are formed by a process that is the opposite of back formation. Give the etymology of the following four words and then describe the process of word formation that is common to them. Notice that all four words are singular in current English; they require a singular verb like *seems* rather than a plural like *seem*.

bodice _____

chintz _____

news _____

quince _____

PROCESS OF FORMATION: _____

1. Identify the sources from which these blends were produced. There will be two sources for each blend. The origin of some of these words is not completely certain, so you can expect variation among dictionaries.

alegar = _____ + _____
blotch = _____ + _____
blurt = _____ + _____
extrapolate = _____ + _____
hassle = _____ + _____
magnetron = _____ + _____
positron = _____ + _____
prissy = _____ + _____
scratch = _____ + _____
scroll = _____ + _____
simulcast = _____ + _____
splatter = _____ + _____
splutter = _____ + _____
tangelo = _____ + _____
travelogue = _____ + _____
vitamin = _____ + _____

2. Some blends are deliberate, intentional creations like *racon* from *radar* plus *beacon*, but others result from unconscious slips of the tongue. In rapid speech, the talker may have in mind two words of partly similar meaning and sound; the speech process gets short-circuited and instead of choosing between the two words, the speaker combines them into a single form. Thus *slick* and *slimy* may blend as [ˈslími], *drip* and *dribble* as [drípəl], or *stockings* and *socks* as [stɑks]. Occasionally such a *lapsus linguae* becomes established in the language, but most of them are hardly noticed by either the speaker or his audience.[2] Try to collect a few examples of inadvertent blending by listening to the speech of those around you.

10.18   *ACRONYMS AND INITIALISMS*

1. Initialisms are abbreviations that make use of the initial letters in a phrase, and are pronounced by sounding the letter names. Such abbreviations are extremely common in contemporary English, often supplanting the unabbreviated term in general usage. Widely used initialisms, in addition to those cited in Pyles's *Origins and Development*, are AA, BTU, CIA, DT's, ESP, FCC, GI, HMS, IQ, JP, KO, LA, MD, NG, OCS, PTA, QED, RSVP, SRO, TNT, USA, VIP, and WCTU. List ten or fifteen similar initialisms in common use. _____

_____

2. The pronunciation of the letters in initialisms such as the ones listed above sometimes gives rise to new written words. What is the origin of each of these terms?

ack ack _____

emcee _____

---

[2] A good discussion of unconscious blends can be found in E. H. Sturtevant, *An Introduction to Linguistic Science* (New Haven, Conn., 1947), pp. 110–16.

jeep _____

kayo _____

veep _____

3. Acronyms are also formed from the initial letters (or sometimes syllables) of a phrase, but they are pronounced as though the letters spelled out a normal word. Give the full phrases from which the following acronyms have been abbreviated.

conelrad _____

Delmarva _____

futhorc _____

loran _____

napalm _____

shoran _____

sial _____

sonar _____

teleran _____

4. English is not unique in forming acronyms. Some words that we have borrowed from foreign tongues were originally abbreviated phrases. Identify the unabbreviated source of each of these words:

kolkhoz _____

comintern _____

flak _____

Gestapo _____

5. Trade names are very often acronyms, for example, *Amoco*, *Nabisco*, *Panagra*, *Socony*, and *Sunoco*. List a few other such trade names. _____

_____

_____

6. Pseudo-acronyms like *Wave* are becoming increasingly common. The following phrases, in which the capital letters spell an acronym, have been recorded.[3]

*F*ilm *O*ptical *S*canning *D*evice for *I*nput to *C*omputers

*E*lectronegative *GA*s *D*etector

*I*nstrumentation *DI*gital *O*n-line *T*ranscriber

*A*utomatic *D*igital *I*nput-*O*utput *S*ystem

In each case it seems likely that the supposed abbreviation had some influence on the creation of the full phrase. List a few other pseudo-acronyms. _____

_____

_____

_____

10.19 FOLK ETYMOLOGY

1. Give the correct etymology of these words and indicate the probable basis for the folk etymology, following the pattern on pages 303–04 of Pyles's *Origins and Development*.

andiron _____

barberry _____

[3] Milton Goldstein, *Dictionary of Modern Acronyms and Abbreviations* (Indianapolis, 1963).

blunderbuss_____

chick-pea_____

demijohn_____

forlorn hope_____

gymkhana_____

mangrove_____

rosemary_____

sty 'swelling on eyelid'_____

teapoy_____

turtle 'reptile'_____

2. If we consider the earliest forms of the italicized words, the answer to each of the following questions is "no." Give the correct etymology for the words. Although the misunderstanding illustrated by some of them is too learned to be of the folk, the principle involved is the same as that of folk etymology.

Was the *gopherwood* from which Noah built the ark named for gophers?

_____

Is a *chipmunk* so called because he chips?

_____

Is an *outrage* a raging out?

_____

Are *nightmares* brought on by horseback riding?

_____

Is a *comrade* someone with (Lat. *com-*) whom one does something?

_____

Is *kitty-cornered* the way a kitten walks?

_____

Is the bridge term *tenace* a combination of a ten and an ace?

_____

Is the *hold* of a ship so called because it holds the cargo?

_____

Is a *ham* radio operator so called because he is an (h)amateur?

_____

Do *Jordan almonds* come from Jordan?

_____

Is the *albatross* so called because it is white (Lat. *alba*) in color?

_____

Is a *posthumous* work one published after (Lat. *post*) the author has been put under the earth (*humus*)?

_____

Is the *ptarmigan* a creature named from Greek, like the pterodactyl and the pteropod?

_____

Is an *argosy* named for the *argonauts*?

_____

Are *purlieus* so named because they are a kind of place (Fr. *lieu*)?

_____

3. Much folk etymology, like the Chester drawers (chest of drawers) and Archie Fisher snow (artificial snow) mentioned in Pyles's *Origins and Development*, is so ephemeral that it never

achieves lexicographical record. Some of it is deliberately humorous. Here are a few additional examples of such folk etymology; add to the list from your own experience.

car porch 'an open-sided shelter for an automobile' (properly *carport*)
Creak Car Lake 'a resort lake near St. Louis, Missouri, reached by a squeaking trolley car' (properly *Crèvecoeur Lake*)
dashhound 'a dog of German origin' (properly *dachshund*)
lowbachi 'a small charcoal brazier in the Japanese style' (variant of *hibachi*)
very coarse veins 'swollen veins' (properly *varicose*)

_____
_____
_____
_____

10.20 COMMON WORDS FROM PROPER NAMES

1. These common nouns were taken without change from the names of actual persons. Explain briefly how each personal name came to be applied to the thing it now denotes.

braille _____
diesel _____
hooligan _____
leotard _____
negus _____
quisling _____
roentgen _____
sequoia _____
silhouette _____

2. These common words are derivatives or altered forms of personal names. Identify the historical person from whose name each word derives.

algorism _____   guillotine _____
(deci)bel _____   klieg (light) _____
boysenberry _____   macadam _____
euhemerism _____   magnolia _____
fuchsia _____   saxophone _____

3. These common words were taken from the names of literary, mythological, or Biblical persons. Identify the source of each.

ammonia _____
euphuism _____
hermetic _____
lazar _____
museum _____
philander _____
procrustean _____
syphilis _____
termagant _____
veronica _____

4. These common words are given names used generically. Identify each word by the usual form of the name from which it comes.

dickey	_____	jockey	_____
dobbin	_____	jug	_____
doll	_____	magpie	_____
(play) hob	_____	marionette	_____
jimmy	_____	zany	_____

5. These words were taken without change from the names of places. Identify the nation in which each place is to be found.

angostura	_____	duffel	_____
ascot	_____	jodhpur(s)	_____
bantam	_____	madras	_____
castile 'soap'	_____	magenta	_____
donnybrook	_____	spa	_____

6. These words are derivatives or altered forms of place names. Identify the place from which each word derives.

attic	_____	muslin	_____
baldachin	_____	palace	_____
buckram	_____	peach 'fruit'	_____
cantaloupe	_____	seltzer	_____
capitol	_____	spruce	_____
currant	_____	tabby	_____
denim	_____	tangerine	_____
jimson(weed)	_____		

7. These common words are derived from the names of tribes or national groups. Identify the sources.

arabesque	_____	hooch	_____
cravat	_____	lumber	_____
frank	_____	slave	_____
gothic	_____	vandal	_____
gyp	_____	welch	_____

8. These common words are derived from various kinds of proper names. Identify the sources.

blucher	_____	protean	_____
cambric	_____	raglan	_____
canary	_____	robin	_____
cretin	_____	shillelagh	_____
loganberry	_____	sienna	_____
majolica	_____	sousaphone	_____
melba toast	_____	vaudeville	_____

10.21 *SLANG*

1. Much slang enters general use from the jargon of particular occupations. Thus the recently popular (*rat*)*fink* has its origin in underworld argot, in which it means 'informer.' Baseball has contributed such terms as *batting average, to be benched, bush leagues, double-header, grandstand play, off-base, far out* (*in left field*), *pinch-hitter, put one over, safe at home, shut-*

out, south-paw, strike-out, and *throw a curve,* all of which are used in discussing subjects other than sports. A batting average may be for tests, checks from home, or women as well as for baseballs. List ten or twelve slang terms that have passed into general use from some area such as crime, the military, jazz, college life, show business, card-playing, or some other familiar activity. _____

_____

_____

_____

_____

2. Reduplication often appears in slang terms. The second element may rime with the first, as in *hanky-panky,* or it may show consonance, as in *chitchat.* Supply the second element in each of these reduplicating compounds:

even- _____ flip- _____

heebie- _____ mish- _____

hoity- _____ slip- _____

razzle- _____ tip- _____

super- _____ wishy- _____

3. Another device by which slang adds to the lexicon is rime. We have already seen that many reduplications make use of rime, but it is likely that rime has also played a part in the coining of slang terms like *gimp* (cf. *limp*), *potted* (cf. *sotted*), *razzamatazz* (cf. *jazz*), *no soap* (cf. *hope*), and *it's a breeze* (cf. *with ease*). Moreover, rime figures conspicuously in phrases such as "See you later, alligator," which at one time spawned a number of imitations of the type "In a while, crocodile."

One of the more complex uses of sound-repetition is Cockney riming slang, which has contributed several phrases to the general vocabulary. This form of slang originated among the London Cockney and spread to Australia and the United States, although it has never been particularly widespread in this country. For a word, such as *wife,* the Cockney substitutes a riming phrase which is semantically appropriate, preferably in a sardonic way, for example, *trouble and strife.* The phrase is often clipped to its first member, thus effectively disguising its origin and serving a function of all slang, to mystify those in the "out-group." A common and unusually complex example of Cockney riming slang is *duke* 'fist,' as in "put up your dukes." *Duke* is a clipping of *Duke of Yorks,* riming slang for *forks; forks* in turn is a slang metaphor for fingers or, collectively, a fist. Here are a few of the better known Cockney slang words. Identify the word on which the riming phrase is based.[4]

Let's get down to *brass tacks.* _____

In his business, he makes a pile of *sugar.* (clipped from *sugar and honey;* compare the poker term "to sweeten the pot") _____

I don't care a *ding-dong* for what they think. (clipped from *ding-dong-bell*) _____

She's a pert little *twist.* (clipped from *twist and twirl*) _____

After one too many, you may feel a bit *tiddly.* (clipped from *tiddlywink,* by way of "I want a little tiddly") _____

When he gets mad, you should hear him *rip.* (clipped from *rip and tear,* common in the phrase *let rip*) _____

Good thinking, that's using the old *loaf.* (clipped from *loaf of bread*) _____

You're tired, you need a little *Bo-peep.* _____

[4] These words and many others can be found in Julian Franklyn, *A Dictionary of Riming Slang* (London, 1960).

4. Slang, by its very nature, is poorly represented in standard dictionaries. For early slang, the *Oxford English Dictionary* is useful and can be supplemented by John S. Farmer and William Ernest Henley, *Dictionary of Slang and Its Analogues*, 7 vols. (New York, 1890–1904). More recent British slang is recorded in Eric Partridge, *A Dictionary of Slang and Unconventional English*, 7th ed. (New York, 1970), and American slang in Harold Wentworth and Stuart Berg Flexner, *Dictionary of American Slang* (New York, 1960) and in Lester V. Berrey and Melvin Van den Bark, *The American Thesaurus of Slang*, 2nd ed. (New York, 1953). Use these works or other available dictionaries to answer the following questions, and note the source of your information for each answer.

What did a seventeenth-century *cony-catcher* catch? _____

_____

When Dickens wrote in *Martin Chuzzlewit*, "She was only a little screwed," with what debility did he imply the lady to be afflicted? _____

_____

Although it is known in America, *smarmy* is more common in British English. What is its meaning? _____

_____

When an Australian is *waltzing Matilda*, what is he doing? _____

_____

What is the meaning of the obsolete American term *ish kabibble*? _____

_____

What is the apparent source of American *sockdolager*? _____

_____

The acronym *snafu* spawned a number of imitations like *fubar* 'fouled up beyond all recognition.' List a few of its other progeny. _____

_____

What are some slang terms for various kinds of auctions? _____

_____

10.22 *LITERARY COINAGES*

1. There are a few words that can be traced with some confidence to a literary origin or to a specific act of coinage. Consult the *Oxford English Dictionary* to find the source of each of these words:

agnostic _____

blatant _____

ignoramus 'ignorant person' _____

knickerbockers _____

Lilliputian _____

malaprop(ism) _____

namby-pamby _____

Peeping Tom _____

potter's field _____

sensuous _____

serendipity _____

simon-pure _____

spoof _____

tam(-o'-shanter) _____

yahoo _____

2. Most of the following words are too recent, at least in their current uses, to be entered in the *OED*. Consult *Webster's Third New International Dictionary* for their origin.

babbitt(ry) _____

bazooka _____

boondoggle _____

fedora _____

Frankenstein _____

goop 'boor' _____

jabberwocky _____

Milquetoast _____

scrooge _____

Shangri-la _____

3. Who, according to the *OED*, was the first person to use each of these words in writing? Note also the year of the word's first appearance in English.

anesthesia _____

blasé _____

electricity _____

environment 'surrounding region' _____

Gotham 'New York City' _____

muckrake _____

ragamuffin _____

rodomontade _____

salad days _____

superman _____

10.23 *ONE PART OF SPEECH TO ANOTHER*

1. For each of these words, write two or more sentences using the word as a different part of speech in each sentence.

back _____
_____

best _____
_____

feature _____
_____

gross _____
_____

slow _____
_____

split _____
_____

total _____
_____

try _____

up _____

while _____

2. According to the citations in the *Oxford English Dictionary*, as what part of speech was each of these words first used?

blemish _____   fun _____

coin _____   idle _____

eavesdrop _____   matter _____

faint _____   pressure _____

fossil _____   shampoo _____

3. Identify the part of speech of the italicized words.

The Recreation Center is hosting a community *sing*. _____

And also loke [look] on schrewes . . . how gret peyne *felawschipith* [fellowships] and folweth hem [them]. (Chaucer, *Boece*, IV, p. 3) _____

Let me *wise* you up. _____

Lady, you are the cruell'st *she* alive. (Shakespeare, *Twelfth Night*, I.v) _____

It might be a *fun* thing to go to one of their parties. _____

The sweets we wish for turn to loathèd *sours*. (Shakespeare, *The Rape of Lucrece*, l. 867) _____

Manufacturers often *package* according to the price instead of pricing according to the package. _____

My heart in hiding / Stirred for a bird,—the *achieve* of, the mastery of the thing! (G. M. Hopkins, "The Windhover") _____

It was an invitation for Clay to *up* and clobber him. _____

Who shall . . . through the palpable *obscure* find out his uncouth way? (Milton, *Paradise Lost*, II, 406) _____

10.24   VERB-ADVERB COMBINATIONS

1. Consult the *Oxford English Dictionary* to find when each of these verb-adverb combinations was first used in the sense indicated. In addition, mark those which originated in America with the abbreviation *U.S.* For some of the phrases, you will need to use the supplementary volume.

bring forth 'give birth to' _____

call down 'reprove' _____

do in 'bring disaster upon' _____

get over 'finish with' _____

hang back 'show unwillingness to advance' _____

lay by 'store up, save' _____

look after 'take care of' _____

put on 'affect, pretend' _____

send out 'issue' _____

take up (for) 'defend, stand up for' _____

2. Combine the verbs listed on the left with the adverbs listed on the right to make as many idiomatic verb-adverb combinations as possible.

cut	down
give	in
put	off
take	out
turn	up

_____

_____

_____

_____

_____

3. Which of the combinations from the preceding question can be converted into nouns by a shift of stress? For example, _to cût úp–a cútùp._ _____

_____

_____

_____

4. Stress may indicate parts of speech for words other than verb-adverb combinations. Write the primary stress of these words with an acute mark over the stressed vowel. Record your own pronunciation.

NOUNS	VERBS	NOUNS	VERBS	NOUNS	VERBS
commune	commune	forecast	forecast	overhaul	overhaul
contest	contest	inlay	inlay	present	present
decrease	decrease	insult	insult	rebel	rebel
discount	discount	object	object	survey	survey
extract	extract	offset	offset	undercut	undercut

10.25 *NEW WORDS FROM OLD: A SUMMARY*

Identify the processes of word-making that have produced these words by writing the appropriate number, from 1 through 10, in front of each word. For some of the items you will need to consult a dictionary; others should be transparent.

1. onomatopoeia		6. blending	
2. use of affixes		7. formation of acronym	
3. compounding		8. folk etymology	
4. clipping		9. derivation from proper name	
5. back formation		10. conversion of part of speech	

_____ curio

_____ emote

_____ gillyflower

_____ halfback

_____ marathon

_____ maser

_____ noncash 'credit'

_____ pop 'sudden noise'

_____ psychic 'a medium'

_____ slanguage

_____ Amerind	_____ jaw 'talk volubly'
_____ cordovan	_____ mongoose
_____ creak	_____ refreeze
_____ glamazon 'chorus girl'	_____ roughneck
_____ intercom	_____ televise
_____ baloney	_____ mike
_____ cusec	_____ primrose
_____ discussant	_____ surrey
_____ handwrite	_____ swimsation
_____ kéy clùb	_____ swish
_____ Benelux	_____ laze
_____ cicerone	_____ mangrove
_____ corner 'get a corner on'	_____ mumble
_____ hiss	_____ sexsational
_____ shóut shòp 'advertising agency'	_____ tot 'add'
_____ academy	_____ grapheme
_____ balletorio 'choral music with dancing'	_____ guffaw
_____ cajun	_____ high-muck-a-muck
_____ VISTA	_____ jell
_____ muscleshirt 'sleeveless T shirt'	_____ orate
_____ caper 'plant'	_____ enthuse
_____ chartreuse	_____ lackadaisical
_____ chirp	_____ oleo
_____ construct 'something constructed'	_____ parsec
_____ optiman 'man in optimum condition'	_____ tough 'rowdy person'

11

Foreign Elements
in the English Word Stock

11.1 QUESTIONS FOR REVIEW AND DISCUSSION

1. Define each of the following terms, illustrating with examples when they are appropriate.

    loan-word   transmission   doublet
    borrowing   ultimate source   hybrid formation
    popular loan-word   direct or immediate source semantic contamination
    learned loan-word   derivative   loan translation (calque)
    provenience   etymon (pl. etyma)   external history

2. Loan-words reflect the contacts that have existed between two languages. What events in the history of the English-speaking peoples account for lexical borrowing from Latin, Greek, Celtic languages, Scandinavian, French, Spanish, Italian, Low German, High German, African languages, American Indian languages, Asiatic languages, and East European languages?

3. What language has had an influence on the English vocabulary over the longest period of time? Why has that language, more than any other, had such an influence?

4. Explain the relative paucity of Celtic loan-words in English.

5. Scandinavian has contributed a large number of common, homely words to the English vocabulary. Explain this fact.

6. During what historical period was the rate of adoption of French loan-words at its highest? How do you account for the fact that French words entered English in such large numbers at that time?

7. Prepare a list of the languages from which English has borrowed words, and for each language indicate the semantic areas most prominently represented by loans.

8. Although English has borrowed a surprisingly large amount of its vocabulary from other languages and has undergone a great many changes during its history, the tongue we speak preserves a recognizable continuity with the English of King Alfred. List some significant bits of evidence which could be used to support this statement.

11.2 LOAN-WORDS AND THEIR SOURCES

Identify the language from which each of these words was borrowed into English.

amuck   _____   booby   _____
ballot   _____   bosh   _____
blouse   _____   cheroot _____

ghoul	_____	okra	_____
gull	_____	picnic	_____
hominy	_____	pus	_____
kid	_____	sargasso	_____
kink	_____	tonic	_____
lens	_____	turn	_____
oil	_____	veneer	_____

_____

atoll	_____	raffia	_____
awe	_____	robot	_____
buffalo	_____	smuggle	_____
chit 'note'	_____	snorkel	_____
cola (kola)	_____	sofa	_____
ditto	_____	spade	_____
dodo	_____	'card suit'	
hickory	_____	squadron	
huckster	_____	thug	_____
penguin	_____	typhoon	_____
punch	_____		
'beverage'			

_____

air	_____	marmalade	_____
banshee	_____	mufti	_____
call	_____	parasol	_____
canasta	_____	persimmon	_____
cosmetic	_____	pilaf	_____
cosmopolite	_____	selvage	_____
deckle	_____	slim	_____
duplex	_____	tom-tom	_____
fan-tan	_____	traffic	_____
lingo	_____	tyro	_____

_____

anger	_____	paraffin	_____
bar 'piece'	_____	polo	_____
barbecue	_____	pylon	_____
cake	_____	raccoon	_____
cheetah	_____	rum	_____
gong	_____	'odd, dangerous'	
guerrilla	_____	sash	_____
hustle	_____	'band of cloth'	
kiosk	_____	spy	_____
lamp	_____	veranda	_____
loot	_____	zinc	_____

_____

bungalow	_____	decoy	_____
caucus	_____	gambit	_____
cedilla	_____	gusto	_____
cozy	_____	lope	

marimba	_____	rock 'stone'	_____
pathetic	_____	root	_____
pathos	_____	safari	_____
posse	_____	shebang	_____
protein	_____	sketch	_____
quip	_____	soil	_____
	_____		
attar	_____	orangutan	_____
ballast	_____	profile	_____
contraband	_____	purse	_____
cup	_____	rob	_____
furnace	_____	silk	_____
garrote	_____	sled	_____
ill	_____	tank	_____
jute	_____	tryst	_____
knapsack	_____	vizier	_____
myth	_____	zither	_____
	_____		
bluff	_____	mugwump	_____
coco(nut)	_____	ombre	_____
extravaganza	_____	sago	_____
fruit	_____	sock	_____
furlough	_____	'footwear'	
hawker	_____	therm	_____
'peddler'		tsetse	_____
humoresque	_____	tungsten	_____
kabob	_____	tutti-frutti	_____
loquat	_____	ugly	_____
lotto	_____	yak	_____
	_____		
babel	_____	manage	_____
beast	_____	renegade	_____
beleaguer	_____	roster	_____
bulwark	_____	scum	_____
casino	_____	succotash	_____
dago	_____	uvula	_____
eugenics	_____	vim	_____
joss (stick)	_____	wing	_____
junket	_____	yen 'desire'	_____
kudos	_____	yogurt	_____

Some words have come ultimately from exotic sources but have entered English directly from more familiar European tongues. For each of the following words, identify first the ultimate source and then the immediate source.

arsenal	_____	camel	_____
arsenic	_____	canoe	_____
borax	_____	carafe	_____
cabal	_____	caviar	_____

hammock	_____	sack 'bag'	_____
jar 'vessel'	_____	sequin	_____
jubilee	_____	spinach	_____
julep	_____	talc	_____
mummy	_____	tiger	_____
petunia	_____	tomato	_____

11.3 DOUBLETS

A doublet is one of two or more words that have come from the same source but that followed different routes of transmission. Doublets have a common etymon, or earliest known form, but different etymologies. Give the etymology for each of these doublets, tracing the members of each set back to the same etymon.

sure _____

secure _____

regal _____

royal _____

poor _____

pauper _____

place _____

plaza _____

piazza _____

cipher _____

zero _____

frail _____

fragile _____

count _____

compute _____

wine _____

vine _____

poison _____

potion _____

palaver _____

parable _____

parabola _____

parole _____

lodge _____

loge _____

lobby _____

loggia _____

corpse _____

corps _____

corpus _____

corse _____

ennui _____

annoy _____

chamber _____

camera _____

respect _____

respite _____

spice _____

species _____

filibuster _____

freebooter _____

caste _____

chaste _____

tradition _____

treason _____

valet _____

varlet _____

vassal _____

11.4 *LOAN TRANSLATIONS*

Instead of borrowing a foreign word that is composed of several meaningful parts, English has sometimes translated the parts. Thus the French *ballon d'essai* has become an English *trial balloon.* Such forms are known as loan translations or calques.

1. Identify the foreign terms of which the following English expressions were translations:

   commonplace _____

   free verse _____

   loan-word _____

   selvage _____

   superman _____

2. Give the loan translations that are sometimes used for these foreign terms:

   fait accompli _____

   Lebensraum _____

   porte-cochère _____

   raison d'être _____

   vis-à-vis _____

11.5 *LATIN LOAN-WORDS*

The loan-words that English has borrowed from Latin can be conveniently divided into four periods: (1) words borrowed while English speakers still lived on the continent, (2) words borrowed during the Old English period, (3) words borrowed in Middle English times, and (4) words borrowed into Modern English. Here are four groups of words; all the words within each group belong to the same period of borrowing. Judging from the form and meaning of the words you should be able to guess the period of each group. You can, however, check your guess in the *Oxford English Dictionary*. Identify the period (Gmc., OE, ME, Mod E) of each group and be prepared to explain how each group is typical of its period.

PERIOD: _____ _____ _____ _____

aborigines	allegory	cope	belt
consensus	apocalypse	cowl	pan
forceps	desk	creed	pillow
propaganda	diaphragm	monk	pipe
referendum	digit	noon	Saturday
specimen	elixir	nun	toll

11.6 *LATIN DOUBLETS*

Below are a number of doublets, all of which are Latin loan-words; the Latin source-words are in parentheses. In each pair of doublets, one of the words is an early borrowing; the other is more recent. The form of the doublets should enable you to tell the relative order of their borrowing. Circle the earlier member of each pair, and be prepared to explain your decision.

vinous (vinosus)   minster (monisterium)   scribe (scriba)
wine (vinum)   monastery (monasterium)   shrive (scribere)

caseate (caseatus)   vallation (vallationis)   dish (discus)
cheese (caseus)   wall (vallum)   disk (discus)

stratum (stratum)   secure (securus)   mint (moneta)
street (strata)   sicker 'safe' (securus)   monetary (monetarius)

11.7 *LATIN LOAN-WORDS*

When English has borrowed Latin nouns, it has usually taken the nominative case form (for example, *index*, *alumnus*, *crisis*, *data*), but in a few instances it has chosen one of the other case forms instead. What case and number of the Latin noun is each of these English words derived from? Be prepared to explain why the English noun is based on an oblique rather than on the nominative case.

innuendo _____   rebus _____
limbo _____   requiem _____
omnibus _____   specie _____
quarto _____   subpoena _____
quorum _____   vice 'deputy' _____

Some English nouns are derived from the inflected forms of Latin verbs and preserve the verbal endings of person, number, tense, mood, and voice. For example, *affidavit* is Latin for 'he has made an oath'; it occurred in legal documents as a formula introducing a record of sworn testimony when all such documents were still written in Latin. Subsequently it was understood as a title and thus as a name for a statement made under oath. For each of the following

English nouns, give the meaning of the Latin verb form from which it was borrowed. Be prepared to explain how a Latin verb became an English noun.

caret	_____	incipit	_____
caveat	_____	mandamus	_____
credo	_____	memento	_____
deficit	_____	placebo	_____
exit	_____	query	_____
fiat	_____	recipe	_____
habeas corpus	_____	tenet	_____
habitat	_____	vade mecum	_____
imprimatur	_____	veto	_____

Some English nouns are derived from Latin pronouns, adjectives, and adverbs. Give the etymology of each of these words, including the Latin part of speech.

alias _____
alibi _____
bonus _____
ego _____
integer _____
interim _____
item _____
nonplus _____
nostrum _____
quantum _____
quota _____
tandem _____

11.8 FRENCH LOAN-WORDS: PERIOD AND DIALECT

All the following words have been borrowed from French, but at various times. Their pronunciation should indicate whether they were borrowed from older French or from Modern French. Use the words *old* and *new* to indicate the period of borrowing, and be prepared to explain your decision.

chair	_____	route	_____	gender	_____
chaise	_____	crochet	_____	genre	_____
sachet	_____	crotchet	_____	marquee	_____
satchel	_____	chalet	_____	marquess	_____
chaplet	_____	chasuble	_____	liqueur	_____
chapeau	_____	moral	_____	liquor	_____
pellet	_____	morale	_____	tableau	_____
platoon	_____	negligee	_____	tablet	_____
damsel	_____	negligent	_____	montage	_____
mademoiselle	_____	critic	_____	mountain	_____
rout	_____	critique	_____		

All the following words are loans from French, but some were borrowed from Central French, others from Norman French. Their pronunciation should provide a clue to the original dialect. Use the abbreviations *CF* and *NF* to indicate their provenience, and be prepared to explain your decision.

catch	_____	caldron	_____	guile	_____
chase	_____	chaldron	_____	wile	_____
cant 'jargon'	_____	regard	_____	castellan	_____
chant	_____	reward	_____	chatelain	_____
case 'box'	_____	guardian	_____	castle	_____
enchase	_____	warden	_____	château	_____
market	_____	guerdon	_____	guise	_____
merchant	_____	waste	_____	wicket	_____

11.9 *FRENCH LOAN-WORDS: RATE OF ADOPTION*

In *Origins and Development* Pyles mentions that a number of studies, notably one by Otto Jespersen, have been made to determine the period during which French loan-words entered the English vocabulary in the largest numbers. You can check Jespersen's findings by making a similar study.

1. In the *Oxford English Dictionary* choose at random for each letter of the alphabet ten or more words of French origin. You may find it necessary to skip some letters, for example *K*, for lack of words.

2. Note the first recorded date of use in English for each word.

3. Tabulate the number of words borrowed during each half-century, and figure the percentage by dividing the total number of words into the number for each half-century.

	NUMBER OF WORDS	PERCENT OF TOTAL		NUMBER OF WORDS	PERCENT OF TOTAL
			Subtotal brought forward	_____	
before 1050	_____	_____	1501–1550	_____	_____
1051–1100	_____	_____	1551–1600	_____	_____
1101–1150	_____	_____	1601–1650	_____	_____
1151–1200	_____	_____	1651–1700	_____	_____
1201–1250	_____	_____	1701–1750	_____	_____
1251–1300	_____	_____	1751–1800	_____	_____
1301–1350	_____	_____	1801–1850	_____	_____
1351–1400	_____	_____	1851–1900	_____	_____
1401–1450	_____	_____			
1451–1500	_____	_____			
SUBTOTAL	_____		TOTAL	_____	

4. Compare your findings with those of Jespersen, who describes his method and tabulates his results in Chapter 5 of *Growth and Structure of the English Language*, 9th ed. (Oxford, 1954). Do your results differ significantly from his? If so, can you explain the discrepancy?

11.10 *FRENCH AND LATIN LOAN-WORDS IN MIDDLE ENGLISH*

Studies like Jespersen's have been based on the *Oxford English Dictionary* and thus tell nothing about the frequency with which the newly adopted words were being used. You can make a very rough estimate of the increasing use of loan-words from French and Latin by using the Middle English passages given in Pyles's *Origins and Development* and in this workbook. A chart for this purpose is provided at the bottom of this page.

1. Count the total number of words in each passage (omitting purely proper names, the frequency of which varies greatly depending on the subject matter).

2. Count the total occurrences of French and Latin loan-words in each passage. Because the exact provenience, French or Latin, of some words is doubtful, it is more convenient to lump together the borrowings from these two languages. If a word like *manere* occurs nine times in the same passage, as it does in Trevisa, you should count it nine times. Again, omit proper names from your count. See the end of this exercise for a list of the loan-words.

3. For each passage, divide the total number of words into the number of occurrences of French and Latin loan-words to find the percentage.

4. Compare the percentages from each of the passages and determine the historical period that saw the greatest increase in use of French and Latin loan-words.

	TOTAL NUMBER OF WORDS	NUMBER OF FRENCH AND LATIN LOANS	PERCENT OF LOANS
ca. 1150 *Peterborough Chronicle*			
ca. 1200 *Ancrene Riwle*			
ca. 1300 *Chronicle of Robert of Gloucester*			
ca. 1350 Rolle's *The Form of Living* (Pyles's *Origins and Development*, pp. 178–79)			
ca. 1400 Trevisa's *Polychronicon*			
ca. 1400 Chaucer's "The Former Age"			
ca. 1400 Chaucer, General Prologue to the *Canterbury Tales*			
ca. 1450 Anonymous, *Polychronicon*			

(If a word occurs more than once, the number of occurrences is given in parentheses.)

Peterborough Chronicle: sancte, pais

Ancrene Riwle: parais, lescun, Seinte, engle, ancre(n) (2), deouel, peoddare, noise, mercer, salue, merci, religuise

Chronicle of Robert of Gloucester: contreyes

Rolle's *The Form of Living:*   cristen, actyve (2), contemplatyve (2), travel, peryle, temptacions (2), sykerar, delitabiler, joy (2), savowre, present, passes, merites, freelte, regarde, deserve, verrayli, contemplacion, quiete

Trevisa's *Polychronicon:*   manere (9), peple (3), dyuers(e) (4), longage(s) (9), i-medled, naciouns (3), confederat, straunge (3), comyxtioun, mellynge, contray (5), apayred, vseþ, garrynge, apayrynge, scole(s) (4), vsage, compelled, construe(þ) (2), lessouns, gentil (3), broche, i-vsed, (i-)chaunged (2), maister, gram(m)er(e) (5), construccioun, secounde, conquest, auauntage (2), disauauntage (2), passe, trauaille, places, sown (2), reem (2), scarsliche, partie, acordeþ, sownynge, parteners, specialliche, frotynge, i-torned, noble, citees, profitable

Chaucer's "The Former Age":   age, apaied, destroyed, desceyued, outerage, medle (2), clere, piment, clarre, contre(s) (3), venym, manar(es) (2), purper, pyne, straunger, merchaundyse, dyuerse, cruel(y) (3), clariouns, egre, armurers, enmys, moeuen, armes, turne, anguissous, mountaigne, allas, gobets, couered, precious(nesse) (3), peril(s) (3)

Chaucer, General Prologue to the *Canterbury Tales:*   the words italicized in Pyles's *Origins and Development* (pages 327–28) plus *Aprille* and *martir*, which are of Latin provenience

Anonymous, *Polychronicon:*   clerely, diuersites (2), langage(s) (12), nacion(e)s (3), propre, inpermixte, perauenture, parte(s) (9), communicacion, confederate, inhabite, barbre (2), tripartite (2), procedenge, peple (2), commixtion, corrupcion, natife, cause(de) (3), schole, compellede, constru, consuetude, nowble, laborede, meruayle, propur, diuerse, yle, pronunciacion, vniuocate, remaynethe, sownde(the) (2), acorde, clyme, marches, participacion, nature, extremities (2), collateralle, arthike, anthartike, specially, cuntre, distaunce, vse, returnenge, costes, multitude, assignede, habundante, fertilite, nowmbre, plesaunte, portes

CONCLUSIONS

11.11 FRENCH AND LATIN LOAN-WORDS IN OTHER PERIODS

Following the directions given in the preceding exercise, determine the percentage of French and Latin loan-words in one of the Old English and one of the Modern English passages given in Pyles's *Origins and Development* and in this workbook. Compare the three periods in the history of our language with respect to the frequency of such loans.

11.12 LOAN-WORDS AND CULTURAL CONTACT

The following words are in four columns, each of which has a common area of meaning. After each word write *OE* if it is a native word; if it is a loan-word, write the name of the language from which it was borrowed. Be prepared to discuss these questions: Do you detect any pattern for the borrowing within each set? What does the pattern indicate about cultural relations among the languages? What kind of word is least likely to be replaced by a borrowed term?

father	_____	horse	_____	day	_____	house	_____
mother	_____	mare	_____	night	_____	floor	_____
son	_____	colt	_____	morning	_____	roof	_____
daughter	_____	foal	_____	evening	_____	door	_____
brother	_____	filly	_____	week	_____	bed	_____
kin	_____	gelding	_____	year	_____	stool	_____
sister	_____	stallion	_____	month	_____	window	_____
aunt	_____	charger	_____	decade	_____	rug	_____
uncle	_____	mount	_____	century	_____	ceiling	_____
nephew	_____	courser	_____	noon	_____	chair	_____
niece	_____			hour	_____	table	_____
cousin	_____			second	_____	chimney	_____
relative	_____			minute	_____	cellar	_____
				moment	_____		

In addition to the Japanese loan-words listed on page 337 of Pyles's *Origins and Development*, a number of others have entered English, some as early as the seventeenth century but most quite recently. All of them are still distinctly exotic.

1. Look up these words in the *Oxford English Dictionary* and note the date of their first recorded use in English. Many of the words have been borrowed too recently to be included in the *OED*; which of the recent loans are listed in *Webster's Third New International Dictionary*? Mark them "*ca.* 1950."

FROM THE TEXT				ADDITIONAL LOANS			
banzai	_____	kamikaze	_____	benjo	_____	samisen	_____
geisha	_____	kimono	_____	geta	_____	satori	_____
hara-kiri	_____	sake	_____	go 'a game'	_____	sayonara	_____
(jin)ricksha	_____	samurai	_____	haiku	_____	shogun	_____
judo	_____	soy(a)	_____	hibachi	_____	sukiyaki	_____
jujitsu	_____	tycoon	_____	kabuki	_____	sumo	_____
				mikado	_____	tatami	_____
				noh	_____	zen	_____
				obi	_____		

2. Add any words you can to this list.

3. How do these words and their time of borrowing reflect cultural relations between Japan and the Occident? _____

_____

4. Can you account for the common pronunciation of *hara-kiri* as [hæ̀rikǽri]? What is your explanation? _____

_____

5. Choose another exotic language from which English has borrowed, and collect as many loan-words as you can, together with their dates of borrowing. Write a paper describing what these words reveal about the external history of English, that is, about the cultural contacts of English speakers with the foreign language.

11.14 *LOAN-WORDS IN THE TOTAL VOCABULARY*

Because of the immense size of the English vocabulary and its ever changing content, no one can definitively count the number of loan-words in our language. It is possible, however, to estimate the percentage of borrowed words within the total vocabulary.

Make a random sampling of the words listed in one of the standard desk dictionaries; you might use the first word on every second page or on every fifth page, and so forth, depending on how large a sample you wish to use. Omit proper names and any word for which no etymology is given. For each word you choose, note whether it is a part of the native vocabulary (in which case it will be traced no further back than to Old English) or whether it has been borrowed. If the word has been borrowed, note the source-language from which it entered English and ignore any earlier history which may be given. Distinguish carefully between sources and cognates: A source is a direct ancestor; a cognate is merely a relative. You will be interested in sources only. Read carefully the prefatory material on etymology in the dictionary that you are using, and be sure that you understand the abbreviations you will find in the main body of the dictionary.

Since the history of some English words is not perfectly known, you are likely to encounter various difficulties in identifying sources. You should handle such problems in whatever way seems best; consistency of treatment is as important as the actual method.

As examples, a few words are considered here to illustrate sources and problems. The etymologies cited are from *Funk & Wagnalls Standard College Dictionary*, Text Edition, published by Harcourt Brace Jovanovich, Inc. (New York, 1963).

hem *noun* [OE]   COMMENT: The word is native.

hem *interj.* [Imit.]   COMMENT: This is an echoic word; it is native.

howitzer [< Du. *houwitzer*, ult. < Czechoslovakian *houfnice* catapult]   COMMENT: The source-language is Dutch; the earlier history is irrelevant to English.

funnel [Earlier *fonel*, ult. < L *infunibulum* < *infundere* to pour < *in-* into + *fundere* to pour]   COMMENT: The earlier spelling *fonel* is irrelevant; the exact history of the word is not known, but it derives ultimately from Latin. Either omit the word or give the source-language as Latin.

boy [ME *boi*; origin unknown]   COMMENT: The word is found in Middle English, but its earlier history is obscure. Give the source-language as Middle English or as unknown, or omit the word.

gloat [cf. ON *glotta* to grin]   COMMENT: The word is cognate with the Old Norse verb, but the source is not known. Give the source-language as unknown, or omit the word.

After you have selected the words you are going to use as a sample and have identified the source of each of them, prepare a table like the one on the next page summarizing the number of words that can be traced to each language and the percentage of the total that they represent.

Percentages are found by dividing the total number of words of your sample into the number of words for any given source. If your total sample consisted of 320 words and it included 8 words borrowed from Italian, the percentage of Italian words would be 8 divided by 320 = .025, or 2.5%.

Your report on this research might include the following parts:

1. STATEMENT OF PURPOSE: a random sampling of words in the English vocabulary to determine the percentage of native words and the percentage of loan-words from various languages.

2. STATEMENT OF PROCEDURE: What dictionary did you use? How did you select the words for the sample? What problems did you encounter in determining sources? How did you handle these problems?

3. RAW MATERIALS: List the words you selected and give the source-language for each. For example:

abase OF	anabatic Gk.
achieve OF	antecedent Lat.
advowson Anglo-French	apprehend Lat.
akimbo ME	arrow OE
alternative Med. Lat.	atman Skt.

4. SUMMARY OF RESULTS: as below.

5. CONCLUSIONS: a short paragraph describing your results and drawing whatever conclusions seem relevant.

Your instructor may prefer that you omit from the report one or more of the parts described above.

	NUMBER OF WORDS	PERCENT OF TOTAL
Native English (incl. OE, ME, imitative)		
Latin (incl. Vulgar Lat., Med. Lat., Late Lat., Neo-Lat.)		
Greek		
French (incl. Anglo-French, Anglo-Norman, OF, Middle Fr., Provençal)		
Spanish (incl. American Sp., Catalan)		
Portuguese		
Italian		
Scandinavian (incl. Old Norse, Danish, Icelandic, Swedish, Norwegian)		
High German (incl. German, Old HG, Middle HG, Yiddish)		
Low German (incl. Dutch, Afrikaans, Flemish)		
Celtic (incl. Welsh, Gaelic, Irish, Cornish, Breton)		
Semitic (incl. Arabic, Hebrew, Aramaic)		
Persian (incl. Avestan)		
Sanskrit (incl. Prakrit, Pali, Hindi, Hindustani, Bengalese)		
Dravidian		
Chinese (incl. Cantonese)		
Japanese		
Malay-Polynesian (incl. Javanese, Tagalog)		
African		
Slavic (incl. Russian, Polish, Bulgarian, Czech)		
Turkish		
American Indian (incl. Eskimo)		
Others (incl. Australian, Hungarian, Armenian, and so forth)		
Unknown		
TOTAL		100

It is obvious that different words occur with different frequencies. *Angle, line,* and *barn* are words of fairly high frequency; *hade, raphe,* and *byre* are considerably less common. We may legitimately ask whether the active vocabulary, words which are common in normal discourse, contains the same percentage of loan-words as the total vocabulary of English.

To investigate the question, follow this procedure:

1. Choose a passage of 300 to 500 words. The best sort of passage will be one that reads easily, a straightforward narrative or exposition from a popular magazine or a book intended for the general market.

2. Count the exact number of words in the passage.

3. Ascertain the source-language for each word, as in the preceding exercise.

4. Prepare a summary of the number and percentage of words for each source, also as in the preceding exercise. To arrive at percentages, divide the total number of words in the passage into the number of words from each source-language. Count each occurrence of a word as a separate word; that is, if *the* occurs twenty times, it should be counted as twenty words.

5. In reporting your findings, compare the results of this study with the results you obtained in the preceding exercise, and draw appropriate conclusions.

As a variation on this exercise, you might classify the words from your passage according to their part of speech (noun, pronoun, adjective, verb, preposition, and so forth) and prepare a separate summary for each part of speech. In your conclusion, compare the parts of speech with respect to their ratio of loan-words. Which part of speech has the highest percentage of loan-words? Which the lowest?

As another variation, you might compare the percentage of loan-words in two passages. Compare a passage from a Hemingway novel with one from *Scientific American*, or a passage from a Salinger short story with one from Kroeber's *Anthropology*, or a passage from the King James Bible with one from Sir Thomas Browne's *Hydriotaphia*. Choose two passages that seem very different in style and decide whether the presence of loan-words contributes to the difference.

Words and Meanings

12.1 QUESTIONS FOR REVIEW AND DISCUSSION

1. Define the following terms:

semantics	pejoration	sound association
semantic change	amelioration	taboo
etymological sense	vogue word	euphemism
generalization	metaphor	intensifier
specialization	synesthesia	

2. What devices for signaling meaning does a language have?

3. What value is there in the study of words? In answering this question, consider one of the conclusions reached by Charles Carpenter Fries in his germinal study *American English Grammar: The Grammatical Structure of Present-Day English with Especial Reference to Social Differences or Class Dialects* (New York, 1940): "In vocabulary and in grammar the mark of the language of the uneducated is its poverty."

4. What is meant by the statement that every word has "a certain field of meaning" rather than a "fixed" or "real" meaning? How does the concept of a "field of meaning" help to explain why meaning varies?

5. What is the relationship between a word's etymology and its meaning?

6. Some of the ways and circumstances in which meaning may change are listed here. Notice that the various ways are not all mutually exclusive; there is much overlapping. Supply an example to illustrate each way.

   (1) a widening of the scope of reference (generalization)
   (2) a narrowing of the scope of reference (specialization)
   (3) a lowering of value judgments involved in the reference (pejoration)
   (4) a raising of value judgments involved in the reference (amelioration)
   (5) a shift in meaning from one social group to another (specialized class usage)
   (6) a shift in meaning from one set of circumstances to another (contextual variation)
   (7) a change in the aspect of the meaning upon which a word focuses (shift in point of view)
   (8) a popular adoption of technical language, often motivated by the quest for prestige (popularization)
   (9) a shift in meaning based on an analogy or likeness between two things (metaphor)
   (10) a transference of meaning from one kind of sense-perception to another (synesthesia)
   (11) a shift from concrete reference to abstract reference (abstraction)
   (12) a shift from abstract reference to concrete reference (concretion)
   (13) a shift in reference from the subjective to the objective (objectification or externalizing)
   (14) a shift in reference from the objective to the subjective (subjectification or internalizing)

(15) a shift in meaning due to the association of ideas (synecdoche and metonymy)

(16) an influence of the semantics of one language upon that of another (calque)

(17) a semantic association between two words due to a similarity in sound (sound association)

(18) a religious or moral taboo which requires new words to replace others thought to be too dangerous, too indecent, or too painful for common use (euphemism)

(19) an exaggerated use of words for mild intensification or emphasis (hyperbole)

7. In 1712 Jonathan Swift published *A Proposal for Correcting, Improving and Ascertaining the English Tongue*,[1] in which he wrote,

> The *English* Tongue is not arrived to such a Degree of Perfection, as, upon that Account, to make us apprehend any Thoughts of its Decay: And if it were once refined to a certain Standard, perhaps there might be Ways to fix it for ever . . . . I see no absolute Necessity why any Language should be perpetually changing; for we find many Examples of the contrary . . . But what I have most at Heart, is, that some Method should be thought on for *Ascertaining* and *Fixing* our Language for ever, after such Alterations are made in it as shall be thought requisite . . . . What *Horace* says of *Words going off, and perishing like Leaves, and new ones coming in their Place*, is a Misfortune he laments, rather than a Thing he approves: But I cannot see why this should be absolutely necessary.

Discuss the goal that Swift sets up in this extract in terms of its desirability and practicality.

12.2 *DEVICES FOR SIGNALING MEANING*

Every language can be said to have two kinds of meaning: lexical meaning, the sense that words have as they are listed in a dictionary, and grammatical meaning, the added sense that words acquire when they are put together in a sentence. Certain words, the function words mentioned on page 15 of Pyles's *Origins and Development*, are so fundamental to the grammatical meaning of a sentence that it is best to consider them as part of the grammar as well as part of the lexicon of English. One way to demonstrate the difference between these two kinds of meaning is with sentences like these:

Oll considerork meanork, ho mollop tharp fo concernesh bix shude largel philosophigar aspectem ith language phanse vulve increasorkrow de recent yearm engagesh sho attentuge ith scholarm.

In prefarbing torming, we cannot here be pretolled with those murler dichytomical optophs of flemack which have demuggingly in arsell wems exbined the obburtion of maxans.

If you are asked what the sentences mean, your first response may be that neither means anything. If further pressed, you might suggest that the first sentence is about language, about something that is recent, and perhaps about philosophy. A careful reading will reveal several other probable bits of information, but at best the sentence remains a farrago of nonsense.

With the second sentence, however, matters are quite otherwise. There is a great deal of meaning in it; for example you can tell from it

1. that, whatever an optoph is, there are more than one of them;
2. that the optophs we are concerned with are dichytomical ones and more murl than other possible optophs;
3. that an optoph is something we might be pretolled with;
4. that optophs are things and not people;

[1] Reprinted in Herbert Davis, ed., *The Prose Works of Jonathan Swift* (Oxford, 1957), Vol. IV.

5. that the obburtion of maxans can be exbined by optophs;

6. that the exbining we are talking about took place in the past.

These six observations are only a few of the many bits of meaning the second sentence will convey to any speaker of English. Indeed, our reaction to the second sentence might be that of Alice to the poem "Jabberwocky": "Somehow it seems to fill my head with ideas—only I don't exactly know what they are!" The first sentence uses real English for its lexically important words, but substitutes nonsense elements for the function words and the word-endings. Therefore we have some idea of what it is talking about, but no notion whatever of what is being said about the subject. The second sentence reverses the procedure by preserving function words and suffixes, but using nonsense syllables for the main lexical items. Thus even though we have no idea of what *optophs* and *maxans* are, we do know what is being said about them.

1. Six observations were made about the meaning of the second sentence. Tell, as precisely as you can, how each of these observations can be inferred from the sentence.

    (1) _____
    _____

    (2) _____
    _____

    (3) _____
    _____

    (4) _____
    _____

    (5) _____
    _____

    (6) _____
    _____

2. Which of the following observations are valid inferences from the second sentence? Write *V* before each valid conclusion and *I* before each invalid conclusion.

    _____ Obburtion belongs to or is characteristic of more than one maxan.
    _____ We probably prefarb torming.
    _____ Flemack does exbine the obburtion of maxans.
    _____ The exbining of the obburtion of maxans by murler dichytomical optophs of flemack is demugging.
    _____ We do not pretoll some optophs.
    _____ The action of exbining the obburtion of maxans has taken place in more than one wem which is arsell.

3. In each of these sentences, underline the function words and circle grammatically relevant endings.

    The merkly boppling dorn quanks all puggles in the scritches.

    A tagmeme is the correlation of a grammatical function or slot-class with a class of fillers or mutually substitutable items occurring in that slot.

    Night's candles are burnt out, and jocund day stands tiptoe on the misty mountain tops.

    But the Idols of the Market-place are the most troublesome of all: idols which have crept into the understanding through the alliances of words and names.

    The generall end therefore of all the booke is to fashion a gentleman or noble person in vertuous and gentle discipline.

    His notions fitted things so well/That which was which he could not tell.

4. Identify the devices which are used for changing the meaning in these pairs of sentences. Write the appropriate numbers in the blanks. The last three pairs involve two devices each.

1. function words
2. intonation
3. suffixes
4. word order

It is time to go.
_____ It is time to go?

She liked the red hat.
_____ She liked the *red* hat.

He invested in stock theater.
_____ He invested in theater stock.

They found the girl in the car that needed washing.
_____ They found the girl in the car who needed washing.

He bought a picture of Rembrandt for two dollars.
_____ He bought a picture of Rembrandt's for two dollars.

The travelers stopped to eat.
_____ _____ The travelers stopped eating.

They said it was a fun time.
_____ _____ They said it was fun-time.

He died happily.
_____ _____ Happily, he died.

12.3 *VARIATION IN MEANING: WORD-PLAY*

In each of these quotations there is a pun or a play on meaning involving the italicized words. In some cases the word-play is due to a word's having a broad field of meaning; in other cases, it is due to an accidental similarity of sound between two different words.

What two meanings are combined to produce each pun? Consult the *Oxford English Dictionary* if you cannot recognize the word-play.

1. For him was levere have at his beddes heed
   Twenty bookes, clad in blak or reed,
   Of Aristotle and his philosophye,
   Than robes rich, or fithele, or gay sautrye.
   But al be that he was a *philosophre*
   Yit hadde he but litel gold in cofre.   (Chaucer, General Prologue to the *Canterbury Tales*)

   _____

   _____

2. For thy sweet love remembered such wealth brings
   That then I scorn to change my *state* with kings.   (Shakespeare, Sonnet 29)

   _____

   _____

3. [As a joke, Falstaff's horse has been hidden.]

Falstaff   What a plague mean ye to colt me thus?
Prince   Thou liest; thou art not *colted*, thou art uncolted.

(Shakespeare, *1 Henry IV*, II.ii)

_____

_____

4. *Hostess*   Marry, my lord, there is a *noble*man of the court at door would speak with you,
he says he comes from your father.
Prince   Give him as much as will make him a *royal* man, and send him back again to my
mother.   (Shakespeare, *1 Henry IV*, II.iv)

_____

_____

5. [Prince Hal and Bardolph, a gluttonous thief, are discussing what is portended by Bardolph's nose, which is as red as a meteor.]

Bardolph   Choler, my lord, if rightly taken.
Prince   No, if rightly *taken*, halter. [that is, 'noose']   (Shakespeare, *1 Henry IV*, II.iv)

_____

_____

6. [In the midst of battle, Prince Hal asks Falstaff for his pistol.]

Prince   Give it me; what, is it in the case?
Falstaff   Aye, Hal; 'tis hot, 'tis hot; there's that will *sack* a city.

[Hal, taking the supposed pistol from the case, finds that it is a bottle of wine.]

(Shakespeare, *1 Henry IV*, V.iii)

_____

_____

7. [Hippolito is confused about the identity of his caller. Why?]

Servant   Here's a *parson* would speak with you, sir.
Hippolito   Hah!
Servant   A *parson*, sir, would speak with you.
Hippolito   Vicar?   (Dekker, *The Honest Whore*, Part I, IV.i)

_____

_____

8. *Fortunatus*   Let none speak to me, till you have *marked* me well.
Shadow   [Chalking Fortunatus's back] Now speak your mind.

(Dekker, *Old Fortunatus*, II.ii)

_____

_____

9. *Viola*   Musician will he never be, yet I find much music in him, but he loves no *frets*, and
is so free from anger that many times I am ready to bite off my tongue . . .

(Dekker, *The Honest Whore*, Part I, I.ii)

_____

_____

10. *Shadow*   But what shall we learn by travel?
    Andelocia *Fashions.*
    Shadow   That's a beastly disease: methinks it's better staying in your own country.

    (Dekker, *Old Fortunatus*, II.ii)

_____

_____

11. Must I, who came to *travail* thorough you
    Grow your fixed subject, because you are true?   (Donne, "The Indifferent")

_____

_____

12. Dull sublunary lovers' love
    (Whose soule is sense) cannot admit
    Absence, because it doth remove
    Those things which elemented it.   (Donne, "A Valediction: Forbidding Mourning")

_____

_____

13. Swear by Thy self, that at my death Thy *Son*
    Shall shine as he shines now and heretofore;
    And, having done that, Thou hast done,
    I fear no more.   (Donne, "A Hymn to God the Father")

_____

_____

14. [This poem is a prayer for God's grace.]

    The dew doth ev'ry morning fall;
    And shall the dew outstrip thy dove?
    The dew, for which *grasse* cannot call,
    Drop from above.   (Herbert, "Grace")

_____

_____

15. And now, unveiled, the toilet stands displayed,
    Each silver vase in mystic order laid.
    First, robed in white, the nymph intent adores,
    With head uncovered, the *cosmetic* powers.   (Pope, *The Rape of the Lock*)

_____

_____

12.4 *ETYMOLOGY AND MEANING*

If the italicized words are taken in their etymological senses, each of the following statements is redundant. Cite the etymological meanings that create the pseudo-redundancies.

They began the *inauguration* by observing the entrails of a sacrificial bull. _____

_____

The *escaping* convict slipped out of his coat, by which the guard held him._____

_____

His *stamina* having been exhausted, the Fates clipped his thread of life. _____

_____

The general *harangued* his soldiers as they gathered about him in a circle. _____

The *candidate* was dressed in a white suit to symbolize his purity._____

A *mediocre* mountain-climber, he never got more than halfway up any peak._____

The *miniature* was painted in shades of red._____

The butcher's shop, especially the bench on which he cleaved meat, was a *shambles*.

The infantry withstood fierce punishment from the *strafing* of the enemy aircraft.

The housemother *controlled* the coeds by checking their names against her register to be sure they were present at lights-out._____

There is an etymological contradiction in each of these statements. Cite the etymological meaning of the italicized word that creates the pseudo-inconsistency.

The *cadre* is the core around which a military unit forms, as a circle around its center.

Although her hair was neatly arranged, she looked *disheveled*._____

He *endorsed* the proposal by signing his name with a flourish across the front of the document.

The archeologist *arrived* at his destination, a ruin in the midst of the Sahara. _____

Although the two men were *companions* of long standing, they had never shared a meal.

The team *scampered* onto the field, eager to meet their opponents. _____

The ship's passengers were *quarantined* for two weeks._____

The use of automation by American *manufacturers* promises to effect a new industrial revolution._____

The short, skinny girl had a great deal of *poise*. _____

You may write on any *topic* you like except a person or a place. _____

12.5   CHANGES IN MEANING

He was a happy and *sad girl* who lived in a *town* forty miles from the closest neighbor. His unmarried sister, a *wife* who was a vegetarian member of the WCTU, ate *meat* and drank *liquor* three times a day. She was so fond of oatmeal bread made from the *corn* her brother grew that she *starved* from overeating. He fed nuts to the *deer* that lived in the branches of an

apple tree which bore pears. A *silly* and wise *boor* everyone liked, he was a *lewd* man whom the

general *censure* held to be a model of chastity.

The paragraph above is logically incoherent if we understand all of the words in their current meanings. If, however, we take each of the italicized words in a sense it had in earlier times, the paragraph contains no inconsistencies at all. Above each of the italicized words, write an earlier meaning that will remove the logical contradictions created by the current sense. The earlier meanings need not be contemporary with one another. They can be found in the *Oxford English Dictionary*.

12.6 *SOME EXAMPLES OF SEMANTIC CHANGE*

The italicized words in the following quotations have lost the meaning that the quotation demands. In the blank to the left of each quotation write a word that will gloss the italicized item for a modern reader. Try to guess the meaning from the context, but if you are unsure, consult the *Oxford English Dictionary*, where you will find most of the quotations used as citations.

_____ He *addressed* himself to go over the River. (Bunyan, *Pilgrim's Progress*)

_____ He had *approved* unto the vulgar, the dignitie of his Science. (Raleigh, *The History of the World*)

_____ *Falstaff* Shall we have a play extempore?
  Prince Content; and the *argument* shall be thy running away. (Shakespeare, *1 Henry IV*)

_____ A Brazen or Stone-head . . . so *artificial* and natural, that . . . it will presently open its mouth, and resolve the question. (Worcester, *A Century of Inventions*)

_____ Yes, and after supper for feare lest they bee not full gorged, to have a delicate *banquet*. (Cogan, *The Haven of Health*)

_____ Doth she not count her blest . . . that we have wrought so worthy a gentleman to be her *bride*? (Shakespeare, *Romeo and Juliet*)

_____ Thus we *prevent* the last great day, and judge ourselves. (Herbert, *The Temple*)

_____ Upon that day either prepare to die . . . or on Diana's altar to *protest* for aye austerity and single life. (Shakespeare, *A Midsummer Night's Dream*)

_____ The exception *proves* the rule. (Proverbial)

_____ But you, my lord, were glad to be employ'd, to show how *quaint* an orator you are. (Shakespeare, *2 Henry VI*)

_____ What lawful *quest* have given their verdict up unto the frowning judge? (Shakespeare, *Richard III*)

_____ If I attain I will return and *quit* thy love. (Arnold, *The Light of Asia*)

_____ Abate the edge of traitors . . . that would *reduce* these bloody days again, and make poor England weep in streams of blood! (Shakespeare, *Richard III*)

<table>
<tr><td>_____</td><td>My ships are safely come to *road*. (Shakespeare, *The Merchant of Venice*)</td></tr>
<tr><td>_____</td><td>Thou wilt never get thee a husband, if thou be so *shrewd* of thy tongue. (Shakespeare, *Much Ado About Nothing*)</td></tr>
<tr><td>_____</td><td>I think you have as little *skill* to fear, as I have purpose to put you to it. (Shakespeare, *The Winter's Tale*)</td></tr>
<tr><td>_____</td><td>Satan . . . insatiate to pursue vain war with Heaven, and by *success* untaught, his proud imaginations thus displayed. (Milton, *Paradise Lost*)</td></tr>
<tr><td>_____</td><td>To be my queen and *portly* emperess. (Marlowe, *Tamburlaine, Part I*)</td></tr>
<tr><td>_____</td><td>There they alight . . . and rest their weary limbs a *tide*. (Spenser, *The Faerie Queene*)</td></tr>
<tr><td>_____</td><td>—I dreamt a dream *tonight*. —And so did I. (Shakespeare, *Romeo and Juliet*)</td></tr>
<tr><td>_____</td><td>So said he, and forbore not glance or *toy*, of amorous intent, well understood of Eve. (Milton, *Paradise Lost*)</td></tr>
<tr><td>_____</td><td>Heaps of pearl, inestimable stones, *unvalued* jewels, all scattered in the bottom of the sea. (Shakespeare, *Richard III*)</td></tr>
<tr><td>_____</td><td>Princes then . . . [were] trained up, through piety and zeal, to prize spare diet, patient labour, and plain *weeds*. (Wordsworth, *Prelude*)</td></tr>
<tr><td>_____</td><td>This God is most mighty thing that may be, the most *witty* and most rightful. (*Lay Folks' Catechism*)</td></tr>
<tr><td>_____</td><td>O Eve, in evil hour thou didst give ear to that false *worm*. (Milton, *Paradise Lost*)</td></tr>
</table>

12.7 GENERALIZATION AND SPECIALIZATION

Each of the semantic developments described below is an example of either generalization or specialization. Identify the process illustrated by writing in the blank *G* for generalization or *S* for specialization.

_____ *aisle:* earlier 'passage between the pews of a church,' later 'passage between rows of seats'

_____ *bereaved:* earlier 'robbed,' later 'deprived by death'

_____ *business:* earlier 'state of being busy,' later 'occupation, profession, or trade'

_____ *butler:* earlier 'male servant in charge of the wine cellar,' later 'male servant in a household'

_____ *chap:* earlier 'customer,' later 'fellow'

_____ *coast:* earlier 'side,' later 'sea shore'

_____ *discard:* earlier 'throw out a card,' later 'reject'

_____ *disease:* earlier 'discomfort,' later 'malady'

_____ *flesh:* earlier 'muscular tissue,' later 'muscular tissue, not viewed as comestible'

_____ *fowl:* earlier 'bird,' later 'barnyard fowl'

_____ *frock:* earlier 'monk's loose-fitting habit,' later 'loose-fitting outer garment'

_____ *frock:* earlier 'loose-fitting outer garment,' later 'woman's dress'

_____ *ghost:* earlier 'soul, spirit,' later 'soul of a dead man as manifested to the living'

_____ *go:* earlier 'walk, travel by foot,' later 'move, travel'

_____ *ordeal:* earlier 'legal trial by a physical test,' later 'a difficult experience'

_____ *passenger:* earlier 'passer-by, traveler,' later 'one who travels by vehicle or vessel'

_____ *spill:* earlier 'shed blood,' later 'waste a liquid'

_____ *thing:* earlier 'legal matter,' later 'any matter'

_____ *wade:* earlier 'go,' later 'walk through water'

_____ *wretch:* earlier 'exile,' later 'unhappy person'

12.8 PEJORATION AND AMELIORATION

Each of the semantic developments described below is an example of either pejoration or amelioration. Identify the process illustrated by writing in the blank *P* for pejoration or *A* for amelioration.

_____ *brook:* earlier 'enjoy, make use of,' later 'endure, tolerate'

_____ *crafty:* earlier 'skillful, clever,' later 'cunning, wily'

_____ *dizzy:* earlier 'foolish,' later 'vertiginous'

_____ *err:* earlier 'wander,' later 'go astray'

_____ *fair:* earlier 'beautiful, pleasant,' later 'moderate, tolerable'

_____ *fame:* earlier 'report, rumor,' later 'celebrity, renown'

_____ *flibbertigibbet:* earlier 'name of a devil,' later 'mischievous person'

_____ *fond:* earlier 'foolish,' later 'affectionate'

_____ *glamour:* earlier 'spell, enchantment,' later 'attractiveness, allure'

_____ *grandiose:* earlier 'large, stately,' later 'pompous'

_____ *impertinent:* earlier 'not pertinent, unrelated,' later 'presumptuous, insolent'

_____ *inquisition:* earlier 'investigation,' later 'persecution'

_____ *luxury:* earlier 'lust,' later 'sumptuousness'

_____ *minister:* earlier 'servant,' later 'government official'

_____ *mischievous:* earlier 'disastrous,' later 'playfully annoying'

_____ *notorious:* earlier 'widely known,' later 'widely and unfavorably known'

_____ *reek:* earlier 'smoke,' later 'stink'

_____ *smirk:* earlier 'smile,' later 'simper'

_____ *sophisticated:* earlier 'overly complex or refined,' later 'sufficiently complex or knowing'

12.9 CHANGES DUE TO SOCIAL CLASS, CIRCUMSTANCE, OR POINT OF VIEW

Changes due to social class, circumstance, or point of view are similar rather than opposite kinds of change. Examples can be found on pages 350–51 of Pyles's *Origins and Development*.

1. The word spelled *Mrs.* in one meaning and *missis* in another meaning shows semantic variation according to social class. Define the two meanings and indicate what the social difference is. _____

_____

_____

2. The word *fee* 'payment for services,' for example, a lawyer's fee, acquired its present meaning in accordance with changes of the circumstances in which the word was used. What was the earliest English meaning of the word? _____

_____

3. The word *attic* 'garret' acquired its present meaning as a result of a shift in point of view. What was the earlier meaning of the word? _____

_____

4. Classify each of the following semantic developments as due either to circumstance, that is, technological, cultural change (*C*), or to point of view (*P*).

_____ *boon:* earlier 'prayer, request for something,' later 'gift, favor, benefit granted to a petitioner'

_____ *glee:* earlier 'pleasant musical entertainment,' later 'pleasure, joy'

_____ *navigator:* earlier 'one who steers a boat,' later 'one who directs the flight of an airplane'

_____ *pen:* earlier 'quill pen,' later 'fountain pen'

_____ *satellite:* earlier 'one celestial body that orbits another,' later 'a man-made object that orbits the earth'

_____ *tide:* earlier 'time,' for example, of the sea's ebb and flow, later 'regular ebb and flow of the sea'

12.10 *THE VOGUE FOR WORDS OF LEARNED ORIGIN*

Popularization, the process by which a learned word enters the general vocabulary and undergoes various kinds of semantic change as it does so, is very common. Here are a number of vogue words the technical meanings of which have been altered in popular use. Define each word (1) in the popular sense illustrated by the sentence in which it is used and (2) in the technical sense that underlies the popular use.

He is strongly *allergic* to any form of modern music.

1. _____
2. _____

At every party there's one loud-mouthed *extrovert* who dominates the group.

1. _____
2. _____

She is such a kind-hearted soul that she *identifies* with every panhandler she sees on the street.

1. _____
2. _____

Crowds make him *inhibited*.

1. _____
2. _____

The poor thing was a *martyr* to her insomnia.

1. _____
2. _____

He plays golf every Sunday; it's an *obsession* with him.

1. _____
2. _____

In New York, she lost her *personal identity* amid the crowds.

1. _____
2. _____

He has a *phobia* about Christmas shopping.

    1. _____

    2. _____

Television sponsors are *psychotic* about having other products mentioned on their programs.

    1. _____

    2. _____

Knowing a little French will give you *status* in the garden club of any midwestern town.

    1. _____

    2. _____

He *sublimated* his desire to smoke by eating lemon drops.

    1. _____

    2. _____

The *tragedy* is that despite our rush, the train has already left.

    1. _____

    2. _____

12.11 *ABSTRACT AND CONCRETE MEANINGS*

Words may change in meaning by shifting (1) from the abstract to the concrete or (2) from the concrete to the abstract. Identify the kind of change exemplified in each of these words by writing the appropriate number, 1 or 2, in the blank.

_____ *chair:* earlier 'a seat,' later 'professorship'

_____ *complexion:* earlier 'temperament, disposition,' later 'color and texture of the facial skin'

_____ *construction:* earlier 'action of constructing,' later 'something constructed'

_____ *engine:* earlier 'native intelligence, ingenuity,' later 'mechanical apparatus'

_____ *libel:* earlier 'a derogatory pamphlet,' later 'a false and derogatory statement'

_____ *nimble:* earlier 'quick-witted, clever,' later 'quick-acting, agile'

_____ *slapstick:* earlier 'instrument that makes a loud noise, used to simulate heavy blows,' later 'farce, broad comedy'

_____ *sloth:* earlier 'laziness,' later 'an arboreal mammal'

_____ *to stomach:* earlier 'digest, retain in the stomach,' later 'put up with, tolerate'

_____ *zest:* earlier 'lemon peel,' later 'enjoyment, relish'

12.12 *SUBJECTIVE AND OBJECTIVE MEANINGS*

Words may change in meaning by shifting (1) from the subjective to the objective or (2) from the objective to the subjective. Thus the earliest, and still the most common, meaning of *sorry* is 'feeling regret,' as in "When Joseph saw it, he was very *sorry*." Such a meaning is said to be subjective because the word describes the person who experiences the sorrow. Later *sorry* came to mean 'evoking regret or disdain,' as in "It was a *sorry* sight." This use is called objective because the word now describes a thing that causes sorrow in someone. The shift in meaning was from the subjective to the objective, from the perceiver to the object perceived.

Identify the kind of change exemplified in each of these words by writing the appropriate number, 1 or 2, in the blank.

_____ *angry:* earlier 'troublesome, causing sorrow,' later 'wrathful, raging'

_____ *anxious:* earlier 'feeling anxiety about something,' later 'causing anxiety in someone'

_____ *careful:* earlier 'painstaking, showing care for,' later 'showing the results of care'

_____ *excitement:* earlier 'something that causes activity or feeling,' later 'the state of being active or emotionally aroused'

_____ *hateful:* earlier 'filled with hate,' later 'inspiring hate'

_____ *joyous:* earlier 'experiencing joy, delighted,' later 'causing joy, delightful'

_____ *knowledgeable:* earlier 'capable of being known,' later 'possessing knowledge'

_____ *like:* earlier 'cause someone to feel pleasure,' later 'feel pleasure about something'

12.13 *METAPHOR, SYNESTHESIA, AND ASSOCIATION OF IDEAS*

Words sometimes acquire new meanings through their use as figures of speech, four of the more common of which are

    1. metaphor,
    2. synesthesia (a kind of metaphor),
    3. synecdoche, and
    4. metonymy.

Identify the figure that was responsible for the new meaning of each of the following words by writing the appropriate number, from 1 through 4, in the blank.

_____ *bar:* earlier 'barrier in the Inns of Court which separated students from senior members,' later 'legal profession'

_____ *blue:* earlier 'a color,' later 'melancholy in sound'

_____ *board:* earlier 'table,' later 'daily meals'

_____ *bottle:* earlier 'a glass container,' later 'alcoholic drink'

_____ *cloud:* earlier 'hill,' later 'condensed water vapor floating in the air'

_____ *cool:* earlier 'moderately cold,' later 'emotionally restrained'

_____ *cork:* earlier 'bark of an oak tree,' later 'stopper'

_____ *crane:* earlier 'a bird with a long neck and bill,' later 'a machine for lifting weights'

_____ *crotchet:* earlier 'a small hook,' later 'idiosyncrasy, whimsical notion'

_____ *fret:* earlier 'eat, gnaw,' later 'worry, be distressed'

_____ *hand:* earlier 'grasping terminal part of the forearm,' later 'employee, laborer'

_____ *harsh:* earlier 'rough to the touch,' later 'discordant in sound'

_____ *high:* earlier 'extending upward in space,' later 'shrill, sharply pitched'

_____ *kite:* earlier 'bird of prey,' later 'toy, flown in the air'

_____ *lousy:* earlier 'infested with lice,' later 'contemptible, worthless'

_____ *sour:* earlier 'acid in taste,' later 'off key'

_____ *tin:* earlier 'a metal,' later 'a can sometimes made of tin'

_____ *triumph:* earlier 'victory procession,' later 'card of a suit that temporarily ranks higher than any other suit'

_____ *vestry:* earlier 'a room in a church used for storing vestments and for meetings,' later 'a body of laymen who administer the business of a parish'

_____ *vise:* earlier 'screw,' later 'tool with two clamps operated by a screw'

12.14 *TWO MINOR CAUSES OF SEMANTIC CHANGE*

Below are some words together with meanings that they have had at various times. The dates are of the earliest recorded use of the word in the senses indicated. Answer the questions that follow each group of words.

aisle,	1370	'wing of a church' (ultimately from Lat. *ala* 'wing')
alley,	1388	'passageway'
alley,	1508	'passageway between rows of pews in a church'
aisle,	1731	'passageway between rows of pews in a church'

What apparently caused the word *aisle* to acquire its 1731 meaning? _____

_____

buxom,	1175	'obedient, meek'
buxom,	1362	'obliging, affable, kind'
buxom,	1589	'attractive, plump, jolly' (used chiefly of women)
buxom,	after 1900	'full-busted, with large breasts'

Buxom probably acquired its most recent meaning through an association in sound with what English word? _____

care,	before 1000	'worry, anxiety, trouble'
Latin *cura*		'pains, trouble, worry; attention, management, guardianship'
care,	after 1400	'responsibility, direction, guidance'

What apparently caused the word *care* to acquire its post-1400 meaning? _____

_____

bloody,	before 1000	'characteristic of blood'
	1117	'covered with blood, bleeding'
	1225	'concerned with bloodshed'
	1563	'bloodthirsty, cruel'
	1676	'very' (an intensifier freely used by fashionable members of society, common in Restoration literature)
	after about 1750	'very' (an intensifier freely used by members of the lower classes, but considered vulgar and taboo in polite society)
French *sanglant*		'bloody, covered with blood, cruel; *figuratively*, outrageous, keen, *used as an abusive epithet*'

John Orr in *Old French and Modern English Idiom* (Oxford, 1962) has suggested that the English use of *bloody* as an intensifier is due to the imitation of a similar use in French of *sanglant* from the fifteenth century on. How do the dates of the semantic development of *bloody* lend plausibility to his theory? What political and social events in English history coincide with the 1676 change in meaning? _____

_____

_____

_____

12.15 *TABOO, EUPHEMISM, AND PEJORATION*

We are all familiar with verbal taboos that require that an offending word be replaced by a kinder, purer, or more elegant substitute. The substituting euphemism acquires the meaning of the old word and as often as not undergoes pejoration and becomes taboo itself, thus requiring a new euphemism. The process seems to continue without end.

1. The subject of smells is one that is surrounded by mild social taboos. Arrange the following seven words in order beginning with those that have the most unpleasant connotation and ending with those that have the most pleasant meaning. Follow your own judgment in ordering the list. All these words originally had neutral or favorable meanings. By looking in the *Oxford English Dictionary* find the earliest recorded date for each of the words.

aroma	smell (v.)
odor	stench (sb.)
perfume	stink (v.)
scent (sb.)	

WORD: _____ _____ _____ _____ _____ _____ _____

DATE: _____ _____ _____ _____ _____ _____ _____

What general correlation is there between the length of time a word has been used to refer to smelling and its tendency to pejoration? _____

_____

2. Some undertakers, doubtless inspired by kindly motives, have promoted euphemisms for burial. The loved one, the last remains, or the patient is given a leave-taking or memorial service in the mortuary chapel, reposing room, or crematorium before interment, inhumation, inurnment, or immurement in the columbarium, memorial park, or resting place. The survivors or waiting ones, as Evelyn Waugh calls them in *The Loved One*, are reminded to make Before Need Arrangements (that is, pay now, die later). English speakers, however, have not needed professional assistance in coining euphemisms for the verb *to die*. Add as many as you can to those given on pages 357–58 of Pyles's *Origins and Development*.

_____

_____

_____

3. Choose any of the subjects discussed on pages 358–61 of Pyles's *Origins and Development* and give other examples of euphemisms used in connection with it. _____

_____

_____

_____

_____

12.16 *THE FATE OF INTENSIFYING WORDS*

1. Among the intensifiers that have come to mean little more than *very* are *absolutely, astonishingly, extremely, horribly, perfectly, superbly, tremendously,* and *utterly*. Add a few other examples to this list. _____

_____

2. Words other than intensifiers share the diminution in force that results from hyperbole. How have the following words paled in meaning?

adore _____

amazing _____

ecstatic _____

fascinate_____

rapt_____

ravenous _____

sorry_____

spill_____

starve _____

swelter _____

12.17 SEMANTIC CHANGE: A SUMMARY

Investigate the semantic history recorded by the *Oxford English Dictionary* for some of these words. For each word you investigate, summarize in a paragraph the principal changes in meaning that the word has undergone. For some of the words, the *OED* will list many senses and subsenses; you will need to be selective in deciding which changes of meaning are major ones. For each change in meaning you note, identify the process of change that it illustrates (generalization, pejoration, euphemism, and so forth).

aftermath	coroner	hag	lust	siege
bane	cunning	hallmark	magazine	smug
bead	curious	handsome	marshal	snob
bird	cute	harlot	mawkish	stool
brat	danger	hazard	mettle	strange
budget	dean	héctic	moot	surly
bug	diaper	henchman	oaf	taint
buxom	dismal	hermetic	pioneer	talent
chapel	disparage	hobby	presently	threat
check	doom	ilk	pretty	trivial
churl	expect	imp	propaganda	umbrage
coarse	fanatic	influence	quell	urchin
coax	frank	jaunty	quick	varlet
cockney	fret	jest	racy	verve
cocksure	genteel	journey	radical	vignette
cohort	girl	junket	road	villain
colossus	gist	lady	sad	virtuous
comfortable	glee	leer	sanctimonious	wedlock
commonplace	groggy	libel	shimmy	wench
constable	hackneyed	lumber	shroud	zealot

5
6
F 7
G 8
H 9
I 0
J